THE KALAMARI UNION: MIDDLE CLASS IN EAST AND WEST

The Kalamari Union: Middle Class in East and West

Edited by
MARKKU KIVINEN

Routledge
Taylor & Francis Group

LONDON AND NEW YORK

First published 1998 by Ashgate Publishing

Reissued 2018 by Routledge
2 Park Square, Milton Park, Abingdon, Oxon, OX14 4RN
711 Third Avenue, New York, NY 10017, USA

Routledge is an imprint of the Taylor & Francis Group, an informa business

Publisher's Note
The publisher has gone to great lengths to ensure the quality of this reprint but points out that some imperfections in the original copies may be apparent.

Disclaimer
The publisher has made every effort to trace copyright holders and welcomes correspondence from those they have been unable to contact.

A Library of Congress record exists under LC control number: 97045894

ISBN 13: 978-1-138-35078-6 (hbk)
ISBN 13: 978-1-138-35080-9 (pbk)
ISBN 13: 978-0-429-43568-3 (ebk)

Contents

v

PART III: MANAGERS AND PROFESSIONALS

PART IV: IDENTITY AND LIFESTYLE OF
THE MIDDLE CLASSES

List of Contributors

Alanen, Ilkka
Senior Research Fellow, The Academy of Finland, Department of Social Sciences and Philosophy/Sociology, University of Jyväskylä, Finland

Ben-Porat, Amir
Professor, Department of Behavioral Sciences, Ben-Gurion University, Israel

Blom, Raimo
Professor, Department of Sociology and Social Psychology, University of Tampere, Finland

Bystrova, Alla
Dr., Researcher, Institute of Sociology, Russian Academy of Science, St. Petersburg, Russia

Bäckman, Johan
M.Soc.Sc., Researcher, National Research Institute of Legal Policy, Ministry of Justice, Helsinki, Finland

Cesnavicius, Aleksandras
Assistant, Institute of Philosophy, Sociology and Law, Vilnius, Lithuania

Chernysh, Mihail
Dr., Senior Research Fellow, Institute of Sociology, Russian Academy of Science, Moscow, Russia

Eremicheva, Galina
Researcher, Institute of Sociology St.Petersburg Branch, Russian Academy of Science

Fairbrother, Peter
Dr., Director, Senior Lecturer, Centre for Comparative Labour Studies, Department of Sociology, University of Warwick, Coventry, United Kingdom

Helemäe, Jelena
Dr., Institute of International and Social Studies, Estonian Academy of Sciences, Estonia

Ilyin, Vladimir
Dr., Research Fellow, Syktyvkar State University, Syktyvkar, Russia

Kivinen, Markku
Dr., Head of Finnish Centre for Russian and East-European Studies,
Finnish Centre for Russian and East-European Studies, Helsinki, Finland

Liuhto, Kari
Dr., Research Fellow, Institute for East-West Trade, Turku School of
Economics and Business Administration, Turku, Finland

Melin, Harri
Dr., Assistant Professor, Department of Sociology and Social Psychology,
University of Tampere, Finland

Nikula, Jouko
Lic.Soc.Sc., Assistant Professor, Department of Sociology and Social
Psychology, University of Tampere, Finland

Piirainen, Timo
Dr., Assistant Professor, Department of Social Policy, University of
Helsinki, Finland

Saar, Ellu
Dr., Researcher, Institute of International and Social Studies, Estonian
Academy of Sciences, Estonia

Semenova, Victoria
Dr., Researcher, Institute of Sociology, Russian Academy of Science,
Moscow, Russia

Slomczynski, Kazimierz M.
Professor, Department of Sociology, The Ohio State University, Columbus,
USA

Solovieva, Nina
Researcher, Institute of Sociology, St.Petersburg Branch, Russian Academy
of Science

Taljunaite, Meilute
Dr., Vice-Director, Institute of Philosophy, Sociology and Law, Vilnius,
Lithuania

Toivonen, Timo
Professor, Turku School of Economics and Business Administration,
Turku, Finland

Introduction:
Class Analysis in East and West

The Kalamari Union is a film by Finnish film director Aki Kaurismäki. It tells the story of 17 men, all of them called Frank, who are trying to make their way from the working class district of Kallio in Helsinki to an upper middle class paradise in Eira. It's a hard and violent journey which begins with a hi-jacking of an underground train. However, none of the Franks make it. They all die, one by one, until only two remain. Where Eira of their dreams used to be, they take a rowing boat and set off to Estonia. Why? Because the world has changed. Paradise is true only in their dreams.

The point that Kaurismäki is making in *The Kalamari Union* is that Finland is still emphatically a society of class differentiation. But what are the implications for Estonia or Eastern Europe in general? Are new social classes in the making in Eastern Europe? Are there signs of a withering away of class issues? How do different classes organize their lives and what kind of political strategies do they adopt in East and West?

This volume includes not only empirical analyses but also brings together different theoretical perspectives on social classes and stratification in East and West. Some of the assumptions of mainstream sociology regarding the death of social class in Eastern European are challenged in the articles. The book represents a multidisciplinary approach, providing descriptions of entrepreneurs and managers and professionals, highlighting economic, sociological and politological aspects of their situation. The class structure in East and West is analysed comparatively at different levels of class analysis.

This book has three aims:

1. To bring Eastern Europe into the class debate;
2. To bring new moral and political issues into scientific and political discussions on social structure;
3. To bring together a variety of theoretical and empirical analyses for a better understanding of the many ways in which classes and class practices are produced.

Recent sociological debates on classes have touched upon Eastern Europe only very provisionally. On the other hand, old analyses of social stratification under conditions of actually-existed socialism, are obviously more or less

ix

irrelevant in the current situations. Theories of the class structure that prevailed during Soviet socialism can be divided into three broad categories:

1. The standard Soviet view, which said that class relations in socialist society are essentially non-antagonistic and that all class differences are gradually withering away (cf. Glezerman 1949; Semjenov 1962; Rutkevich 1978).

2. The power-theoretical view on class relations of socialist society, which describes it as a society ruled by bureaucrats, the intelligentsia, or managers. In this category we have such theorists as Trotsky, Djilas and Burnham (cf. Trotsky 1937; Ticktin 1973; Djilas 1957; Burnham 1941).

3. The attempts by analytical Marxism to define socialism and 'state-bureaucratic socialism as specific forms of exploitation' (cf. Roemer 1981; Wright 1985; Blom and Kivinen 1990).

None of these approaches has any explanation for the processes going on in the transitory period. The particular contribution of this book is to analyse processes of class relations in Eastern Europe comparatively from new theo-retical aspects, using up-to-date empirical data. Throughout the volume, empirical findings and theoretical arguments will be set in the broader context of class debate.

In socialism power was said to be held by the working class. However, there was a constant tension between the 'holy proletariat' and the real life of the working class. Now, all the political forces in Eastern Europe, and especially in Russia, leftist and liberal alike, are hankering for the middle classes in moral undertones. The middle classes are said to be hard-working, law-abiding and full of the 'spirit of capitalism'. The 'New Russians' are often described in the Russian media as 'a sign of excellence of human quality'; and their skills, knowledge and wealth are said to 'multiply our general richness and enhance our possibilities as a state'.

This book explores the real processes behind the economic bases, the lifestyles and the political participation of the middle classes both in East and West. This, inevitably, leads to more concrete political and moral issues. The new 'sacred middle class' is challenged. We are looking at the concrete processes in which social positions are produced and reproduced; we are looking at the construction of class-based practices in working life, in education and in lifestyles.

Adopting several different conceptual approaches and perspectives, the contributors to this volume enter into an interesting debate with each other. The following empirical issues are covered in the book:

— survey analysis of social structure;
— emerging entrepreneurship in official statistics;
— social mobility in East and West;
— case studies on trade unions;

— in-depth interviews concerning middle class lifestyles;
— survey analysis of class identities;
— historical and statistical analysis of consumption patterns; and
— focused interviews on survival strategies.

One of the specific contributions of the book is to bring together analyses of entrepreneurial and wage labouring middle classes both in Western and Eastern Europe.

In the West, the imminent death of class analysis has now been debated in several major sociological journals for many years (Holton and Turner 1989; Pahl 1989; Crompton 1991; Marshall 1991; Mullins 1991; Pahl 1991; Goldthorpe and Marshall 1992; Clark and Lipset 1991; Pakulski 1993a and 1993b; Waters 1994; Hout, Brooks and Manza 1993; Clark, Lipset and Rempel 1993; Holton and Turner 1994; Saunders 1995; Pakulski and Waters 1996; Lee and Turner 1996; Holmwood 1997; Wright 1997). In this book the issue is tackled in the context of post-socialist change.

Jan Pakulski and Malcolm Waters argue in their article (1996) that class is too crude a concept, incapable of handling the nuances of the new identity politics. The class perspective, they say, has become a political straitjacket which prevents an accurate understanding of contemporary social, cultural and political processes. Our line of argumentation differs from this position. If there were a universal tendency towards a fragmentation of stratification and a decomposition of classes, then post-socialist societies would be far more advanced in this respect than the advanced capitalist countries. But instead of postulating this kind of universal tendency, we want to specify the crystallizing and decomposing tendencies and try to analyse them both theoretically and empirically.

In their defence of class analysis John Goldthorpe and Gordon Marshall (1992) define class analysis as a major sociological 'research programme' in the sense of Lakatos (cf. e.g. Lakatos 1970).

> Class analysis in our sense, has as its central concern in the study of relationships among class structures, class mobility, class-based inequalities, and class-based action. More specifically, it explores the interconnections between positions defined by employment relations in labour markets and production units in different sections of national economies; the processes through which individuals and families are distributed and redistributed among these positions over time; and the consequences thereof for their life chances and for the social identities that they adopt and the social values and interests that they pursue (Goldthorpe and Marshall 1992, 382).

As a whole, Goldthorpe and Marshall conclude, class analysis does not imply a commitment to any particular class theory, or even less so, to any theory about history. In this vein class analysis should not make too strong conceptual commitments.

1. Class analysis as a research programme is not committed to the view that class struggle is the moving force in history. The working class does not have an 'historical task' of getting rid of capitalism. Class formations and actors have a contingent, country-specific role in the divergent paths of modernization.

2. Class analysis does not commit itself to the labour theory of value, nor to any other particular theory of exploitation. Conflicts exist between classes, but class interests do not imply mutually exclusive zero-sum games. They can be connected to positive sum games based on joint interests.

3. Nor does class analysis imply any commitment to a 'Winter-palace model' or to a 'communal activity model' for the working class. Instead, one should try to show the particular conditions which make class-based activity probable.

4. Class analysis does not imply a reductionist theory on political action. Belonging to particular class positions only brings forth potential class interests. Whether these interests will show up or be shadowed by others, depends on social identities. Although the demographic identities of classes are relevant in the process of identity formation, the crucial role here is played by political movements and parties themselves, their ideologies, programmes and strategies.

If we are supposed to look upon class analysis as a research programme, a loosening of the inevitable conceptual commitments within the effort should not lead to empiricism. Conceptual disputes and disagreements are an integral part of the research programme, but not all conceptual issues are fundamentally relevant to the fate of the whole programme. Every move in the conceptual development cannot be regarded as a fundamental anomaly for the whole research programme (this kind of approach can be seen especially in the recent work of Pakulski and Waters 1996). Consequently, criticism must be aware of its level of argumentation. On the other hand, class analysis should be aware of the fact that some conceptual issues are more open than others. And, last but not least, even if the commitment to the criticism of exploitation is not an inevitable part of class analysis, the effort is linked to various forms of social criticism. These aspects of the programme should also be discussed in connection with particular theoretical and empirical problems.

The 'death of class' line of argumentation is open to several criticisms.

— When the argumentation is based on philosophy of science, the link to substantive theoretical problems becomes completely arbitrary. For example, the idea of the accumulation of anomalies in class analysis (Holmwood 1997) remains a programmatic statement without any connection to the real conceptual development in the field. A close reading of Kuhn (1970) and Lakatos

(1970) does not as such help to find any substantive anomalies, let alone to evaluate their significance.

— We do not really know enough about the development of the social sciences to argue that it is characterized by rapid changes of paradigms or research programmes. For example, different approaches to studying power do not lead to a rejection of the basic concept. From decision-making power (Dahl 1961) to non-decision making power (Bachrach and Baratz 1962) and further to hegemonic (Laclau and Mouffe 1985) and discoursive forms of power (Foucault 1977), each approach has its own conceptual tools and empirical scopes. But it would be misleading to consider this development as an indication of power analysis withering away; on the contrary, a broadening of the scope and specifying the limits of each approach would seem a more adequate characterization. And this has been going on in class analysis, too (see Wright 1997).

— Class analysis is not completely independent of other fields of social research. Traditionally, it used to be closely connected to political economy, but these ties have now been loosening during the last two decades. New challenges and conceptual connections have been emerging from the sociology of work in the vein of analysing the 'politics of production' (Burawoy 1979; Kivinen 1989) or from cultural analysis (Thompson 1968; Bourdieu 1979).

— In many critiques of class analysis a fundamental paradigmatic example is seen in either Marx or Weber. However, neither have a research programme proper based on the concept of class. Modern class analysis is by now well aware of the fact that neither Marx nor Weber developed a view on the wage-earning middle class, and that neither developed a systematic view regarding the scope of class analysis in the contemporary sense.

Class analysis consists in much more than just a mapping out of classes. Class analysis operates at several different levels and it calls for a genuine analysis of many different variables. Class analysis is indeed a complex process that involves numerous different levels. A basic distinction that has to be made is that between class position and class situation (Kivinen 1989; Blom et al. 1992). Class position has to do with the structural relations of domination within production, whereas the concept of class situation refers to more concrete phenomena: reproduction situation (income, education, position in the labour market) and working conditions.

In post-socialism all social classes are weak. A social class is in a strong position when it has achieved stability (1) in terms of ownership or power resources and (2) class situation and (3) when it has powerful organizations to lean back on. In these terms all major classes — the bourgeoisie, middle classes and the working class — are rather strong in Western Europe. In these countries ownership based on capital is well established, and professional and managerial groups have definite and undisputable privileges over and above the working class. On the other hand the working class has its own powerful organizations and in this sense forms an important part of civil society. In post-socialist countries, by contrast, the structures of ownership are still in the process of taking shape, the wage-earning middle class is weak, and the working class also lacks its own organizations through which it could have become incorporated into civil society (Kivinen 1994a and Kivinen 1994b).

However, to deal with East European societies as 'a status bazaar' (Pakulski and Waters 1997, 157), neglecting all the issues of class research, would be highly misleading.

(1) When the nomenclature turns its organizational assets into private ownership, as is the case in post-socialism, it would be a rather strange conceptual strategy to argue that the question of ownership is irrelevant for structural analysis. We could of course conclude that 'the kleptoclature is simply more lucky or talented than the others'. But for the absolute majority of people in Russia and East Europe, this kind of reasoning might sound rather absurd.

(2) Neither in the Eastern European context, nor in general, does class analysis exclude research on networks or consumption patterns (see e.g. Lonkila 1997). It would be rather strange to study the life chances of Russian workers exclusively on the basis of their consumption patterns when large fields of industry and huge enterprises are dying or under radical reconstruction (see Clarke 1993, 1995 and 1996).

(3) When large parts of the middle classes live in poverty, this is a genuine anomaly for class analysis (Piirainen 1997). This does not, however, imply that issues connected with managerial hierarchies or professionalization are completely irrelevant. New kinds of contradictory class locations can be discovered when, for instance, an engineer or an academic scholar is earning a living as a taxi driver. In this context we should also try to identify the new processes of skill degradation. Traditional conceptions of proletarianization or middle class formation are not relevant in transitional systems.

(4) Class interests cannot be identified without taking into account the level of class situation. For example, in order to analyse the potential interests of the current Russian middle class, we have to start out with a study of its concrete and historical living conditions.

(5) Classes are both socio-economic realities and cultural constructs (Kivinen 1997). During the Soviet period a constant tension prevailed between the 'holy proletariat' and the actual Russian working class. Whereas the former was supposed to be disciplined, organized, hard-working etc., the latter turned out to be rural, carnevalistic, heavy-drinking, etc. Nowadays an almost analogical situation can be seen in the case of the idealized middle class. All Russian political forces hanker for the middle class. By reducing

class analysis to a cultural level, we lose the possibility of secularization and deconstruction of such sacred codes.

(6) Class analysis does not imply class reductionism or essentialism. Other identities and other 'imagined communities' are also relevant in Russia. They are even more relevant than in Western societies because of the weakness of classes.

One of the real problems caused by the debate on the death of class may lie in its uncivilizing effects on middle class academic culture. Back in the mid-1980s when we published a comprehensive book on class in Finland, one of my civilized colleagues (who has since published fascinating titles on consumption and body) asked in a public debate about the book: 'But what if the effects of class are not visible anywhere?'

I remember replying to him that it is absurd to answer this kind of question when one has just published 700 pages of analysis of these effects. But my colleagues were no longer reading these kinds of books. Every now and then, glancing through their office window, they might see an ordinary worker passing by; and the conclusion is that these must be the last workers in the world. But they are wrong. These people down there are Franks making their way to Eira.

PART I: Entrepreneurs

One of the obvious specific features of contemporary East European middle classes is that entrepreneurs, who in Western conditions would be regarded as old middle classes, are genuinely the new middle classes; the professional and managerial 'new middle classes' have already existed during the Soviet period. In this book entrepreneurs are analysed from the point of view of the economy, politics and lifestyle. The special issues of farming are also raised. Emerging East European entrepreneurship is compared with the situation in the West.

Kari Liuhto's article on the transformation of the Estonian enterprise sector offers a detailed analysis of the development of Estonian entrepreneurs. The current situation has several links with historical developments during the previous era of independence. Common features include the loss of Eastern markets and manufacturing contacts, a strong orientation to the West, an increase in foreign investment, and the need to build up the national economy.

The structuration of entrepreneurial middle classes in the Baltic countries remains surrounded by much ambiguity. Careful statistical analyses reveal that in present-day Estonia there are large numbers of non-active or phantom organizations. The role of foreign investment is increasing since the economy is not yet overheated. In their article Meilute Taljunaite and Alexandras Cesnavicius challenge the concept of middle class in the Baltic context. They point at the difficulty of identifying clear-cut class groups in the present situation of class structuration. On the other hand, participation in the privatization process seems to lead to the formation of new proprietary classes. The authors describe participation in the privatization process is considerable detail. The article concludes with some generalizations about entrepreneurship and privatization processes in Lithuania.

The nouveau riche in Russia, the 'New Russians' (novye russkie) are attracting much attention in the mass media both in Russia and the West. Johan Bäckman's article sets out to pull down the myth of New Russians and to proceed towards a sociologically more tenable concept. Are the 'New Russians' really the builders of a Russian economic miracle or a new leisure class? Bäckman has interviewed the nouveau riche in St.Petersburg and draws a particular ethos of them. They seem to be workaholics who do not have the time or the desire to consume. They also feel a deep sense of guilt of their privileges and fear the 'others'.

Although entrepreneurs in St.Petersburg and all over Russia are still combining traditional Soviet features with a new orientation in their lifestyle, they are beginning to form an independent and fairly well-organized political force. Business elites are seeking means to influence public processes on both the local and national level. In the article by Galina Eremicheva and Nina Solovieva, people running for seats in the City Assembly are characterized according to their background and interests. Obviously entrepreneurs have more influence on the political scene than their mere numerical force would imply.

In a broader historical view the entrepreneurial middle classes in the West have been divided into two parts, the urban petty bourgeoisie and peasants. In his article Ilkka Alanen analyses the formation of private agriculture in the Baltic countries. Baltic agriculture is marred by the general problems of the transition period and uncertainty about future agricultural policy. There is a long way to go before the goal of the present policy, a system of family farms, is reached. The prospects may be somewhat better in Lithuania, whereas in Estonia the chances of even primitive small farming are meagre. On the other hand, capitalistically organized production seems to be possible in Estonia. Nevertheless, the only really viable unit of agricultural production in all the Baltic countries is the garden plot.

PART II: Wage-Earning Middle Classes in Formation

Comparative analysis of occupational structures in the former Soviet Union and in the West does not reveal very many differences in the sizes of wage-earning middle class occupations. In the Soviet Union there were at least as many engineers, doctors and teachers as in the United States. The differences lay elsewhere, in the nature of the processes of class relations and in the structuration of the class situation. Professionalization was never as effective in state socialist societies as it has been in developed capitalist societies. Professional and managerial middle classes have not had such undisputable and established privileges as they have in the West.

There are two basic aspects of class formation: the creation of class structures and the allocation of people in positions within these structures. Consequently, one of the most fundamental conceptual distinctions within class analysis is that between 'positions' and 'people'. During the state socialist regimes we have seen at least three different policies concerning the middle classes. Stalin regarded the positions of middle class wage earners as 'cadres of science and technology' as an inevitable phenomenon, but he did not accept the particular people in these positions. Consequently, the bourgeois specialists were to be replaced by 'red experts'. Pol Pot accepted neither middle class positions nor the people. The strategy of Khrushchev and Brezhnev was to make the positions less relevant but to allow middle class kids get middle class jobs.

In the current situation the wage-earning positions are also under transition. Kazimierz M. Slomczynski's article is devoted to two issues of class formation. The first issue pertains to the disintegration of the most typical elements of an 'old' communist structure and the integration of the most typical elements of a 'new' emerging social stratum. In particular, the analysis demonstrates to what extent people from the nomenclature stratum have been able to convert their political assets and become a new privileged business class. The second issue addresses the question as to which social classes are most distressed. The analysis is based on various surveys conducted in Poland, Hungary and the Czech Republic, and the results are also compared with Western Europe.

In his article Vladimir Ilyin examines the process of middle class formation in Russia from several points of view. Referring to empirical data on salaries, he argues that most professionals and managers cannot be regarded as a real middle class group in the current situation. He also emphasizes the difference between profitable and unprofitable firms in middle class formation, and points out how some core groups are struggling for privileged positions.

Amir Ben-Porat's article highlights the case of Israel.

Three parameters determined almost every process after the Second World War in Israel. These were: the import of labour in the form of mass immigration, the import of capital, and the domination of the state in every instance of society.

The second 'realm' began in the early 1960s and ended during the 1970s. It was characterized by the consolidation of a capitalist type of class structure mainly by the shrinking of the petty bourgeoisie and expansion of the new middle class. The third realm began in the early 1980s and is characterized by the growing domination of market economy, a deliberate withdrawal of the state from certain aspects of economy, and the declining power of the labour unions. Both components of the middle class were influenced mainly by the economic options typical of each realm.

The formation of the old middle class was supportive of the sociological 'minorities', sephardim females and Arabs, although in absolute terms, Azhkenazim, males and Jews dominated this class as well. These results raise important issues concerning the class formation in the Baltic states, where the intertwining of ethnic and class processes is seen as a key issue.

The article by Ellu Saar and Jelena Helemäe looks at patterns of intragenerational mobility in two cohorts during the early stages of economic reform in Estonia. Were people stable or mobile? What kind of mobility predominates, structural or circulation, upward or downward? The authors use data from two longitudinal studies concerning the most educated parts of two birth cohorts, i.e. those born in 1948-49 and 1964-65. The main result is that the emergence of the private sector as the most important dimension of economic life in Estonia did not bring about crucial changes as regards movement into professional positions. The changes were only very minor in the case of managers as well. This would seem to indicate that positions move into new systems of social co-ordinates rather than people change their positions.

PART III: Managers and Professionals

The structuration of classes in the former Soviet Union fundamentally differed from that in the Western societies. At the level of class situation the middle class was clearly distinguished from the working class as far as conditions of work were concerned. On the other hand middle class incomes were not considerably better. One fundamental difference was a clear absence in the Soviet Union of distinct profiles of class consciousness and action of the kind we are accustomed to seeing in advanced capitalist countries. However, the habitus and lifestyle of the middle class was clearly distinguished from the working class.

The articles in this section highlight the current change of class relations in post-socialist Eastern Europe. They focus on three particular aspects:
— Managerial structures from a class perspective;
— Professionalization in East and West;
— Dimensions of class formation.

The focus of Peter Fairbrother's paper is on a specific type of social stratum, namely unionized non-manual workers in two prototypical industries. While there is the long tradition of examining such workers in the West, this has not been the case in Russia. The question is whether the unionization of non-manual employees constitutes a new middle class in the making. The case studies indicate that this is not the case. The unions acted to defend their interests in the context of division and struggle over the future of industries. In this respect this was not the process of middle class in the making at the point of production.

Harri Melin's article examines the process of managerial change in post-socialist Estonia in a broad historical and theoretical perspective. The traditional Soviet type of management was based on the plan and a complex network of interdependencies. Analysing two case studies in Estonian industry, it is argued that managers in Estonia have already undergone fundamental changes towards a capitalist kind of structures. In this respect the difference between Russia and Estonia is considerable indeed.

Russian professionals in transition is the subject of the analysis by Victoria Semenova. The main argument is that professionals in the private sector differ quite fundamentally from those of the state sector. The empirical part combines both quantitative and qualitative data (longitudinal survey data and life story analysis).

At some stages the Revolution in Eastern Europe seemed to take on features of a real attack against the nomenclature. The summer of 1991, when the CPSU was closed down, proved to be an uneasy time for party functionaries. Overnight, they lost both their social status and their job. What happened to these people? Alla Bystrova's article provides an answer on the basis of 20 semi-structured in-depth interviews. The respondents seem to have lost their interest in politics but almost all of them have entered on promising managerial careers.

Markku Kivinen argues that from the perspective of post-socialist transition, we have to face the ultimate problems of class analysis in a new light. Many theories of the new middle class take into consideration only one form of mental labour. This way class may be conceptualized, for example, as bureaucrats, technocrats or as intelligentsia. In these terms class can be seen in moral overtones as 'good' or 'bad'. The article problemizes this approach in the current post-socialist conditions.

Using new empirical data on the Baltic societies, it is shown that the middle classes are much weaker in these countries than they are in Finland. In fact, all classes in post-socialism are weak. However, it would be too straightforward to conclude that classes are withering away. Rather, we would need to have a more analytical approach to processes of class relations.

PART IV: Identity and Lifestyle of the Middle Classes

Class consciousness is not an easy subject for analysis. At least four different but complementary theoretical concepts are employed in the following analysis:
— habitus and lifestyle;
— consciousness and organization;
— class identity; and
— class culture.

The idea that the middle classes are worthy of admiration because of their lifestyle is bound up with professionalism, and because their political attitudes lean towards democracy, it has deep roots in social theorizing. One of the traditional issues discussed in the West has been the middle class support for the Nazi government during the economic crisis and 'status panic'. In his article Michail Chernysh asks whether the middle class vote in Russia today could go to the Communists. However, basing his argument on new survey data, Chernysh argues that the Russian middle class shows the same inclination to support liberal causes as its counterparts in other countries. On the other hand, its numerical weakness does not allow it to act as a real stabilizing force.

In his article Jouko Nikula analyses the situation in the Baltic countries in the sphere of politics and interest representation. The picture is quite bleak: the political field remains very unstable and fragmented, social movements are weak, and large segments of the population are disenchanted with the results of the reforms. In all the Baltic countries the nature of politics has been elitist and technocratic, with very weak links to the grassroots level. The results of several surveys indicate that people generally have nothing against private ownership or market economy, but they are not convinced by the statements of 'ultra liberals' who say that the total dismantling of state ownership is a precondition for future prosperity. The state and markets are not seen as contradictory, but rather as complementary institutions, and in all the post-socialist countries the state is expected to be active in the social sphere.

Referring to recent survey data from all the Baltic countries, Raimo Blom problemizes the possibility of middle class society or middle class hegemonic projects in these states. Middle class groups seem to be the main losers in the ongoing transformation process, at least in the short term. The results also suggest that the consciousness of these groups is more or less dispersed. Because of the high level of uncertainty, we can expect the future to be characterized by slow and cyclical social development.

Timo Toivonen's study compares the relative level of leisure consumption at three points of time, i.e. in 1955, 1966, and 1971. This is a particularly interesting period of time because it saw an extraordinarily rapid proliferation of certain modern consumer durables, such as television sets and cars. The aim of the study is to find out whether there occurred any changes in the connections between consumption expenditure and social backgrounds. In general, the results show that during the period under review, consumption differences between social groups increased considerably. Contradicting several earlier theories, the conclusion is that class differences are smaller at the beginning of mass consumption than during the take-off period of mass consumption. This provides an interesting aspect for analysing the processes in contemporary East Europe.

The theoretical point of departure in Timo Piirainen's paper is a Weberian view on stratification. In a study of the transformation of the social structure in post-socialist countries, the change can be thematized as a shift from an 'estate society' to a class society. The notion of 'asset' is a central concept in the analysis; assets are defined as resources, properties or activities that can be used to enhance an actor's life chances. Another key concept is that of 'strategy'. The study is based on an extensive interview data set collected in St.Petersburg during 1993-95.

Piirainen argues that a middle-class habitus is formed through a closer integration into the monetary economy, and this integration requires a sufficient amount of valid assets. Households that do not have a sufficient amount of assets that are valid in market capitalism rely on an opposite strategy: instead of integrating into the monetary economy in order to form middle-class lifestyles, they strive to withdraw from the monetary economy and to compensate the gap between the devaluated wages and rising prices by increasing activity in the sphere of the unofficial economy. Piirainen's analysis brings forth people as actors. His view could be seen to complement the analysis of the birth of positions, based on structural processes and collective power resources.

Bibliography

Bachrach, P. and Baratz, M.S. (1962), 'Two Faces of Power', *American Political Science Review*, Vol. 56, pp. 947-952.

Blom, R. and Kivinen, M. (1990), 'Analytical Marxism and Class Theory', in S. Clegg (ed.), *Organization Theory and Class Analysis. New Approaches and New Issues*, De Gruyter, Berlin and New York.

Blom, R., Kivinen, M., Melin H. and Rantalaiho L. (1992), *The Scope Logic Approach to Class Analysis. A Study of the Finnish Class Structure*, Avebury, Aldershot.

Burnham, J. (1941), *The Managerial Revolution*, Doubleday, New York.

Clark, R. and Lipset S. (1991), 'Are Social Classes Dying?', *International Sociology*, Vol. 6, 4, pp. 397-410.

Bourdieu, P. (1979), 'La Distinction. Critique sociale du jugement', *Les Editions de Minuit*, Paris.

Clark, T., Lipset, S. and Rempel, M. (1993), 'The Declining Political Significance of Social Class', *International Sociology*, Vol. 8, 3, pp. 279-293.

Clarke, S. et al. (1993), *What about the Workers. Workers and the Transition to Capitalism in Russia*, Verso, London.

Clarke, S. (ed.) (1995), *Management and Industry in Russia: formal and informal relations in the period of transition*, Edward Elgar, Aldershot.

Clarke, S. (ed.) (1996), *Conflict and Change in the Russian Enterprise*, Edward Elgar. Aldershot.

Crompton, R. 'Three Varieties of Class Analysis: Comment on R.E. Pahl', *International Journal of Urban and Regional Research*, Vol. 15, pp. 108-113.

Dahl, R.A. (1961), *Who Governs? Democracy and Power in an American City*, Yale University Press, New Haven.

Djilas, M. (1957), *The New Class*, Thames & Hudson, London.

Foucault, M. (1977), *Discipline and Punish. The Birth of Prison*, Penguin, Harmondsworth.

Giddens, A. *The Class Structure of Advanced Societies*, Hutchinson, London.

Glezerman, G.E. (1949), *Likvidatsiia ekspluatatorskih klassov i preodolenie klassovyh razlitshii v SSSR*, Moskva.

Goldthorpe, J. (1980), *Social Mobility and Class Structure in Modern Britain*, Clarendon, Oxford.

Goldthorpe, J. and Marshall, G. (1992), 'The promising Future of Class Analysis. A Response to Recent Critiques', *Sociology*, Vol. 26, 3, pp. 381-400.

Holmwood, J. (1997), *The Problem of Inequality and Class in Contemporary Debates*, paper presented at the VIII International Meeting of the Comparative Project on Class Structure and Class Consciousness, Canberra 1-3 August 1997.

Holton R. and Turner B. (1989), *Max Weber on Economy and Society*, Routledge, London.

Holton R. and Turner B. (1994), 'Debate and Pseudo-Debate in Class Analysis: Some Unpromising Aspects of Goldthorpe and Marshall's Defence', *Sociology*, Vol. 28, 3, pp. 799-804.

Hout, M., Brooks, C. and Manza, J. (1994), 'The Persistence of Classes in Post-Industrial Societies', *International Sociology*, Vol. 8, 3, pp. 259-278.

Kivinen, M. (1989), *The New Middle Classes and the Labour Process. Class Criteria Revisited*, Department of Sociology, University of Helsinki, Research Report 223, Helsinki.

Kivinen, M. (1994a), 'Perspektivy razvitija srednego klassa v Rossii', *Sociologicheskii zhurnal*, 2, pp. 134-141.

Kivinen, M. (1994b), 'Class Relations in Russia', in Piirainen, T. (ed.), *Change and Continuity in Eastern Europe*, Dartmouth, Aldershot.

Kivinen, M. (1997), *Sosiologia ja Venäjä*, Hanki ja Jää, Jyväskylä (forthcoming).

Kuhn, T.S. (1970), *The Structure of Scientific Revolutions*, University of Chicago Press, Chicago.

Laclau, E. and Mouffe, C. (1985), *Hegemony and Socialist Strategy*, Verso, London.

Lakatos, I. (1970), 'Falsification and the Methodology of Scientific Research Programmes', in I. Lakatos and A. Musgrave (eds.), *Criticism and Growth of Scientific Knowledge*, Cambridge University Press, Cambridge.

Lee, D. and Turner, B.S. (eds.) (1996), *Conflict about Class*, Longman, London.

Lonkila, M. (1997), 'Informal Exchange Relations in Post-Soviet Russia: A Comparative Perspective', *Sociological Research Online*, Vol. 2, 2.

Lukes, S. (1974), *Power: A Radical View*, Macmillan, London.

Marshall G. (1991), 'In Defence of Class Analysis: A Comment on R.E. Pahl', *International Journal of Urban and Regional Research*, Vol. 15, pp. 114-118.

Mullins, P. (1991), 'The Identification of Social Forces in Development as a General Problem Within Sociology', *International Journal of Urban and regional Research*, Vol. 15, pp. 119-129.

Nikula, J. (1997), *From State-Dependency to Genuine Worker Movement? The Working Class in Socialism and Post-Socialism*, Tampere University Press, Tampere.

Pahl R. (1989), 'Is the Emperor Naked?', *International Journal of Urban and Regional Research*, Vol. 13, pp. 709-720.

Pahl R. (1991), 'R.E. Pahl Replies', *International Journal of Urban and Regional Research*, Vol. 15, pp. 127-129.

Pakulski, J. (1993a), 'Mass Social Movements and Social Class', *International Sociology*, Vol. 8, 2, pp. 131-158.

Pakulski, J. (1993b), 'The Dying of Class or of Marxist Class Theory', *International Sociology*, Vol. 8, 3, pp. 279-292.

Pakulski, J. and Waters, M. (1996), *The Death of Class*, Sage, London.

Piirainen, T. (1997), *Towards a New Social Order in Russia. Transforming Structures and Everyday Life*, Dartmouth, Aldershot.

Roemer, J.E. (1981), *A General Theory of Exploitation and Class*, Cambridge University Press, Cambridge, Mass.

Rutkevich, M.N. (1978), 'O ponjatii sotsialnoj struktury', *Sotsiologicheskie issledovaniia* 4/1978.

Saunders, P. (1995), 'Might Britain be a Meritocracy?', *Sociology*, Vol. 29, 1, pp. 23-41.

Semjenov, V.S. (1962), *Preobrazovanija v rabotshem klasse i intelligentsii v protsesse perehoda k kommunizmu. Iz istorii rabochego klassa SSSR*, Leningrad.

Ticktin, H. (1973), 'Towards a Political Economy of the U.S.S.R.', *Critique* 1994, 1, pp. 1-23.

Trotsky, L. (1937), *Revolution Betrayed. What is Soviet Union and where it is going?*, London.

Waters, M. (1994), 'Succession in the Stratification Order: A Contribution to the Death of Class Debate', *International Sociology*, Vol. 9, 3, pp. 295-312.

Wright, E.O. (1978), *Class, Crisis and the State*, New Left Books, London.

Wright, E.O. (1985), *Classes*, New Left Books, London.

Wright, E.O. (1997), *Class Counts: comparative studies in class analysis*, Cambridge University Press.

PART I

ENTREPRENEURS

1 Transformation of the Estonian Enterprise Sector from a Planned System towards Market Economy[1]

KARI LIUHTO

Transformation of the Enterprise Sector in Soviet Estonia

The Soviet Union, notorious for its history of failed economic reforms, ventured out in the mid-1980s on a new socio-economic reform known as *perestroika*: the aim was to avoid the impending economic collapse of the Soviet system. Ultimately, the purpose of *perestroika* was to improve the efficiency of the Soviet economy through similar measures that were first introduced during the NEP period (Nove 1992, 331-394).[2] One of the new steps taken was the creation of a foundation for small state enterprises with less than 50 employees during 1985-87.

> Although the new small businesses remained state property, they enjoyed far more rights than other state firms, who functioned in strictly regulated conditions. This was the first step towards decentralization of organization and what is more important, of state enterprise management (Venesaar and Vitsur 1995, 190).

Perestroika tested out these economic reforms in the most advanced Soviet republics, such as Soviet Estonia (Van Arkadie and Karlson 1992, 103-104).[3] However, while Soviet Estonia served as a 'laboratory' for small state-owned enterprises, only 800 such firms were established in the country by 1990, employing 13 000 people and showing total sales of no more than 300 million roubles (Lugus et al. 1991, 13; Kilvits 1994, 4). The economic significance of the reform, therefore, remained rather modest. The allowance of small state enterprises was only a small step for the national economy, but a significant move indeed for overall business development: it signified a departure from the *one big factory* concept towards real entrepreneurship (Kozminski 1993, 7).

The next step taken on the road towards a market economy was the introduction of producers' cooperatives.[4] The first cooperatives were founded

3

in Soviet Estonia in late 1986, although it was not until May 1988 that the relevant legislation was passed in the Soviet Union (Lugus et al. 1991, 3; Venesaar and Vitsur 1995, 190). The Decree on Cooperatives paved the way for private entrepreneurship in the Soviet Union for the first time since the NEP period — but not quite without difficulty.

The problems were chiefly caused by the failure to integrate producers' cooperatives into the planned economy and by the absence in the Soviet Union of a free market. In practice this meant that cooperatives had constant difficulties with the acquisition of commodities. Many of them had to resort to the unofficial market to keep their operation going, and there were frequent accusations in the press of speculation and government property being stolen (Cockburn 1989, 176-179; Slider 1991, 797-821).

The cooperatives had only limited impact on the Soviet economy: they represented less than one per cent of total industrial production, only three per cent of the total turnover of Estonian enterprises and around five per cent of the labour force (Van Arkadie and Karlson 1992, 264; Kilvits 1994, 4). Moreover, two-thirds of the cooperatives registered in Soviet Estonia were still in state ownership (Lugus et al. 1991, 31). More important, however, than their economic significance was the fact that the private producers' cooperatives signalled the arrival of private entrepreneurship in the Estonian economy after a break of almost 50 years.

Another major reform that came with *perestroika* was the Decree on Joint Ventures (January 1987), which gave all foreign companies the right to set up subsidiaries within the Soviet borders (Xueref 1988).[5] However, contrary to the expectations of Soviet reformists, there was no rush of foreign companies into the Soviet Union. Interest was undermined, among other factors, by delays in registration, Soviet bureaucracy, high exchange rates, lacking business legislation, and a lack of investment guarantees (Yhteisyritykset Neuvostoliitossa 1989, 18-36; Kallio 1990, 67-74). As a consequence only 1,180 joint ventures were registered in the Soviet Union — 82 of them in Soviet Estonia — by the end of 1989 (PlanEconReport 1989, 16; Katila 1990, 10; Laurila 1993, 44).

Within two years the number of foreign companies in Soviet Estonia increased almost fourteen times over to 1,118 foreign-owned organizations (Liuhto 1995b, 509-512).[6] The sharp increase in joint ventures originated in the Decrees on Joint Stock Companies adopted in 1989 and 1990, which created a solid legislative basis for private entrepreneurship in Soviet Estonia (Sorainen 1993, 61).

These legal reforms did away with the obstacles that had kept many foreign investors outside of Soviet Estonia (Informare 1992b, 28-29). Although the significance of foreign companies remained quite limited in terms of the Soviet Estonian economy, they did bring the economy and entrepreneurship of Soviet Estonia closer to the world economy. Foreign-owned companies also brought along Western management knowledge into Soviet Estonia. Thirdly, foreign companies added to the variety, particularly within trade and services (Liuhto 1995b, 507-525).

Despite their minor economic significance, the reforms were fundamental steps towards market economy. To begin with, small state organizations were the first phase in the creation of small and medium-sized entrepreneurship. Then, producers' cooperatives provided an opportunity for the emergence of private entrepreneurship. Finally, the Joint Venture Decree gave Western companies the right to own subsidiaries within the Soviet borders. The seeds for the transition of the organization sector in Estonia were thus sown before the country gained independence, but the organization sector began to grow rapidly when Estonia declared independence from the Soviet Union.

Transformation of the Organization Sector in Independent Estonia

New organizations were set up in huge and growing numbers in Estonia in late 1991: by the beginning of 1992 the total number of organizations exceeded 35,000. Since then the pace of registrations has settled to around 15,000 new organizations a year. By mid-1996, the total number of registered organizations in Estonia was almost 100,000 (Figure 1).

Figure 1. Growth of the Estonian organization sector

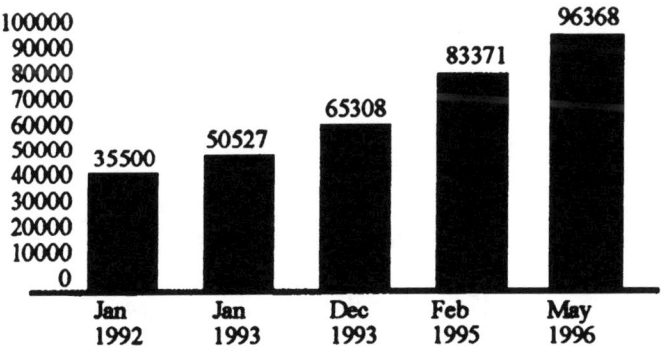

Looking at the level of business activity in the Estonian organization sector, it is important to note that only 65,153 of the total of 96,368 registered organizations are business organizations (enterprises) — the rest are various kinds of institutions and associations. In addition, it must be pointed out that many of these business organizations are inoperative. In mid-1996 the number of active business organizations in Estonia stood at no more than around 30,000.

Personnel numbers in Estonian business organizations are very low: almost 90 % of these organizations employ less than 20 workers. The statistics indicate a decrease in the proportion of small organizations, whereas that of medium-sized organizations is growing (Table 1).

Table 1. **Transformation of organizations by personnel size**[7]

Personnel	1/1992 All registered organizations	2/1995 All registered organizations	5/1996 Business organizations
0-9	78	88	76
10-19	7	5	11
20-49	7	4	8
50-199	5	2	5
over 200	3	1	1
TOTAL	35,500	83,371	65,153

The changes that have taken place have implied a reduced direct role for the state in the Estonian organization sector. Whereas state organizations accounted for around one-quarter of the total organization sector in 1992, the figure in mid-1996 was down to no more than 5 %. Although the number of state organizations is fairly insignificant, it is important not to underestimate their economic importance. State organizations still account for a considerable proportion of industrial production, and they employ significant numbers of workers. The importance of the private sector is clearly illustrated by the statistic that it accounts for 65 % of Estonian GDP (Pautola 1996, 25).

The role of foreign ownership must also be given due attention in examining the transformation of the Estonian organization sector. The proportion of foreign-owned organizations in Estonia today stands at almost 10 % of all registered organizations, having doubled from the beginning of 1992. The foreign impact on the Estonian economy should not be underestimated: FDIs accounted for some 10 % of the country's GDP in 1994 (Pautola 1996,

28). The role of FDIs is further highlighted by the fact that in 1995, over 60 % of them were engaged in manufacturing, which has suffered during the economic transition (Ministry of Economic Affairs 1996, 43).[8]

The major foreign investors in Estonia are Sweden and Finland, together accounting for approximately 40 % of total foreign capital investments. However, the Nordic dominance in Estonia is now decreasing as other countries are showing a growing interest in the Baltic States. Capital investments from Russia/CIS countries remain significant at 9 % of total foreign capital investment (Table 2).

Table 2.   Transformation of registered foreign companies in Estonia (%)

	1/1993	1/1994	7/1995	1/1996
Total number	3,814	6,799	8,344	8,886
Direct foreign investment (DEM million)	225	288	513	575
Main investors:				
Finland	29	26	23	20
Sweden	37	35	21	18
Russia/CIS countries	7	7	10	9
USA	4	8	8	7
Ireland	1	1	7	6
United Kingdom	1	1	6	6
Others	21	22	25	34

Sources: Liuhto 1994a, 93-100; Estonian Investment Agency 1995, 16; Ministry of Economic Affairs 1996, 40-42.

The interest shown by Russian investors in the Estonian market is seen as a double-edged sword. While the Estonian economy needs the injections of foreign capital, the Estonian authorities are keeping a close eye on the development of Russian-owned organizations in Estonia. Some authorities consider Russian organizations a potential threat that might be used as a political weapon against Estonia if relationships between Russia and the Baltic countries were to cool down.

Looking at FDIs as a whole, the statistics indicate that foreign companies have invested more in Estonia than in Latvia and Lithuania together. In addition, among the former planned economies, the level of FDIs per capita in Estonia ranks second-highest after Hungary. The high level of activity of foreign companies in Estonia may appear somewhat surprising in view of the fact that Estonia is a small country with very limited natural resources. One probable explanation for the foreign interest lies in the country's stable and developed business environment and its strategic status as a foothold to other Baltic States and Russia (Ministry of Economic Affairs 1996, 44).

In mid-1996 almost 40 % of all registered organizations in the Estonian organization sector operated in the wholesale and retail business; at the beginning of 1992 the sector accounted only for one-fifth. The number of organizations in wholesale and retail trade has multiplied five times since 1992, and now exceeds 35,000. Unfortunately, large numbers of these organizations are inoperative (Table 3).

Table 3.   Transformation of organizations by field of activity (%)

	1/1992[9]	5/1996	
FIELD OF ACTIVITY	All registered organizations	All registered organizations	Business organizations
Agriculture & forestry	13.0	16.0	6.0
Fishery	0.3	0.5	0.6
Mining	0.1	0.1	0.2
Manufacturing	13.4	9.8	16.7
Energy	0.4	0.5	1.2
Construction	7.9	4.7	8.6
Wholesale and retail trade	20.8	37.2	39.6
Hotel and catering	7.2	4.1	4.7
Transport & communication	4.6	3.7	4.9
Finance	0.9	0.9	0.7
Real estate & business services	12.2	11.4	11.2
Social insurance & services	19.1	11.1	5.6
TOTAL	34,678	96,368	65,153

In a regional analysis, organizations in Estonia are quite heavily concentrated around the capital city of Tallinn and the surrounding Harju county: together, they accounted for half of all registered organizations in mid-1996. This level of concentration is surprising in that one might have predicted to see the process of economic transformation dismantle the dominating status that the capital city held during the Soviet era and a decentralization of economic activities to other regions (Table 4).

Table 4. **Transformation of registered organizations by location (%)**

| | 1/1992 | | 5/1996 | |
LOCATION	All registered organizations	All registered organizations	Business organizations	Business organizations per 100 people
Harju county	40.8	46.6	59.4	7.0
Hiiu county	1.4	0.9	0.6	3.5
Ida-Viru county	8.3	6.6	6.2	2.0
Jôgeva county	2.9	2.2	1.3	2.0
Järva county	3.9	2.5	1.4	2.1
Lääne county	2.5	2.2	1.8	3.7
Lääne-Viru county	3.9	3.7	3.0	2.6
Pôlva county	1.9	2.8	1.3	2.4
Pärnu county	8.0	6.2	5.3	3.5
Rapla county	2.3	2.9	1.7	2.8
Saare county	2.8	3.0	2.4	3.8
Tartu county	11.4	11.2	10.0	4.2
Valga county	2.2	2.3	1.6	2.6
Viljandi county	5.6	4.2	2.5	2.5
Vôru county	2.2	2.7	1.5	2.2
TOTAL	35,500	96,368	65,153	4.4

There are several possible explanations for the present concentration around the capital city. Firstly, the administrative bodies that are crucial to business operations are all situated in Tallinn. Secondly, those Estonian companies that have foreign trade benefit from their location in the capital region where over 60 % of all foreign-owned companies are registered. Thirdly, about one-third of the Estonian population lives in the capital region (Liuhto, 1994a, 28).

Looking at the number of business organizations in different regions relative to the population in the respective regions, the capital region has by far the highest ratio with seven business organizations per 100 inhabitants. The lowest number of active organizations is found in the counties of Ida-Viru and Jôgeva, where only two business organizations have been registered per 100 inhabitants. It is important to observe here that Ida-Viru has a large Russian population: in Narva, for instance, ethnic Estonians represent only a few per cent of the town's total population.

It is hard to provide any unambiguous explanation for the lack of entrepreneurial spirit in Ida-Viru. Some Estonian experts believe that the lower level of entrepreneurial spirit in the Russian population is explained by the fact that Russians have not registered their organizations in Estonia, even though they are involved in unofficial trade between Estonia and former Soviet republics. Another possible explanation is the lack of entrepreneurial know-how among Russian industrial workers.

This question requires closer and more systematic research attention. One should bear in mind that the rising levels of unemployment in the ethnic Russian population in Estonia are adding to their sense of dissatisfaction towards the process of economic transformation, and this for its part may be badly reflected in relationships between Estonia and Russia.

The Future Development of the Estonian Organization Sector

The development of the Estonian organization sector in the near future will be greatly affected by legislation adopted in September 1995 according to which all joint stock companies registered in Estonia must have a minimum stock capital of DEM 50,000. Joint stock companies established before the entry into force of this act have to raise their stock capital to DEM 25,000 by September 1997 and to DEM 50,000 by September 1999 (Viron uusi liike-toimintalaki 1995, 31-79).

In this context it is important to remember that 85 % of all Estonian organizations are joint stock companies (Kaubaleht 1995; Rozental 1995, 17). Moreover, 1995 statistics indicate that 70 % of these organizations had an initial stock capital of less than DEM 1,250. In practice what this means is that most Estonian organizations will have to raise their stock capital, change their company form or close down. The authorities have estimated that some 50,000 organizations may have to be closed down unless they manage to raise their stock capital or change their company form (Hirv 1996, 9).

There is reason to believe that as a consequence of this legal change, most of these 50,000 organizations will change their company form in order to keep their capital requirements down. In other words, there are no grounds to expect a massive wave of bankruptcies among active organizations. On the other hand, the reform will get rid of the inoperative organizations from the Estonian statistics and thus allow for a more reliable description of the real state of the organization sector.

If the current trend in development continues, the Estonian organization sector will comprise 40,000-60,000 active business organizations by the end of the decade. The majority of these organizations will probably remain small even though the proportion of medium-sized organizations will grow. Although the trade and services orientation is expected to continue in the near future, one can anticipate a gradual concentration of the trade sector as a result of bankruptcies, takeovers and the formation of trade chains.

Estonia's relationship with Russia and the European Union will be a major determinant of the future development of the Estonian organization sector. Closer relationships with Russia would have a positive impact on the Estonian organization sector, as the dismantling of trade barriers between these countries would probably increase their mutual trade.

If Estonia is accepted as a full member of the European Union at the end of this decade, the country's organization sector will be very much influenced by the development of the relationships between the European Union and Russia. Estonia's membership of the European Union and good relations between the EU and Russia would provide an opportunity for Estonian companies to take advantage of their geographical location in-between the EU and Russia. If Estonia and the other Baltic States are accepted as full members, this will in the long term affect Finland's current role as the European Union's foothold to Russia.

Conclusion

Following the dismantling of a system of state monopoly which was based on a few hundred giant organizations, the Estonian economy today depends very much on its small organizations. By mid-1996 the entrepreneurial spirit in the country has generated almost 100,000 registered organizations.

Unfortunately, only one-third of these 100,000 organizations are active business organizations. The situation in the other Baltic States is very similar: only 30-40 % of all registered organizations are operative. In Latvia, for instance, only 26,000 organizations of the total of 80,000 registered in the country were active in mid-1996. However, Estonia differs from the other Baltic States in the sense that it has by far the highest ratio of active business organizations per capita.

The second consequence of economic transformation is the diminishing direct role of the state in the organization sector. The role of foreign companies should be given close attention in the analysis of ownership transformation. Although Nordic companies continue to hold a dominant position in Estonia, other foreign investors are now becoming more active in the Baltic States.

The third significant outcome of transformation is the structural change of the Estonian organization sector: the Soviet system in which the accent was on industrial production, has been replaced by an economy that relies heavily on trade. As a consequence almost 40 % of all business organizations are registered within wholesale or retail trade.

In a regional analysis, very little has changed in the Estonian organization sector since the Soviet era: the organization sector remains heavily centralized around the capital city. The role of country capitals is expected to gain in importance in the future.

To summarize, the factor that looms in the background of the transformation of the Estonian organization sector is not so much the privatization of state organizations, but rather the establishment of new organizations. This means that research on organizational transformation is not only about change, but also and importantly about development.

Notes

1. This research was undertaken with support from the European Commission's Phare ACE programme 1995.
2. NEP is an abbreviation for Novaya Ekonomicheskaya Politika, which was applied in Soviet Russia during 1921-28. The NEP system was introduced after the collapse of War Communism, which forced the state to retreat one step in the construction of socialism and adopt typically capitalistic measures, such as private entrepreneurship and foreign capital, on Soviet territory (Nove 1992, 78-144; Liuhto 1994b, 18-29).
3. The transformation of the Estonian enterprise sector was chosen as the subject for this study because Estonia has managed to transform its economy towards a market-oriented system perhaps faster than any other post-Soviet republic.
4. Self-employment will not be studied in this context because it should be regarded as a profession rather than entrepreneurship: the self-employed did not have the right to employ other people. Furthermore, self-employment has only limited economic significance. In 1990 there were only about 600 registered craftsmen in Soviet Estonia (Lugus et al. 1991, 32-35). Similarly, 'entrepreneurial activity' in the shadow economy will not be examined in this study because it does not meet the criteria of official entrepreneurship (Grancelli 1988).
5. From 1983 onwards, enterprises from socialist countries had the right to start joint ventures on Soviet territory (Matejka 1988, 171-189).
6. Estimates of direct foreign investment on the eve of independence vary from USD 84 to 150 million (Informare 1992a, 29; Borsos 1995, 12). The figures differ so widely because of rampant inflation of the rouble, very much complicating the task of estimation (Liuhto 1995a, 102-117).
7. In this context one needs to underline that the 1992 and 1995 statistics include all registered organizations because no reliable statistics were available on active business organizations during these particular years. The 1996 statistics presented in the Table cover only active business organizations. These differences may undermine efforts at detecting a reliable trend in development.
8. Industrial output in Estonia dropped by 35 % in 1992, by 19 % in 1993, and by 3 % in 1994 but showed an increase in 1995 of 1.4 % (Ministry of Economic Affairs 1996, 10).
9. The number of registered organizations in Estonia in 1992 varies to some extent because some organizations operated in more than one field.

Bibliography

Borsos, J. (1995), *Domestic Employment Effects of Finnish FDIs in Eastern Europe*, The Research Institute of the Finnish Economy, Helsinki.

Cockburn, P. (1989), *Getting the Russia Wrong — The End of Kremlinology*, Verso, London.

Estonian Investment Agency (1995), *Invest in Estonia Factsheets*, Estonian Investment Agency, Tallinn.

Grancelli, B. (1988), *Soviet Management and Labor Relations*, Allen and Unwin, Boston.

Hirv, D. (1996), 'Aasta pärast suletakse 50,000 ettevõtet', *Kaubaleht* 7.10.1996, p. 9.

Informare (1992a), *Foreign Economic Relation of Estonia*, Informare Ltd., Tallinn.

Informare (1992b), *Invest in Estonia*, Informare Ltd., Tallinn.

Kallio, M. (1990), *Suomalais-neuvostoliittolaiset yhteisyritykset*, SITRA publication, Helsinki.

Katila, R. (1990), *Suomalais-neuvostoliittolaiset yhteisyritykset SNTL:ssa — oikeudelliset ongelmat*, Finnish-Soviet Chamber of Commerce publication, Helsinki.

Kaubaleht (1995), 'Väga väikese põhikapitaliga ettevõtted domineerivad', *Kaubaleht* 23-29.1.1995.

Kilvits, K. (1993), *Current State of Estonian Industry*, The Research Institute for the Finnish Economy, Discussion papers no. 500, Helsinki.

Kozminski (1993), *Catching Up? — Organizational and Management Change in the ex-Socialist Bloc*, State University of New York Press, Albany.

Laurila, J. (1993), 'Suoran sijoitustoiminnan kehittyminen Venäjällä ja Suomen lähialueilla', *Review of Economies in Transition* 10/1993, Unit for Eastern European Economies, Bank of Finland, pp. 33-61.

Liuhto, K. (1994a), *Ulkomaiset investoinnit Viroon — tilastoja ja totuuksia*, Turku School of Economics and Business Administration, Institute for East-West Trade, Turku.

Liuhto, K. (1994b), *A Comparison of Foreign NEPmen and Contemporary Joint Ventures in Russia — A Historical View in Predicting Future Development*, Turku School of Economics and Business Administration, Institute for East-West Trade, Series C1, Turku.

Liuhto, K. (1995a), 'Statistical Illusions of Joint Ventures in Russia, St. Petersburg: New Klondyke or Unusual Flower-Growing Swamp?', *SLOVO: A Journal of Contemporary Russian and East European Affairs* 8/1, pp. 102-117.

Liuhto, K. (1995b), 'Foreign Investment in Estonia: A Statistical Approach', *Europe-Asia Studies (formerly Soviet Studies)* 47/3, pp. 507-525.

Lugus, O., Venesaar, U. and Vitsur, E. (1991), *Development of Entrepreneurship in Estonia*, Estonian Small Business Association, Institute of Economics, Estonian Academy of Sciences, Reprint 36, Tallinn.

Matejka, H. (1988), 'More Joint Enterprises within CMEA', in J. Hardt and C.H. MacMillan (eds.), *Planned Economies: Confronting the Challenges of the 1980s*, Cambridge University Press, Cambridge, pp. 171-189.

Ministry of Economic Affairs (1996), *Estonian Economy 1995-1996*, Ministry of Economic Affairs of the Republic of Estonia, Tallinn.

Nove, A. (1992), *An Economic History of the USSR*, New and final edition, Penguin Books, London.

Pautola, N. (1996), 'The Baltic States and the European Union — on the Road to Membership', *Review of Economies in Transition* 4/1996, pp. 21-40.

PlanEconReport (1989), 'Update on Soviet joint ventures', *PlanEconReport* 5/41.

Rozental, V. (1995), 'Pooled registeeritud firmadest on Tallinnas', *Äripäev* 03.10.1995.

Slider, D. (1991), 'Embattled Entrepreneurship: Soviet Cooperatives in an Unreformed Economy', *Soviet Studies*, vol. 43, no. 5., pp. 797-821.

Sorainen, A. (1993), *A Foreign Investor in the Baltics*, Lakimiesliiton kustannus, Helsinki.

Sutela, P. (1991), *Economic Thought and Economic Reform in the Soviet Union*, Cambridge University Press, Cambridge.

Van Arkadie, B. and Karlson, M. (1992), *Economic Survey of the Baltic States: The Reform Process in Estonia, Latvia and Lithuania*, Pinter Publishers, London.

Venesaar, U. and Vitsur, E. (1995), 'Development of Entrepreneurship', in O. Lugus and G.A. Hachey Jr. (eds.), *Transforming the Estonian Economy*, Institute of Economics, Estonian Academy of Sciences, Tallinn pp. 187-207.

Xueref, C. (1988), *Guide to Joint Ventures in the USSR*, International Chamber of Commerce publication, Paris.

Yhteisyritykset Neuvostoliitossa (1989), KPMG-Wider publication, Helsinki.

2 'New Russians' and Social Change

JOHAN BÄCKMAN

Introduction

Russia is very much virgin territory for social scientists. In the fieldwork I have done within this territory, I have been concerned not so much with strict methods or theories, but rather with the methods of pure exploration. Given the difficulties involved in making interpretations on the basis of Western classifications, concepts and theories, I have considered it wiser to start out with simple questions. The main question I have wanted to address is this: *How does the development of market relations affect the relationships between people?* The rapid changes that have been taking place in Russia in recent years provide fruitful soil for such an examination: the society of market reforms serves as a valuable laboratory for sociology.

This article is concerned to examine the changes sweeping Russian society from the vantage-point of one particular elite group. The focus is on the new business managers of the private sector, the so-called 'New Russians' (*novye russkie*). The position of an elite is seen here as determining the overall development of society, as one of the models for forecasting how the general conditions in society will change (Babaeva et al. 1994). The purpose of this article is to provide, by way of an experiment, the material required for a scientific evaluation of social change. It is based on my forthcoming monograph *New Russians — In Search of Social Change*, in which I will be exploring processes of social change on the basis of an analysis of ten focused qualitative interviews with representatives of the business elite ('New Russians') during 1995 and 1996, as well as on the basis of a wide range of secondary sources (Bäckman 1997).

This article is based on a qualitative analysis of the ten semi-structured focused interviews with top business managers. These interviews served primarily as a learning process for myself: the 'New Russians' to whom I spoke were in the position of teachers of the process of social change, describing and evaluating the changes as they had experienced them.[1]

'New Russians' as a Stereotype

While the (journalistic) stereotype of 'New Russians' seems to be a rather vague mixture of idealistic admiration and heavy prejudice, all the informants were asked to define in their own words how they understood the concept. Their definitions repeated the emphatically dualistic nature of the concept, but it still remained vague. A bank manager in his thirties described the concept as follows:

> There are two meanings for New Russians, on the one hand it refers to real businessmen, bankers, new industrial managers, private owners, real estate agents. Then there are those New Russians who are simply bandits [*bandity*]. They are different New Russians, in a negative, ironic sense. [...] New Russians are associated with leather jackets, crew-cut, golden jewellery, mobile phones, Mercedes Benzes. [...] They usually operate small businesses and have no other way to bring themselves forward. [...] The New Russian is someone who just one year ago was nobody and who had nothing. Then, within the space of one year, by whatever means, he has made enough money to buy an imported car, a mobile phone [...] fancy clothes. But they still don't know what taste is. They are not gentlemen. [...] Within a short period of time he has earned a great deal of money. He has no background, no knowledge on how to spend that money [...] This is why they usually do not have a very good house, but they do have their Mercedes and mobile phone and they go to casinos, spend money on women etc. [...] This is the image of a New Russian. He has no culture or education on how properly to spend his money. One way to spend all that money is to travel to the Canary Islands, to the USA, to the Maldives, to the Bahama Islands, to drive a Mercedes or a BMW. Often it is very difficult to make the distinction between a New Russian and a bandit because so far they have been closely interconnected.

A manager of a major American-owned company defined the concept of New Russian as contradictory. He considers it mainly in negative terms, but points out that it probably does have some positive aspects about it depending on the person who is speaking:

> People who work in Western companies earn less money than those working for Russian firms. [...] It is understandable that this is how the concept of New Russians is defined. I myself do not feel I belong to this category [...], because I am not working for a Russian company engaged in grey *biznes* and making huge profits [...]. The concept of New Russian refers to those people who are making easy money in the black and grey markets and are not involved in proper *biznes* at all. [...] Perhaps somewhere New Russians are understood as people who also do legal *biznes* [...]. In general I would say the concept refers to the new generation, which emerged and got involved in [...] *biznes* ... and of course succeeded ... when you talk about New Russians, you would probably want to talk about success as well. [...] Those who like New Russians will say that they

are new, energetic people engaged in *biznes* and who have lots of money; others will say they have struck it rich easily and through the grey markets. I myself do not like to talk about these things in positive or negative terms. We should talk about Russians, ordinary Russians.

A 60-year-old manager of an insurance company considered 'New Russians' as pioneers of the market economy, as the first private entrepreneurs of the late 1980s. However, the meaning of the concept has since then changed and taken on a negative slant. He argues that the concept can refer, or at least should refer, to a 'middle class':

The notion of New Russians has several meanings. First of all it refers simply to the entrepreneur who left the state sector and decided to put his own money and health on the line in order to do *biznes*. This is the starting-point for the meaning of the concept. [...] New Russians are in fact those who immediately went to the cooperatives. The meaning of New Russians has changed since then, ... from a scientific point of view New Russians should represent a middle stratum, a middle class. It is possible that they now do in fact represent it. [...] Among entrepreneurs there are large numbers of people who are involved in the shadow economy and even criminal activities. [...] New Russians have huge amounts of money, deposited in foreign accounts [...]. The New Russian entrepreneur does exists, but the concept is broader than the ideological term. Ideologically speaking it is a negative stereotype. [...] It now has negative meaning.

A manager in his thirties observed that the concept of 'New Russians' has nothing whatsoever to do with business, since the concept 'originates from the sphere of moral relations':

To an extent it is the same thing that happened in America [...] when people struck it rich with oil. That is where this understanding comes from, new money and old money ... old money, European aristocracy ... showing off is not acceptable, especially if you've got lots of it, but new money, people want to show the whole world ... how much they have earned. In my opinion this concept does not come from the realm of *biznes*, but ... from the realm of human behaviour ... from the circle of social life. I myself do not like the concept of New Russian, it gives the impression of splashing out big money all around, and the money is usually earned by different means, not always honestly. [...] I do not consider myself a New Russian. [...] The question is not about *biznes*, the concept of New Russian itself has nothing to do with doing *biznes*. The concept originates from the sphere of moral relations.

A manager in his forties considers the concept of 'New Russians' in negative terms only:

The concept, to me, has a negative tone about it. I think it is understood as referring to young people who are making lots of money, by whatever means, and who do not know how to use that money ... they have not reached an adequate level of culture [*uroven kultury*].

The idea of 'New Russians' that emerged from the interviews had two sides to it, with the accent clearly on the negative side. The meaning of the concept seems to be in a constant process of flux, reflecting the problems stemming from increasing inequality in society. The dualistic properties of the concept are highlighted in the following table:

Table 1.   Dualistic stereotype of 'New Russians'

Positive	Negative
Cultural	Non-cultural
Honesty	Dishonesty
Pioneers of market economy	Ruthless criminals
Stable business	Economic crime
Earned prosperity	Unearned prosperity
Long-term investments	Short-term investments
Good taste	Bad taste
High education	Low education
Prudent consumption	Extravagant consumption
Middle class	Criminal class
High professionalism	Lack of professionalism
Social ascent	Unstable social position
High-level relations	Low-level relations

This study is concerned exclusively with the positive side of the myth. Although stereotypes do not generally provide a sufficiently solid basis for scientific analysis, *everyday speech* about 'New Russians' does offer a reliable foundation in that it clearly manifests the changes taking place in the social structure, the increasing inequality and the emerging position of the new social group(s). In general, the concept of 'New Russians' remains *beyond strict definition*. The only way to unravel it is to look at its manifestations, the individuals concerned and their social lives, and develop sociological constructs on the changing social structure, tracing at least at one level the impacts of the emerging market economy on relationships between people.

Itineraries of Social Mobility

Two different forms of social mobility could be identified in the informants' life histories as they emerged from the interviews. The younger informants (usually aged 20-35 years) experienced a rapid *vertical* social ascent, usually from talented students through a doctorate to top business positions. However, there were also businessmen from the older generation (usually aged between 40 and 60) who had switched from academic circles or from political elites to the business world, thus representing *horizontal* social mobility.

However, all successful business managers had several basic qualifications in common, such as *intelligence, managerial skills, the ability to adapt to new conditions and to succeed in those conditions, a high level of education, work experience and ambitions for individual success*.

On the other hand, the informants attributed their success primarily to the 'period of limitless opportunities' or to 'living in a successful period'. During this period, they said, almost anyone could achieve considerable success, although the situation was now getting more difficult with the stiffening competition on the market.

Without going into the details of their life histories (which shall be discussed in depth in my forthcoming monograph), some comments need to be made about the factors lying behind the trends of social ascent.

Although the 'period of limitless opportunities' was clearly a significant factor in social ascent, educational background played a very major part as well. Top business people usually had a very strong educational background, often coming from elite educational establishments in Moscow and often with post-graduate qualifications. However, this education was rarely in business economics and administration. Instead, education typically served as a foundation for learning something new; as one of the informants pointed out, 'the university teaches you the skill of studying, it teaches you flexibility and an understanding of problems'. Work experience was also considered an important asset for social ascent: this was the only way to learn the practices of the world of business.

'Friends organizing business together' were often mentioned as an important 'initial social capital' for the business. The principal conditions for success were thought to be education and relationships; indeed during the early phases of privatization the markets consisted mainly of 'good relationships'. However, several informants indicated that ambitions of individual success were also a major driving force in their career, although some of them still emphasized the role of the 'work collective' or a 'good team', thus underrating the role of individual achievement.

The old party organizations were not very prominent in the informants' explanations. One of the young managers pointed out that he had resented all youth organizations from the outset: 'we felt it was false, and we didn't like it'. Some older informants, however, felt that these organizations had provided some 'moral direction'.

In the cases of horizontal social mobility, the older representatives of the business elite used to work as part of the regional political elite or in academic circles. During and after *perestroika* they wanted to get into something new and different; their contacts often saw them move into private business. It is clear then that these organizations, and party membership in particular, offered a significant foundation for 'good relationships'.

The main driving force of social mobility among 'New Russians', it appears, lies is individual achievement, although the favourable economic conditions did make the road to individual success relatively easy. In conclusion then, it may be argued that apart from stories of individual ambitions, the rest could be purely a structural phenomenon, a huge market-building process, a short 'period of limitless opportunities' during which virtually anyone could gain success without specific qualifications.

On the other hand, experience in certain managerial skills or in 'Russian business philosophy' was considered as one of the most important factors. The specific practices were described as the 'ability to talk with people', to inject stability, confidence and predictability into business operations by means of *interpersonal relationships* between the managers in the yet undeveloped institutional surroundings.

New Labour Ethics

The informants stressed that even though they had the cash to buy expensive things, they would usually refrain from consumption in order to support the business, often quite simply because they did not have the time to spend the money. When a young manager in his twenties working for a leading real estate agency was asked about the chances of getting rich, he answered without hesitation: 'It's not the money, but the process.' For him, the 'art of making money' was the most interesting aspect of the profession, not the money or the possibilities to spend it. The fact that business managers are chiefly concerned to make a profit for a company gives some indication of their attitude towards conspicuous consumption. In order to succeed in their job they not only have to work hard and restrict consumption, but they also have to invest the profits in the further development of the business.

One of the informants, a bank manager in his thirties, said that he should not be called a 'successful Russian businessman', but an ordinary professional manager in a 'conservative and peaceful' bank. However, he pointed out that there are some really successful individuals who have made fortunes in a short space of time and who are 'absolute workaholics':

> I cannot be considered a successful Russian businessman. I am an officer in a very conservative and peaceful bank [...] which makes a 20 per cent profit and is growing slowly [...] because we avoid taking risks. For me, many Russian businessmen who have had success are those who five years ago started out with 100 dollars and who now have hundreds of millions of dollars. [...] They are absolute workaholics [...] they have time for nothing.

The question concerning the business elite's leisure activities was revealing. On the one hand the managers admitted that they did engage in some sporting activities such as tennis, on the other hand they said they rarely had time for anything else except work:

> Quite frankly my thoughts are on the job all the time, not because I like it but let's say because it is expected. I am simply interested in it. [...] I start at nine in the morning and finish at eight or nine in the evening, working 12-13 hours a day.

A young entrepreneur in his thirties explains that he is like any 'normal person', watching TV in the evenings and playing tennis once in a while with his 'business partners'. Even in the summer it is only during the weekends that he finds the time to go to his summer cottage:

> Unfortunately I have no particular leisure interests, I like to lie on the sofa and watch television like all ordinary people. Twice a week, in the evenings, I play tennis for three hours ... with friends, partners, they are also businessmen [...] during the weekends I go out with the family to our *dacha* [summer cottage]. During the summer my family lives at the *dacha* and I go out there every weekend.

A managing director of a major insurance company says that he has to work so much because he has no education in law or in economics and business administration. The difficult economic situation also requires hard work:

> Because I am not professional in the insurance business, because I am not a lawyer, not a financier, for me all this is difficult. But I am a professional manager. I have, firstly, extensive practical experience in management, secondly I know about the theory of management and I teach management. [...] I work 10-14 hours a day. I lecture from 4pm to 6pm, and still come back to the office after that. This is a kind of milestone in life, the financial situation is difficult, the economic situation in the country [...] a lot depends on my private contacts.

A manager in his forties admits that he works at least ten hours a day, but emphasizes the importance of 'inner management' (the better the management, the less you have to work). In general, however, the unstable situation and *endless flow of new information about the markets calls for constant work:*

> I work a lot. Sometimes 10, sometimes 15, but never less than 10 hours a day. [...] If company management is good, then one does not have to work so much. Inner management [*vnutrennyi menedzhment*] will suffice. There are plenty of workaholics in Russia. [...] The branch where we work is very difficult. The changes are coming thick and fast, a great deal of new information is flowing in all the time, you have to work hard to find the time to react to it all.

Mainly because of workaholism and perhaps some traditional aspects, 'New Russians' are not familiar with Western-style hedonist consumption. At least the romantic ethic of endless willingness to obtain new and to fulfil illusions, as described by Colin Campbell, cannot be applied in the Russian context. This labour ethics also resembles an ideology of sacrifice of work and willingness to make personal sacrifices. (Campbell 1990).

In a study which compared the attitudes of Russian and American entrepreneurs, one of the results was that the Russian respondents *scored significantly lower on hedonism* than their American counterparts. The following conclusion was drawn:

> Seven decades of shortages, an environment in which resources and decisions have been controlled, and a pervasive orientation toward subsistence may explain the Russian response as a suppression of expectations beyond social entitlements. [...] Human helplessness is not uncommon in developing economies, and often behavioral norms reflect a general suppression of expectations. The extent to which people in these societies can be motivated due to low expectations for potential rewards is questionable. Yet in affluent societies, the opposite phenomenon occurs: expectations are nurtured psychologically by the environment toward greater pleasures and self-gratification. (Holt et al. 1994).

Semenova has studied the professional strategies of young intellectuals who have switched from the state to the private sector in order to get ahead and develop their professionalism. The switch was motivated by a desire to escape one's dependent status, to become 'independent and free'. The young intellectuals who decided to make the move were more oriented toward risk and adventure, and their key motivation was a *new working ethics*, individual achievement, risk and success. Some of them wanted to 'stand up in protest to the command economy'. According to Semenova, the main driving factor behind the switch was an ethics of independence, a willingness to work on one's own and to take risks (Semenova 1995).

Consumer Behaviour

Consumer-oriented happiness has never been an ideological goal in Russia. Now, for the first time, Russians can see themselves as consumers in the sense that those who are above subsistence level have access to a greater range of goods and services than ever before, and they also have greater experience in exercising choice. A more thorough investigation of consumer behaviour will be presented in my monograph on *New Russians*, but some comments are in order here.

Some estimates suggest that a person who earns USD 5,000 a month or more can in Russia be considered 'rich'. The income of the urban business elites in the top income bracket is estimated at around USD 120,000 a year. However, as one of my young informants pointed out when asked about the meaning of a high standard of living, 'it is not the standard of living that counts, but the standard of relations'. In his opinion contacts or 'good relations' were a more valuable asset than any material property. The problem thus centres on the definition of 'rich' in the Russian context. One of the informants described the prospects of 'being rich' as follows:

> [...] The new rich can go abroad to fancy places twice a year or more [...] If you have the money, you can have two or three lovers, buy them expensive clothes, furs that cost 10,000-15,000 dollars [...] expensive cars that cost 300,000-400,000 dollars, apartments furnished with quality western furniture, personal hairdressers and masseurs [...] summer cottages outside the city that cost 100,000-200,000 dollars. They can have guards at summer cottages, who are paid at least 2,000 dollars [...]

A young manager, only just over twenty, pointed out that the most important purchase for the 'new rich' was a car; that, he said, was even more important than the house or flat. However, he also said that after buying a Mercedes, these people would still drive around in their domestic and cheap *Zhiguli* in order to observe people's reactions:

> Mercedes is the most important thing, the new rich are really not too bothered about where they live. [...] If you have a Mercedes, you still use a Zhiguli for a couple of months and watch people's reactions, to find out what people think. Zhiguli is more practical.

Conspicuous consumption tends to be interpreted in the sense of the old Russian proverb 'from dirts to princes' (*iz gryazi v knyazi*): for the most part businessmen tend to label such behaviour as showing off, as 'uneducated' or 'uncivilized':

If you have nothing to show, that is obviously not nice. It is a mindless way of behaviour [*durnoi ton*]. [...] These are usually people who do not have enough education, who do not have enough inner culture.

A consultant in his forties says that *the question of conspicuous consumption is a question of business honesty*. If you are running an honest business, you will not be afraid to show off your success:

If you have an honest *biznes*, you do not have to be afraid of showing it. If your *biznes* is not so honest, then you will always be afraid of showing it. ... [...] If you have an honest *biznes*, then it depends on what the person is like ... on the psychological aspect. Does he need to be something to feel comfortable, does he need to ... boast [*hvastatsya*] ... does he need something like that [...] in order to be societally acknowledged [*priznanno obshchestvenno*] or needless.

On the other hand, even if you do have an honest business, you will always run the risk of blackmail if you show off. Criminals are on the look-out to find well-to-do people or profitable companies that they can blackmail:

The *mafiya* knows a lot, but it doesn't know your income unless you show off. If they knew, they would come back and blackmail more.

One of the reasons why those who are better off do not always sleep so well, lies in their uncertainty about the future, fears of one further new deal of property. A young manager in his thirties does not want to speak about himself when asked about conspicuous consumption, but he suggests that some businessmen are reluctant and unable to invest in the future because it is not known what the future holds. His comment that 'it is difficult to plan for tomorrow', helps to explain all the extravagant consumption, even though he does point out that features of consumption depend on the consumers' educational standards:

I do not want to speak about myself, but in general. Usually they [Russian businessmen] spend their money on themselves ... on a car, an apartment, at this stage they will not invest in their business. [...] I think that this has to do first of all with the economic situation. In situations of great economic instability it is quite difficult to plan ahead. I would not prepare a business plan for two or three years ahead even though I know what should be done. To an extent you can understand them. Of course it boils down to their not having enough education, but on the other hand there is the recognition that your chances are here and now, it is difficult to plan for tomorrow. ... This is the general understanding.

On the other hand a young manager says that when their business was growing rapidly, the friends who had put together the initial capital decided that 'the less we take out for private consumption, the more we can invest into further development':

> I ended up [*popal*] ... I was invited to work at [company name], a commercial company where at the time one of my friends was working [...] he was director of the laboratory, he brought me in as an operator. At that time the salaries were high. It was a commercial company, we were paid [...] 10-20 times more than [...] the average pay. In the first shop we paid for the facilities, the real estate, almost 60 square metres, we paid almost 8,000 dollars altogether, 8,000 dollars for the business premises, for the rest of life ... 5-6 people can easily put together that sort of money [...]. We leased our first printing machine. We agreed that the less we take out for private consumption, the more we can invest into further development.

A young manager of a chain of shops says that being rich means first of all 'freedom', especially in terms of tourism:

> I like to be rich because it means I can feel myself free. I like to travel to South Africa for holidays with my wife, to Egypt, I like to travel to warm places twice a year. The air quality is poor here, it's dirty, but down there the sun is always shining. [...] The income means you can feel free. [...] Money is not of course enough, but without money it is difficult to be free. There are people such as artists who can be free even if they have no money at all. But they live in a different world, they do not need prosperity at all.

The 'New Russian' consumer culture seems to be a rather odd mix of workaholism, luxurious lifestyles, and fear of criminals and 'others'. On the other hand, despite their freedom of choice, the new rich will typically opt for a lifestyle that is quite similar to the lifestyle of the former privileged Soviet elite. Consumption patterns are not compulsive, escapist or numbed by the abundant satisfaction of false needs. Moreover, this consumer culture is an odd heritage of Soviet consumer culture, to which the idea of a never-ending fulfilment of hedonist dreams can hardly be applied (at least for the time being).

On the basis of the informants' descriptions and other sources, several factors can be identified behind the consumption patterns of the 'New Russians' during social change. (1) 'New Russians' often refrain from consumption at the expense of long-term business investment, thus giving priority to business interests. Sometimes they will 'collect a fortune' during economic instability, sometimes simply spend all the money out of concern over the instability. (2) 'New Russians' are afraid of criminals and blackmailers, restricting their consumption when appearing in public. (3) They are also afraid of tax officials because extravagant consumption is usually associated with economic crime. (4) In general business managers do not want to identify themselves with the negative side of the myth of 'New Russians', but to underline the distinction to 'uncultural, uncivilized criminals'. (5) The traditions of collective sociability did not allow for differentiation, thus restricting consumer behaviour. (6) In general hedonist consumption remains alien to Russian consumer culture. (7) 'Social capital' (contacts and good relations) is generally appreciated more than material wealth. Social capital is also one of the foundations of social differentiation, serving often as initial capital for the business. (8) To some extent the consumption patterns of 'New Russians' resemble the luxurious lifestyle of the privileged elites during the Soviet era, which means they often have negative connotations in the eyes of ordinary people. (9) Consumption is restricted by the lack of free time. Many successful business managers can be described as 'workaholics' (*trudogoliki*), which is why purchase decisions are often made by housewives. (10) There is no established consumer culture for the emerging middle class or the 'New Russians'.

Privatization of Private Life

Social change is a complex sociological concept; indeed sociology is always, in one way or another, concerned with processes of social change. The study of social change can apply the whole range of sociological methods and theoretical perspectives. It has been said in various contexts that contemporary Russian society is facing an extraordinary 'social change'; but what, exactly, could that mean?

The new, emerging positions in the changing social structure cannot be defined within set, traditional frameworks, for example on the basis of labour market positions; we need to look at aspects relating to consumption patterns and way of life. The process of social change, in the context of the 'New Russians', refers first and foremost to the *emergence of an individualized and privatized life-world*, which is closely associated with the emergence of new consumption patterns, labour ethics and emerging professionalism.

The hypothesis of the privatization of social life has been fruitfully studied by Goldthorpe et al. (1969) in the British *Affluent Worker* study. Their idea was to study whether the social life of well-to-do British workers was undergoing a process of privatization. The basic dichotomy was between two hypothetical forms of sociability, called the 'working class perspective' and the 'middle class (bourgeois) perspective'. The working class perspective emphasized, firstly, that collective action has a strong role, and mutual aid and solidarity are the most significant aspects of social life. Secondly, the orientation consists of a strong willingness to make a dichotomy between 'us' and 'them', i.e. between the workers as 'us' and political or other authorities as 'them' having merely fatalistic connotations. The third argument emphasized that individuals with a working class orientation are heavily focused on maintaining their standard of living and style of life, not on developing or widening their experiences. And finally, working class individuals are living in and for the present rather than showing ambitions or concern about the future.

The hypothetical middle class or bourgeois orientation included an individualistic social ethic, where the prime value and crucial indicator of the individual's moral worth was individual achievement. Secondly, middle class individuals were future-oriented, they were looking ahead in time and tended to plan their future by making present sacrifices in order to ensure greater benefits in the future. Thirdly, the middle class understanding of the social order was hierarchical, and finally, the central feature of the orientation was an aspiration to ascent in this order both in terms of work career and living standards. The shift from the working class perspective towards the middle class one was described as a process of *embourgeoisement*.

The results of the study showed that a family-centred and privatized way of life was merely a norm among the affluent workers, and that economic advancement was a matter of paramount importance for the households. The solidaristic attitudes were absent not only in life out-of-work, but also in working lives, causing instrumental attitudes towards work. In addition, the commitment to the collective means of achieving economic goals was weakening, and the affluent worker developed a preference for individual independence.

Since the features of the working class orientation, as described in the *Affluent Worker*, closely resemble the collectivist forms of sociability in Russia, it should be interesting to discuss whether a similar kind of privatization of private life and individualization of the life-world is now taking place among the 'New Russians'. The analogy I have drawn is of course rather simple, but I would still insist that there are close similarities between Russian collectivity, which came about for historical reasons and which were developed by the shadow economy, and the sociability of the 'working class perspective' described in the *Affluent Worker*.

As noted earlier, prosperity begins to set the affluent businessmen apart from the surrounding world. The main driving force in this social change is represented by new consumption patterns. While new meanings, values and social patterns begin to take shape around the new rich, they also have to take distance from the surrounding people, for various reasons, all of which are more or less intentional by nature. New attitudes towards work, new consumption patterns, a new housewife institution, detachment from collectivist traditions, and fear of 'others' are all interwoven to create a process of social change that can be described as the emergence of the modern private, or the privatization of private life.

This reminds us of the social change outlined in the *Affluent Worker*. The modern private, new forms of sociability that separate private life from the public, and changes of sociability at work, resemble the change towards middle class models of sociability. The main idea of the privatization of the private life is '[...] how increasing affluence and its correlates can have many far-reaching consequences — both in undermining the viability or desirability of established lifestyles and in encouraging or requiring the development of new patterns of attitudes, behaviour and relationships.' The change chiefly implied a shift away from community-oriented social life and towards the recognition of the conjugal family and its fortunes.

To some extent the social change taking place among the new rich does of course differ from the corresponding processes in the case of the *Affluent Worker*. Firstly, the new rich are not alienated in the same way as the affluent worker in that they do not exhibit instrumental attitudes towards work. While one of the main results of the *Affluent Worker* project was that the idea of alienation was closely applicable to respondents' experiences of their work and to the meaning and place that work typically held in their social lives, it seems that for the new rich work is still primarily a privatized form of social life under development. For the new rich, work is not only means of satisfying needs, but a goal in itself. As was pointed out in the *Affluent Worker* study, privatization did not only concern the domestic life or the domestic space, but the relations at the workplace also became more private by nature.

Perhaps the most fundamental feature of social change among the 'New Russians' is a shift from solidaristic and collectivistic orientations towards an individualized life-world. This implies a *radical break from the collectivist traditions of social networks* and a move towards Western-type sociability. In a collectivist community, however, it is extremely difficult to make distinctions, and the outcome of becoming rich might be loneliness and isolation.

In the Soviet Union, both official socialization and the shadow economy created a distinctly collectivist culture which has been strengthened by traditions of communal living, for instance. Collectivity can also be traced back to religious traditions. As Srubar has noted, real socialism created a society that is similar to modern Western societies in a statistical sense, but *different in terms of social relations*, creating an 'archipelago of networks' (Srubar 1991). These social relations can mainly be described as social networks through which almost everything at all levels of society can be obtained *po blatu*, by means of 'good relations'.

However, one of the most significant factors in privatization is the willingness to work independently. In a study where she examined the biographies of young professionals in Moscow, Victoria Semenova discovered that most young people preferred to work independently, *samostoyatelno*. This expression is particularly interesting. Oleg Kharkhordin considers the significance of this search in his article *The Ethic of Samostoyatelnost and the Spirit of Capitalism*, where he points out that this willingness is one of the significant factors in social change and market-building (Semenova 1995; Kharkhordin 1994).

Success at work and social ascent also changed the social lives of managers. Change in status has been described as a 'change of one's entire life', including daily schedule, attitudes towards money and expenditure, and friendship relations (Boikova 1996).

A successful young manager in the real estate business described the situation as follows:

> It is difficult to communicate with your old friends because they cannot afford the same as I can. They have different interests in life. But I want to help my student friends. [...] I have two close friends, and I know they would do anything for me.

A 33-year-old managing director considers the changes that have happened in his relations to other people during social ascent as 'dissonance'. This has to do with the fact that people who have not achieved a high standard of living cannot take up the invitation to spending their time off in comfortable surroundings:

> Of course we had some problems. You always have people around you who come from different social positions. And if that position changes in two or three years, if someone suddenly begins to earn much more, then yes immediately you see unpleasant things beginning to happen, for example when you have to invite people over to your home, for a good meal, to a restaurant, they cannot come [*otvetit*] because there is not enough money. [...] You can feel this dissonance, especially in the beginning. But now, first of all I was lucky because ... my closest friends work in *biznes*, it doesn't really matter how much do you earn, whether it's 5,000 dollars a month or 3,000 dollars a month, that's the region we're in. If you earn 3,000 a month and your friend earns 40 dollars a month, then that's a big difference.

This answer points at two aspects of social change: new consumption patterns influence the social relations, and the social sphere begins to move apart from the surrounding world, towards a more homogeneous sphere structured according to profession, social positions and living standards (consumption patterns).

However, the 33-year-old manager points out that this 'dissonance' is not of major significance because most of his friends and acquaintances work for new private companies:

All my friends and acquaintances belong to this circle of society, in one way or another: either they have become businessmen, they have opened their own businesses, or they work in commercial organizations where they have a good, normal salary. [...] Ninety percent of my friends work in commercial organizations.

A manager in his fifties who had set up a private research institute explained that the change in the social sphere concerned most particularly the privacy of the home, where new social norms of privacy have begun to control behaviour, making some old practices less 'normal' than before:

You used to be able to phone people up at night, or drop by without calling in advance [...] That was normal, everybody considered it normal. I myself could make calls until two o'clock at night and from eight in the morning. [...] But that's no longer normal.

The process of change also concerned social relations at the workplace. The main reason why relationships with colleagues have changed lies in the fact that working hours have become a more valuable asset than before. Time is regarded as a commodity that is always in short supply:

It used to be like this at the institute that if I had a problem, I could always drop by in the neighbour's room and ask him to explain this or that, 'you're familiar with this problem aren't you, could you help me solve it'. Then I might ask him out for a smoke or a cup of coffee'. Today, time is a more valuable resource [...]

One of the informants observed that although the standard of living of some of his friends is well below the standards of affluent businessmen, it is always possible to try and help others, for instance by offering them a job:

I cannot help my friends by handing them money, but I can possibly help them in some other ways, by helping them find a job, perhaps in my own company, perhaps in my partners' company.

As regards relationships with relatives, one manager noted that 'earlier they used to feed me, now I feed them':

To relatives? No, not usually, except that earlier they used to help me, now I help them. You always get this situation where your parents feed you and then you begin to feed them. That's quite normal.

However, there are exceptions, as is clear from the following excerpt. In the case of clear horizontal social mobility, an informant in his fifties explained that his small private social sphere had remained entirely intact:

My private circle of friends has remained the same throughout my life. It is not a big circle, no more than ten people [...] in my first job at the *Komsomol*, these people come from a long way back, over the years our relationships have been refined [...] Only three persons came to this private circle from *biznes*.

The Unwritten Rules of Business

On the one hand, the private sphere of managers' social lives has become narrower, more selective and more homogeneous; at the same time the public sphere, i.e. the social sphere of colleagues, clients and partners, has become wider. This again highlights the importance of *personal relations in the public sphere in terms of business stability.*

A manager in his forties stresses that a stable social network in the public sphere is conducive to a stable and 'civilized' business where 'relations are in order':

Of course the circle of friends widened when I became engaged in *biznes*, and its nature changed as well. But I switched to a civilized *biznes*, and I always do everything in my power to keep these relations in order [...] there are no chance relations.

Contacts and social networks play an important part in personnel recruitment. One manager openly admits he has hired all his staff through personal contacts; he has also found all his business partners in the same way. This strategy provides all-important guarantees for business activities:

It is very difficult for us to get guarantees on business partners, that's why they come through private contacts. For me nobody works simply from the street. [...] All the rest work through some acquaintances.

Holden has noted in a research for which 150 Russian top industrial managers were studied that the importance of relationships for business development among managers in Russia was seen in *highly personalized terms*. Holden concluded:

The Russian attitude to relationships is to do with grooming and using people for their influence. This is perfectly logical in a society like Russia, in which power and privilege — over the centuries — has been more important that the acquisition of wealth (Holden 1995).

Contacts, 'good relations' are appreciated even more than material aspects; in fact they are seen as the most valuable capital asset of all. When a young successful businessman was asked about his material wealth, he reacted with some embarrassment and pointed out that the most important things are contacts and relationships, not one's standard of living:

> It is not about your standard of living but your contacts. Top circles are an important source of information for me. For instance, I can go to speak to Mr. [name]. The economy of relationships is not a bad thing, it is simply a fact of life.

The inadequacies of the Russian legal system have thus given rise to special strategies among business managers that are geared to the *creation of independent mutual predictability and trust between actors within business relationships*. These semi-institutionalized forms of behaviour are based on unofficial social norms and sanctions. Interpersonal relationships can help managers to minimize their risks, avoid corruption and interventions by organized crime. One may speak about an institutionalized system of personal relations which has features of a predictable institution, a predictable system of rules which is used by the majority of business managers. Trust between companies is based on trust between people, on a certain form of 'business friendship'.

Personal relationships have several significant functions in business, securing the continuity, stability and predictability of the business environment. A distinction can be made between five main functions of personal relationships: (1) Interpersonal relationships are a special form of social capital, a precondition for any business operation with a major influence on the prestige of the actors involved. (2) Since the privatization of public information on the markets, interpersonal relationships have assumed a significant role in terms of obtaining information. (3) Even passive interpersonal relationships can serve as insurance in crisis situations: contacts are invaluable in predicting and avoiding risks. (4) Statements and recommendations obtained via personal relationships are very important for evaluating the reliability of potential business partners. (5) Personal relationships can help to create new relationships that are essential for business activities and (6) change services within networks (see Cunningham and Turnbull 1982).

One of the principal factors of social ascent has to do with managerial skills. Although emphasizing the role of the two elite educational establishments in the country, a young senior manager of a bank stresses that he has learned everything he knows through experience at work. Experience, in his opinion, was the most important thing of all, not background, family, education, friends or money. He says that the basic education he obtained in economics merely 'helps me understand the problems'; the way they are resolved comes through experience. By experience he does not only mean concrete professional skills and abilities in decision-making (to which he attaches much importance), but some kind of 'business philosophy', an ability to talk with people, an ability to create, develop and maintain interpersonal relationships in the yet undeveloped institutional surroundings:

> Here in Russia the main thing is that you have to talk to people because there is not a lot of printed information; although there is plenty of gossip in newspapers, sometimes pure bullshit, and information can only be acquired by talking to people. And the way you talk to people is extremely important. You must have the ability to raise questions. That's all. And to get answers. In my opinion this is very important. It comes with experience.

One of the main problems of business managers is coping with organized crime and with the *mafiya*. This issue falls beyond the scope of the present article, but is investigated in detail in my forthcoming monograph *New Russians*. I have also examined the world of organized crime in Russia in another context (Bäckman 1996).

Concluding Remarks

The interview material on which the present article largely rests, calls for a systematic sociological analysis and interpretation which is not possible within the confines of this short article. As I pointed out at the beginning of the paper, I have wanted simply to take some careful, tentative steps in the jungle that is the constant flux of social change in Russian society. The interviews offered a wide range of clues for further research and more thorough analysis, which I shall pursue in *New Russians*. My intention here has been to put forward the idea of the explorer-sociologist rather than a hypothetical scholar operating in the 'virgin territory' of changing Russian society.

It would seem that one of the core processes of social change lies in the emergence of *economic independence* among individuals. For the most part people still live in fluctuating social networks of relatives, friends, acquaintances and neighbours, who can always replace their networks if help is needed, but this strategy is now changing within the new emerging social groups (particularly the 'New Russians'). Economic independence requires that individuals have one regular job that guarantees them a living. Unlike before; their salary is now paid on the basis of personal qualifications and other measurable assets. Consumer goods are in better supply than earlier, and consumption takes place entirely within the public sphere, not partly through networks as used to be the case. This changes the function of money as a medium of exchange. Suddenly, one is no longer dependent on networks of friends and relatives. Showing off one's affluence takes on an extraordinary symbolic meaning. Sometimes, however, businessmen have to contend themselves with nothing more than showing off: the young markets still largely lack such things as company histories, annual reports, reputations or any other similar features.

As regards the sociological definition of 'New Russians', I venture to propose the thesis that *all people who are involved at the epicentre of social change, in the emergence of a privatized life-world, can be described as 'New Russians'*. This simple starting-point will hopefully offer interesting ideas for further research. At least it is one of the answers I have tried to give to the fundamental question of how the development of market economy affects relationships between people.

Note

1. I conducted the interviews myself in Russian, tape-recorded and translated them into English. The informants were recruited through private channels on location. For reasons of anonymity only the following information is provided on the ten informants: they occupied the positions of financial manager (age approximately 30 years), senior manager (30), managing director (30), sales manager (30), chairman of the board (55), managing director (55), managing director (35), general director (40), general director (22), and director (55). They represented the branches of trade, banking, consultancy, insurance, food industry, real estate, and research.

Bibliography

Babaeva, L.V., Tarshis, J.J. and Reznichenko, L.A. (1994), 'Metodologicheskie problemy izucheniya rossiiskoi elity' [Methodological Problems of Studying the Russian Elite], *Obshchestvo i ekonomika* No 11-12.

Boikova, T. (1996), 'My nash, my novyi mir postroim!' [We Are one of Us, We Are Building the New World!], *Ogonjok* No. 3, January.

Bäckman, J. (1996), *Venäjän organisoitu rikollisuus* [Organized Crime in Russia], National Research Institute of Legal Policy, Publication Series No. 137, Helsinki.

Bäckman, J. (1997), *New Russians — In Search of Social Change*, forthcoming.

Campbell, C. (1990), *The Romantic Ethic and the Spirit of Modern Consumerism*, Basil Blackwell.

Cunningham, M.T. and Turnbull, P.W. (1982), 'Inter-Organizational Personal Contact Patterns', in H. Håkansson (ed.), *International Marketing and Purchasing of Industrial Goods: An Interaction Approach*, Wiley, New York.

Goldthorpe, J.H., Lockwood, D., Bechhofer, F. and Platt, J. (1969), *The Affluent Worker in the Class Structure*, Cambridge University Press.

Holden, N.J. (1995), *Experiences of applying the IMP interaction approach in the transfer of western marketing know-how to Russian industrial managers*, paper prepared for the proceedings of the 11th IMP conference, Manchester, Sept. 1995.

Holt, D.H., Ralston, D.A. and Terpstra, R.H. (1994), *Constraints on Capitalism in Russia: The Managerial Psyche, Social Infrastructure, and Ideology*, California Management Review 1994, 36(3), pp. 124-141.

Kharkhordin, O. (1994), *The corporate ethic, the ethic of samostoyatelnost and the spirit of capitalism: reflections of market-building in post-Soviet Russia*, International Sociology vol. 9 no. 4, pp. 405-429.

Srubar, I. (1991), *War der reale Sozialismus modern? Versuch einer strukturellen Bestimmung*, Kölner Zeitschrift für Soziologie und Sozialpsychologie, 43:3, pp. 415-432.

Semenova, V. (1995), *On Transition to the Middle Class: Professional Strategies of Young Intellectuals in Russia*, paper presented to the Second Seminar on Middle Classes in Comparative perspective — East & West, Tallinn, 13-15 November.

3 Entrepreneurs in Contemporary Political Structures

GALINA EREMICHEVA AND NINA SOLOVIEVA

The city of St. Petersburg in Russia today has over 48 commercial banks, 56 bank affiliates, and over 65,000 private companies and joint ventures. The entrepreneurial climate in the city is also rapidly changing: attitudes towards 'businessmen' are now more respectful than before. The change is fundamentally due to the growing influence of the private sector on the city's economy. Over one-third of the working population is currently employed in the private sector. The fact that there are more than 150,000 'New Russians' (i.e. people in the top income bracket) among the locals is perceived with less agitation.

There is no doubt that entrepreneurs in St. Petersburg as indeed elsewhere in Russia are now emerging as an independent and reasonably well-organized force. This is clear from the tendency to set up associations, companies, consortia, holding companies etc., which are engaged not only in purely commercial activities but also in creating conditions for the development of business in Russia and in safeguarding the interests of business people. International congresses and seminars have been hosted to discuss the problems and prospects of business development. As members of political parties and various other organizations, business people also take an active part in political life. It is obviously of great interest for entrepreneurs to enter the power structure — the State Duma, governmental bodies, the City Assembly. Indeed the business elite today is concerned not only to work out a general strategy for the development of business, but it is also looking for ways in which to influence public processes at both the local and national level.

Business in Russia has now reached a qualitatively new level where its interests need to be represented in politics. Political engagement among top-ranking businessmen is considered quite natural and well-grounded both theoretically and practically.

The current state of affairs in society — the ongoing social and economic reforms, their social background and political context — is resulting in a stratification of the population according to the political interests of different groups. Each group wants to ensure that its political interests are represented on the political scene.

Experts insist that the government's faltering economic policies, haphazard budget structure, and lack of funding for the structural transformation of the economy are largely to blame for trends of deindustrialization, which is set to give rise to large numbers of bankruptcies and eventually to a further decline in standards of living, an increase in unemployment and growing discontentment among virtually all strata in society.

Rigid, inflexible financial and tax policies also run counter to the goal of business development. The state has taken on itself the responsibility of confiscating the monies of the rich in society, but not the responsibility to improve policies as such.

Misconduct and malpractice among high-ranking officials in the securities market are also detrimental. The mechanisms of speculation in stocks and shares is well-known in macroeconomics. The Ministry of Finance itself resorts to the same ruses to strip people of their earnings: first it issues bonds and then buys them back with money raised from subsequent emissions. The outcome of speculation is all too obvious: a financial crash and a severely destabilized stock market. The course of action adopted by the government organs connives at the speculative practices in the financial market, provokes a further decrease in industrial investments, and drains resources from material production.

St. Petersburg, the city which hopes to emerge as a financial, banking and stock market centre, can do nothing but be concerned about its representation in the power structure, about the professional and personal qualities of those who are representing and safeguarding the interests of the business community at all levels. Lobbying by different bank associations and by particular players in the securities market has already proved detrimental to the national economy, which needs to have more effective methods of operation.

One of the avenues into political life is through the Noitia elections. Since the beginning of genuinely free elections in Russia, people from all walks of life have wanted to put themselves to the test in this arena. The latest elections to the Duma in 1995 and particularly to the City Assembly showed that the days of populist politicians are now over and that the electorate prefers to vote for professionals who have achieved success by hard work. Polls conducted by sociologists confirm that the electorate expect only experts and entrepreneurs to show a genuine commitment to addressing the problems of the city and its citizens rather than simply working for their own best interest. So what are the businessmen represented in the City Assembly striving for? And what kind of plenary power can the Assembly vest them with?

On the one hand, a representative power structure is absolutely essential for the city; without it the people will not have access to unbiased information about how the local authorities are addressing local problems, nor will they be able to express their opinion about decisions taken by the Mayor's office or take part in governing the city.

On the other hand, there must be clear-cut boundaries between the functions of legislative and executive branches of interaction and the formation of local self-government. St. Petersburg is a competent subject of the Russian Federation, and a stable legislative foundation is needed in order that the city can independently resolve its problems and completely realize its huge potential. All this bears on the interests of the local business community.

The local entrepreneurs who made a bid for seats in the City Assembly represent businesses of different sizes and a wide range of political views and positions. Each of the different groups of local businessmen engaged in politics have specific features.

The programmes adopted by the government make it clear that gas and oil as well as agricultural industries are the priority targets for state investment. A much smaller proportion of state resources will be allocated to the development of small and medium-sized business. Analysis of pre-election publications in the mass media and the programmes put forward by the candidates as well as by parties and unions allows us to gain a good idea of the political aims and tasks of the representative groups of businessmen participating in the elections.

4 Petty Production in Baltic Agriculture: Estonian and Lithuanian Models

ILKKA ALANEN

Introduction

This article[1] shows that as a result of decollectivization, two theoretically different types of agricultural systems are currently emerging in the Baltic States: the Estonian and the Lithuanian model. As we will see, these systems are not based on the Western type of 'family farm',[2] but on large-scale production intertwined with primitive petty production. The article is based on a survey material that was collected at the end of 1994; a complementary material from spring of 1995; and on a local community study.

Changes in the Agrarian System From a Formal Point of View

Three Phases of Transformation

My analysis focuses on the rural economy and on agricultural primary production, although the latter forms part of a more extensive agro-industrial complex. It therefore needs to be borne in mind that some of the problems related to the socialist and to the present transition period originate from this broader context (World Bank 1992, 15, 42; Zhurek 1991, 299; Sepp and Terk 1995, 2-3; cf. Clarke 1993).

As will be shown in the article, there are certain differences between the three countries concerned. However, in terms of their natural environment, recent historical background and the general juridical features of the privatization process, they do form a relatively coherent group irrespective of whether they are compared with the other republics of the former Soviet Union (e.g. Wegren 1991) or with the former socialist states of eastern or central Europe (e.g. Summary Report 1995). Nonetheless the Estonian, Latvian and Lithuanian agricultural reforms can be illustrated in one single figure. Figure 1 describes the three phases of the ongoing system change.

Figure 1. Changes in the Baltic agrarian system

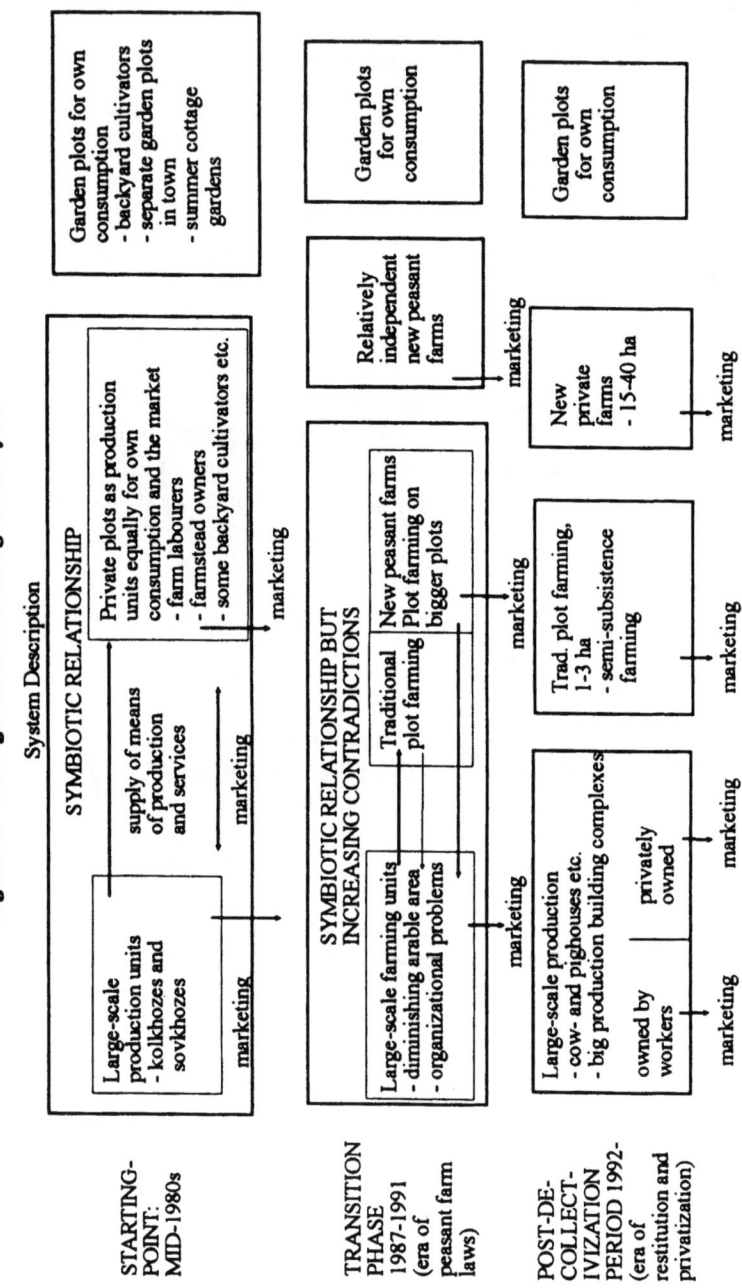

The Starting Point 1987-1991

This phase is characterized by the symbiotic nature of the agricultural system before the beginning of privatization, implying a complementary and rather uncompetitive relationship between large-scale farming and plot farming (McIntyre 1991 and 1992; Swain 1993; Hann 1993, 102). This was indeed a general characteristic of Soviet-type agriculture. Private plots made use of the large labour reserves and effectively increased the supply, quality and variety of foodstuffs and helped collective farms reach their production targets. On the other hand, the collective farm routinely offered plot farmers various infrastructure services, including (in the same way as in Western contract cultivation) cattle feed, corn, fertilizers, calves, ploughing, sowing, marketing channels, and covered a large part of their costs. The acreage of the plots and the number of livestock were restricted by legislation, even though there were differences in this regard between the Baltic countries. In practice, however, the legal norms were flexible, probably in all the Baltic countries. According to Põder (1996), Estonian plot farmers had access to all kinds of land that could not be cultivated by machine (stony fields, littoral and forest meadows, outlying fields) or otherwise unproductive lands. From the 1960s onwards cattle breeding was allowed to the extent that it was possible to feed the cattle, to provide the necessary cow sheds and enough family members to tend the cattle. Many agricultural and even non-agricultural workers in the Soviet countryside had a better life than their urban counterparts (cf. Selden 1994, 429-430; McIntyre 1992, 82-84, 86-88; Wegren 1991, 134-135; Povilianus 1993, 22; Palm 1992, 289). The formal division into the social and the private was thus to a large extent abolished, and people enjoyed a relatively comfortable life.

While the symbiotic relationship was in its general structure the same, there were considerable internal differences between the various parts of the former Soviet Union and even between the Baltic republics. According to the World Bank (1992, 193), in 1989 Lithuanian plot farmers possessed 10.5 % of the cultivated land and accounted for 30.6 % of gross production value. The figures for Latvia were as low as 5.2 % and 24.5 %, and for Estonia even lower, 4.5 % and 21.3 %. The differences between the republics were biggest in animal husbandry. Lithuanian plot farmers accounted for almost one-third of the gross production value of animal husbandry, while their Latvian and Estonian counterparts made up only one-fourth and one-sixth, respectively. The data collected from different sources by Wegren (1991, 121, 124) are consistent with the former, although it only applies to kolkhozes. Wegren also completes the picture drawn by the World Bank. The Lithuanian kolkhonics spent much more time in plot farming than did their Estonian and Latvian colleagues (ibid. 123). They concentrated markedly more on animal husbandry or on the production of milk and dairy products rather than milk only, and the families made almost a double income (ibid. 123, 126, 134). Similarly, the study highlights the differences of the relationships between collective farms and plot farms. While in Estonia and Latvia milk was marketed through kolkhozes, in Lithuania it went directly to the state and the cooperatives. Thus, plot farming in Lithuania does not seem to be as strictly organized by kolkhozes as in the neighbouring countries, and the Lithuanians might have been more market-oriented, selling a large proportion of their production on the kolkhoz market (ibid. 132).

From the point of view of research on post-socialism it is worth noting that Lithuania came closer to the Hungarian model of Soviet-type agriculture, whereas Estonia had more in common with former East Germany and Czechoslovakia (Poviliunas 1993, 22; Raun 1989, 250; Répàssy and Symes 1993, 83-84). It is easy to foresee that these country differences will also be reflected in the agrarian system originating in the decollectivization of agriculture.

However, outside the symbiotic relationship described above, the rest of the population — even in the capital cities — were also able to cultivate garden patches either in rural kitchen gardens, in gardens of summer cottages or in garden plots of urban dwellings. According to our survey,[3] almost two-thirds of the Estonian, Latvian and Lithuanian economically active population practised gardening. This consisted mainly of the production of root crops, vegetables, berries and fruit for one's own (plus relatives' and acquaintances') direct consumption. Gardening was indispensable especially in the country, because not even the most basic root crops were available in the shops. At the same time gardening developed into a strong cultural heritage in the Baltic countries and was not practised for any actual economic reason (cf. Lieven 1993).

The Transition Phase 1987-1991

The first family farms were set up during the years of *perestroika* (from 1987 onwards). At the same time restrictions on production and on the acreage of private farming plots were gradually lifted. However, even after the mid-1980s, before the beginning of decollectivization, the number of private farms in the Soviet Union continued to decline. At the same time the number of livestock was increasing, giving rise to what Wegren (1991, 136) called the 'resurgence of plot'.

This development was mainly to take place within the old system, for most private farms and even some new family farms remained closely integrated with the old system. This is why the development can be described partly as a turn towards the Hungarian model. It did, however, go somewhat further, leading to increasing conflicts within the old system and sowing the seeds of a new system in the form of rather independent farms. The outcome, however, was not yet a system of independent family farms (see e.g. Alanen 1996a; Sepp and Terk 1995, 3-5).

The Decollectivization Phase 1992-1996 (Ongoing)

The current land reform is creating a new agricultural system on the basis of private ownership. The system is characterized by two main principles, the primary of which is the restoration of pre-socialist land ownership rights, the secondary, complementary one consisting of the privatization of the residual property (residual land, production plants, machines, cattle, etc.) of the collective farms. At the same time this policy has been supplemented by the creation of new plot farms of 1-3 hectares and making the old ones independent, as illustrated in Figure 2.

The privatization process has, firstly, led to a differentiation of the agricultural and non-agricultural functions of former sovkhozes and kolkhozes. Non-agricultural functions involved various industrial, trading, welfare, cultural and other services. Some of these industrial and trade functions (construction industry, power production units, sawmills, collectively owned shops) today constitute the basis of private entrepreneurship; a large number of these services have been transferred to the state and have been effectuated by local (municipality) governments. At the same time and for economic as well as political reasons, it has been necessary to abolish or reduce to the extreme minimum many of these services.

Secondly, privatization has resulted in the following kinds of specific agricultural units (empirically, types of agricultural production units): (1) Large-scale farming units based on major complexes of production buildings. Some of these are owned by their workers (so-called neo-collectivistic enterprises), others are privately owned (capitalistically organized enterprises). Typically, these have no agricultural land of their own. This is due to the fact that, on account of restitution, land is usually restored to its former owners. In all Baltic countries these units are, as highlighted by Sepp and Terk (1995, 14) in an analysis focusing exclusively on Estonia 'a somewhat unplanned transitional product of Estonia's economic reform. [...] Hundreds of cooperatives, limited liability companies and joint-stock companies grown out of collective and state farms, which want to continue the traditional agricultural production and resist the logic of the liberal economic model, are an anomaly for a large part of Estonian politicians and international financial organizations, which could be temporarily tolerated at best and for which they can find no practical use.' (2) Family farms, either farms originating in the peasant

Figure 2. Allocation of production buildings, machines and livestock through privatization (internal auctions, apportionments etc., including informal, even illegal actions)

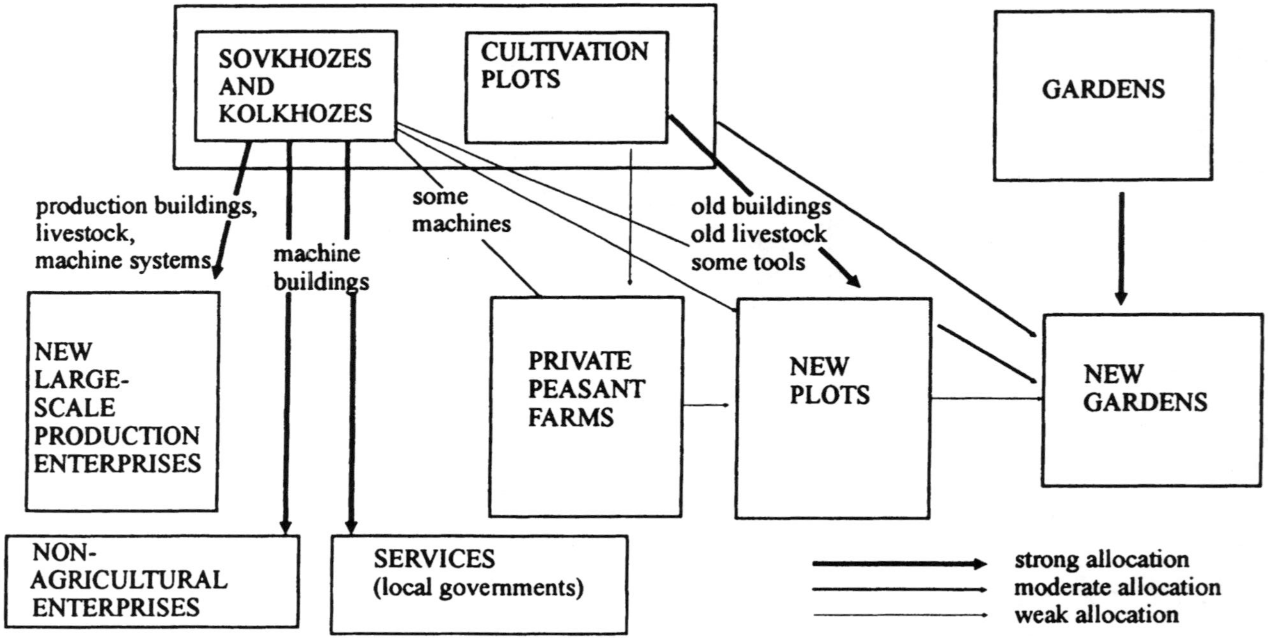

farms of the transition phase or restored old farms dating from the period of independence. (3) Traditional plot farms of 1-3 hectares are still often former private farms originating from the symbiotic system. Part of their production is still marketed. In addition, a considerable number of these farms have come into being as people have started to cultivate land that either belongs to nobody or that is in the possession of their relatives or acquaintances. Leaseholds are still another possibility. Likewise, part of those people who have obtained land through restitution start producing on lands that have nothing to do with the private farms (or the residential and production buildings pertaining to them) of the symbiotic system. (4) Furthermore, garden plots cultivated for personal consumption only remain a separate production unit type. They have a similar foundation as before, but given the increase in food trade a more common reason for cultivating them nowadays is the low level of income and short-comings in social security — or simply cultural heritage. Namely, now that people no longer have access to the cheap or free resources of collective farms (machines, seeds, feed, etc.), they tend to find the cultivation of these plots laborious and often unprofitable. It has to be emphasized, though, that the reform is still in its transitional phase and that these different unit types have not yet been properly established as fixed elements of the overall system.

The formal result of the reform, from the viewpoint of land ownership, is illustrated below on the basis of the rural survey material[4] collected in Estonia in spring 1995.

Table 1. Self-reported proportion of land (in hectares) owned by people working primarily within and outside the agri-cultural branch in 1995

	Engaged in agriculture (N=101)		Not engaged in agriculture (N=448)	
	Cultivated land %	Total amount of land %	Cultivated land %	Total amount of land %
Not at all	21	11	44	36
0.3 ha or less	20	21	21	29
0.31-3 ha	26	23	17	17
3.1-8.9 ha	8	9	5	4
9 ha or more	21	7	7	10
	100	100	100	100

The material was collected in a situation where Estonia's land reform was far advanced. The difference between possession and ownership is a crucial distinction with regard to the interpretation of the results. In compliance with the land reform, land is first conveyed to the land owner. However, it is only after a relatively long and complicated procedure that ownership is authenticated. Generally speaking, virtually all people who possessed land in Estonia during the period of independence or those who live in the countryside are entitled to land.

As we can see from the results, large numbers of households have land in their possession. This is not to say that all land owners will acquire land even during the later phases of the land reform, for anyone has the possibility to lease and, in principle, buy land. Moreover, in addition to the prospective owners, other people also have access to the land that has not yet been restored to its owner. Likewise, our local community study carried out in southern Estonia shows that many of both the prospective and the present owners have placed their land at the disposal of other households.[5]

The results reveal that the majority of households had land in their possession. However, most of these land possessors were only occupants of small garden plots (0.3 hectares at most) or of patches of cultivated land (0.31 to 3 hectares). It is of course only exceptionally (e.g. in greenhouse gardening) that real business can be based on small plots like this.

Of particular interest are those 101 households where the interviewees said they were engaged in the agricultural branch, i.e. that they belonged to the part of population engaged in farming and animal husbandry. Although working in the agricultural branch, 11 % of them had no land in their possession, while 55 % owned areas smaller than 3 hectares in size. In other words, two-thirds had areas of land that were too small for anyone to make a living. In any case, one-fifth were not involved in cultivation of any sort, and the amount of land cultivated by another one-fifth suggested it was used primarily as a garden plot. One-quarter of those working in agriculture may even have practised small-scale farming, but this was not usually a primary activity. Who else could these people engaged in agriculture be except farm workers or possibly those out of work?

These were of course households with the largest areas of land under cultivation, i.e. those who reported that a minimum of 9 hectares of arable land in their possession was cultivated. These were the same people who had the best chances of being independent farm operators, accounting for 37 % of the households engaged in agriculture. Still, out of the 46 households within the study possessing a minimum of 9 hectares of land, only 28 cultivated it. And although fields are not the only type of landed property (others including forests and swamps), land areas as large as these usually comprise fields as well. Therefore, it is clear that a considerable number of people leave their

Figure 3.   Land allocation to different kinds of production units during the privatization of agriculture

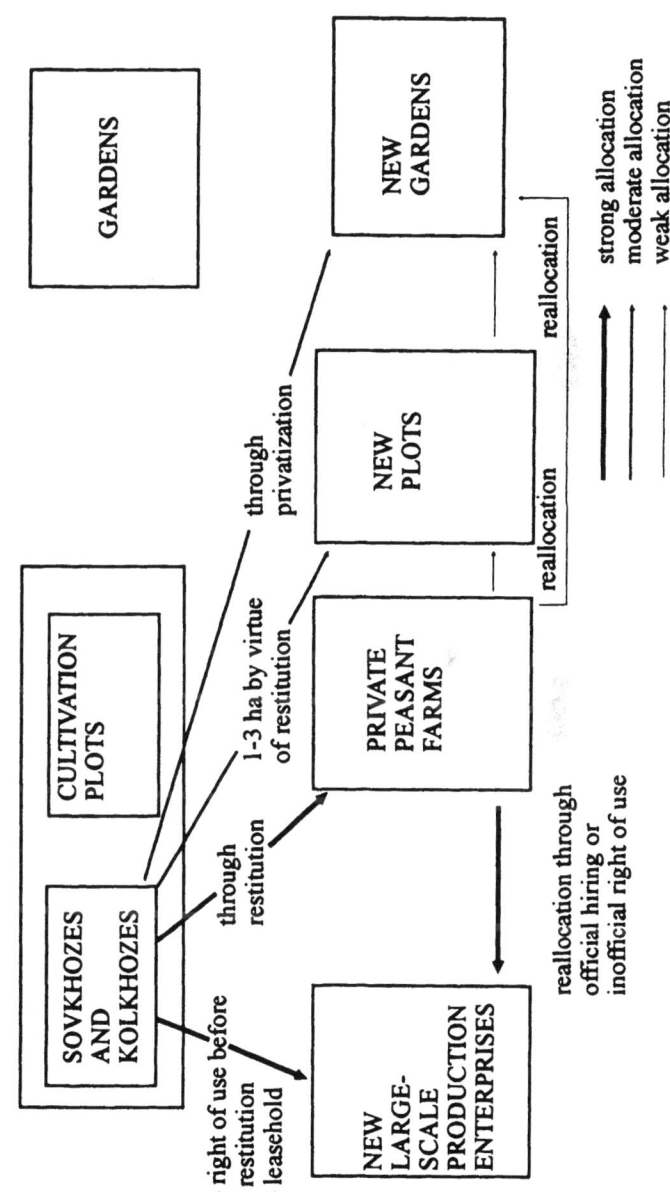

lands completely uncultivated and, quite as evidently, many others only cultivate part of their land.

Hence, the results indicate that (1) people were able to acquire arable land. As a rule, however, (2) the amount of cultivated land was so small that it was not fit for full-time farming, i.e. (3) cultivation was based on some other reasons, such as earning extra income or cultural heritage, or was in fact necessitated by a low level of income level or shortcomings in social security. And vice versa, (4) the small amount of cultivated land may partly be explained by the fact that the transformation from the earlier agricultural system is still under way, and therefore landowners have not yet had the time to begin cultivation or (5) they are unable or (6) unwilling to do so. I shall revert to these results later on in this paper. In the meantime suffice it to note that, on the basis of the empirical results, it seems clear that the ongoing transitional phase can be no more than a marginal reason for there being only small amounts of land under cultivation.

What about large-scale agriculture, the foundation of which lies in the major farm production buildings of former collective farms? According to our community study in southern Estonia, these large-scale enterprises lease or actually use free of charge the land that has not yet been privatized or that the new occupants/owners are not able or willing to cultivate. Thus, as a whole, the land reform seems to have led to a reallocation of land between different types of enterprises, as indicated in Figure 3.

The land reform has thus resulted in an agricultural system dominated by small-scale farming. According to the original theory of agricultural reformists, small farms and family farms should have good prospects for development within this system. Under the prevailing circumstances, however, land resources obtained through restitution are immediately exposed to a redivision. These land resources either remain the property of or are transferred to large-scale farms, at least temporarily. This is because some potential family and small farms are simply never established, some remain or are reduced to plain gardens and still others give up cultivating altogether.

The Decollectivization of Agriculture and the Models of Agricultural and Rural Development

The Survey Material from the Baltic Countries

The hypothesis presented in Figure 3 can be further specified by means of the survey material that was collected at the end of 1994. The survey material also allows comparisons to be made between Estonia, Latvia and Lithuania. In addition, the analysis will largely draw on the preliminary results of the community study carried out in the countryside of southern Estonia.

To provide a background for the correlation matrix I created a considerable number of variables. Of these, however, only those which best describe the Baltic agricultural systems and the differences between them will be included in the analysis. Furthermore, for reasons of simplicity, the discussion is restricted to the countryside and the economically active rural population. The empirical key terms of the presentation are the agricultural and the non-agricultural branch of the rural economy, large-scale and small-scale farming, market-oriented and independent small farming, plot farming and gardening, the agricultural proletariat and different kinds of semi-proletariats. These will be defined in greater detail at the end of this section and in the fourth section. As the same questions were asked in all three Baltic countries, we will also be able to look at the differences between these countries.

The Decollectivization of Agriculture and the Birth of the Estonian and Lithuanian Models

The spring of 1993 was a crucial time for the Baltic countries with regard to the decollectivization of agriculture: this was when Estonian kolkhozes and sovkhozes had to be privatized. As to the relative and absolute percentage of the farming population, the starting point is the same in these countries. In all these countries, 19.5 % of the economically active population were engaged in agriculture during the previous year. However, 1993 saw a radical change in the situation. In Estonia the size of the farming population dropped by 45 % to a mere 9.7 % of the total population. In Latvia, too, the farming population decreased by 10 %, but its proportion of the total population remained at 19.5 %. In Lithuania, however, the farming population increased by 13 % and its relative proportion amounted to 22 % of the total population (Baltic States in Figures 1994, 15). In fact, agriculture has gained a stronger footing in present-day Lithuania and Latvia than in Estonia. It is well-known that the general economic trends in Estonia have been more favourable than in the other two countries. However, during this critical year, there was only a slight decrease in the Estonian and Latvian farming population but a marginal increase in the Lithuanian farming population (ESA 1995, 43; Statistical Yearbook of Latvia 1995, 52; Statistical Yearbook of Lithuania 1995, 36).

The decollectivization of agriculture in Estonia has thus led to a drastic change within the rural population. In Latvia and especially in Lithuania, however, decollectivization has not changed the population's occupational structure. The following provides an overall picture of the scope of the research material, the interviewees' occupational branch and the households' primary sources and forms of income.

Table 2.   Classification of the material by interviewee's occupational branch and by household's primary form of income[6] in the Baltic countries[7]

1. ESTONIA	Agriculture	Non-agriculture	Total	
Interviewee's	%	%	(N)	%
occupational branch	24	76	305	100
Households by primary source of income	%	%	%	%
wage income	75	88	(260)	85
entrepreneurial income	18	5	(24)	8
mainly plot farming	7	7	(21)	7
Total	100	100	(305)	100

2. LATVIA	Agriculture	Non-agriculture	Total	
Interviewee's	%	%	(N)	%
occupational branch	34	66	(253)	100
Households by primary source of income	%	%	%	%
wage income	61	90	(202)	80
entrepreneurial income	15	3	(18)	7
mainly plot farming	20	7	(33)	3
Total	101	100	(253)	100

3. LITHUANIA	Agriculture	Non-agriculture	Total	
Interviewee's	%	%	(N)	%
occupational branch	52	48	(286)	100
Households by primary source of income	%	%	%	%
wage income	46	86	(186)	65
entrepreneurial income	14	5	(27)	9
mainly plot farming	41	9	(78)	27
Total	101	100	(291)	101

The results of the survey are consistent with official Baltic statistics in that in Estonia, those engaged in agriculture make up only a small part of the rural population. In Lithuania, on the other hand, the proportion of this population is large. Likewise, in Estonia the proportion of households whose primary source of income is agricultural wage work is clearly bigger than it is in Lithuania. When the unit of analysis is the household (rather than the individual as in the official Baltic statistics), Latvia seems to come closer to Estonia than to Lithuania. The third feature that most clearly distinguishes between Estonia and Lithuania, viz. plot farming — which is of much greater importance in Lithuania than it is in the other two countries — further accentuates this difference. Nevertheless these countries have much in common. Considered from a Western point of view, agricultural wage work has a prominent position in all Baltic countries, whereas entrepreneurial incomes — agricultural as well as non-agricultural — are of minor importance.

Large-Scale and Small-Scale Agricultural Enterprises

Large-scale agricultural enterprises are defined as those with a staff of ten or more, small-scale enterprises as those with a staff of nine or less. In all three countries large-scale enterprises were mainly neo-collectivistic (often major companies with more than 50 employees), less frequently state-owned and only in a few rare instances capitalistic private enterprises (in private ownership). One outcome of the first phase of decollectivization, despite a measure of reluctance on the part of the Baltic political and cultural elites (Alanen 1996a), has thus been a relatively widespread process of neo-collectivization. This is, in many ways, only natural. Former collective farms left behind such resources as cow sheds, piggeries and henhouses together with their machinery and equipment that were suited to large-scale production but not as easily converted for use in small-scale production. Furthermore, the manpower reserves available had been trained for large-scale production and its division of labour. Despite all the criticism, these people were accustomed to their way of life. On collective farms there were also employees who could not expect very much from the process of restitution. According to our local community study most employees had a sceptical or even firmly negative attitude towards the splitting up of large farms. They had very little to gain (some land and no more than a few machines), but a great deal to lose.

Since the privatization of the means of agricultural production was divided into two separate processes (restoring land to its former owners and selling buildings, cattle and machinery to workers of collectives by vouchers) large-scale farms have no land of their own. However, these farms generally use the old machinery of kolkhozes and sovkhozes to cultivate large areas of land. And even though large-scale enterprises do not actually own land, they do have vast areas of land at their disposal because restitution is still under way. Moreover, farmers willingly lease out restored land at reasonable prices or, in a few rare instances, cede it to these enterprises for nothing.

Most companies in the category of small agricultural enterprises were family business. This also applies to Estonia, where there was at least one regular paid employee on a few farms obtained through restitution. Working on a small farm usually implies working on one's own or one's family's farm. At the same time, however, people often work as wage earners on large farms — this work usually being their and their families' primary source of income. Likewise, judging by the correlation coefficients, a large number of these entrepreneurs in the Baltic countries are market-oriented. Besides, entrepreneurial income is the most important source of income in many enterprises. This is the form of income typical of petty producers in particular, highlighting the fact that the entrepreneur and his family fail to draw any specific wage income from this job; rather, they simply live by the undifferentiated income they get from the enterprise. The categories of wages and profits belong to large-scale production only; in this sector, even managers typically draw their incomes as salaries, which are thus separated from profits in practice (see Alanen 1991, 277-315).

Those doing their (main) work on their farms were divided (country by country) into those working on large and those working on small farms as shown in Table 3.

Table 3. **Percentage of interviewees working on small-scale and large-scale farms**

	ESTONIA		LATVIA		LITHUANIA	
	N	%	N	%	N	%
Small farms	20	31	15	24	53	51
Large farms	45	69	48	66	55	49
Total	65	100	63	100	108	100
Percentage of rural population	21%		25%		38%	

In Estonia and Latvia large-scale production is thus more important to the agricultural branch. In Lithuania, on the other hand, those doing their main work on farms constitute a considerably larger proportion of the whole rural population.

Restituted Farms

Farms obtained through restitution form an independent category of their own, correlating only vaguely with that of small farms. According to our survey, these farms have been entrusted with a reasonable amount of land (often more than 20 hectares of cultivated land). Nonetheless the local community study in southern Estonia suggests that in most cases these farms have no modern tools or production buildings. Farms with a reasonable amount of both have usually been founded before the period of independence or, at the very latest, during the rouble phase at the beginning of that period. At that time prices of the means of production were low and old machinery, still fit for use, could be acquired free of charge from abroad or at bargain prices from collective farms. In addition, the state assisted in the creation of the necessary infrastructure by granting low-interest loans (which were soon devoured by galloping inflation). Of course, these farms usually come under restitution as well. However, the majority of farms that originated with restitution, are completely new farms (Alanen 1996b).

Market-Oriented Farms and Agricultural Small-Scale Entrepreneurs

Two relatively clear-cut variables allows us to examine agricultural small-scale enterprises in more detail. One of them consists of farms engaged in market-oriented agriculture, this being the general feature of those farms. On the basis of our local community study, however, it seems that a fair number of these farms either specialize in animal husbandry alone or combine animal and crop husbandry into a mixed form of farming (cattle farms). Unfortunately, the survey material does not allow a distinction to be made between cattle farms and other farms. The other variable is closely related to independent agricultural petty production in that the family's or the interviewee's primary income is entrepreneurial income (independent petty producers). Numerically, these can be classified, country by country, as shown in Table 4.

As we can see, differences in private farming dating from the Soviet era are still reflected in the number of market-oriented farms. During the Soviet era the number of cattle farms was lowest in Estonia and (clearly) highest in Lithuania. In Lithuania, in contrast to the situation in Estonia and Latvia, not even marketing was in the hands of kolkhozes. Lithuanian statistics indicate that there were livestock on some 70 % of the half a million or so Lithuanian

Table 4. **Number of market-oriented and independent petty producers in the survey material**

	Market-oriented farms	Independent petty producers
Estonia	12	13
Latvia	21	13
Lithuania	54	20

private farms and dairy cattle on two-thirds of them. These figures have remained remarkably stable throughout the 1990s (Statistical Yearbook of Lithuania 1995, 313).

From this alone it could be deduced that some of these farms are quite similar to post-war small farms in the West: a cow or two, a few pigs if any, sheep, hens, sometimes even a workhorse. According to our local community study in southern Estonia, these farms were for the most part of this kind. Usually, it is not possible to increase the number of livestock to any significant extent because of the limitations imposed by the production buildings and the outdated machinery. These limitations exist notwithstanding the fact that typically, these farmers are descendants of old peasant families, they inhabit old family houses and have been or will be restored old areas of land. These limitations are ultimately economic by nature for — though willing — the entrepreneurs lack the resources they would need to set up a modern agricultural enterprise. Judging by the small number of market-oriented farms and independent petty producers in the sample, only a few of these farms can be regarded as technologically sophisticated family farms modelled on the West. Unfortunately, these cannot be distinguished from the rest of the material. Still, both in Estonia and Lithuania there are regular paid employees on two-cattle farms. The yield from the farm is usually the main source of income for the cattle farm, but one-quarter or one-fifth of the households draw their primary income from wage work, mostly on agricultural large farms.

Furthermore, according to my correlation analysis (Alanen 1996b, 22, and Appendix 2), market-oriented farms in these countries differ from one another. Compared with Estonia, farm production equally for one's own use and consumption is much more widespread — and is of almost equal significance — in both Latvia and Lithuania. This suggests that in Latvia and Lithuania, private plot farms dating from the socialist period have a better chance of survival.

In conclusion then, agricultural petty production in the Baltic countries is keeping up the tradition of socialist private farming. In this sense it is relatively traditional and primitive. Estonia differs to some extent from its neighbours by virtue of its somewhat more up-to-date farming practices. This cautious generalization takes no account of plot farming, however.

Plot Farming

The term 'plot' refers here to a land area on which the interviewee and his family practise agriculture. The term has a legal meaning in the context of the agrarian reform: Baltic statistics on agriculture usually define it as comprising farms of 1-3 hectares. The term is somewhat ambiguous, though. A plot may be in one's own possession or it may have been placed at one's disposal temporarily on grounds that it has not yet been conveyed to any legal person. Plot farming is also practised on a smaller scale in the gardens of detached houses and summer cottages. Moreover, many land owners have given the use of their land to someone else — often but not always to close relatives. Land sometimes changes hands against payment (in most cases not exceeding the land tax paid by the owner), sometimes for nothing. One paradox of privatization that emerges clearly from the survey and local community study carried out in Estonia is that land and the means of production often fall into separate hands. Those who have a tractor and a thresher often lack land, whereas land owners do not have the money to purchase their services. For the time being, however, those with machines do have plenty of land. Therefore, plot farming is largely a phenomenon linked with the transition period and will most likely cease to exist as a separate form with the stabilization of new social relations in agriculture. The scope of plot farming and its economic significance to those engaged in it can be seen from the following tables. In these countries, the numbers and percentages of families for whom plot farming was the most important, second most important or third most important source of income were as follows (see Table 5).

As we can see, plot farming is extremely common in the economically active rural population in all three countries. In addition, it is typically the second most important source of income. On the other hand, there are also some clear differences between the countries. In Lithuania and Latvia almost three-quarters of all families are engaged in plot farming. Its relative significance to households is clearly greatest in Lithuania. In Estonia only one-third of all rural households count plot farming among the three most important sources of income (the other being wage income and entrepreneurial income). However, even to those practising plot farming its significance is clearly the lowest. The distinction between the three countries revolve around the most important source of income. Plot farming is rarely the most important source of income in Estonia, very often in Lithuania, while Latvia stands somewhere

Table 5.   **Number and percentage of families for whom plot farming was the most, the second and the third most important source of income**

	ESTONIA		LATVIA		LITHUANIA	
	N	%	N	%	N	%
Most important	10	8	27	14	75	36
Second most important	108	81	104	55	103	50
Third most important	16	12	57	30	30	14
Total	134	101	188	99	208	100
Percentage of households analysed		33		74		73

in-between these two extremes. The high frequency of plot farming in Latvia is explained by the fact that in this country, plot farming is (compared with Estonia and Lithuania) more often only the third most important source of income.

As far as the households are concerned the different sources of income are complementary to one another. A cross-tabulation of plot farming with the interviewee's occupational branch gives some idea of how this works out.

It is clear from the table that plot farming adds to a family's income differently depending on whether it is the second or third most important source of income. Naturally, when it is ranked second, plot farming is of greater significance to the household. When the complementary nature of plot farming is strongest, approximately two-thirds of the interviewees work outside agriculture, and there are no major differences between the countries. As the inclusion of the third most important source of income complicates things rather than helps to clarify them (cf. the position of Latvia compared with the other countries), the following analyses on complementariness will concentrate on plot farming as the second most important source of income. Before that, however, we should highlight possibly the main result of the table: practising plot farming in order to supplement the family's income is also very common in the non-agricultural population. This is clear in the next tables.

The second inference we can draw from the tables is that plot farming increases the livelihood of those working outside agriculture more frequently in Latvia and Lithuania than it does in Estonia. This may have to do with the fact that in Estonia the non-agricultural population is less frequently forced to fall back on plot farming, although our local community study suggests

Table 6.   Interviewee's occupational branch according to the importance of source of income in Estonia, Latvia and Lithuania

COUNTRY	IMPORTANCE OF SOURCE OF INCOME	INTERVIEWEE'S OCCUPATIONAL BRANCH				TOTAL	
		Agriculture		Non-agriculture			
		N	%	N	%	N	%
1.ESTONIA	The second	35	32	73	68	108	100
	The third	11	69	5	31	16	100
	Total	46	37	78	63	124	100
2.LATVIA	The second	39	38	65	63	104	100
	The third	11	19	46	81	57	100
	Total	50	31	111	69	161	100
3.LITHUANIA	The second	35	34	73	71	103	101
	The third	14	47	16	53	30	100
	Total	49	37	89	67	133	100

Table 7.   Those adding to the family's income by plot farming as a proportion of the agricultural and non-agricultural population country by country

	Percentage	(All economically active)
1. ESTONIA		
- agricultural population	64	(72)
- non-agricultural population	34	(233)
2. LATVIA		
- agricultural population	31	(87)
- non-agricultural population	69	(166)
3. LITHUANIA		
- agricultural population	33	(148)
- non-agricultural population	65	(138)

that land would be available for all those interested in Estonia. Besides, the picture drawn by the tables of the significance of plot farming to Latvians is slightly exaggerated in that in this particular country, plot farming was more often only the third most important source of income.

What has been said above applies only to those families where the interviewee was engaged in the non-agricultural branch. Even so our attention is drawn to the thesis proposed by dependency theorists (Wallerstein, Amin, de Janvry, etc.), who say that dependency plot farming as practised in the family circle (see Alanen 1995) is characteristic of the proletariat in developing countries. All the same, this also applies to the agricultural proletariat. In this respect Estonian agriculture seems at first glance to rest more on plot farming than Latvian and Lithuanian agriculture. Estonian agriculture thus seems to conform best to the hypotheses of dependency theorists. Nevertheless, Latvian and especially Lithuanian agriculture fits in better with the dependency theorists' model for the developing countries. Especially in Lithuania but also in Latvia the number of households for whom plot farming was the primary source of income was much higher than it was in Estonia.

A detailed analysis of the correlation matrices (see Alanen 1996b, 27-29) leads to the following conclusions:

(1) On the basis of plot farming, a significant group of independent or relatively independent agricultural petty producers has come into existence especially in Lithuania, to some extent also in Latvia but practically speaking not at all in Estonia.

The relatively independent nature of plot farming, its considerable popularity in Latvia and Lithuania and its almost total absence in Estonia is most apparent if we analyse plot farming as the household's most important source of income. In no country did households making their living mainly from plot farming correlate with (the interviewee) working on a large farm. In Latvia and Lithuania these households correlated weakly with working in a small agricultural enterprise, more strongly with agricultural entrepreneurial income and market-oriented farm production and even more strongly with the interviewee regarding agricultural entrepreneurship as his most important source of income. In Estonia all these correlations were missing.

(2) In general, however, plot farmers are characterized by straightforward proletarianism rather than semi-proletarianism. Wage work either on a large farm or in the non-agricultural branch constitutes the second most important source of income for a large proportion of Lithuanian and Latvian households as well as virtually all Estonian households making their living mainly from plot farming. In Estonia independent and relatively independent agricultural petty producers are actually not included in this class. Therefore, even if cultivated 'for sale', a plot (as a supplementary source of income) is not usually taken as being equivalent to a farm — and in that respect to a

market-oriented enterprise. In the light of the local community study carried out in Estonia, this peculiarity is explained by the fact that the family breaks the tradition of socialist private production with its modest production buildings and storehouses, insignificant amounts of livestock and manual working methods. Especially in the case of keeping up a small private cattle farm of the socialist period, production is practised 'equally for sale and consumption'. This relates either to cultivating a farm obtained through restitution by means of rented machinery or to cultivating a no-man's-land or a leasehold by means of machinery obtained in connection with privatization. Even a restituted farm can be large, but the yield is negligible. As the mere keeping up of a field obtained through restitution requires cultivating it and as one's own and one's relatives' hopes of starting an independent farm have the same effect, one spares no labour or pain despite the insignificant outcome. According to the local community study in Estonia, however, this kind of cultivation will often be given up after just one or two years of experimentation. And if we look at both the farms — engaged in plot farming — where the interviewee had been working in the agricultural branch and the farms where he had been working in some other economic branch, the results are revealing. Plot farming practised on restituted farms is only slightly more important than plot farming in terms of economic supplementariness. Those practising plot farming as their second most important source of income are for the most part members of wage worker families.

Farm production by wage worker families does not, however, consist simply of mechanical crop husbandry on vast areas of land and the selling of crops — as will be made clear by the survey material collected in the Estonian countryside.

(3) For the most part, plot farming is characterized by manual cultivation of small land areas for direct consumption. For this reason, plot farming could almost be called gardening. However, one reservation has to be made: gardening merges partly with relatively independent petty production especially as far as the Lithuanian model is concerned (more on this later).

Gardening

Those visiting the Baltic countryside soon become aware of the fact that courtyards and the immediate surroundings of detached houses are full of patches of root crops, vegetables, berries and fruits, some of which are cultivated in modest greenhouses. Even around blocks of houses one will typically find 20-30 well-tended patches with a variety of plants. In addition, former plot farming areas are often to be found outside population centres. Land owned by relatives and acquaintances give large numbers yet another opportunity to engage in cultivation. On the whole, acquiring land for gardening is no problem, particularly in the countryside. The survey results on the amount of time spent in gardening indicate that gardening is very widespread indeed in the Baltic countryside.

Table 8.   **Number of hours per week spent in gardening outside regular working hours, country by country**

Hours per week spent in gardening	ESTONIA		LATVIA		LITHUANIA	
	N	%	N	%	N	%
More than 5 hours	112	37	129	51	129	45
Less than 5 hours	143	47	91	36	120	42
not at all[8]	50	16	33	13	37	13
Total	305	100	253	100	286	100

It needs to be borne in mind here that the respondents were asked specifically how much time they spent gardening outside their regular working hours, in other words these figures exclude the amount of time invested by other family or household members. This would surely be greater than the figures indicated — and accordingly the proportion of families not engaged in gardening is smaller than is suggested by the table.

According to the table only one-tenth of the rural population in the Baltic countries is not engaged in gardening. This, however, is only the first observation; the second observation concerns the huge amount of time that is devoted to gardening: in Estonia over one-third and in Latvia one half of the rural population put in almost an extra working day through gardening. It is obvious then that without economic motives, people would hardly spend so much of their spare time in plot farming.

The third finding is again related to the Estonian and Lithuanian models. Ultimately, the difference in the amount of time devoted to gardening in Estonia and Lithuania can only be explained by reference to the differences between the two evolving agricultural systems. This difference is clearly seen in Table 8, which shows that 45 % of the Lithuanians but only 37 % of the Estonians spent more than 5 hours a week in gardening. In Latvia the percentage is even higher than it is in Lithuania. As a whole, however, the Latvian features discussed above fall in-between the Estonian and Lithuanian models of agricultural systems.

More generally, it has to be noted that the distinction made between plot farming and gardening was dependent on the interviewee's and to some extent on the interviewer's semantic interpretation. The cultivation of small patches and a few apple trees in the courtyard would obviously be defined as gardening; while the cultivation of several hectares is equally obviously considered to be plot farming. But how does one classify a detached and enclosed garden plot comprising 30 acres at the back of a block of flats? Those keeping up the socialist tradition of cultivating private plots usually have both: a kitchen garden, 2-3 hectares of arable land and some livestock. This often makes it difficult to distinguish between these two different types of farming. Besides, a household may simultaneously be engaged in both of these distinctive forms. This as well as the difference between Estonia and Lithuania and Latvia can be seen in Table 9.

Table 9. **Proportion of rural population engaged in plot farming and gardening**

	ESTONIA	LATVIA	LITHUANIA
Percentage of households engaged in plot farming	30	74	73
Percentage of gardeners	84	87	87

The minor overlap between Estonian plot farming and gardening further suggests that gardening and plot farming also differ from one another at least in this country. This is also evident from the fact that 37 % of the Estonian rural people interviewed spent more than 5 hours a week in gardening — a higher proportion than the number of households engaging in plot farming. In my opinion the differences and similarities between the Baltic countries are best interpreted as an indication that at least in Estonia, the clear tendency for gardening and plot farming to drift apart as independent production units is simply a symptom of a more general model, which is characterized by a differentiation between the agricultural branch and the other industries as well as the insignificant volume of independent petty production based on plot farming.

In Lithuania plot farming (such as market-oriented petty production, Alanen 1996b, 31-32) is typically viewed as a multipurpose activity. The prospects for development in this sort of activity are better in Lithuania than in the other Baltic countries thanks to the socialist tradition of private farming, characterized by the production of dairy produce for marketing and for own consumption. This — in the absence of other alternatives — constitutes the very essence of survival strategies and is supplemented by both plot farming and other means available. In Estonia people are less dependent on plots. This is due to the fact that other rural industries are sufficiently developed to allow people to make a living outside agriculture. On the other hand, people in Estonia who work for wages in the agricultural branch are more often than people in Lithuania forced as well as able to make extra money through both plot farming and gardening. According to the local community study, these kinds of farms are often former private plots of kolkhozes and sovkhozes, even in Estonia. Furthermore, even if one of the members of the family — having lost his/her job, for instance — worked full-time on the farm, the incomes of other family members would be large enough to make plot farming only the second most important source of income.

Agricultural Wage Work

Small-scale farms are more prevalent in Lithuania than they are in Estonia and Latvia, and consequently agricultural wage labour is less important in this country as well. This is clearly highlighted in the following table which compares the relative importance of agricultural wage work but also with wage work in general and other rural occupations. The empirical criteria for the family classification were the interviewee's occupational branch and the family's main source of income.

Table 10. Proportion of rural families drawing their primary income from agricultural wage work (%)

	ESTONIA	LATVIA	LITHUANIA
Proportion of population engaged in agriculture	73	61	46
Proportion of all families with wage income as primary source of income	21	26	37
Proportion of economically active rural population	18	21	24

It is clear then that wage labour has a prominent position in the economically active population in all three Baltic countries. However, the Estonian and the Lithuanian models differ from one another. Agricultural wage work on large-scale farms (Alanen 1996b, 33), the agricultural branch and the future of large-scale farms are closely linked together especially in Estonia but also in the other Baltic countries. In Lithuania there has been a stronger movement towards splitting up large farms than in the other two countries. This is clearly seen in the predominance of plot farming and in the undeveloped state of the agricultural branch in today's Lithuania. Therefore, the splitting up of large-scale farms in these countries and particularly in Lithuania will in all probability leave yet a greater part of the rural population dependent on different forms of agricultural petty production. This is very likely even though the amount of time that Estonian agricultural wage workers spend on their small farms or in plot farming is at least the same as the corresponding amount of time spent by their southern counterparts (see Alanen 1996b, 33). This is due to the fact that in Estonia, this part of the population, besides being agricultural petty producers, also have other ways of making their living.

One dimension of this connection between plot farming and the survival of large-scale agriculture is to be seen in Table 8 above, which illustrates the prevalence of plot farming within and outside agriculture. In Estonia plot farming is the rule only among those who draw their main income from the agricultural branch, in the other countries it is the rule among those who draw their main income from outside agriculture. The interpretation offered is that working within non-agricultural branches is a real alternative to working within the agricultural branch only in the Estonian countryside.

This freedom of choice open to Estonians is also seen in the paradox reflected in Table 10. Estonian families who work as paid labourers in the agricultural branch are at least equally tied up with agricultural petty production as are their counterparts in the other Baltic countries. Nevertheless, their proportion of both all agricultural wage workers and the total economically active rural population is noticeably smaller than in the case of Lithuania — while Latvia once again falls in-between these two developmental models. But to what exactly do these models refer?

Theoretical Core of the Estonian and Lithuanian Models

The differences between the Estonian and Lithuanian models can be outlined on the basis of radical, mostly neo-Marxist theories (Amin, Wallerstein, Meillassoux, etc.). In spite of their considerable differences, all these theories consider the small peasantry as an object of exploitation. The first theoretical accounts of this relationship were offered by French economic anthropologists in the 1960s (Meillassoux, Rey, Terrain). According to Claude Meillassoux (1981), the problems of the developing countries arise from a unique articulation with each other of the capitalistic and the (as he termed it) domestic mode of production. The mechanism of exploitation between these had its origin in two distinct movements.

Firstly, direct and indirect wages are one form of exploitation. The capitalistic sector, which in addition to industrial and mining enterprises also included agricultural large-scale farms, was able to hire extra labour from the non-capitalistic sector. This was due to the fact that (1) this labour, cultivating small patches which did not yield enough for a living, was forced to do wage work in capitalistic enterprises, and that (2) the oversupply of labour forced rival employees to reduce their wage demands to an absolute minimum. The capitalistic employer paid out in wages no more than was necessary for reproduction. On rural large farms, for instance, Baltic agricultural large-scale enterprises are thus in a position to pay wages below the average because families supplement their incomes through plot farming and gardening. According to Meillassoux's theory the employees of these enterprises are therefore rural semi-proletarians or de facto proletarians. This, however, is confined to direct wages only. Capitalistic enterprises and the power elite also profit from the shortcomings in social security, for people are paid indirect wages in the form of unemployment benefits, health services and pensions. As part of these costs can be charged to households (and in the developing countries to the wider family and other communities), indirect wages are also cut. A seasonally unemployed family member can thus go back to his/her farm and work there while other family members stay at home to look after their sick and aged relatives. In the community study in Estonia one example was provided by a case where a family member who was made redundant, took up plot farming on a full-time basis while another family member with an insufficient disability pension dedicated himself to gardening ('so that we won't go hungry').

Second, exploitation is fuelled by petty producers who bring their food-stuffs to the local market and sell them cheaply, which further pushes down the costs of labour reproduction. An example is again provided by the material for the Estonian local community study (even though the element of exploitation does not seem particularly significant at least in Estonia). Among the interviewees there was one family which had received some livestock, including two cows, from the socialist private economy. Milk was sold at below the going price direct to the people in the surrounding village; but they got more for their milk than they would have received from a dairy.

The hypotheses of this theory originate with Russian economist Alexander Chayanov, whose writings have also inspired the theory of a specific peasant mode of production. The thesis put forth by Chayanov (1966) — and by the populistic movement connected to agricultural petty production in general — is that peasant families/family farms do not seek to make a profit but simply to satisfy their own needs. I have pointed elsewhere (1991) to the inaccuracy of this premise. At the same time, however, I have acknowledged that petty farming may contribute to a specific mechanism of exploitation in a way analogous to Meillassoux's articulation theory. Let us move on now to describe the Estonian and Lithuanian models of agricultural development in the light of the above theory.

All three Baltic countries were characterized during the research by quantitative stability of their rural populations and — despite decollectivization — a predominance of large-scale production (wage labour) within agriculture. In all countries the peasantry was widely engaged in gardening and relied to a significant extent on plot farming. However, the paths of development also diverged to some extent, the extremes being represented by the Estonian and Lithuanian models (the position of Latvia in-between these two extremes is omitted from the discussion below for the sake of simplicity). The differences between the Estonian and the Lithuanian models can be summarized as follows:

(1) Large-scale production and wage labour are more dominant in Estonia's agricultural branch than they are in Lithuania. However, Lithuania's small-scale farms, far more numerous than in Estonia, are not usually technologically sophisticated family farms. In all probability they are mainly continuations of socialist private households with their modest production buildings and small amounts of livestock. Even if it were possible to expand production on the strength of additional land obtained through restitution, this would probably be foiled by economic reasons (e.g. the need to invest in production buildings, livestock and machinery). The same applies by and large to Estonia's petty production — less prevalent though it is and possibly somewhat more up-to-date.

(2) The Estonian countryside is far more differentiated than the Lithuanian countryside in terms of industrial structure. This is clearly seen in Figure 4 in that the proportion of those engaged in the rural agricultural branch is considerably lower in Estonia (24 %) than it is in Lithuania (52 %).

(3) The main factor accounting for the predominance of agriculture in Lithuania's rural population is not, however, agricultural petty production as such. Rather, it is plot farming both as the family's primary source of income and as a supplement to wage work. Empirically, plot farming is also the most important clue when separating these two models from each other theoretically.

Figure 4 highlights the following three facts: Firstly, families engaged in plot farming in Lithuania account for a much larger proportion (73 %) of all rural households than they do in Estonia (30 %), i.e. Lithuanians add to their incomes more often by plot farming than do Estonians. The fact that Estonians spend less time in plot farming is not explained by loss of land. (Lithuanians also devote somewhat more time to gardening, although gardening as a whole is almost equally common in both countries.) The greater amount of time that

Figure 4. Estonian and Lithuanian models of agricultural and rural development

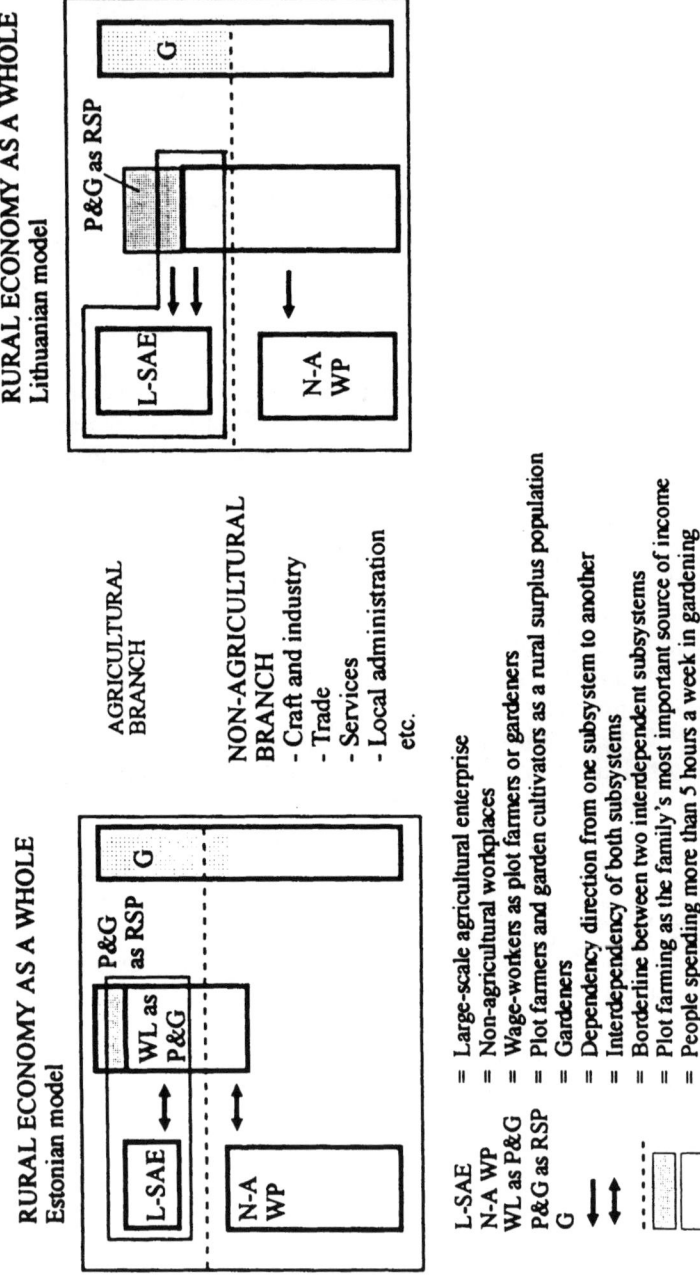

RURAL ECONOMY AS A WHOLE
Estonian model

RURAL ECONOMY AS A WHOLE
Lithuanian model

AGRICULTURAL
BRANCH

NON-AGRICULTURAL
BRANCH
- Craft and industry
- Trade
- Services
- Local administration
  etc.

L-SAE	=	Large-scale agricultural enterprise
N-A WP	=	Non-agricultural workplaces
WL as P&G	=	Wage-workers as plot farmers or gardeners
P&G as RSP	=	Plot farmers and garden cultivators as a rural surplus population
G	=	Gardeners
↓ ↓	=	Dependency direction from one subsystem to another
↕	=	Interdependency of both subsystems
----	=	Borderline between two interdependent subsystems
▨	=	Plot farming as the family's most important source of income
▢ ▢	=	People spending more than 5 hours a week in gardening

Lithuanians spend in plot farming (and gardening) is probably due to their greater need to supplement their other sources of income.

Secondly, over one-third (36 %) of Lithuanian plot farmers consist of households for whom plot farming is the main source of income. The corresponding figure for Estonians is one-tenth (10 %) or, in a closer analysis, even lower than that (the approximate 5 % in Figure 4). These plot farmers are a large rural surplus population who have been left with no better alternative but to live on undeveloped plot farming. Estonia's more differentiated industrial structure as such is indicative of the fact that these 'better' alternatives do in fact exist. One alternative that Lithuanians have evidently lost for good are workplaces on former kolkhozes and sovkhozes.

Thirdly, in both countries those wage worker families who have retained jobs on large farms seem to resort equally to plot farming in order to earn an extra living in conformity with the neo-Marxist theories of developing countries. In Estonia there were 54 employees (including managers and supervisors) and 46 plot farmers (plot farming as the family's second and third most important source of income) — engaged primarily in the agricultural branch — working on large farms. The corresponding figures for Lithuania were 68 employees and 50 plot farming families. But this is where the formal similarities end. The number of families for whom plot farming was the most important source of income and wage income within the agricultural branch the second most important source of income, was much higher in Lithuania than it was in Estonia (Alanen 1996b, Appendix 1). The most likely inference from this (and from the additional argumentation presented later on) is that the interdependence between wage work within large-scale agriculture and plot farming is not of the same kind in Estonia and Lithuania, after all — rather, it corresponds to Figure 4. Lithuanian plot farmers are more dependent on agricultural large-scale production than their Estonian counterparts, which will probably also result in a decrease in their wage level. With respect to Estonia, the relationship between these two agricultural production units has therefore been represented as an interdependence between large-scale and small-scale production, respectively. It appears from the local community study carried out in Estonia (in keeping with Estonian state statistics) that the wage level of agricultural employees (as well as that of supervisors and managers) is clearly below the average and that employees often resort to plot farming and gardening to make extra money. However, in Estonia this is of a more voluntary nature than it is in Lithuania, for it is easier for Estonians to find alternative workplaces in the countryside. This is manifested in the far more differentiated industrial structure of the Estonian countryside compared to that of Lithuania. In addition, Lithuania's greater dependency on plot farming is seen in the fact that those families where the interviewee was engaged in non-agricultural branches often had to rely on plot farming — much more often, indeed, than their Estonian counterparts.

From the foregoing we can draw the following conclusion with regard to the differences between the Estonian and Lithuanian models. In Estonia plot farming is a complement to agricultural production and may contribute to the survival of this branch of production and particularly that of large-scale agriculture during the transition phase. In Lithuania, on the other hand, the surplus population which has its origin in decollectivization, is caught up in the trap of plot farming and is forced to act within the limits imposed by the economically troubled large-scale agriculture and by the undeveloped agricultural production structure. In keeping with the theories of developing countries, it is — to use Meillassoux's terminology — a most potential object of 'super exploitation'.

But how did these two models come into being? I have offered a tentative answer to this question as well as to the question of the impacts of these models on the development of the Baltic countries in a manuscript (1996b) on the basis of which I am now writing a more extensive monograph.

Notes

1. This article is based in part on papers presented to the 'Second Seminar on Middle Classes in Comparative Perspective — East & West', Tallinn 13-15 Aug 1995 and to the workshop 'Implementation of Agri-Environmental Policy Instruments in a Changing Political Environment — Exchange of Nordic and Baltic Experiences'. Vilnius, Lithuania, 9-12 May 1996. The latter (1996b) is a comprehensive study on the basis of which I am currently writing a book in English. The article is partly based on the empirical and theoretical argumentation presented in this book.

2. On this and more generally on my thinking about these policy problematics, see Alanen (1995) and Blom et al. (1996a).

3. A total of 4,500 individuals — 1,500 from each Baltic country — were interviewed at the end of 1994.

4. Based on a sample of 1,000 respondents living in the Estonian countryside, this survey was carried out by a group of Finnish and Estonian researchers in the context of the research project on 'The Privatization of Agriculture in the Baltic Countries'. Some small towns, including Viljand with a population of over 20,000, are also included in the survey.

5. This study is carried out by a group of Finnish and Estonian researchers participating in the project on 'The Privatization of Agriculture in the Baltic Countries' (an independent research under the Baltic—Nordic Project).

6. Occupational branch was classified on the basis of self-report. Households were classified by their primary sources of income. The figures for entrepreneurial income also include cases where this income is the primary form of income of the interviewee only.

7. Although the sample gives a somewhat distorted picture of the proportion of Lithuania's and Latvia's rural population in particular, it is the internal division of the rural population

that is most relevant for the present concerns. In this light I am not aware of anything that would essentially undermine the value of the material.

8. In each country only 1 to 3 interviewees gave incomplete answers; they have been included in the class 'not at all'.

Bibliography

Agricultural Situation and Prospect in the Central and Eastern European Countries (1995), Summary Report, European Commission, Directorate General for Agriculture, Working Document.

Agriculture 1994 (1995), Statistical Office of Estonia, Tallinn.

Alanen, I. (1991), *Miten teoretisoida maatalouden pientuotantoa*, Jyväskylä Studies in Education and Social Research, No 81, Jyväskylän yliopisto, Jyväskylä.

Alanen, I. (1995), 'The Family Farm Ideology, the Baltic Countries, and Theories of Development', *Eastern European Countryside* 1(1): pp. 5-21.

Alanen, I. (1996a), 'The Privatization of Agriculture and the Family Farm Ideology in the Baltic Countries', in B. Raimo et al. (eds.), *Between Plan and Market. Social Change in the Baltic States and Russia*, Walter de Gruyter, Berlin, pp. 141-168.

Alanen, I. (1996b), *The Change in the Baltic Agricultural Production System Brought About by the Privatization of Agriculture*, paper prepared for the workshop on 'Implementation of Agri-Environmental Policy-Instruments in a Changing Political Environment — Exchange of Nordic and Baltic Experiences', Vilnius, Lithuania, 9.5.-12.5.1996.

Baltic States in Figures '94, Estonia, Latvia, Lithuania (1994), Statistical Offices of Baltic States, Statistics Finland, Helsinki.

Chayanov, A. (1966), 'The Theory of Peasant Economy', in D. Thorner, B. Kerbley and R.E.F. Smith (eds.), Richard D. Irwin, Homewood/Ill.

Clarke, S. (1993), 'The Contradictions of the State Socialism', in S. Clarke, P. Fairbrother, M. Burawoy and P. Krotov (eds.), *What about the Workers? Workers and the Transition to Capitalism in Russia*, Verso, London.

Economic and Social Development in Lithuania. 1995, January-December (1996), Department of Statistics to the Government of the Republic of Lithuania, Vilnius.

ESA. Statistical Yearbook 1995 (1995), Statistical Office of Estonia, Tallinn.

Hann, C. (1993), 'Property Relations in the New Eastern Europe: the Case of Specialist Cooperatives in Hungary', in H. de Soto and D. Anderson (eds.), *The Curtain Rises. Rethinking Culture, Ideology, and the State in Eastern Europe*, Humanities Press, New Jersey.

Lieven, A. (1993), *The Baltic Revolution. Estonia, Latvia, Lithuania and the Path to Independence*, Yale University Press, New Haven.

McIntyre, R.J. (1991), 'Eastern European Success with Socialized Agriculture: Developmental and Sovietological Lessons', *Review of Radical Political Economics*, Vol. 23, Nos 1-2.

McIntyre, R.J. (1992), 'The Phantom of the Transition: Privatization of Agriculture in the Former Soviet Union and Eastern Europe', *Comparative Economic Studies*, Vol. 34, Nos 3-4.

Meillassoux, C. (1981), *Maidens, Meal and Money. Capitalism and the Domestic Community*, Cambridge University Press, Cambridge.

O'Reilly, S. (1995), 'Rural Development in the Baltic States', *Eastern European Countryside* 1(1), pp. 23-35.

Palm, T. (1992), 'The Suurupi Program: Estonian Economic Policy for the Transition', *Journal of Baltic Studies*, 23, No 3.

Põder, H. (1996), *Historical background of the municipality of Kanepi from the viewpoint of the agricultural reform*, manuscript.

Poviliunas, A. (1993), 'Economic and Social Factors Influencing Lithuanian Agricultural Development', in *Agricultural Development Problems and Possibilities in Baltic Countries in the Future*, Finnish-Baltic Joint Seminar, Saku, Estonia, 1993, Agricultural Economics Research Institute, Finland, Research Publications 72.

Raun, T.U. (1989), *Viron taloushistoria*, [The Economic History of Estonia], Otava, Helsinki.

Répássy, H. and Symes, D. (1993), 'Perspectives on Agrarian Reform in East-Central Europe', *Sociologia Ruralis*, Vol. 33, No 1.

Selden, M. (1994) 'Pathways from Collectivization. Socialist and Post-Socialist Agrarian Alternatives in Russia and China', *Review* (Fernand Braudel Center), 17(4), pp. 423-449.

Sepp, J. and Terk, E. (1995), *Privatisation in Estonian Agriculture and Employees Ownership*, mimeo.

Statistical Yearbook of Latvia, 1995 (1995), Central Statistical Bureau of Latvia, Riga.

Statistical Yearbook of Lithuania, 1994-1995 (1995), Methodical Publishing Centre, Vilnius.

Swain, N. (1993), 'Transitions from Collective to Family Farming in Central Europe: a Victory of Politics over Sociology', *Eastern European Countryside*, Torun.

Unwin, T. (1995), 'Agrarian Change in Estonia: Historical Context and Contemporary Restructuring', *Eastern European Countryside*, 1(1), pp. 37-51.

Wegren, S.K. (1991), 'Regional Differences in Private Plot Production and Marketing: Central Asia and the Baltics', *Journal of Soviet Nationalities*, Vol. 2, no 1, pp. 118-138.

World Bank (1992), 'Food and Agricultural Policy Reforms in the Former USSR. An Agenda for the Transition', (Country Department III: Europe and Central Asia Region), Studies of Economies in Transformation, Paper Number 1, Washington.

Zhurek, S.J. (1991), 'Intra-SCEO Food Trade. Implications for USSR', *Food Policy*, Vol. 16, No 4.

5 Attitudes towards Privatization: Winners and Losers

MEILUTE TALJUNAITE AND ALEKSANDRAS CESNAVICIUS

Transformation of the Structure of Social Reproduction and Social Consequences

The development of small and medium-sized businesses has been the aim of all government programmes adopted during the past five years. However, even in today's political situation the importance of middle strata formation is still not adequately emphasized. This is probably due to the remaining ideological shades of the 'historical middle class' in post-socialist societies.

Rapid social change in our society has inspired sociologists to investigate the various consequences of changes in the macrostructure and in the formation of a new class structure. They are also analysing the new mechanisms of social stratification. Some of the brightest examples of this are the processes of restitution and privatization and the formation of the entrepreneurs' group and a financial elite.

In this paper we wish to touch upon these issues from a particular angle; hence the approach will undoubtedly be a limited one. We address the topic primarily from the angle of privatization as the new mechanism for middle strata formation. We use the form 'middle strata' instead of 'middle classes' because its meaning is free of the ideological burdens of the 'historical middle class'.

Our baseline assumption is that every concrete empirical or theoretical investigation of every social stratum in today's society helps to revise class criteria, on a theoretical level. Today we can only guess about the formation of new classes or about the re-establishment of old ones, for instance the bourgeoisie or capitalists. We find it impossible to believe that all class criteria or definitions existing in Western sociology can automatically be applied to our society today. A good example is provided by the 1995 paper of Krzysztof Jasiecki and Wlodzimier Wesolowski, in which they examine the question of whether or not an entrepreneurial class is taking shape in Poland.

The first obvious difference between modern orthodox theory and neo-Marxist class theory lies in the systematics of their class criteria. Erik Olin Wright's (1978) work focuses on the control of labour, on the authority to make decisions. This seems to be quite an important distinguishing class criterion in the current, very mixed labour situation, even for people of the same profession. Special importance should now be attached to the organization of labour control. There should also be attempts to work on the concept of mental labour in order to problemize the process of proletarianization and to establish closer links between the analysis of class criteria and class analysis as a whole (Kivinen 1989). It is obviously difficult to dispute the new view of Marxist class theory that the conceptualization of social classes must begin at the forces of production. In the case of class structure in a bourgeois society, the most important criteria are those that can be derived from the categories included in Marx's presentation of the process of economic production. In a bourgeois society people can be pigeonholed into one specific class position on the basis of whether they are engaged in productive or unproductive labour and whether their wages are paid directly from capital or by the state, through taxes. This line of theorizing is highly unsatisfactory because it concerns itself only with the general societal form of labour and it abstracts from the content of work.

Some authors argue that classes must be understood on the basis of the development of job descriptions. This process may produce contradictory results for certain groups of people in that their positions may combine the criteria of several different social classes. Wright formulated this idea into his theory of class structure where central processes include the separation of ownership and possession, the development of complex managerial hierarchies, and the loss of autonomy of direct producers. Wright defines the new middle classes on the basis of control over three types of capital: financial capital, physical capital, and labour (the labouring activity of wage workers).

Two popular findings related to the influence of systemic change upon stratification, have been given almost equal weight and space in publicist writings and perhaps even in the social sciences. One of them has emphasized the influence of systemic change on ownership structures and on the spread of private ownership, and discovered the progress of embourgeoisement and the development of the middle classes. The other thesis pointed at the process of polarization in the decline of broad social strata and the erosion of the middle strata.

However, it should be noted that clarity cannot be achieved with the current 'soft' approach to the concepts. They even frequently merge: two such problems are the interpretation of embourgeoisement and the development of the middle strata as synonyms and the lack of differentiation between the traditional ('petite bourgeois') and the new middle strata. As far as the former problem is considered, in our view the processes of embourgeoisement and the growth of the middle strata do not always bring about a simultaneous strengthening of the 'bourgeoisie' and the 'middle strata'. The concept of 'middle strata' also comprises rather different social situations.

We link the traditional middle strata to small ownership, where the new middle strata are associated essentially with 'white-collar workers', the strata of employees.

In Lithuania, the picture is further complicated by decades of a 'semi-petite bourgeois' of the second economy, which breaks the clear formula of the 'traditional middle strata'. In contrast to typical Western tendencies (where the emergence of the 'new middle strata' paralleled the withdrawal of the traditional petite bourgeois strata, but the middle strata as a whole broadened due to the economic growth) our case involves the opposite developments.

In February 1995 there were 130,000 enterprises in Lithuania, about 4,000 of which remained in state ownership. The Secretary of the Ministry of Economics, Mr V. Navickas, claimed that in the near future, our country would have only 208 state enterprises, and that the list of these enterprises had been approved by Seimas (parliament). World bank experts reported that the privatization of living space was proceeding very smoothly in Lithuania. According to data gathered by the World Bank experts from a survey of 200 top executives, the greatest hindrances were financial and juridical limits: constantly changing laws, taxes, high norms of interest and competition with unofficial enterprises. The experts also noted that the majority of top executives in our country do not succeed in the international market and rely too much on help from the state. They find it unacceptable that taxes are gathered retroactively.

During the past decade the stratum of small owners and entrepreneurs has significantly expanded but so far the precise size of the stratum remains unknown. While this traditional or newly born social group has significantly strengthened the base of the middle strata, the typical semi-petite bourgeoisie of the 'Lithuanian mode' — those who profit from the second economy — have lost their earlier position. The way of life of the white-collar new middle strata has been shaken. This is partly due to the moderation of the economic role of the state and partly to the deteriorating economic situation (the decreasing domestic product). In the final analysis these processes run counter to each other: even if the strata of owners and entrepreneurs are growing, this is counterbalanced by the shrinking of the second economy and of the state sphere. It may sound somewhat paradoxical, but it could be true that the expansion of the 'old middle strata' has not been on such a scale that it could have compensated for the sinking of the 'new middle strata' (and of the 'semi-petite bourgeoisie').

At the same time, there can be no doubt that the objective processes mentioned above do not entirely cover the conceptual sphere of the development of the middle strata. Changes in class consciousness may also influence the dynamics of the processes. Some researchers make a distinction between the objective and the subjective aspects of the development of the middle strata. We are also somewhat sceptical about theories that conceptualize the new middle classes primarily on the basis of their consciousness.

A simple but not negligible index of the growth of the middle strata is provided by the proportion of people who regard themselves as belonging to them. The related empirical approaches are of course different. An important characteristic of the development of the middle strata (either in the objective or in the subjective sense of the term) is found in the social determinants hidden behind it. It is an important cornerstone of thought on the subject of embourgeoisement that ownership and economic position join (or may even become decisive) in the traditionally leading dimensions with status and occupational and educational positions.

System Transformation: Economic versus Social Imperatives

The decisive ideology understood that the state and co-operative sectors essentially have to disappear and this political message was fully understood by the leaders of economic enterprises and co-operatives. The management of enterprises and co-operatives, disregarding certain profitable and productive companies, started to transfer state and co-operative property into private ownership. This led directly to the collapse of the socialized sector. The general trend of disintegration had an even stronger effect on agriculture. Economists mention the following effects: agricultural growth slowed down, there was a decline in production, the income-generating capacity of production also deteriorated significantly, and the rate of inflation began to fluctuate.

The society of Lithuania today does not correspond to the model of a stable democratic society. According to our economists 80 % of the citizens of Lithuania today live in poverty (1995), 15 % belong to the middle strata and 5 % are rich.

In 1995 the highest average salaries in Lithuania were paid to financial middlemen (1321.04 litas), followed by electrical engineers (930.24), officers at ministries, departments and services (799.36), suppliers of electricity, gas and water (778.9), producers of cellulose, paper and paper products (770.74), transport workers and shopkeepers (766.01), and gas producers and distributors (764.33).

There are practically no middle strata in Lithuania in the same sense as in Western countries. Our middle strata do not play an exceptional role in political, economic and social life.

In the Soviet era there was, according to the official class definition, no middle stratum. Society had a structure that was formed according to very different criteria of social status than in the West.

The middle stratum forms the majority of the economically active population who have the opportunity to work productively. First of all, these are
the best of workers, standing out for their knowledge, qualifications and
ability to work well — in other words, professionals.

Secondly, the middle stratum differs from all other social strata in terms
of its standard of living and lifestyle. The main attributes of the middle stratum
are proper housing, proper maintenance of the home, a second residence, a
car, and a bank account.

Thirdly, the middle stratum exercises political influence, i.e. it influences
political processes in one way or another. It also participates, directly or
indirectly, in the government of the state.

The only recipients of social welfare are pensioners and invalids (this is
how it was before, and this is how it is now), as if they were the entire society
in this country. But there are more poor people among wage earners than there
are among pensioners. These include single mothers, young families and
families who earn little.

The former middle stratum in Lithuania — the basis of which was formed
by highly qualified specialists and professionals — engineers, industrial
workers, doctors, teachers, scientists — is disappearing as they join the ranks
of poor people. This process is particularly rapid in the villages.

The level of consumption of the greater part of the population has been
thrown back 10-15 years in time. In 1993, the amount of meat consumed in
Lithuania was only 70 % of the 1975 level; the corresponding figures for milk
were 71 % and for fish 53 %. In 1989, alimentary expenses accounted for 35
% of the cost of living, in 1993 they soared to 62 %.

The income ratio of 10 % of the richest and 10 % of the poorest sections
of the population used to be 3.5 — 4, now the figure is as high as 12 and in
rural villages 14, much higher than in developed countries (6-8).

As is clear from the distribution of incomes, the rich and the poor are
already separated by a wide gulf. However, the worst thing of all is that there
is no transition between these extreme poles: the percentage of people in the
middle is very small indeed.

In our view any approach is rather limited if it takes economic realities
into consideration but considers the development of the middle strata as
something less than accomplished — still discovering definite signs of it in
habits and aspirations.

In the search for concrete criteria for classes or social strata in our current
society in transition, there are contradictions to be faced at two levels: the rise
between objective indexes of social strata, and the contradictions between
objective and subjective aspects.

The main hypothesis we follow in our examination of the social stratification of our society goes as follows: In post-socialist society, there emerged

a major contradiction between social and economic status; in other words, the most glaring contradiction in society splits the traditional Duncan's SEI (Social Economical Index), and therefore it is not directly applicable here. On the other hand, the substance of these two parts, i.e. of social and economic status, has changed as well. In social status, in addition to the occupational and educational hierarchies, social origin plays a certain role. And this social origin is not based solely on one's grandparents class dependence, but it is also, to some extent, related to one's possibilities to get private property and the right of restitution. There remains the problem of how to describe economic status: undoubtedly, in public opinion, economic status is directly related to material welfare, income, and working in the private or state sector. It should be kept in mind that the former shadow economy is still alive and probably even stronger than in the Soviet era, and that it has now expanded on all three levels: the level of the individual, the level of firms, and even on the level of the state. It is difficult to rank the economic positions of different social groups. We have attempted to describe our hypothesis in Figure 1.

Figure 1. Searching for the middle strata

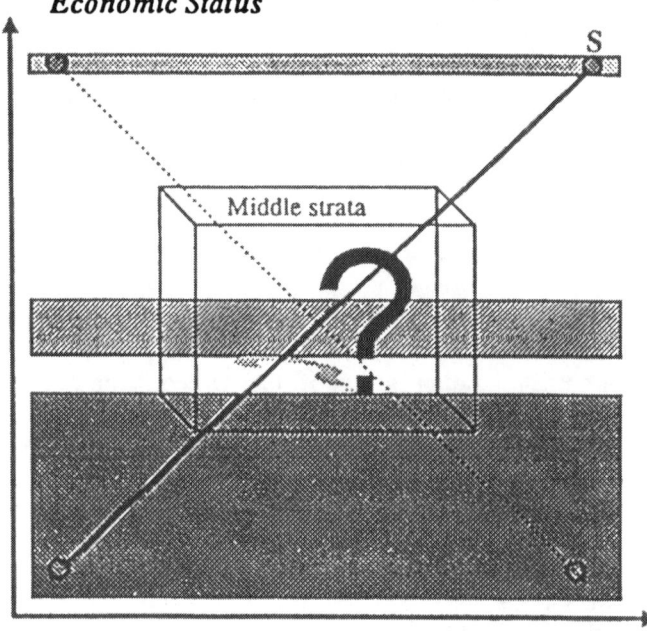

If occupational and educational hierarchies rank more or less evenly (line S), then the distribution of economic status in society cannot be marked as adequate or equal to this line of social status. One group, classified by their social characteristics, can comprise people with totally different indicators of economic position. For instance, in our household survey conducted in Lithuania in 1995, people who had no professional training and an education of only eight grades, indicated their current profession as 'middleman' but had a very high level of economic welfare: a detached house, several cars, such a high level of income that they did not even want to specify sums, enough money to support a housewife, children and pensioner parents. The middleman's mother has been a housewife all her life, the father worked as a builder. Before the restitution of independence, the young man had had nothing except a two-roomed apartment left by his parents. At the other end of the scale we have a professor, academic scholar, former adviser for the President. There are many examples of educated people who have a profession but who now have to trade in the Gariunai market.

Some classical schemes of social structure have now been actualized, although at the same time we are also witnessing the formation of new classes such as a 'ruling class', the 'class of the rich' or the 'dominating class'. Elements of the classes of capitalists, a financial elite and an economic and political elite are now becoming apparent in Lithuania. This raises the question of where entrepreneurs stand. Our argument is that, with some exceptions or at least if society continues to develop in the same direction, it will be possible to speak not only of small businessmen and petty bourgeoisie formation, identified with the middle class, but also of big businessmen and business class segments.

It is clearly evident that these are indexes linked to occupational and educational hierarchy and to the cultural environment, which are a dominant factor in class consciousness. For instance, some authors suggest that the concept of middle stratum is characteristically linked to white-collar society.

As yet we have found no precise data on the social demographic characteristics of entrepreneurs in Lithuania. It should be noted, almost as a secondary hypothesis, that occupational status no longer has clear or equal criteria in all cases; this is particularly true with regard to entrepreneurs and managers. Here we have not only certain contradictions between the objective indicators of the profession of entrepreneur, but also an even greater contradiction between the objective and the subjective aspects (with personal identification with entrepreneurs).

Opinions and attitudes are influenced not only by the objective situation but also by cultural patterns. Therefore it is very important for sociologists to see whether the factual differences are paralleled by differences in identification, satisfaction, the incidence of psychological problems, anomie and alienation. Only then can they aim to prove that the level of dissatisfaction is more or less positively correlated with the factual standard of living and life circumstances. It must be concluded that the level of satisfaction does not depend only on the level of and changes in income and life circumstances. That, however, does not mean that information about the level of dissatisfaction can be neglected, as it expresses very real social facts. The picture is also coloured by well perceived ideological motives.

Privatization as the New Mechanism of Stratification

Our examination of the privatization process raised many questions: one of these questions is whether there is a class of entrepreneurs taking shape in Lithuania. We have described the course and stages of privatization in an earlier article (Taljunaite 1995); here we can only add a short review. As from June 1, 1995, it has no longer been possible to privatize against investment cheques.

One privatized litas in 1994 brought Lithuania almost USD 2.5, and nearly half of that in 1992 and 1993. Last year's results of privatization for hard currency were the worst since the beginning in autumn 1992. Local entrepreneurs preferred objects privatized for investment cheques, and foreigners who had been interested in the enterprises for sale did not dare to enter the competition at all, having seen all the old technology and the factories neglected. Investment joint-stock companies have now purchased about 25 % of all privatized state capital.

A total of 5,158 enterprises were privatized in Lithuania between the beginning of privatization and January 8, 1995; 2,497 of these were large and medium-sized enterprises that were privatized through a public issue of shares, 2,616 were small businesses that were auctioned. Ten enterprises were sold by declaring a competition for the preparation of the best business plan; 42 were sold for hard currency (seven of these were privatized through a public issue of shares, limiting the level of privatization to 30 %).

By April 20, 1995, 4,546 businesses had been privatized. These account for approximately 70 % of all businesses to be privatized and for 47 % of the value of the capital expected to change hands in privatization. Could it be possible to not only stop this process, but to start it all over again, from the beginning? Such an idea promises a new stage of disorder.

Former Prime Minister Vagnorius says that by 'evading the laws and services of privatization, our state enterprises have started to re-register as private joint-stock or closed joint-stock companies'. This is a very comfortable generalization to which there is no reason to object; there are numerous examples. However, one important point seems to have been ignored here: what power legitimized this?

In accordance with article 31 of the State Enterprises Law (1990) and the January 27, 1992 Government resolution 'On the state and the state joint-stock companies initial capital enlargement from their own means', enterprises were increasing their initial capital out of their profits, later re-registering as joint-stock companies or closed joint-stock companies. Everything was done legally. The profits were huge due to massive inflation, and the enterprises took advantage of the difference between the prices of materials and production. Some might view this as a waste of resources.

The second stage of privatization was initiated by Prime Minister G. Vagnorius, although his plans were thwarted by the rising of new powers. Participation was possible only to those with litas.

Consumers (potential customers) accumulated 7 billion roubles. In exchanging them to litas, they received 70 million litas: In other words, the savings of the population, the most important potential for the development of the economy, were wiped out, just as in Russia. At that moment, the consumer was demolished, and that was echoed most painfully in the internal market, industry and agriculture.

Here are some evaluations of the privatization process:

— This is 'Bolshevik' privatization with an agenda 'to divide to all'.
— One people is using others.
— Silently 'worthless' cheques were bought.
— 'Everything was given free', when it had to be privatized for money.

There were differences because the amount of investment cheques partly depended upon the savings that people had in those days.

— Who had roubles in those days?
— In the early stages of privatization the distribution of cheques among the citizens of Lithuania was the only safeguard and reasonable way out.
— The ratio of distribution is disputable.
— At the second stage, the plan was to privatize for litas.
— Not everyone waited until this stage.
— It was not allowed.

Not surprisingly there was widespread dissatisfaction with such privatization. It has now become clear that the chosen way of privatization was based on evolutionary political motives, not on economic ones. The aim of cheque privatization in Lithuania was to take the right to manage capital away from those who managed it in the socialist era, and to take it fast. However, lack of professionalism meant that this goal was not fully achieved. In fact the opposite happened: in the chaos that prevailed those who managed the property took what they wanted.

What are the greatest causes for dissatisfaction? Some people are dissatisfied because they did not get all of their property back; others are dissatisfied because what they got was not in the right place; yet others are dissatisfied because it is impossible to return their land since a town has been built in its place; and some complain that there is nothing out of which to pay compensations.

Two ways of returning concrete property were planned and applied in Lithuania:

— Attempts were made to compensate the owners by money or cheques. This was the easier way, but returning the property would have had symbolic value.

— Property was returned according to earlier land boundaries; houses were returned if they had been nationalized.

The process of giving property back was evaluated as follows:

— Not everything was put into practice as the organizers had planned.

— Such a reform could have been performed successfully in a country where parliament, government and municipalities were loyal and worked effectively.

— The organizers also failed to carry out the reform at a fast enough pace: several stages of privatization took for too long, creating ideal ground for corruption. The supreme council of Lithuania clearly opted for a fast avenue to privatization in handing out cheques to all inhabitants. Supporters of this choice tried to liquidate state property as soon as possible, because private property is much more rational. They did not care about the prices at which state property was sold or to whom it was going to belong; what the investment potential of the new owners might be; what their levels of professionalism were, etc. Such privatization could have been justified if the flow of money had come to Lithuania, where it was needed for the re-structuration of the economy, modernization, new investments and the building of new areas.

Unfortunately, rapid privatization tends to be followed by a decline in production, rising unemployment, significant cuts in social welfare and income disparities. Therefore large numbers of people are today dissatisfied with their economic situation, with the reform itself and with the political forces that now rule Lithuania. Different strata of society have different interests. Former owners are calling for the return of their property or proper compensation. People who worked hard and had small deposits are calling for the return of real purchasing power.

The most difficult thing is to return land. The main reason for this lies in faulty privatization methods. One of the main evils in this process is the use of administrative means where market forces should be at work. In general, where the market is changed by administration, there will inevitably be situations that have not been anticipated by the law, and in order to return the status quo new administrative means will be necessary. The process and its results become extremely complicated. The amount of administrative means increases fast. Finally they begin to overgrow the aim.

There are two vices of administration that stand out here: the prices of the businesses to be sold are fixed by officials, and the mechanism of registering property sold is clumsy.

Having passed the law, the government decided that the means had taken on the meaning of the aim. Their response to the argument that current privatization cannot solve the problems was that privatization is making rapid headway, as confirmed by foreign experts.

But where are the proceeds from the privatized state businesses? The money from the sale of the 'Vilnius' hotel alone, at going prices, should suffice to build not one but several fully-equipped modern hospitals. The state should be rolling in money. But all these proceeds have also vanished. The reasons are the same.

The Factor of Participation in Privatization

The index of participation in privatization was also included in the further analysis of the social map of the middle strata. Although participating in privatization (which appears to be linked to a 'bourgeois' identity and the category of the self-employed) appears to affect the categories, the influence is as yet rather weak. The lack of support in the categories of skilled workers and peasants indicates that the acquisition of property by the lower strata has not been an effective social bridge leading towards the middle strata.

Legislation pertaining to privatization is already in force. The Lithuanian privatization modalities draw largely on the models of the former Czechoslovakia and Poland. Like the former Czechoslovakia, Lithuania opted for 'mass privatization' by distributing free vouchers to Lithuanian citizens. There is also an 'age element' to the privatization system in Lithuania: given that older people have worked longer time in the service of the state, it is felt that they should be given a larger share of the assets than younger people. As in the former Czechoslovakia, privatization began with the auctioning of small-scale enterprises; this was followed by the sale of large-scale enterprises using a voucher system. As in Poland, state enterprises were first transformed into state-owned joint-stock companies and then privatized. Up to 30 % of the shares of those joint-stock companies could then be bought by the workforce on very favourable terms. The problem of lack of private capital seems to have been resolved in the same way as in the Czechoslovakian model: vouchers were distributed to Lithuanian citizens in the form of 'special investment accounts' at the Savings Bank. Every Lithuanian citizen was given a minimum capital of 5,000 roubles for investment. This also helped the government to promote participation in the privatization scheme by all social groups.

We tried to classify people into four groups according to how they used their cheques (see Table 1). More detailed sociological surveys might help to give more precise figures for the proportions of these four groups.

The winners and losers are easy to identify in the table. We have attempted to divide the four strata of the rich according to the history of their wealth — in most cases more than just participation in the process of privatization. The first group or stratum is represented by the old party bosses, the old nomenclature. Their money comes from the Soviet era. The second wealthy group is the more recent nomenclature, including top officials. Both these groups are fed by politics. The more confused the laws, the better for them. A third group is formed of the servants of the old nomenclature. They were born at a time of shortage, when it was necessary to 'offer' cash or cognac to guests in order to make money. The fourth group, the true new rich, were quick to begin trading, to re-sell and re-export. The real capitalist system is good for them. They need both the police and order, and they are even willing to pay taxes.

Banks today have quite a lot of capital because they gave credit to entrepreneurs. Entrepreneurs profit most in periods of shortage. Today there are more and more varied commodities in shops, the period of shortage is over, and the profits made by entrepreneurs will soon settle down at the level of 5-6 %. The economic 'scales' will become more balanced. Those who can offer unseen, unheard of commodities will be winners. The need for new ideas will return to Lithuania.

Privatization proceeded most rapidly in small and medium-sized enterprises and in separate units of major industrial enterprises. In these enterprises, career mechanisms and socio-economic positions will be modified by the stabilization of the private sector, which always happens when there is a polarization and differentiation of entrepreneurs. A sharp decrease in the income of small entrepreneurs was noticed in 1995. Also observed in the stratum of small entrepreneurs were their lower level of education and falling level of aspirations. This puts a number of these entrepreneurs on a par with the hired worker. Overall the private sector in Lithuania is very split and its distribution in various state structures is very uneven. This sector has been hardest hit by state policy lately. It is dominated by small firms requiring manual labour, service and small-time trade; firms that go under the general label of 'small business'. The first to come to these conclusions were the commercial banks of Lithuania, which have recently started to merge with the larger enterprises.

Table 1. Groups of people as classified by their use of cheques

First Group 'The Cheated'

At the outset of privatization, these people regarded the cheques they received as worthless and sold them to other people for valueless roubles. (The buying of cheques was then officially forbidden by law; later it was made legal again.)

The causes for this were:

— wrong attitudes

— unacceptable information about businesses to be privatized and estimation of possible perspectives

— inability to participate in privatization and to 'work'

(People were not psychologically prepared for privatization).

Second group 'Non-economists'

Those who took the cheques and gave them to joint-stock investment companies, often without any obligations or reservations, to relieve themselves of the uneasy burden of thinking and knowing and again of the need to 'work' in privatization. Today they have nothing and will receive nothing in compensation.

Third group 'Of delayed action'

These people did not sell their cheques, they did not trust anyone, and they are inclined to keep their money with them.

Their use of cheques was divided as follows:

Private apartments, workshops, land, co-operative gardens	Invested into enterprises Bankrupted	— Receive dividends — Had some shares that they sold at a favourable opportunity, e.g. when two interests were competing (their second stage of privatization).

Fourth group 'The Resourceful'

These people emerged as winners from the process of privatization. They remain in 'the black box' of scandalous bankers' cases, murders of entrepreneurs etc. In this sense the term 'winner' is not always appropriate. However, all of them have achieved what they have through their own 'actions'; these are people of action. Many of them are sometimes called 'professional' privatization people.

Legislation in Lithuania defines small enterprises as firms with less than 100 staff, medium-sized firms are those with no more than 200 employees. According to register data for the situation at the beginning of March, 1994, a total of 40,620 enterprises or 36 % of all Lithuanian firms were in the category of small enterprises. The vast majority, almost 30,000, were private enterprises.

There is no single strategy for the development of the economy and no agreement on the main questions of the economy. National priorities have not been defined. Therefore entrepreneurs prefer to concentrate on short-term business interactions, while only a small part of firms are engaged in production. Survey data on entrepreneurs show that 50 % have no intention of changing their line of business during the next 12 months, nor do they expect their business to grow. One of the main difficulties for business development is the shortage of turnover means, mentioned by 40.2 % of the entrepreneurs who took part in the survey. Other obstacles included the small size of the Lithuanian market (32.4 %), small premises (29.1 %), and lack of information (26.7 %).

In comparison with other countries where taxes are at a similar level, the tax revenue in Lithuania is much lower. The conclusion is that the tax system does not work as it should do, i.e. not all potential taxes are collected. Lithuanian entrepreneurs do their level best to avoid paying taxes because the state has failed to take into consideration their wishes and suggestions.

It is necessary to create and expand the middle stratum in Lithuania, in agriculture, in business and elsewhere.

Our small state has an economic interest in finding its place in the international division of labour — to create products requiring high-quality, careful work. Entrepreneurs have to search for niches in the market and the state has to let them do this. It is necessary to encourage new businesses, especially small and medium-sized businesses. This should be made an urgent priority because new jobs are a significant factor in the growth of the national economy. Small and medium-sized businesses are not only important for strengthening the national economy; it is also significant that these entrepreneurs are the most self-sufficient citizens in the state. They do not depend upon state capital, they earn their own living and they are free to make their own choices. The development of small and medium-sized businesses is particularly important from the point of view of creating a new society.

When it became apparent that privatization was based on defective methods and was not succeeding to create a market economy, attentions shifted to small production and small businesses.

The new entrepreneurs are expressing ever greater dissatisfaction. They struck it rich quite easily in the chaos that followed after the collapse of the Soviet Union, and now it is becoming more and more difficult for them to make money. They do not want to see their profit margins reduced. It is difficult for them to understand that in a normal society, it is not the profit from average sales that has to be large, but the volume of sales; i.e. it is necessary to sell more and cheaper, not to sell little but at a high price.

This is how small production plays a crucial role in the market economy of developed countries. But this is not enough. More fundamental learning is necessary. As surveys have shown, large sums of capital are invested into small enterprises in the developed countries. By our standards, the only criterion by which they can be considered small is the number of staff. In addition, the majority of such enterprises have close ties with large-scale production and are originally units of major firms. In contrast, such production as can be organized with the credits offered here finds its equal only in the least of the developing countries of the Third World.

In the near future our economic orientation will probably turn towards large-scale industry, which is currently beset by outmoded technology, just as many other branches of industry. However, it has the potential and large numbers of qualified people working for it. This is an important asset. In Western countries huge sums are invested in human capital. The experience of developing countries shows that the accumulation of human capital is one of the most difficult tasks of economic progress.

The processes outlined above will bring new mechanisms into middle strata formation.

Bibliography

Harcsa, I., Kovach, I. and Szelenyi, I. (1995), 'The price of privatisation. In Review of Sociology of the Hungarian Sociological Association', *Special Issue 1995*, pp. 47-63.

Jasicki, K. and Wesolowski, W. (1995), *Formovanie sie klas przedsiebiorcow w Polsce*, paper presented at the conference 'Sector privatny w Polsce', 22 June 1995, Warszawa.

Kivinen, M. (1989), *The new middle class and the labour process: class criteria revisited*, Research reports no. 223, University of Helsinki.

Taljunaite, M. (1995), 'Shift in the proportion of the two sectors: the process of privatisation', *Lithuanian society in social transition*, Vilnius.

PART II

WAGE-EARNING MIDDLE CLASSES IN FORMATION

6 Formation of Class Structure under Conditions of Radical Social Change: An East European Experience[1]

KAZIMIERZ M. SLOMCZYNSKI

Introduction

World political events during the past decade have changed the theoretical perspective of sociologists on social structure. In a sense, structure-based components can be found in all internal conflicts in societies undergoing rapid transformation. Particularly in Eastern Europe, studies of social structure must be adjusted to the social transition of the 'post-communist era' and the various conflicts generated by conditions of radical social change. In Eastern Europe all major processes — the decay of the Communist Party, the emergence of pro-capitalist parties, the formation of non-communist governments, the gradual implementation of market rules and the 'privatization' of the economy — are associated with new cleavages between basic segments of society. Thus, the change of theoretical approaches must be reflected in a sharper focus on social conflict, including the formation and articulation of group interests — specifically, class interests.

In this paper it is assumed that *social classes* are defined through economic power, which in turn is used to refer to specific political and ideological functions in society. In this interpretation, classes are distinguished on the basis of certain *relations* rather than attributes, and considered as *social groups* with their own history, in contrast to aggregates. Ownership of the means of production, control over the work process, and economic exploitation are constitutive relationships of social classes. These relationships form the basis on which the political and cultural identity of classes is established.

Social stratification means the existence of inequality among persons with respect to generally desired goods. Formal education, occupational rank and job income are the main dimensions of social stratification. According to modern sociological theory, the degree of social inequality is in a statistical sense strongly determined by class position. In this framework, stratification can be identified as a *secondary characteristic of class structure*.

89

There is no doubt that classes and stratification have much in common. But are they sufficiently distinct so that they can be differentiated in empirical analysis? What is the hierarchy of social classes according to average indices of formal education, occupational rank and job income? To what extent are social classes consistently stratified? Is the pattern of class order identical in different countries? How do East European countries compare with those of the West? These are the questions that shall be addressed in this paper.

Questions related to social class are linked to questions concerning social status. In particular, we can ask whether the relationship between formal education, occupational rank and job income changes over time. This issue leads us to an analysis of status inconsistency. Are individuals with inconsistent statuses 'deviant cases', or do they fit the usual patterns for the distribution of status characteristics? Again, how do East European countries compare with those of the West?

The core of this paper is devoted to two issues of class formation. The first issue pertains to the disintegration of the most typical elements of an 'old,' communist structure and the integration of the most typical elements of a 'new', emerging social structure. On the one hand, I will focus on the nomenclature stratum and, on the other hand, on an emerging business stratum. In particular, the analysis will link both strata, demonstrating to what extent persons from the nomenclature stratum have been able to convert their political assets and become part of the new privileged business class. In this context, I will also analyse the extent to which communist party membership in the pre-1989 period affects entrepreneurial activity in a market economy.

The second issue of class formation pertains to mental state. Class formation has important psychological consequences. It is assumed that well-established classes differ with respect to the outlook of their members. I will focus here on one of the most important facets of mental state: a sense of distress versus a sense of well-being. Distress is an underlying dimension of orientation to self and society, reflecting people's psychic discomfort or pain. Distress refers not to the active tone of particular life conditions, but to a much more pervasive sense of unhappiness with self and society. Adopting this understanding, we can ask: Is distress determined, in a statistical sense, by social class? Which social classes are most distressed, and which social classes are least distressed?

I also investigate the extent to which social classes differ with respect to subjective assessments of changes in people's life during the period of 1988-1993. Subjective evaluation of these changes, rooted in an individual's mental state, is linked to the individual's interests implied by position in the social structure. During radical social transformation, various types of interests and experiences may reduce or enhance the individual's positive opinion of social change, depending on social class.

Generally, this paper aims to demonstrate that social classes — those that were formed during the communist era and those that are emerging in the new system — differ by the objective measure of inequality and the subjective measure of well-being. Recent discussion in sociology is questioning the importance of social class not only in leading industrial countries but also in countries of the 'second world'. The main thesis of this paper is that class structure generates social inequalities and differentiated interests under conditions of radical social change.

Empirical Basis

In this paper I use various surveys on social structure and mobility conducted in Poland, Hungary and the Czech Republic. I also rely on previously published data. All data — both from surveys and the literature — pertain to the period from 1964 to 1993. I have chosen these data because they cover an extensive range of topics, they are based on large samples, and their quality is much higher than average. Data sets from all surveys analysed in this paper (Domanski and Slomczynski 1994; Slomczynski, Janicka, Mach, and Zaborowski 1992; TARKI 1992; Mateju and Rehakova 1993; ISSP 1992; ISJP 1991; Cichomski and Sawinski, 1994) are in the public domain. Particularly important are data from the project 'Social Stratification in Eastern Europe after 1989: General Population Survey' (Szelenyi and Treiman 1994).

Background data from the West are mainly from the ISSP (1992) project. Here I restrict our re-analysis to the most advanced capitalist countries in Europe. I also refer to data published in West European countries (Treiman and Roos 1983) and in the United States (Kohn and Slomczynski 1990).

From Simplified to Complex Class Schemes

Detailed and innovative analyses of Marx's theory of social structure in a capitalist society affected various conceptualizations of social classes in the *transitional period from capitalism to socialism*. Most of these conceptualizations, relevant to East European societies, share the premise that at early stages of the development of a socialist society the class structure is to some extent inherited from the previous formation; class structure formation is also affected by both the division of labour and factors characterizing centrally planned and state controlled economies (e.g. Wesolowski 1979; Widerszpil 1978; Hryniewicz 1983; Hegedus 1981; Konrad and Szelenyi 1979; Adamski 1985). I will elaborate on these conceptualizations as they are applied in the empirical analysis.

The Process of De-Structuralization

Commonly accepted conceptualizations of class structure in a socialist society are based on the assumption that the state's control of the economy reduces the importance of the defining distinction involving the ownership of means of production. The sense in this assumption is that in a socialist society such classes as the working class or intelligentsia are former classes rather than still existing classes. *In the strict sense, in a socialist society social classes based on the criterion of ownership of the means of production should be considered as remnants of the previous socio-economic period, that is, of capitalism.*

Consequently, in the 1950s and 1960s the Marxist understanding of the structure of a socialist society was based on the assumption of special changes in the 'early communist period' — changes that took place as a result of agricultural reform, nationalization and the expansion of industry. According to this assumption, after the elimination of the landed aristocracy and bourgeoisie, three classes survived the post-revolutionary period: the working class, the white-collar workers, commonly known as the 'intelligentsia', and peasantry.

This simplified class structure was not an invention of Marxists. It was accepted by sociologists, historians and economists of various persuasions who looked at East European societies through the prism of the past. The fact that a working class, a peasant class and an intelligentsia existed in East European societies was standard socio-historical knowledge, and Marxists incorporated this knowledge into their theory of the building of a socialist society.

East European sociologists often applied in their empirical analyses a class scheme based on a distinction between the working class, the intelligentsia and the peasantry. In terms of occupational groups the core of the working class is composed of skilled and unskilled factory workers. The intelligentsia consists of professionals, technicians and office workers. The peasantry includes individual and collective farmers.

Earlier empirical research shows that dividing the population into three basic classes captures some social inequalities expressed in terms of education, occupation and income. However, these classes were internally differentiated (for a review, see Wesolowski and Slomczynski 1977). In the early 1970s it was documented that the interclass variation of basic stratification variables was not greater than intraclass variation (Slomczynski 1972). *The hypothesis of stratification relevance of the three basic classes in real socialism was rejected on statistical grounds.* This was a motivation for further research into the occupational basis of stratification rather than its class basis.

Criteria of Class in a Centrally Planned Economy

The scheme described thus far mirrors class divisions that do not stem directly from the social organization of production in a socialist society: *central planning and state control of the economy*. Slomczynski and Kohn (1988; see also Kohn and Slomczynski 1990) conceived class structure in terms of predominant features of the mode of production in socialist countries in the late 1970s. They used the following criteria:

1. *Control over utilization of the means of production*. This is a crucial class criterion in the nationalized and centralized economy. Managers are distinguished from other state employees by their decision-making over what is to be produced and what specific methods are to be involved in the production process. Managers form the most influential and a decisive group involved in the process of economic planning; they can be seen as an extension to the state-power apparatus. In contrast to other socio-economic systems, managers in the socialist system implement ideological goals and cannot subjugate them to a technical or economic rationale. The importance of political goals in administering the economic system affects the managers class interests and their relation to other classes.

2. In a socialist economy, *immediate control over labour* separates supervisors from supervisees in such a way that the former must defend their actions, not only with respect to the latter but also with respect to managers. In socialist enterprises first-line supervisors exercise their power on the basis of an organization of production in which the coordination of work is delegated to them. They have very limited means of executing power. They are distinguished from managers since they do not make any decisions concerning what should be produced and how the work should be done; however, their immediate control over labour identifies them as a class exercising control over others.

3. *The mental component of performed work* is a criterion used to distinguish non-manual subordinates from all manual workers in a nationalized economy. This criterion is understood here in both absolute and relative terms: firstly, the mental component of work is an asset associated with the autonomy of a job; secondly, it is 'capital' used in contacts with people to demonstrate one's value on the labour market. Non-manual subordinates constitute a class which does not have its antagonistic counterpart. This class appears alongside the other classes and tries to avoid confrontation with them.

4. *Production and non-production work* divide all manual workers of a nationalized economy into manual factory workers, the core of the working class, and a peripheral element, which takes in the rest. There are two reasons for conceiving manual factory workers as a separate class; these reasons are political and economic. In Poland, factory workers have been the main force

in the immediate bargaining process with the state government because of their concentration and the established means of struggle available to them, such as strikes and demonstrations. Economically, manual factory workers have been the main force of socialist industrialization.

5. *Ownership of the means of production*, the basic category of Marx's theory of social classes in the so-called antagonistic formations, does not differentiate people in a socialized economy. In particular, both state and cooperative forms of ownership of the means of production are of little consequence in a socialist economy. Excluding agriculture, the only class owning their means of production is the petty bourgeoisie. This is a residual class in any socialist country. It should be included in the class scheme, not only to complete the class division of the population but also because of its link with traditional forms of economic activity.

The resulting six classes are presented in Table 1. Slomczynski and Kohn (1988; Kohn and Slomczynski 1990) demonstrated that *social classes distinguished on the basis of the above criteria differ substantively with respect to social status*, expressed as a linear combination of formal education, occupational rank and job income. In Poland in the 1970s, the eta coefficient, measuring the relationship between class membership and social status, was high and statistically significant (cf. Table 1, Panel A). This proves that the applied class criteria played an important role in the distribution of unequally divided goods.

In Eastern Europe during the 1970s the correlation between class on the one hand and status and its components — education, occupation and income — on the other, were no lower than the corresponding correlation in the West. The eta coefficients for the United States, West Germany, Netherlands, and several other countries range from .54 to .79. Thus, we have to refute any argument of a 'classless society' during the communist era.

Extensions in the Late 1980s

An analysis of Polish data from 1988 demonstrated that two categories are heterogeneous: white-collar workers and production workers. Using these data, my collaborators and I have decided to distinguish office workers from experts and professionals. We have also delineated workers in private enterprises from those employed in state industry. All class categories used in our more recent analyses are included in Table 1, Panel B. Again, the eta coefficients, measuring the relationships between class membership and formal education, occupational rank, and job income, seem high and statistically significant.

Table 1.   Relationship of social class to social status, for economically active men, in Poland, Hungary, and Czech Republic

Social Class	Social Status	Status Components		
		Formal Education	Occupational Rank	Job Income
	Average value standardized by its maximum and minimum			
A. Poland, 1978				
Managers	1.00	1.00	1.00	1.00
First-line supervisors	.53	.55	.53	.51
Non-manual subordinates	.62	.76	.60	.27
Factory workers	.05	.01	.05	.18
Non-production workers	.00	.00	.00	.00
Petty bourgeoisie	.34	.21	.36	.61
(Farmers)	(.14)	(.09)	(.11)	(.16)
Eta coefficients	.82	.69	.78	.43
B. Poland, 1988				
Managers	1.00	.87	1.00	.80
First-line supervisors	.65	.63	.67	.17
Experts	.97	1.00	.96	.09
Office workers	.47	.57	.50	.00
Factory workers	.14	.21	.22	.12
Service workers	.00	.17	.00	.02
Petty bourgeoisie	.71	.43	.42	1.00
Farmers	.13	.00	.18	.33
Private-enterprise workers	.20	.33	.13	.15
Eta coefficients	.83	.70	.85	.34
C. Poland, 1993				
Managers	1.00	.91	1.00	1.00
Supervisors	.69	.62	.71	.59
Experts	.98	1.00	.98	.79
Office workers	.47	.53	.43	.10
Factory workers	.14	.24	.25	.11
Service workers	.00	.19	.00	.00
Employers	.80	.74	.62	1.00
Self-employed	.19	.27	.31	.42
Farmers	.15	.00	.16	.24
Private-enterprise workers	.24	.28	.18	.16
Eta coefficients	.80	.69	.83	.38
D. Hungary, 1987-1992				
Eta coefficient, 1987	.86	.81	.75	.40
Eta coefficient, 1992	.71	.60	.76	.38
E. Czech Republic, 1984-1992				
Eta coefficient, 1984	.86	.81	.75	.40
Eta coefficient, 1992	.71	.59	.77	.33

Sources: Slomczynski (1994) and ISSP (1992).

Since economic planning and management in a socialist society takes place within political and administrative structures, participation in such processes is correlated with a person's access to positions of power. At the same time, the degree to which power — both as a generalized form of ownership and as an autonomous factor — determines the nature and extent of cultural and ideological domination should be ascertained empirically. The question of the influence which affiliation to economic classes has on political life and on submission to cultural and ideological domination is an important topic. My previous analysis demonstrates that classes represent different class interests. In particular, persons from these classes have varied preferences — usually incompatible — for solutions to dealing with state interventions, welfare state provisions, and reform programmes (Shabad and Slomczynski 1994). More-over, these classes differ greatly with respect to the influence of their members in the workplace — influence on rewarding policy, organization of work and personnel matters.

Class Structure in a Period of Transition

In our analysis of the transition from state socialism to capitalism, we preserve the basic class distinctions we made for the 1980s, but in some cases we introduce a new interpretation for specific categories. For example, the distinction between managers and supervisors becomes more restrictive since managers are meant to be top managers while supervisors are meant to direct the work of at least four other persons. We also make further distinctions that reflect recent changes in class structure. In particular, with an emerging capitalist class it is now possible to differentiate employers from the self-employed.

Is social class, as we have measured it, distinctly different from social stratification, not only conceptually but also empirically? Descriptive statistics demonstrate the validity of the argument made by class theorists that, although social class and social stratification have much in common, they are far from identical (see Table 1, Panel C). In particular, *the relationships of social class with status components are not consistent*. For example, managers rank particularly high on the occupational scale, while experts and profession-als are on the top of the educational hierarchy; managers and employers rank highest in income. First-line supervisors rank lower than experts and profes-sionals on the occupational scale but not on the income scale. In short, these descriptive data justify the contention *that social classes constitute discrete categories and are not arranged on a common continuum*.

Nonetheless, the correlation between social class and status components — as expressed in terms of eta — is very sizeable, especially for education and occupation. Although these correlations represent less than identity, there is no denying that social class and social stratification have a great deal in common. We need to recognize that class and stratification are empirically related. However, we should also recognize that classes are not consistently stratified with respect to basic status components: formal education, occupational rank, and job income.

I should also point out that at the first stage of transition from socialism to capitalism the overall relationship between class and status is not as high as it used to be in the 1980s. The difference in eta coefficients for the 1980s and the 1990s is greater in Hungary and the Czech Republic than in Poland. However, this finding should be interpreted with caution since we were not able to apply exactly the same class schema for the three countries. In particular, for Hungary and the Czech Republic we did not have enough information to retain the same distinctions of managers and supervisors, and employers and self-employed.

Social Status and its Components

Social status is usually measured on the basis of the relationship between education, occupation and income. This tripartite relationship can be expressed by the statement that occupation is the intervening force linking education to income. From this point of view, occupation forms a mechanism by which the influence of education is translated into differences in income. In more general terms, work roles in the economy constitute a balance between skills possessed by individuals and the remuneration obtained. To some extent this balance is governed by central planning in socialist societies and the labour market in capitalist societies.

If we look at the absolute impact of status components, we can observe some substantial changes in the period from the mid-1960s to the beginning of the 1990s. Two points should be made:

(1) We observe some increase in the correlation between formal education and occupational rank. At present, differences in education explain about 40 % of the variance in occupational ranks. In Eastern Europe the relationship between formal education and occupational rank is even stronger than those found in various West European societies (cf. Table 2). Thus, labour allocation in the present economy imitates that of market economies. However, this may be interpreted as a legacy of the communist era. In Eastern Europe, various plans of 'who should work where' were aimed at increasing the matching of personal skills and qualifications with job requirements.

Table 2. **Correlation between formal education and occupational rank in Poland, Hungary, Czech Republic and West European countries**

Sample	Occupational Rank Measure	Correlation Men	Women	Total
	A. Poland			
Urban, 1964-1967; N=2,400	SEI	.47	-	-
National, 1972; N=13,000	Prestige	-	-	.48
National, 1975; N=4,903	SEI	-	-	.48
National, 1988; N=5,357	SEI	.61	.59	.60
National, 1992; N=1,500	Prestige	.69	.61	.65
	B. Hungary			
National, 1981; N=5,561	Prestige	.51-.74	-	-
National, 1987; N=1,557	SEI	.65	.59	.61
National, 1992; N=3,200	Prestige	.58	.53	.56
	C. Czech Republic			
National, 1967; N=13,215	SEI	.65	-	-
National, 1984; N=6,000	SEI	.57	.62	.65
National, 1991; N=3,200	Prestige	.61	.68	.65
	D. West European Countries			
National, 1958-1976	SEI/Prestige	.55	.48	.51
National, 1991-1992	SEI/Prestige	.58	.51	.54

Sources: Poland, 1964-1967 in Slomczynski (1994, Table 2), Poland, 1972 in Pohoski, Pöntinen and Zagorski (1978, Table 7), Poland, 1975 in Alestalo, Slomczynski, and Wesolowski (1978, Table 3), Poland, 1988 and 1992 in Slomczynski (1994, Table 3); Hungary, 1981 in Peschar, 1984, Appendix), Hungary, 1987 and 1992 in Slomczynski (1994, Table 3); the Czech Republic (Czechoslovakia), 1967, 1984 and 1991 in Slomczynski (1994, Table 3); West European Countries, 1958-1976 — averages from Table 4 in Slomczynski (1994) on the basis of the following: Abramson, Gofin, Habib, and Gofin (1982), Bornshier (1983), Covello and Bollen (1977), Elhardus (1981), Ganzebum (1984), Hope (1983), Peschar (1984), Psacharopulos (1977), Pöntinen (1978), Treiman and Roos (1983); West European Countries, 1991-1992 — averages from ISSP (1992).

There is a definite risk that the relationship between education and occupation will be weakened in the transitional period. The private sector is trying to attract highly qualified labour by offering much higher earnings than those offered by the state sector. This process, which is apparent currently in Poland,

Hungary and the Czech Republic, implies a lowering of the correlation of education and occupation with income.

(2) In Poland, the period from the mid-1960s to the beginning of the 1990s brought *an overall decrease in the correlation between formal education and job income, and between occupational rank and job income*. The main change occurred at the beginning of the 1980s when, according to official statistics, the average earnings of non-manual workers were lower than those of manual workers (GUS 1986). Note that even in today's Poland each of the crucial stratification variables — education and occupation — account for less than three per cent of earnings.

Table 3. Correlation between education and earnings, and between occupational rank and earnings in Poland, Hungary, Czech Republic and West European countries

Sample	Correlation	
	Education and earnings	Occupational rank and earnings
A. Poland		
Urban, 1964-1967	.38	.40
National, 1972	.32	.31
National, 1975	.37	.38
National, 1982	.21	.16
National, 1988	.20	.19
National, 1991	.23	.24
National, 1992	.33	.28
National, 1993	.26	.25
B. Hungary		
National, 1992	.27	.25
C. Czech Republic		
National, 1992	.26	.21
D. West European Countries		
National, 1972-1976	.34-.55	.35-.58

Sources: Poland, 1964-1967 in Slomczynski (1994, Table 2), Poland, 1972 in Pohoski, Pöntinen and Zagorski (1978, Table 7), Poland, 1975 in Alestalo, Slomczynski and Wesolowski (1978, Table 3), Poland, 1988-1993 in Domanski (1994, Table 1); Hungary and the Czech Republic in Slomczynski (1994, Table 3); West European Countries, 1972-1976 — ranges from Domanski (1994, Table 1) on the basis of Treiman and Roos (1983).

In general terms, two important relationships in the stratification system —
those between education and earnings, and between occupation and earnings
— are much lower in Poland than in West European societies. For the period
of 1982-1993, the correlation between years in education and earnings range
from .20 to .33. Between occupational prestige and earnings they range from
.16 to .28 (Table 3). For West European countries in the 1970s, the same
correlations were in the range of .34 to .55 and .35 to .58. If we look at the
Polish, Hungarian and Czech results from the perspective of a functional
theory of stratification, both these weak relationships should obviously be
treated as serious obstacles to economic development.

Status and Status Inconsistency

In the late 1970s some scholars suggested that the concept of status inconsistency should be abandoned 'after nearly 30 years of less than fruitless usage'
(Crosbie 1979). In the mid-1980s, the proceedings of a conference arranged
by the Research Committee on Social Stratification of ISA, *Status Inconsistency in Modern Societies* (Strasser and Hodge 1986), indicated a revival of
interest in both the theory and research of status inconsistency. A reading of
these proceedings suggests that not all usage of status inconsistency is
'fruitless'. The lively theoretical debate on the function of status inconsistency, for both society and individuals, continues.

Status refers to a 'vertical dimension' of social stratification, which
'captures' most of the variance of its components: formal education, occupational rank and job income. By *status inconsistency* we mean a construct
indexed by the same components but placed orthogonally — a 'non-vertical
dimension' of social stratification. This is the most straightforward interpretation of Lenski's (1954) original definition (cf. Hope 1975).

More than fifteen years ago, Slomczynski and Wesolowski (1977) developed the idea that social policies leading to status inconsistency result in a
reduction of global social inequality. In their paper, 'general status' was
defined as an additive function of an individual's position in various dimensions of social stratification. It can be argued that combining a high position
in one dimension with a low position in other dimensions causes the general
social status to 'regress' to the middle of the social ladder and, therefore,
produces equality. Indeed, measuring inequality in general status, a weak
relationship between status components implies more equality than does a
strong positive relationship.

Taking this observation as a point of departure, Slomczynski and Wesolowski (1977; Wesolowski 1979) posed a question that is particularly relevant
to socialist societies attempting to reduce social inequality: Are individuals

with inconsistent status 'deviant cases' or do they fit the usual patterns of distribution of status characteristics?

During the period of 1978-1992 *the extent of status inconsistency increased substantially in Poland.* In our analysis, we use a principal components model for creating a model of status and status inconsistency as the two axes of stratification space. In this framework, status is identified with the 'vertical' axis while status inconsistency is identified with the axis orthogonal to it, that is the 'non-vertical' or horizontal axis.

Table 4. **Principal component analysis of formal education, occupational rank and job income, for economically active men, in Poland, Hungary and Czech Republic**

Variables	Status	Status inconsistency
	Components weights	
A. Poland, 1978		
Formal Education	.837	.413
Occupational rank	.894	.163
Job Income	.644	-.740
Eigenvalue	1.940	.745
B. Poland, 1992		
Formal Education	.857	.277
Occupational rank	.842	.298
Job Income	.522	-.852
Eigenvalue	1.715	.866
C. Hungary, 1992		
Formal Education	.888	.166
Occupational rank	.834	.403
Job Income	.628	-.771
Eigenvalue	1.879	.784
D. Czech Republic, 1992		
Formal Education	.878	.283
Occupational rank	.825	.241
Job Income	.527	-.846
Eigenvalue	1.729	.843

Sources: Poland, 1978 in Slomczynski (1989); Poland, Hungary and the Czech Republic, 1992 from ISSP (1992).

The principal component models of status and status inconsistency, presented in Table 4, are based on data from Poland, Hungary and the Czech Republic. Consider the model of status first and compare the data for Poland in 1978 and 1992. In the 1978 data occupational rank has the highest weight, while job income has the lowest. The internal structure of the model is very similar, in terms of the weights, for both years. However, in terms of explanatory power, the model for 1978 is stronger: the eigenvalue is higher and the range of proportions of explained variance in status components — formal education, occupational rank and job income — is larger than in 1992.

In status inconsistency both formal education and occupational rank have a positive impact. However, these two variables are dominated by the very strong and negative impact of job income. The distribution of the weights suggests that the non-vertical dimension of social stratification identifies the *unbalanced reward process*. The most educated persons, who work in prestigious occupations but earn little money, score highest; a situation of extreme 'under-rewarding'. Persons who earn most but who have little education and work in non-prestigious occupations score lowest; a situation of extreme 'over-rewarding'.

The overall internal structure of status inconsistency is the same for 1978 and 1992. In 1992, however, status inconsistency accounts for a greater proportion of the total variance in formal education, occupational rank and job income. This means an increase in status inconsistency in the period from 1978 to 1992. Recent data for Hungary and the Czech Republic show status inconsistency in a very similar light as in Poland in 1992 (cf. Table 4, compare Panel B with C and D). From an international perspective, high status inconsistency is a specifically East European feature of social structure.

Social Class, Status, and Status Inconsistency

Table 5 provides mean values for status and status inconsistency for all social classes. In Poland, Hungary and the Czech Republic managers and experts are at the top of the status hierarchy, while the working class and farmers are at the bottom. In all these countries the difference between the top and the bottom is marked: it exceeds two standard deviations. Employers are close to the top; office workers are in a higher position than the self-employed; service workers are closer to the working class than to non-manual workers. This seems to be a universal pattern of status inequality in Eastern Europe.

Table 5. **Mean values of status and status inconsistency for the adult population in Poland, Hungary and Czech Republic, 1993**

Variables	Status	Status inconsistency(a)
		Mean Values(b)
		A. Poland
Employers	+.893	+.339
Self-employed	+.304	+.102
Managers	+1.512	+.186
Supervisors	+.235	+.039
Experts	+1.638	-.613
Office workers	+.414	-.409
Service workers	-.127	-.207
State industrial workers	-.548	+.193
Farmers	-.972	+.423
Workers in private enterprises	-.493	+.017
		B. Hungary
Employers	+.541	+.376
Self-employed	+.085	+.144
Managers	+1.486	+.185
Supervisors	+.323	+.214
Experts	+1.389	-.745
Office workers	+.334	-.420
Service workers	-.330	-.064
State industrial workers	-.681	+.218
Farmers	-.873	+.657
Workers in private enterprises	-.547	+.212
		C. Czech Republic
Employers	+.792	+.630
Self-employed	+.285	+.312
Managers	+1.447	+.212
Supervisors	+.515	-.224
Experts	+1.555	-.616
Office workers	+.386	-.336
Service workers	-.296	-.198
State industrial workers	-.668	-.174
Farmers	-.705	-.396
Workers in private enterprises	-.607	-.209

(a) A plus sign reflects over-rewarding while a minus sign reflects under-rewarding.
(b) Expressed in standardized scores.

Source: Computations for this paper are derived from 'Social Stratification in Eastern Europe after 1989: General Population Survey' (Szelenyi and Treiman 1994).

The international variation pertains only to a small number of social classes and may be explained by the specific circumstances of economic development in different countries. For example, the relatively high position of supervisors in the Czech Republic may be the result of the labour force being concentrated in large factories. The low position of farmers in Poland can be attributed to the ineffectiveness of agriculture in the country. In Hungary the self-employed stand lower than in Poland and in the Czech Republic due to the legacy of the second economy. However, these international differences should be considered as minor deviations from an overall pattern.

If we look at the data pertaining to status inconsistency we see that, in all three countries, experts, office workers and service workers are mostly under-rewarded in the sense that their income is too low relative to their education and occupational rank. In the Czech Republic, supervisors also join the under-rewarded. Other social classes are over-rewarded, although to a varying degree. Among the over-rewarded, two categories stand out: farmers (in Poland and Hungary in particular) and managers (in the Czech Republic in particular). The positions of managers and the self-employed are similar in all three countries: moderately over-rewarded. In Poland, supervisors and those workers who are employed in private enterprises are close to the point of balance between over-rewarding and under-rewarding.

Although state industrial workers and those working in private enterprises do not differ very much in terms of their status, this inner differentiation of the working class is important because it reveals a difference in status inconsistency. This is particularly true in Poland, where state industrial workers are over-rewarded to the same extent as managers, while workers in private enterprises are only marginally over-rewarded. In the Czech Republic, however, workers in private enterprises are over-rewarded to a greater degree than state industrial workers. Again, these international differences should not blur the overall pattern which shows that the core on the non-manual and non-supervisory part of the labour force is under-rewarded while the rest is relatively over-rewarded.

Consequently, social class is related not only to social status but also to status inconsistency. Social class explains about 10 % of the variance of this horizontal dimension of social stratification in each country. The relationship is moderate and statistically significant. It deserves to be noted for both theoretical and political reasons. Theoretically, it is important as it proves the complexity of social inequality in contemporary societies in the context of the meritocracy ideal. It is also important because it can draw the attention of the politicians who are responsible for distribution policies. They aim at providing a balance between investments in human capital (education), labour force structure (occupational rank) and rewards (earnings).

The Destruction of 'Old' Classes and the Formation of 'New' Classes

What has been happening to the former nomenclature in Poland under the current systemic change? In turning our attention to the post-1989 fates of the nomenclature, our aim is to answer the following general question: To what extent are state-socialist assets and resources currently undergoing a conversion process into assets and resources that are effective in the emerging capitalist system?

In East Central Europe, before 1989, *political segmentation of the state-socialist labour market* created inequalities in opportunities, rewards and resources. The labour market inequalities resulted from one of two factors: (1) a managerial status obtained within the administrative system of the ruling economy, or (2) membership of the Communist Party. Both these factors were important in the allocation of human and material resources, brought about by labour market structures and perpetuated by the logic of central planning and strict administration by the political entities. Consequently, labour market segmentation in socialist societies should be treated as a product of politics.

Understood this way, political segmentation was partly a product of the nomenclature system. This system has a set of positions reserved for direct appointment by the party. Nomenclature in itself is simply 'a list of positions, arranged in order of seniority, including a description of the duties of each office' (Harasymiw 1969, 122). However, in reality, it carried significant status and power because these positions required ratification by the appropriate party committee. It served as the 'nervous system of the party', extending to all levels of society, and enabled the party machine to penetrate all ranks of the social system (Lewis 1985). In short, it was a structural arrangement through which the party ensured that important positions went to 'appropriate' people and that these people carried out the party directives efficiently and effectively (Slomczynski and Lee 1993).

I think of the *nomenclature system and party membership* as two interrelated factors through which the political segmentation of the state-socialist labour market came into being and through which it was maintained. The extent of political segmentation in the Polish state-socialist labour market is revealed by the fact that by the late 1980s, the 'national level nomenclature' and the 'local level nomenclature' covered more than one million jobs, including practically all managerial positions at practically all levels. At the same time, the number of party members, though decimated during the 'Solidarity' years, was still around two million.

The labour market segmentation approach to 'asset conversion' during the transition in Eastern Europe allows one to study *general mechanisms through which the political division of the whole state-socialist labour market has been carried over to the new post-communist capitalist system*. In this type of approach, the central research question is to what extent a pre-1989 managerial position and membership of the Communist Party affect one's placement within the post-1989 labour market. An additional question pursued in this research is to what extent that placement is affected by current political affiliations. I have taken this 'political segmentation' perspective.

Table 6 provides information of intragenerational occupational mobility in 1988 and 1993 on the basis of panel data. In this paper the nomenclature positions are defined in three different ways. Firstly, a number of these are positions of top management. Secondly, party membership opens the way to a larger spectrum of managerial and non-managerial positions of the non-manual kind. Thirdly, they are extracted from the published lists of nomenclature positions (see Slomczynski and Lee 1993). It is important to note that the three categories are not mutually exclusive.

Table 6. Outflow mobility from nomenclature positions and positions of experts and office workers in 1988-1993 in Poland

	Position in 1988			
	Nomenclature Positions			Office
	Managerial	Party members	Occupational Titles	Experts	Workers
Social Class in 1993	Percentage distribution				
Top managers	17.9	10.3	10.4	5.5	.7
Middle managers	5.1	6.4	7.3	7.3	3.0
Lower managers	5.1	6.4	8.0	7.3	7.1
Expert	2.6	16.2	6.9	45.5	3.4
Office workers	7.7	10.8	10.0	9.1	50.7
Service workers	2.6	8.0	9.3	.0	1.9
Manual workers	.0	.9	2.0	.0	2.9
Farmers	2.6	1.7	3.5	.0	1.5
Owners	15.4	7.7	10.9	16.4	7.1
Not working in 1993	41.0	29.9	29.2	9.1	21.6
N	39	117	202	55	268

Source: Polish Panel Data (Domanski and Slomczynski, 1994). Column 1, 4, and 5 as presented in Mach and Slomczynski (1994); column 2 and 3 as computed for this paper.

For 1993, three categories of managers are distinguished: 'Top managers' are defined as (1) those executives (and their deputies) who effectively run firms of at least 500 employees and (2) state and party bureaucrats at the central level. 'Middle managers' are those who either have at least 25 subordinates or have subordinates who themselves have subordinates. 'Lower managers' include first-line supervisors with less than 25 subordinates and other low ranking managers.

In Table 6, the outflow percentages for nomenclature positions are compared with analogous outflow percentages for positions of office workers. 'Experts' are defined as those having jobs that require a university education but who at the same time do not have any managerial function. Office workers are non-manual employees performing predominantly clerical tasks.

During the period from 1988 to 1993, a substantial proportion of intragenerational mobility was directed outside the economic system. Depending on the occupational category, up to 40 % of those working in 1988 did not work in 1993. The highest percentage of those who left the occupational system for early retirement is found among 1988 top managers. This, of course, does not necessarily mean that top managers are the main 'losers' of the transition process in Poland. However, this result does suggest that getting rid of the old managerial elite in Poland was more effective than proponents of the theory of elite reproduction would admit.

The percentage of early-retired or unemployed persons in the 1993 data is lowest among those who in 1988 were experts. In this sense, those people who had belonged to the category of experts in 1988 were the most privileged in their occupational trajectories during the transition period. Note that experts also have the strongest 'drive' to enter the 'emerging stratum' of entrepreneurs. However, the tendency to become an entrepreneur can also be seen among those who had been top managers in 1988. Those who had held nomenclature positions (by virtue of party membership) and occupational titles came in-between the top managers and experts in their outflow to the business class.

Thus, answering our first research question, we conclude that the 1988-1993 mobility patterns of the nomenclature do not differ very much from those of experts. Although former top managers entered successful occupational careers in the new system, a significant number of them chose to leave the labour market, opting for retirement. I am therefore reluctant to consider top managers as being equally successful in the new system as were the experts. Another interesting point is that almost 65 % of office workers were able to retain their positions or move up, to managerial and expert positions.

The second question dealt with factors which increased the probability of becoming self-employed in the years between 1988 and 1993. Do state-socialist managers and former members of the Communist Party show a higher propensity of becoming self-employed than the rest of the population? Can traces of state-socialist political segmentation still be seen in the post-communist world of self-employment? Mach and Slomczynski (1994) answered this question by means of logistic regression.

The main result from Table 6, controlling for several important variables, is that former state-socialist middle managers show a significantly higher propensity to become self-employed than do the non-managerial occupational categories. Top and lower managerial categories do not show a similar tendency — being either at the top or at the bottom of the state-socialist managerial hierarchy has not been a factor increasing chances of self-employment. Table 6 does not support the assertion that being a former state-socialist top manager improves one's chances of becoming a capitalist owner.

As far as the impact of membership of the Communist Party is concerned, the most interesting result is shown in the second column of Table 6 where a significant negative coefficient is presented. This means that being in the party has hindered rather than helped in becoming self-employed. The coefficient ceases to be significant when other controls are introduced. Nevertheless, it is important to note that no analysis supports the supposition that former membership of the Communist Party might have positively influenced the choice of an entrepreneurial career under the new system.

My conclusion of this part is as follows: From the two state-socialist assets that used to be important dimensions of political segmentation of the state-socialist labour market — managerial position and membership of the Communist Party — the second is not exchangeable for capitalist ownership, while the first is, provided that the position was neither too high nor too low before the systemic change. This result is contrary to at least some versions of the theory of the reproduction of elite (for a review of the theory, see Treiman and Szelenyi 1993).

Social Classes and Mental State

The viewpoint in this section stems from some basic findings of the comparative Polish-American analyses for the 1970s (Kohn and Slomczynski 1993). In these analyses, the most striking international difference was in the relationship between position in the social structure (expressed in terms of class) and a sense of distress (in contrast to a sense of well-being). In the United States, employers and managers had a strong sense of well-being; manual workers were the most distressed. In the Poland of centralized and planned economy, the opposite was true: manual workers reported a strong sense of well-being while office workers and managers reported a strong sense of distress. Under socialism, manual workers had a greater sense of well-being than did members of any other employee class. Has the present transformation in Poland changed the pattern of this relationship between social class and distress? Is the present-day Polish pattern closer to the American one of fifteen years ago?

In 1987, the correlation (etas) of social class with distress was only modest in magnitude, .14 for Poland and .18 for the United States. In Table 8 we provide the findings for our study of 1992. For Polish men, the magnitude of the relationship has become greater than before: an eta of .23. The pattern of the relationship is nearly a complete reversal from what it was under social-ism; it is similar to that of the capitalist United States, with manual workers now the most distressed social class and managers the least distressed. The experts, classed as non-manual workers in the old categorization are among the least distressed social classes. What is most striking about the pattern for Polish men in 1992 is that it is so similar to the capitalist pattern, and so dissimilar from the earlier socialist pattern.

The dramatic change in the 'class/distress' relationship in Poland cannot be attributed to our adjustment of the class schema for the new conditions of radical social change. In Table 7 we use the same social-class categories for the 1978 and 1992 Polish studies. We have also examined the possibility that this change might be an artefact resulting from differences in the measurement of distress. Alternative measurement models proved either implausible (be-cause of weak differentiation between distress and conformity to external authority) or produced essentially the same results (in terms of magnitude and pattern of relationship) as did our preferred model (Kohn et al. 1995). We consequently conclude that the great change in the relationship of social class with mental distress for Polish men in 1978-1992 is not an artefact of differences in the measurement instruments: it is a real change in how class relates to distress, brought about by contrasting conditions of apparently stable socialism and radical social change.The main international difference evident in our analyses of the data from Poland and the United States concerned distress (Kohn and Slomczynski 1990, 96-97, 212-228). In Poland — contrary to the United States — manual workers were, on average, the least distressed among all social classes. Kohn and Slomczynski (1990) tried to explain this result through the relative improvement of the working conditions of Polish manual workers in the socialist system. They wrote:

> In Poland at the time of our survey, *all* employees of the nationalised sector of the economy — production workers, nonproduction workers, non-manual work-ers, first-line supervisors, and managers alike — by law enjoyed employment security, sick leave, guaranteed vacations, and other job protections [...] Since manual workers enjoyed the same job protections as all other employees of the nationalised sector of the economy, their having such protections does not in itself explain why production and non-production workers were the least distressed of all employee classes. Their having such protections, though, represented a substantial, if gradual, improvement over their past situation, for it was only

during the late 1960s and early 1970s that Polish labour law had been changed to give them the job protections that had previously been enjoyed only by non-manual workers. The full implementation of those laws took place in the early 1970s, approximately five years before our survey. Thus, at the time of our survey, Polish manual workers enjoyed a degree and range of job protections and job benefits that constituted a decided improvement over those they had had in the past. We believe that this helps to explain why production workers and nonproduction workers were the least distressed of employee social classes. (Kohn and Slomczynski 1990 217, 221)

Table 7. **Logistic regression of entrance into entrepreneurship in 1988-1993 by managerial position and Communist Party membership in 1988, controlling for other variables, for Polish panel data**

Independent Variables	Dependent variables			
	Enterprise Ownership		Entrepreneurship(a)	
	Regression Coefficient c	c/s.e. c	Regression Coefficient c	c/s.e. c
Top managers (1988)(b)	.00	.00	.47	.41
Middle managers (1988)(b)	.84	2.36	.85	2.21
Lower managers (1988)(b)	-.24	-.70	-.08	-.23
CP Membership (1988) (1=Yes)	-.58	-1.77	-.13	-.40
Control variables				
Gender (1=Male)	.85	4.13	.76	3.43
Year of Birth	.02	1.76	.02	1.89
Ln Earnings (1988)	-.55	-2.51	-.60	-2.50
Education (Years)	.02	.51	-.01	-.29
Pre-1988 'Solidarity' Membership	-.32	-1.32	-.22	-.82
Pre-1988 Contacts with the West (1=Yes)	.77	2.08	.58	1.57
Entrepreneurship in the family (1=Yes)	.39	2.11	.41	2.00
Intercept	-.25	-.19	-.19	-.13

(a) Entrepreneurship includes employers and the self-employed.
(b) Dummy variable, with reference category 'non-managers'.

Source: Polish Panel Data (Domanski and Slomczynski, 1994) as presented in Mach and Slomczynski (1994). Owners excepting agriculture in 1988, farmers in 1988 or 1993, and the unemployed in 1993 excluded from analysis, N=894.

Table 8. **Mean values of mental distress in common cross-time social class categories, for men, in Poland, in 1978 and 1992**

	Men in 1978	Men in 1992
Variables	Mean Values(a)	
Managers	+.102	-.454
First-line supervisors	+.049	-.183
Office workers	+.193	-.132
Production manual workers	-.091	+.142
Non-production manual workers	-.043	+.014
Self-employed	-.169	-.028

(a) Expressed in standardized scores. Psychological distress is a construct inferred from four psychological scales: self-deprecation (with weight .68), anxiety (.66), self-confidence (-.32), and trustfulness (-.22). The measurement model, based on confirming factor analysis, is presented in Kohn, Slomczynski, Janicka, Khmielko, Mach, Paniotto, Zaborowski and Gutierrez (1994).

Source: Kohn and Slomczynski (1990) and Slomczynski, Janicka, Mach and Zaborowski (1995).

In 1992, the international difference in mental distress disappeared. Changes in working conditions contribute to the current situation of manual workers. Their distress tends to stem from their high degree of skill/education mismatch: they shifted to workplaces that have been subjected to decentralization, they work under various stressful behavioural constraints, and they fear unemployment. In contrast, some classes — managers, supervisors, and non-manual workers — have benefited: They have a greater sense of well-being.

Table 9 provides the mean scores for the class category members' assessments of changes in their life in 1988-1993. It shows clearly that in all three countries — Poland, Hungary and the Czech Republic — social class differentiates the assessment of change. In all countries employers, experts, managers and the self-employed give — on average — positive appraisals of the shift in their life situation while industrial workers, farmers, and workers in private enterprises provide a negative appraisal of the shift in their situation. Although there are some national differences in the overall ranking of classes in this respect, international similarity prevails. A notable difference is visible in the position of the self-employed in the Czech Republic, where this position is much higher than in Poland and Hungary. In contrast, the position of service workers in lower in the Czech Republic than in Poland and Hungary. In Hungary supervisors are much closer to the working class than in Poland and in the Czech Republic. Disregarding these, the results are very similar.

Table 9.   Mean values of own evaluation of social status, for adult population in Poland, Hungary and Czech Republic, 1993

Variables	Mean Values(a)	Standard deviation
	A. Poland	
Employers	+.647	.948
Self-employed	+.193	1.097
Managers	+.252	1.087
Supervisors	+.007	.989
Experts	+.296	.997
Office workers	+.113	.969
Service workers	+.066	.987
State industrial workers	-.162	.924
Farmers	-.300	.887
Workers in private enterprises	-.168	1.014
	B. Hungary	
Employers	+.349	1.108
Self-employed	+.225	1.090
Managers	+.267	.959
Supervisors	-.153	.947
Experts	+.309	1.012
Office workers	+.001	.984
Service workers	+.059	1.089
State industrial workers	-.240	.922
Farmers	-.104	.888
Workers in private enterprises	-.084	.996
	C. Czech Republic	
Employers	+.493	1.023
Self-employed	+.354	.995
Managers	+.123	.998
Supervisors	+.119	.923
Experts	+.282	.925
Office workers	+.108	.918
Service workers	-.112	1.012
State industrial workers	-.352	.924
Farmers	-.408	1.010
Workers in private enterprises	-.289	.963

(a) Expressed in standardized scores. Own evaluation of social status is measured on the basis of answers to the following question: Comparing your life now and in 1988, would you say your life is much better now, a little better, about the same, a little worse now, or much worse now? Recorded on a scale of 1 to 5, where a high score indicates improvements in life situation.

Source: Computations for this paper from 'Social Stratification in Eastern Europe after 1989: General Population Survey' (Szelenyi and Treiman 1994).

The maximum class difference is relatively larger in Poland and the Czech Republic than in Hungary. In Poland this difference — between employers and farmers — is close to one standard deviation. We should note, however, that standard deviation of close to one is present in almost all classes. The relationship between class and the assessment of change in one's life is not very strong. In Hungary class accounts for a little less than 5 % of the variance while in the Czech Republic and Poland for around 10 %. However, the effect of class on our measurement of the citizen's own assessment of change is statistically significant.

Conclusion

After the Second World War, the class structure of the capitalist-type system was destroyed in Eastern Europe. The three remaining classes — the intelligentsia, the working class and the peasantry — were adapted into the socialist-type system. However, in the 1960s these classes became internally differentiated and lost their important role in stratifying society according to social status. In the 1970s and the 1980s, new class divisions were crucial to the stratification process. In our analysis we distinguished the following classes for this late stage of the socialist era: managers, first-line supervisors, experts and professionals, office workers, state-factory workers, service workers, petty bourgeoisie, farmers and private-enterprise workers. The relation of class to the basic stratification variables — formal education, occupational rank, and job income — is very strong. However, in each stratification dimension the distance between the top class and the bottom class is, in relative terms, small.

In the period of transition from a socialist-type system to a capitalist-type system, a dramatic change is required in class structure. The most obvious aspect of change is a new class composition, adjusted to the process of privatization of the economy and to its consequences. We can also expect much greater class inequalities. Some of these inequalities will increase because of the emergence of a capitalist class and the new category of the unemployed.

The relationships between education, occupation, and earnings exhibit a substantial degree of status inconsistency. Although the correlation between education and occupational rank remains high, we observe a very low correlation between education and earnings, and between occupation and earnings. These latter correlations are much lower than in the West.

In a planned and centralized economy, education was a normative criterion for allocating persons to jobs. For example, in Poland, Hungary and Czechoslovakia in the 1960s and 1970s there were prescribed rules specifying the level of education required for a given position. Moreover, education was a criterion for the distribution of social rewards, and the meritocratic principle was commonly interpreted as a specification of the rule that rewards should be distributed on the basis of effort.

In recent years, status inconsistency has increased in East European societies, diverging from the meritocratic ideal. *Ideal-type meritocracy*, in which the relationship between education and earnings is strong, is often seen as a normative construct underlying the labour market of the capitalist system. In industrialized countries, formal education — which provides training in specific skills and general qualifications appropriate for job requirements — has been directly implemented as the main criterion for assigning persons to jobs with appropriate financial rewards. An emerging market economy does not follow this pattern. Thus, sociologists need a new account of gains and losses resulting from status inconsistency during the transition period.

In our analyses we found that political segmentation of the former state-socialist labour market does not exert a strong influence on the placement of individuals within the current post-communist, capitalist labour market. It seems that persons holding nomenclature positions in 1988 did not move into entrepreneurial positions in 1993. We discovered, however, that it has been the former middle managerial status (and not a top or lower managerial status) that has been effectively exchangeable for an advantageous position within the new system — especially for the status of an owner, and for greater economic well-being. Former membership of the Communist Party — an additional dimension of political segmentation — does not have any unique effect on the occupational fates of individuals in the post-communist labour market, after other variables have been controlled for.

The process of economic restructuring in East European societies has obviously influenced all social classes, but not equally so. In Poland, some classes — managers, supervisors and non-manual workers — have benefited: they have a greater sense of well-being. The working class — the proclaimed vanguard under socialist ideology — has been affected negatively. This class is the most distressed, as it is in all capitalist countries. In Poland, the process of bringing the working class back into its 'historically determined place' was quick and effective. This partly explains why the working class is averse to systemic change: members of this class are relative losers and they are aware of this very fact.

Note

1. An earlier version of this paper was presented at the Second Seminar on Middle Classes in Comparative Perspective: East & West, Tallinn, Estonia, October 12-15, 1995. Parts of the paper are based on analyses reported in the following sources: Kazimierz M. Slom-

czynski, 'Class and Status in East European Perspective', pp. 167-190 in Matti Alestalo, Erik Allardt, Andrzej Rychard, and Wlodzimierz Wesolowski, The Transformation of Europe: Social Conditions and Consequences, Warsaw: IFIS Publishers; Bogdan W. Mach and Kazimierz M. Slomczynski, 'What Happened to the Nomenclature System? The Political Segmentation of the Labour Market in Eastern Europe', paper presented at the Conference 'European Society or European Societies? Changes in the Labour Markets and European Integration', Espinho, Portugal, October 22-28, 1994; Kazimierz M. Slomczynski, Krystyna Janicka, Bogdan W. Mach and Wojciech Zaborowski, Struktura Spoleczna a Osobowosc [Social Structure and Personality], Warsaw: IFIS Publishers, 1996; Melvin L. Kohn, Kazimierz M. Slomczynski, Krystyna Janicka, Valery Khmielko, Bogdan W. Mach, Vladimir Paniotto, Wojciech Zaborowski, and Roberto Gutierrez, 'Class, Work, and Personality under the Conditions of Radical Social Change: A Comparative Analysis of Poland and Ukraine', paper presented at the World Congress of Sociology, Bielefeld, Germany, July 18-22, 1994, and Kazimierz M. Slomczynski and Goldie Shabad, 'Systemic Transformation and the Salience of Class Structure in East-Central Europe', paper presented at the Tenth International Conference of Europeanists, Chicago, March 14-16, 1996. From these sources I use some parts of the text to which I substantially contributed. Thanks are due to Tomas Kolosi, Peter Roberts, Petr Mateju, Ivan Szelenyi, and Donald Treiman for allowing me to use their data and to Goldie Shabad, Bogdan Mach, Wojciech Zaborowski, Elizabeth Osborn, Tadeusz T. Krauze, and Markku Kivinen for their comments.

Bibliography

Abramson, J.H., Gofin, R., Habib, J. and Gofin, J. (1982) 'Indicators of social class: a comparative appraisal of measures for use in epidemiological studies', *Social Science of Medicine* 16, pp. 1739-1746.

Adamski, W. (1985), 'Aspiracje — interesy — konflikt' [Aspirations — interests — conflict], *Studia Socjologiczne* 2, pp. 21-40.

Alestalo, M., Slomczynski, K.M. and Wesolowski, W. (1978), 'Patterns of social stratification', in E. Allardt and W. Wesolowski (eds.), *Social Structure and Change. Finland and Poland*, Polish Scientific Publishers, Warsaw, pp. 117-146.

Bronschier, V. (1983), *Status attainment, status allocation or search for status? Models of the process of stratification with special reference to value priority effects: the Swiss case*, paper prepared for the meeting of the Research Committee on Social Stratification, International Sociological Association, October 17-20, Amsterdam.

Cichomski, B. and Zbigniew S. (1994), *Polish General Social Survey*, Machine Readable Codebook, Warsaw, ISS UW.

Covello, V.T. and Bollen, K.A. (1980), 'Status consistency in comparative perspective. An examination of educational, occupational, and income data in nine societies', *Social Forces* 58, pp. 528-539.

Crosbie, P.V. (1979), 'Effects of status inconsistency: Negative effects from small groups', *Social Psychology Quarterly* 42, pp. 110-125.

Domanski, H. (1994), 'New mechanisms of social stratification?', *Sisyphus: Social Studies* IX (2), pp. 139-154.

Domanski, H. and Slomczynski, K.M. (1994), *Social Changes in Poland 1987-1993. A Follow-up Study*, Machine Readable Codebook, vols. 1 and 2., Institute of Philosophy and Sociology, Polish Academy of Sciences, Warsaw.

Elchardus, M. (1981), 'Class structuration and achievement, *Sociological Review* 29 (3), pp. 413-444.

Ganzeboom, H.B.G. (1984) 'Causal models for the intergenerational transmission of social inequality in the Netherlands in 1958 and 1977', in B.F.M. Bakker, J. Dronkers, and H.B.G. Ganzeboom (eds.), *Social Stratification and Mobility*, SISWO, GUS (Central Statistical Office), Statistical Yearbook, 1986, Amsterdam, pp. 109-122.

Harasymiw, B. (1969) 'Nomenclature: The Soviet Communist Party's leadership recruitment system', *Canadian Journal of Political Science* 2, pp. 121-135.

Hope, K. (1975), 'Models of status-inconsistency and mobility effects', *American Sociological Review* 40, pp. 322-343.

Hope, K. (1983), 'Are high schools really heteronomous?' *Sociology of Education* 56 (July), pp. 111-125.

Hryniewicz, T. (1983), 'Metodologiczne aspekty struktury klasowej w Polsce. Stosunki produkcji, wladza, klasy spoleczne' [Methodological aspects of the analysis of class structure in Poland. Relations of production, power, and social classes], *Studia Socjologiczne* 1:(88), pp. 43-83.

ISSP (1992), *International Social Survey Program. Social Inequality*, Machine Readable Codebook.

ISJP (1991), *International Justice Program*, Machine Readable Codebook.

Kaminski, A. (1992), *An Institutional Theory of Communist Regimes*, ICS Press, San Francisco.

Kohn, M.L., Slomczynski, K.M., Janicka, K., Khmielko, K.V., Mach, B.W., Paniotto, V., Zaborowski, W. and Gutierrez, R. (1994), 'Class, work, and personality under the conditions of radical social change: A comparative analysis of Poland and Ukraine', paper presented at the World Congress of Sociology, Bielefeld, Germany, July 18-22.

Konrad, G. and Szelenyi, I. (1979), *The Intellectuals on the Road to Power*, Harvester, Brighton.

Lenski, G. (1954), 'Class crystallization: A non-vertical dimension of stratification', *American Sociological Review* 19, pp. 405-413.

Lewis, P.G. (1985), 'Institutionalization of the party-state regime in Poland', in B. Misztal (ed.), *Poland After Solidarity: Social Movements versus the State*, Transaction Books, New Brunswick.

Mach, B.W. and Slomczynski, K.M. (1995), 'Occupational structure and mobility in the transition from communism to post-communist capitalism', in E. Wnuk-Lipinski (ed.), *After Communism: A Multidisciplinary Approach to Radical Social Change*, ISP PAN Publishers, Warsaw, pp. 135-151.

Mateju, P. and Rehakova, B. (1993), 'Revolution for whom: Analysis of selected patterns of intragenerational mobility in Czech Republic, 1989-1992', *Czech Sociological Review* (English Edition) 1, pp. 73-90.

Peschar, J.L. (1984), 'Comparative social stratification in Hungary and the Netherlands', in B.F.M. Bakker, J. Dronkers, and H.B.G. Ganzeboom (eds.), *Social Stratification and Mobility*, SISWO, Amsterdam, pp. 123-151.

Pohoski, M., Pöntinen, S. and Zagorski, K. (1978), 'Social mobility and socio-economic achievement', in E. Allardt and W. Wesolowski (eds.), *Social Structure and Change: Finland and Poland*, Polish Scientific Publishers, Warsaw, pp. 147-182.

Pöntinen, S. (1978), 'Comparison of social mobility in the Scandinavian countries', in W. Wesolowski, K.M. Slomczynski and B.W. Mach (eds.), *Social Mobility in Comparative Perspective*, Ossolineum, Wroclaw, pp. 251-269.

Psacharopoulos, G. (1977), 'Family background, education and achievement: A path model of earnings determinants in the U.K. and some alternatives', *British Journal of Sociology* 28 (September), pp. 321-335.

Shabad, G. and Slomczynski, K.M. (1994), 'Social structure, group interests, and support for systemic transformation in East-Central Europe', paper presented at the Interdisciplinary Seminar of the Democratization Program, the Mershon Center, Columbus, Ohio, USA, October 6.

Slomczynski, K.M. (1972), *Zroznicowanie spoleczno-zawodowe i jego korelaty* [Socio-occupational Differentiation and its Correlates], Ossolineum, Wroclaw.

Slomczynski, K.M. (1989), *Social Structure and Mobility: Poland, Japan, and the United States. Methodological Studies*, Institute of Philosophy and Sociology, Polish Academy of Sciences, Warsaw.

Slomczynski, K.M. and Kohn, M.L. (1988), *Sytuacja pracy i jej psychologiczne konsekwencje. Polsko-amerykanskie analizy porownawcze* [Work situation and its Psychological Consequences. Polish-American Comparative Analyses], Ossolineum, Wroclaw.

Slomczynski, K.M. and Wesolowski, W. (1977) 'Reduction of social inequalities and status inconsistency', *Polish Sociological Bulletin*: The Structure of Polish Society (special issue).

Slomczynski, K.M. and Lee, J.H. (1993), 'The Nomenklatura system in Poland, 1978-1987: A case of political segmentation of the labor market', *Polish Sociological Review* 4 (104), pp. 281-291.

Slomczynski, K.M., Zaborowski, W. and Mach, B. (1995), 'Social structure and aversion to systemic change: Poland and Ukraine', paper presented at the Vth World Congress of the International Council for Central and East European Studies, Warsaw, Poland, August 6-11.

Slomczynski, K.M., Janicka, K., Mach, B.W. and Zaborowski, W. (1996), *Struktura spoleczna a osobowosc. Psychologiczne funkcjonowanie jednostki w warunkach zmiany spolecznej* [Social Structure and Personality. Psychological Functioning of the Individual under Conditions of Social Change], IFiS PAN, Warsaw.

Strasser, H. and Hodge, R. (eds.) (1986), *Status Inconsistency in Modern Societies*, Verlag der Sozialwissenschaftlichen Kooperative, Duisburg.

Szelenyi, I. and Treiman, D. (1994), *Social Stratification in Eastern Europe after 1989: General Population Survey*, Codebook, UCLA, Los Angeles.

TARKI (1992), *Social Mobility Study*, Machine Readable Codebook, TARKI, Budapest.

Treiman, D. and Roos, P.A. (1983), 'Sex and earnings in industrial society: A nine nation comparison', *American Journal of Sociology* 89 (3), pp. 612-647.

Treiman, D. and Szelenyi, I. (1993), 'Social stratification in Eastern Europe after 1989', NSF Research Proposal.

Wesolowski, W. (19799, *Class, Strata, and Power*, Routledge and Kegan Paul. London.

Wesolowski, W. and Slomczynski, K.M. (1977), *Investigations on Class Structure and Social Stratification in Poland, 1945-1975*, Institute of Philosophy and Sociology, Polish Academy of Sciences, Warsaw.

Widerszpil, S. (1978), 'Problems in the theory of the development of a socialist society', *Polish Sociological Bulletin* 2, pp. 23-36.

7 The New Middle Strata in Modern Russia[1]

VLADIMIR ILYIN

This article aims, firstly, to identify the new middle strata. Secondly, it presents an empirical analysis of the emergence of the new middle strata in the modern Republic of Komi in Russia.

The New Middle Strata

> Class structure is a structure of relatively defined positions filled by individuals (or families) that determines the objective class interests of those individuals. The concept of class structure designates a set of positions distinct from the human individuals who occupy those positions. Class positions are relational positions. This means that specific classes are definable only in terms of the relations that bind them to other classes (Wright 1989, 186).

For purposes of class structure analysis people are pigeonholed into existing class positions. The middle strata are a group of positions within this structure.

For Max Weber, the social space is divided on the basis of different class situations. By the term 'class' he refers to 'any group of people that is found in the same class situation' (Gerth 1991, 181). 'Property' and 'lack of property' are the basic categories of all class situations (Gerth 1991, 182). In principle this approach does not contradict Marx. However, Weber stressed that 'class situation' is ultimately a 'market situation' (Gerth 1991, 182). The core of Marx's analysis of class structure is a market meeting of the capitalist who owns the means of production and the worker who sells his ability to work (Gerth 1991, 182).

> Those who have no property but who offer services are differentiated just as much according to their kinds of services as according to the way in which they make use of these services, in a continuous or discontinuous relation to a recipient (Gerth 1991, 182).

Middle strata formation is the process in and through which these positions are created. The nature of this process is the same as the nature of class formation. These positions are part of market production and they emerge

118

only under capitalism. Social inequality under state socialism has quite different contents and its main types result from administrative relations. If the classical case of class division is connected with capitalist society, then it is better to call the major social groups of Soviet society by another name.

The concept of middle class (or classes) is used by the majority of sociologists. However, white-collar groups are extremely heterogenous in social terms, even more so than wage workers, forming a pyramid in terms of sources of income, income level, power and prestige. It is therefore not possible to bundle all white-collar positions into one single 'middle class': it should not be considered a class status in its own right, especially in post-Soviet societies. 'Strata' is a more adequate concept in this situation.

Following the Marxist tradition, I shall conceptualize class structure and the middle strata as a part of it in terms built around the mechanisms of capitalist market exploitation, capital, and surplus-value. The old or traditional middle strata are made up of self-employed entrepreneurs, including peasants, farmers, small traders, and so on. The status of the new middle strata is contradictory. These are employees with cultural capital; they earn a salary and get dividends on their cultural capital; they are the exploited and the exploiters. 'Labour markets, not control of property', as C. Wright Mills wrote, 'determine their chances to receive income, exercise power, enjoy prestige, learn and use skills' (Vidich 1995, 189). The life-chances of the middle strata are determined by their possibilities to sell their services in the labour market. Their income is an occupational income and includes the cost of their labour power and dividends on their skills or cultural capital.

The concept of 'cultural capital' is used here in a broader sense than it is defined by Bourdieu. Cultural capital is non-material wealth that yields a profit for its owner. It comprises a real education and credentials; working experience and an informal personal network; symbolic capital and organizational ability; discipline and a profitable approach to work. Cultural capital increases the productivity of the workforce and its role is compatible with the role of material or money capital. There is a deficit of cultural capital in the market and there are more jobs than there are professionals or managers who can fulfil these functions on the high level. Owners of cultural capital are in great demand. As a result, owners of cultural capital can now sell their potential for more than the market price of their labour power — they can also demand dividends on their cultural capital. They take part in the appropriation of surplus-value.

Attempts to understand classes on the basis of job descriptions can be fruitful for the study of the new middle strata (Kivinen 1989). Job autonomy is one criterion for social differentiation within the administrative organization. It, too, is correlated with cultural capital. The more cultural capital workers have, the greater their job autonomy. This makes job autonomy an empirical indicator for the invisible thing that is cultural capital. Dividends are paid to professionals for their ability to work autonomously. However, this autonomy is a consequence, not a source of class division.

Kivinen is right in arguing that 'class theory should incorporate the concepts of both alienation and exploitation' (Kivinen 1989, 51). Still, alienation is a consequence of class relations but on the level of administrative organization, which is a secondary level of analysis. Class relations are relations concerning the mode of production; administrative relations concern labour processes and are determined by class relations. These remain two different types of relations.

The elimination of private property and the realization of key socialist principles create a new quality of cultural capital. Engels proposed a way for resolving this problem. He wrote that in a capitalist society all expenses of education are covered by individuals and their families. This way their labour power has a higher price. In socialist society these expenses are covered by society. This way the results created by this labour power belong to society; the worker has no right to demand extra wages (Engels 1986, 186).

This principle became a reality in the Paris Commune (1871) where the salary of public officers was limited to the level of the wages of skilled workers. The same principle was declared by the Bolsheviks in 1917. However, real life forced them to step back and pay higher salaries to the best professionals. The army of ordinary engineers, teachers, managers and so on still had the same income as workers. Their dividends on cultural capital were appropriated by the state. The labour market was replaced with administrative distribution of the labour force. Prices of labour were a result of administrative decision-making. Thus the new middle strata existed in Soviet society mainly as an embryo of elite.

It is difficult to separate the price of labour and dividends for cultural capital. Thus there are no strict class boundaries between the working class and the new middle strata. It is a fruitful approach to try and identify the core of the new middle strata. As Kivinen (1989, 55) points out:

> On the one hand we have the working class and on the other the core of the new middle classes — and in-between these two a number of contradictory class locations whose situations combine features of both of the basic wage-labouring class groups.

However, in order to conduct empirical research of class structure, we need empirical indicators of the boundaries between wages — as a price of labour — and dividends on cultural capital, which are not formally separated from wage. For simple labour force (without dividends on cultural capital) the price could constitute the basic wages of a worker of the first rank (the minimum), the average salary and wage, or the official minimum wage. However, these boundaries are not watertight.

Are Professionals Members of the New Middle Strata or of the Proletariat?

Professionals working in enterprises are usually considered members of the new middle strata (classes). Is this true for modern Russia? I do not think so. Most professionals sell their labour within the limits of its market price and do not get any dividends on cultural capital. As shown in Table 1, the sector with a high concentration of white-collar workers is very close to the minimum wage.

Table 1.   Average salaries and wages in Komi (July 1995)

	Average salary and wage in thousands of roubles	Average salary and wage compared with official minimum wage (N)
The Republic of Komi	929	2.1
productive sector	1,029	2.3
non-productive sector	686	1.5
budget organizations	503	1.1

Source: State Statistical Committee for the Russian Federation, January-August 1995, Stykvar.

Officials of the state apparatus are increasingly becoming part of the labour market. Their incomes are too low to be considered as dividends on cultural capital (see Table 2).

Table 2.   Average income of employees in the state apparatus in Komi in 1994

General income in '000 roubles	Average salaries in '000 roubles.	Average salary of apparatus employees compared to average wage in the Republic of Komi
460,000	395,000	101.5

Source: Statistical Committee for the Republic of Komi, Wages statistics up to 1994.

Table 3. **Average salary of professionals and the wages of workers in core sectors of the Republic of Komi in 1993-94 (roubles)**

	Workers		Professionals	
Coal association Vorkutaugol (state)				
1992	26,153.6	(100.0%)	24,117.4	(92.2%)
1993	208,444.9	(100.0%)	210,181.5	(100.8%)
1994	719,708.8	(100.0%)	772,707.1	(107.4%)
Vorgashorskaya mine (joint stock)				
1992	24,857.6	(100.0%)	24,848.2	(99.9%)
1993	228,041.1	(100.0%)	232,495	(102.0%)
1994	872,606.4	(100.0%)	836,982	(95.9%)
Concern Intaugol (state)				
1993	191,952	(100.0%)	267,862	(139.6%)
1994	752,081	(100.0%)	1,036,724	(137.9%)
Zapadnaya Mine (joint stock)				
1993	187,834	(100.0%)	240,843	(128.2%)
1994	787,997	(100.0%)	1,037,461	(131.7%)
Construction trust Pechorshahtostroy (state)				
1993	142,768	(100.0%)	161,746	(99.3%)
1994	428,045	(100.0%)	611,310	(142.8%)
Ukchta mechanical plant (joint stock)				
1993	58,846.5	(100.0%)	62,767.9	(106.7%)
1994	192,941.9	(100.0%)	221,329.4	(114.7%)
Ukchta engineering company (joint stock)				
1993	63,557.9	(100.0%)	85,546.8	(134.6%)
1994	212,857.7	(100.0%)	266,973.2	(125.4%)
Knyazhpogost engineering company (joint stock)				
1993	41,233	(100.0%)	43,234	(104.9%)
1994	160,334	(100.0%)	188,050	(117.3%)
Syktyvkar engineering company (joint stock)				
1993	52,963.6	(100.0%)	56,471.1	(106.6%)
1994	219,156.5	(100.0%)	290,317.2	(132.5%)
Gas company Severgasprom (All-Russia's joint stock)				
1993	130,490	(100.0%)	197,069	(151.0%)
1994	544,929	(100.0%)	765,881	(140.6%)
Vorkuta Electric and Heating Centre (joint stock)				
1993	170,341	(100.0%)	250,075	(146.8%)
1994	637,280	(100.0%)	857,777	(134.6%)
Sosnogorsk Electric and Heating Centre (joint stock)				
1994	427,271	(100.0%)	611,202	(143.0%)

Source: Statistical Committee for the Republic of Komi, Wages statistics up to 1994.

Table 4.   Average monthly salary of managers compared with workers' wages (roubles)

Enterprises, years	Managers	
Coal association Vorkutaugol (state)		
1993	326,989.0	(156.9%)
1994	1,212,636	(168.5%)
Vorgashorskaya mine (joint stock)		
1992	41,227.1	(165.9%)
1993	375,501.9	(164.7%)
1994	1,351,937.4	(154.9%)
Concern Intaugol (state)		
1993	374,500	(195.1%)
1994	1,533,195	(203.9%)
Zapadnaya Mine (joint stock)		
1993	348,313	(185.4%)
1994	1,423,932	(180.7%)
Construction trust Pechorshahtostroy (state)		
1993	237,021	(166.0%)
1994	746,999	(174.5%)
Ukchta mechanical plant (joint stock)		
1993	102,188.3	(173.7%)
1994	602,927.2	(312.5%)
Ukchta engineering company (joint stock)		
1993	125,217.1	(197.0%)
1994	395,862.9	(186.0%)
Knyazhpogost engineering company (joint stock)		
1993	65,768	(159.5%)
1994	321,293	(200.4%)
Syktyvkar engineering company (joint stock)		
1993	61,566	(116.2%)
1994	281,099.3	(128.3%)

Source: Statistical Committee for the Republic of Komi, Wages statistics up to 1994.

The figures on the salaries and wages at enterprises in the Republic of Komi show that the salary of professionals in 1993-94 was 99 % to 140 % of the wages of workers in the same enterprises. The status of the majority of professionals is thus too close to the status of workers: they cannot be included in the new middle strata. Nor does the average salary of managers differ markedly from that of workers (116 % to 200 % in our sample). Only a small proportion of their income can be regarded as dividends on cultural capital. There are some exceptions, however. Professionals in banks have relatively high incomes and receive high dividends on their cultural capital.

As a result of the emergence of a large number of small new private enterprises, the demand for accountants suddenly increased. This professional group of low prestige and salary was transformed into a prosperous middle stratum. Many of them now work in several enterprises and enjoy a very high salary.

The emergence of the new middle strata has taken place in a very narrow sector of social space. In the future, once the current economic crisis is over, this process will become far more widespread.

Tables 3 and 4 reveal no major gaps between the incomes of professionals and managers. Only enterprises with a relatively high level of profitability are able to pay managers and professionals dividends on their cultural capital. Form of ownership is not a relevant factor.

The Struggle for Middle Strata Positions

The dream of the majority of Russia's white-collar employees is to gain a status position in the middle strata and to 'live as in the West'. The conviction that equal incomes for professionals and workers are an injustice is still widespread, especially among managers and engineers. Under the political regime of the Communist Party it used to be impossible openly to express this position and to defend it. This only became possible in the 1990s.

The first to begin the struggle for a real middle stratum status were the pilots and air traffic controllers in civil aviation. Their enterprises occupy monopolistic positions in many regions of Russia where people do not have a real choice between means of transport, providing an important headstart in the struggle for the right to dividends on cultural capital. Besides, pilots and air controllers occupy key positions in their enterprises. The profits, indeed the very fate of the business depends on them. They are the core workers of aviation enterprises. It is much easier for them to get a rise or new privileges for themselves rather than having to struggle for the interests of all employees. It is similarly easier for the state and enterprise administration to satisfy the demands of their core workers.

The fragmentation of interests led to the creation of a sectional trade union movement within Russia's aviation sector. The pilots and air traffic controllers set up two trade unions, each of them restricted to just one profession. This was an unusual phenomenon for Russia. In principle their struggle was aimed at gaining privileged positions in aviation; this struggle fuelled the separatism of these trade unions.

This struggle was, in part, successful. However, given the severe economic crisis the core positions held by these professional groups gave them only limited possibilities to (1) participate in the distribution of profits and (2) to satisfy their demands to get dividends on cultural capital. Aviation remains a low-profit business, and only a few companies can pay out dividends on cultural capital — indeed some of them have difficulty paying their regular wages. The demand for pilots and air traffic controllers came up against the enterprises' limited economic potential.

However, air traffic controllers have additional sources of income as well: they control not only the flights of Russian airlines but also those of foreign carriers. In the early 1990s when the exchange rate of the rouble was extremely low and unrealistic, even moderate incomes in hard currency were sufficient to pay some dividend. However, this income had to be distributed within a huge sector. In fact, the struggle of air traffic controllers was not just about the separation of their departments from airports; it was principally a struggle for the right to appropriate part of their incomes from foreign airlines without having to involve all employees in this process. This attempt met with strong opposition from the government, airport administration, the pilot trade union and the trade union of aviation workers. Meanwhile, the pilots in some enterprises have the possibility to work abroad and to earn wages that include dividends on their cultural capital.

Favourite Positions in the Labour Market

The market price of workers' skills may vary in different circumstances. This is partly dependent on the market situation. If one type of skill is in scarce supply and in great demand, then the price will be rather high; the value of that skill may be transformed into cultural capital. The transition to a market economy and the deep crisis in Russia have caused radical changes in the structure of demand for different professions. The demand for some has decreased; for some it has increased.

The growth of a huge number of new small businesses has generated a great demand for accountants. The professional group with low prestige and salary was transformed into a prosperous middle stratum. Many of them now work in several enterprises and enjoy a very high salary level. The same transformation took place in banks. Low-paid mental workers became a privileged group. Managers and professionals in gas (and sometimes oil) processing enterprises also gained a middle stratum status. The very high levels of profit for banks, trading companies and gas enterprises allow owners to pay many of their employees dividends on their cultural capital.

Key Administrative Positions as New Middle Strata Positions

The survey on the incomes of directors of 466 state and privatized enterprises (with the controlling interest in the hands of the state) was conducted by the Statistical Department of the Republic of Komi in May-July 1995. Its results show that directors do receive dividends on their cultural capital.

Table 5. Normative ratio of the basic wage of a first-rank worker to a director's salary

Total share of directors, in %	Less than 200 employees. Normative ratio 1:10	200-1500 employees. Normative ratio 1:12	1500-10000 employees. Normative ratio 1:14	Over 10000 employees. Normative ratio 1:16
100	61.4	33.7	3.4	1.5

The incomes of directors are 2-4 times higher than the average earnings in their sector and 2-3 times higher than the wages of workers in the same enterprises. The chief professionals of enterprises have the same status as directors. The key administrative chiefs of enterprises receive dividends on their cultural capital: they are members of the new middle strata. Key leaders of the republican state apparatus are also in a similar position.

The administrative elite of the republic is obviously part of the middle stratum. The basic salary (without regional indexes) of the Head of the Republic was USD 600 in mid-1995. This is 50 times more than the minimum wage. The chairperson of the State Council earned 95 % of the salary received by the Head, the first deputy 90 %. A minister earned USD 200 and the Head of Syktyvkar (the capital of the republic) likewise USD 200. However, the basic salary is only a small part of the visible official income. A minister actually received extra salary for working experience (40 % of the basic salary) and for their position as first officer (50 %). In addition, all officers had monthly bonuses of 20-30 % of their salary, material help, etc.

Limitations of Official Statistics

Official statistics give very limited information on the process of class formation and on social stratification in general. Detailed information is available on the differentiation of incomes, but these data are usually preconceived: they reflect the true level of workers' income but hide parts of the high management incomes. The workers earn almost all their income as wages, and this information is openly available. The incomes of top managers tend to be top secret. Their salary often has two levels: the first level is the official basic salary — which may sometimes be open to employees — and the second level includes secret bonuses. The amount of these bonuses is often much higher than the basic salary.

Table 6.   Bonuses of top management at the N University (from June to October, 1995)

Official positions	in roubles (thousands)	in USD
Rector	7,800	1,733
First pro-rector	9,120	2,026.7
Pro-rector N1	7,950	1,766.7
Pro-rector N2	7,720	1,715.6
Pro-rector N3	7,720	1,715.6
Chief accountant	4,900	1,088.9

This information only covers the formal bonuses paid at the University. Given the extremely tight budget constraints (even the heating had been cut off in the spring and the autumn), most personnel received no bonuses during this period. Almost all of these bonuses were paid out of the 'economic help fund'. In addition, top management received bonuses from commercial firms and banks which had offices in the university building.

Top managers are often entitled to loans at very low interest rates: this is obviously an effective way of hiding part of their incomes at times of high inflation. Workers have very limited opportunities to use this method. The opportunities of enterprises to build houses for their employees, as they did during the state socialist period, are virtually non-existent. People do have a formal right to buy flats, but their incomes are too low for this to be possible without credit. For key managers, things are different: many enterprises — especially those with an authoritarian regime of management — continue to buy apartments for their key managers or to give them loans at very low interest rates. These forms of distributing profits are hidden dividends on cultural capital.

The boundary between means of production and consumption is not often perfectly clear. Workers and engineers have to buy their own cars, whereas top managers have company cars which are also available for private use. In fact, company cars are often a hidden form of dividends on cultural capital. Another such form of dividends is a high level of office comfort, which is not available to the majority of employees but a privilege of a very small group of managers. In many cases business travel by top managers is indistinguishable from tourism: as well as including formal meetings there are also informal parties and excursions. These expenditures are a form of personal consumption but they are all paid by the company.

This should make the social boundaries between workers and the new middle strata more visible; the differentiation, based not only on wage and salary but on hidden forms of dividends on cultural capital, is closed to traditional quantitative analysis — but partly open to qualitative analysis.

The Alternative Personal Strategy of Overcoming the Proletarian Status

Some groups of intellectuals belong to the old or traditional middle strata, e.g. doctors, dentists, writers, artists, etc. They own legal or illegal enterprises founded on their cultural capital. They employ themselves and appropriate the surplus-value. Under state socialism this activity was prohibited, but it did not disappear: instead it went into the shadow economy. Under the post-communist regime, the possibilities for the development of such private enterprises increased considerably.

For many salaried professionals, this social niche is an attractive way to a middle stratum status. A small number of them, mainly lawyers, have registered their own enterprises. The majority of professionals who are able to find a niche for themselves in the market prefer not to submit themselves to entrepreneurial risks. They create a status position for themselves in the shadow economy, but continue to work as employees in state or privatized enterprises. Their position in enterprises gives them relative stability. Its principal function is to allow them to retreat from their private activity, which earns them an essential part of their total incomes.

Such secondary employment is especially widespread in the Russian capital and in other large cities where private teachers, translators, doctors, etc. are in great demand. The scale of this activity is not striking, but it is rather visible. For example, in early 1995 the salary paid to a university teacher

(M.Sc.) for one hour of lessons was 15,000 roubles (USD 3.3); a private teacher preparing schoolchildren for an entrance examination to a university or institute earned 25,000 to 60,000 roubles an hour (USD 5.5 to USD 13.3). This illustrates how one person can occupy two status positions: one as a white-collar worker and another in the social field of the old middle stratum. A small number of white-collar workers use this alternative personal strategy for overcoming their proletarian status.

Note

1. This article summarizes some of the results of the research on social stratification and management which has been conducted in collaboration with sociologists from the University of Warwick. The research has been funded by the Open Society Institute.

Bibliography

Engels, F. (1986), Anti-Duhring, in F. Engels and K. Marx, *Collected works* (in Russian), Izdatelstvo polititseskoi literatury, Moscow.

Gerth, H.H. and Wright, M.C. (1991), *From Max Weber: Essays in Sociology*, Routledge, London.

Kakaja zarplata u gosapparata? (1995), in *Molodez Severa*, 28 Sept., C 1,3.

Kivinen, M. (1989), *The New Middle Classes and the Labour Process — Class Criteria Revisited*, Yliopistopaino, Helsinki.

Vidich, A.J. (ed.) (1995), *The New Middle Classes. Life-Styles, Status Claims and Political Orientations*, Macmillan, London.

Wright, E., Howe, C., Cho, D. (1989), *Class Structure and Class Formation: A Comparative Analysis of the United States and Sweden*, Reprint Series, N21. Dep. of Sociology University of Wiscosin.

8 Non-Identical Twins: The Formation of the Middle Class in Israel

AMIR BEN-PORAT

I. Very serious students of social science once thought that the middle class — the bourgeoisie — was evaporating. Capitalist society, it was argued, had no role for this class. It was doomed and so were its members, save for a very few, and they would become proletarians. The argument that underlay this anticipation was a derivation of the orthodox thesis on the future of capitalism, according to which certain positions in the economy become obsolete with the maturation of the capitalist mode of production. These students argued that this was eventually inevitable and the extinction of the middle class was 'written' in the historical scripts.[1]

However, it appears that history itself disagrees. In present-day capitalist societies, the middle classes are very much alive and kicking (Bradly 1982; on the present day middle class, see Toivonen 1987; Bruce-Briggs 1979; Burris 1980; 1986; Carchedi 1977; Carter 1985; Clegg et al. 1986; Crossic 1977; Dale 1985; Enzensberger 1976; Gagliani 1981; Giddens 1973; Gouldner 1979; Hindess 1987; Johnson 1985; Poulantzas 1975; Rose 1978; Scase 1982; Stenmetz and Wright 1989; Szelany and Martin 1988; Wancquant 1991; Wright 1985). It is true that the old middle class — the petty bourgeoisie — is indeed shrinking, thus supporting Marx's presupposition. On the other hand, the new middle class is growing in every capitalist society, and is even larger than the old one. The point is that, contrary to the orthodox thesis on capitalism, the middle class remains an original component of capitalist society. Moreover, even the petty bourgeoisie has a modest but probable future. These mean three things: Firstly, the existence of the middle class should be acknowledged theoretically, not just empirically. Secondly, structure comes first, that is, the structure or its history, is the 'explanation', and thirdly, although mobility in capitalist society is becoming less promising (see Gruski 1994; Erikson et al. 1982; Goldthorpe 1980), the mobility that concerns the middle classes, that is, entering and leaving the new and the old middle classes, is still effective. The effect of this mobility is asymmetric — it reduces the 'old' component while reinforcing the 'new' one.

The present paper is concerned with this question: What happened to the middle class since the establishment of the State of Israel? The raison d'être of the following discussion centres on the contention that Israel was in the process of becoming a capitalist society. This process, among other things, generated the formation of a definite class structure in which the present and the future of the old and the new middle classes took different directions.

In particular, this paper follows the development of the middle class(es) in Israel. It is anticipated that Israel fits the capitalist model. The peculiarities of this society must have had a definite impact on the formation of the middle class, and this would be evident by the form, by the volume and by the composition of this class. However, these are levelled by the main process of becoming a capitalist society; eventually, the middle class is split into two by the shrinking of the old component and the expansion of the new. In some important respects, the distance between these two components turns them into two different classes in cultural and political terms and, most importantly, in structural positions. The modern literature has already acknowledged this development, and there is no reason to elaborate it here (see e.g. Giddens 1973; Buriss 1980; Clegg et al. 1986).

The point of departure for this study about the formation of the middle class(es) in Israel is the concept of the 'realm of opportunity'. This borrowed concept is slightly elaborated in the following in order to address the present issue of class formation (the initial concept of 'realm of opportunities' is based on Przeworski 1985; see also Ben-Porat 1993). Basically, it is suggested here that the 'realm of opportunities' set up practical 'degrees of freedom': for the actual possibilities of class formation, it determines, for example, the actual 'empty places' at different levels of the economy and specifies the adequate qualifications which are required to fulfil these places. Hence, it set up the actual odds of individuals' mobility in and out of certain classes.

Primarily, the conceptual perspective that is adopted here is much the same as that which is labelled in the literature as the 'deep structure', or just the structuralist perspective. Following this perspective, it is proposed here initially that the process of class formation should be considered as a three-layer hierarchy: a) the deep structure, b) the liaison assets and c) the surface-observed phenomena. Therefore, the study of the formation of the middle class starts with the identification of 'realms of opportunities' that set some options of mobility and specify the proper assets that enhance one's chances of joining, remaining in, or leaving this or that class. The final stage is that of inspecting the surface phenomena; the numbers, the classification and their associations in real life.

II. The social history of capitalist societies demonstrates that the middle class — the petty bourgeoisie — has never disappeared but has gone through some substantive changes. Ever since the beginning of the twentieth century the share of this class in the class structure has been diminishing. After the Second World War, its size stabilized at around 15—20 % of the labour force (Wright and Martin 1987; Beker 1984). A few explanations are offered for this survival. It is argued, mostly by neo-Marxists, that two things may contribute to the survival of the petty bourgeoisie: first, although its function in the capitalist system has diminished, it still fulfils certain necessary roles. Unfortunately, only a few writers specify these roles. Second, the middle class after Word War II is different from the class previously called by this name. It has split into two fractions: a) the old middle class — the traditional petty bourgeoisie — of small businessmen, small merchants, low grade administrators, and so forth. This class came into being before the rise of competitive capitalism. Since then, the old middle class has been in a continual state of decline and has been losing its influence (or role) in the economy and politics; b) the new middle class — a product of developing capitalism — includes a variety of self-employed and employee professionals, high grade administrators in the private sector and in state and public organizations. This class has been growing at an increasing rate in every capitalist society.

Probably, the continual survival of the middle class is misleading. In fact, the 'old' class is really dying, because is has no role in monopoly capitalism. The observed 'old' class positions are the remains of this class. On the other hand, the 'new' middle class is integral to capitalism because of its roles. This explains the persistence and also the growth of this class-component in monopoly capitalism. Nevertheless, we still need some explanation which is not *ad hoc* to deal with the fact that the 'old' component of the middle class is alive, and sometimes even expanding to a certain extent.

The concept of a 'realm of opportunity' signifies a certain historical situation that is distinguished from other sequential situations. Primarily, the concept identifies the concrete realm by specifying two critical parameters: the unique correspondence between the major instances of a society in the realm, and the 'boundaries' of this realm, that is, the particular historical period. It is possible to consider the logic of the history of capitalist society as based on a sequence of certain realms that are embedded in an underlying process of becoming capitalist. In general terms, a historical situation is distinguished by definite economic, political and cultural conditions. The order of these is less important than the distinction between the conditions that determine the particular realm of opportunities (options), and the concrete parameters that dominate the realm. The determinant conditions and the dominant parameters are not necessarily considered. This explains the historic situation in capitalist societies in which class division is 'demoted' or superseded by ethnic or other divisions that dominate society.

In a capitalist society, the economy, or more specifically, the principles of the organization of production, constitutes the determinant factors. Still, in accordance with the practical history of capitalism and its logic, certain realms are distinguished. First, early capitalism is specified by the principles of *competitive capitalism* comprising small enterprises and family-based businesses, and remains a distinct realm of opportunities that favours certain classes. Another realm, that of *monopoly capitalism,* is specified by the domination of big corporations and the coalition between finance and industrial capital. It operates to the benefit of other classes than those of the first realm. In both realms, the determinant conditions are the same — they are the capitalist principles of organization production. However, some parameters are more prominent in each realm, as well as the correspondence between the economy and non-economic instances. For example, the role and practice of the state is clearly different in each of them.

As regards the interest of a research study on class formation, realms may be identified be means of observing the biographical history of the society in question. Thus, the realm of early capitalism in European society, where capitalism emerged and developed under 'natural' conditions, is very different from the realm of the same name in post-colonial societies, where capitalism, or part of it, was imported, or borrowed, or copied. Thus, political, cultural and other parameters make a difference. They specify the realm of opportunities and mark its borders: a situation of post-colonialism is an example of a realm that is embedded in the history of the particular society, and shares some basic principles with other realms. However, the particular domination of political and cultural factors make this realm unique. A realm of mass immigration — which in fact was evident only in a few countries in the nineteenth and twentieth centuries — is clearly distinguished by the particular confrontation between imported characteristics and existing ones, and it enforces certain opportunities or options on the entire society. The first period/realm of the State of Israel was distinguished by a realm the opportunities of which were determined almost totally by two elements, mass immigration and imported capital.

Thus, the methodology that should be adopted in order to study class formation is built on a process of identification that begins with the identification of the realm of opportunities in the history of the studied society, and hence, the options that are available at that definite period. We then proceed to the identification of the class structure and to the characteristics that are assumed to be associated with an individual's chances of occupying a specific position, or degree of class mobility. It is now obvious that the whole concept of realm of opportunities reinforced the 'structural agenda' that, regarding the subject of class formation and class mobility, lays down the principle that 'structure comes first', i.e., that structural conditions should be considered before, and in isolation from, the individual's characteristics and consciousness.

Moreover, in concept and practice, realms of opportunities have priorities over those socio-economic factors that constitute the basic or causal elements in certain models of structural mobility (Gruski 1994; Goldthorpe 1980; Robinson 1984; Simkus 1984; Hauser and Featherman 1977; Hazelring et al. 1976).

III. It follows that in order to deal with Israeli class formation, prior attention must be given to the historical situation in which the formation of the Israeli middle class took place. The section immediately below is intended to offer the basic parameters of Israeli society and to mark the main realm of opportunities of this society since the establishment of the State in 1948 (the division of the entire period into realms is based on Ben-Porat 1993; Barkai 1983; Halevi and Malul 1968; Patenkin 1967).

The First Realm: The situation in Israel after 1948, when the British Mandate in Palestine terminated and the State of Israel came into being, was in many important respects similar to that of a post-colonial situation. Usually, this context provides some opportunities for the middle class people in the economy and in the administration. In Israel, where the state in the early 1950s was 'overdeveloped', these opportunities were utilized by the indigenous population; the expansion of the administration made it possible for some of them to move up the class ladder. More importantly, the state provided the facilities for the emergence of the new middle class (Ben-Porat 1993).

Eventually, three parameters determined almost every process at that time. These were: the import of labour in the form of mass immigration, the import of capital and the domination of the state in every instance of society. One million immigrants came to Israel between 1948 and 1961. Of these, no less than 700,000 came between 1948 and 1952, *doubling the Jewish population.* As a result, the labour force increased by 35 % during the first three years. The available options were very restricted for the newcomers. Within several years, over 60 % of the new immigrants had to change their occupations. Many (about 15 %), who before emigration had belonged to the middle class became proletariat. Quite a few never again participated in the economy.

Capital in substantial amount was being received from three sources: from Jewish communities in the West, from the US government, and from the West German government in the form of reparations for losses suffered under the Nazis, paid to individuals and to the state in instalments over ten years starting in 1953.

For certain historical reasons that had their roots in the pre-1948 period, politics in the first decade continued to constitute a dominant factor. Thus, the state was regulating — virtually controlling — the import of labour and the import of capital. Because of this, the state was highly involved in the formation of the class structure in Israel. This was evident in state policy of industrialization which, inter alia, forced mobility on the labour force, and in the state policy regarding capital. In the first realm of opportunities, then, options of class formation and accordingly of mobility, were not unaffected by state policy.

Two other realms are identified in Israel: The second realm began in the early 1960s and ended during the second half of the 1970s. This realm was characterized by a state policy of industrialization and by the consolidation of a capitalist type of class structure, mainly, as is shown below, by the shrinkage of the petty bourgeoisie and the expansion of the new middle class. This realm was also characterized by the consequences of the Six-Days War. The impact of this on the economy and the class structure was straightforward — it led to the introduction of a cheap Arab labour force from the occupied territories into the Israeli economy — of vital influence on the formation of the class structure. This cheap Arab labour occupied the lower ranks of the economy — the proletarian positions — and inevitably caused the upward mobility of a portion of the Israeli labour.

The third realm began in the early 1980s and is still effective. This realm is characterized by the growing domination of a market economy, a deliberate withdrawal of the state from certain aspects of economy, and the declining power of the trade unions. Essentially, this realm has been dominated by the options that have been made possible by the continual process of becoming a capitalist society. In this realm, politics and ideology have been much more cooperative regarding this process.

By definition, each of the above realms offers certain options for class structure formation in general, and for the formation of the middle class(es) in particular. The identification of realm and some of its more critical options is a necessary condition for any study of class formation. However, the process of class formation also involves two other processes: the process of the creation of class positions — that is, the creation and formation of a class structure — and the process of allocation of people to these positions. The latter is not accidental; mediating factors, such as certain demographic characteristics, delegate certain people — already in class positions, or on a 'waiting list' — to certain class positions. In other words, certain factors determine the odds of some people regarding their mobility up or down the class structure. The realm's influence on class and mobility, is conclusive.

IV. Table 1, which shows the distribution of the class structure in Israel at three points in time that parallel the above realms, serves here as a point of departure for the formation of the middle class in Israel ever since statehood. The class categorization in this table follows that of Olin E. Wright, which already has been used in another study of the Israeli class structure (Wright 1985; Ben-Porat 1989; 1993).

Table 1.　Class structure in 1961, 1972, 1983 (%)

Class/year	1961	1972	1983
Total	100.0	100.0	100.0
Bourgeoisie-capitalists	1.5	1.8	1.9
Petty bourgeoisie	22.5	19.5	12.0
Managers-professionals	15.4	19.8	26.1
Semi-autonomous	18.3	24.3	30.7
Proletariat	42.3	34.6	29.3

The distribution of classes in Israel is based on the information of the labour force as reported by the Israeli Bureau of Statistics. The classification of occupations and positions into classes excludes Kibbutzim members as well as non-Israeli Arabs from the occupied territories. The former — representing about 5 % in 1961 and 3 % in 1983 — may cause a minor underestimation of the size of the new middle class. The non-citizen Arabs from the occupied territories, employed in the Israeli economy since 1967 in proletarian positions but not counted in the statistics, explain the apparently dramatic decline of the proletariat in 1972 and 1983. Evidently, Israelis moved up in the class structure, and this move is demonstrated in the semi-autonomous and the middle class categories.

Table 1 attests to the leading concept of this paper. The real shifts during the entire period in the sizes of all the classes (except the capitalists) reflect the effects of the realms of opportunities: the concrete options in the first realm were quite different from those of the second, and those of the second were different from those of the third: both the instances of economy and politics were involved in specifying the particular and distinct realms, the economy becoming increasingly capitalistic, and politics becoming more supportive of the capitalist system (relative autonomy, etc.).

Two class categories in the above table are relevant to particular discussion of this paper: the petty bourgeoisie — the 'old' middle class — and the managers-professionals, who in effect constitute the 'new' middle class. In this study, the first category includes shopkeepers, small merchants, self-employed artisans, small employers (one or two employees) and so forth. The identification of members of this class (or to use another term, positions) is based on the possession of a small amount of property and ownership of one's own labour. This property is more frequently employed in exchange/commercial relations than in production, but this is not an exclusive criterion that distinguishes the petty bourgeoisie. The new middle class category includes high-ranking managers in industry and in public organizations, self-employed professionals, university professors, high school teachers, and so forth. The relevant literature is still inconclusive about the exact classification of positions in the new middle class. However, there is a broad consensus of opinion in the literature of the major conception of this class. 'Knowledge' is offered as the unique criterion that marks this class category and that makes it a specific and not transitory class in the class structure of capitalist societies.

The following presentation of the formation of the old and the new middle classes in Israel relates to class, realm and certain demographic factors that have been selected because of their assumed effects on individual odds of mobility in capitalist societies in general, and in Israel in particular.[2] These are: gender, ethnic origin, education, nationality and year of immigration. In accordance with the leading concept of this paper, it is argued here that the effect of each of the above factors is contingent on the realm. In fact, these factors may, or may not, act as mediators regarding one's odds of joining or leaving the middle class categories noted above.

Table 1 portrays the general formation of the middle class between 1961 and 1983. The next sections elaborate on the association between class fraction, realm and demographic factor(s), allowing us to estimate the chances of certain individuals joining, remaining in or withdrawing from either the old or the new middle classes. Other possibilities regarding other classes are not dealt with here.

The petty bourgeoisie. The decade of the 1950s — the first realm — was specified by a non-selective mass immigration that was encouraged by the Zionist State of Israel and, indeed, was one of its main raisons d'être. The volume of this class category in 1961 (Table 1) was exceptional in comparative terms of a capitalist state, but it was normal in terms of a post-colonial state with a meagre economy, and most critically, in a realm in which mass immigration was the most effective parameter.

The first period that is summed up in Table 1 (up to 1961) could be considered one of reallocation and temporation from a class formation point of view. At the start of their absorption, few individuals were able to resume their pre-immigration position within the Israeli economy. The petty bourgeoisie were slightly exceptional; some imported a little capital that made it possible for them to start a small business (a shop, a workshop). Others imported their tools and were able to resume their craft as hairdressers, tailors, shoemakers, etc. Mass immigration produces its own demand for personal services. Petty entrepreneurship was possible in Israel for those who were able and ready to seize the immediate opportunities. The petty bourgeoisie at that time included new immigrants and veterans. As is shown in Table 1, the proportion of this class in the first realm was exceptional in comparative terms. However, this class declined in the next two realms: the 'fate' of the petty bourgeoisie was associated with the development of capitalism in Israel.

The effects of the particular realm on the size of this class were also projected on its composition and, in fact, on certain factors that intermediate the allocation of individuals into the positions of this class, that is, on the factors that enhance or inhibit the odds of individuals joining, remaining in, or withdrawing from the class. But the effects of the realm were also proved in another way: by restricting the available opportunities for people and thus forcing them to choose the petty bourgeois position. Table 2 presents the distribution of six demographic factors by the three realms.

Table 2.   Composition of the petty bourgeoisie in 1961, 1972, 1983 (%)

	Nationality		Gender		Ethnic origin		Age		Education		Immigration	
Categ	Jew	Arab	M	F	Seph	Oth	-30	+30	Elem	High	-48	+48
1961	91	9	81	19	19	81	44	56	92	8	55	45
1972	92	8	80	20	31	69	38	62	59	41	44	56
1983	91	9	81	19	43	57	51	49	50	50	45	55

The demographic factors that are considered here as intermediate factors are nationality; gender; ethnic origin, divided into 'Sephardim', i.e. individuals who emigrated from countries in Asia or Africa, and 'Others', those who emigrated from countries in Europe or America, as well as individuals who were born in Israel; age, divided into those aged 30 and under, and those over age 30; education, divided into 'elementary' (primary school) and 'high' (high school, university, etc.); year of immigration, divided into two periods: before the establishment of the state in 1948, and after 1948.[3]

The composition of the petty bourgeoisie in Israel in the 1950s was uniquely characterized by the definite effects of mass immigration: it was mainly composed of people who emigrated from Europe and America (from countries that were modern-capitalist or very close to this mode of society). People aged over 30 with an elementary education and pre-1948 immigrants were overrepresented in this class. The composition of the petty bourgeoisie was determined to a large extent by the realm: year of immigration was at that time a critical factor, being a veteran in the country (immigration before 1948) enhanced the individual's odds in the entire class structure. It helped one to join certain classes, and to avoid others. During the first realm, the number of veterans in the petty bourgeoisie exceeded the number of newcomers. However, the composition of the petty bourgeoisie in the first realm was transitional: the 1950s composition was ephemeral and abnormal, as is shown by the composition of this class in the next two realms.

The second realm, which was characterized by a rapid economic development patronized by the state, had two clear effects on the petty bourgeoisie. First, it caused this class to shrink: its size was reduced by about 15 % (Table 1). Second, it affected the composition of this class. Certain factors such as ethnic origin and education became more (or less) effective than before, thus enhancing or inhibiting the odds of mobility in and out of this class. The composition of the petty bourgeoisie in the second realm anticipated the trend in the third realm.

The third realm was, and still is, embedded within the accelerating process of becoming a capitalist society. The changes in the structure of the economy and other instances caused a dramatic decrease in the share of the petty bourgeoisie, which went down to 12 % of the total labour force in 1983, and continued to decrease in the 1990s.

Looking at the composition of the petty bourgeoisie, it appears that two intermediating factors hardly changed between 1948 and 1983: Jews and males continued to dominate in this class, as indeed their dominance in other classes. On the other hand, the realms' options were more in favour of Sephardim and young people. Time and the reduction in the number of new immigrants (until the early 1990s) increased the share of the 'after 1948' immigrants in the petty bourgeoisie. But the main point was the decrease in the volume of positions in this class by about 40 % from 1972 to 1983. This means that the real options of inflow mobility were also shrinking. The realm of opportunities restricted the options regarding the petty bourgeoisie, but it opened more options for the new middle class.

The new middle class. Though exact information is not available, it is suggested here that in the first decade, the share of managers and administrators in the new middle class component was dominant (Ben-Porat 1993). The professional element in the new middle class was relatively small. But the proportion of professionals and managers was growing steadily. The rate of 15.4 % for the new middle class in 1961 (Table 1) reflects, in part, the state policy of industrialization: managerial positions were created at the initial stage and during the acceleration of industrialization. This also encouraged the growth of professionals. The growing involvement of the state in the economy was accompanied by a growing number of administrators. The impact of this was clearly evident in the second realm.

The information in Table 1 is instructive: between 1961 and 1983, the new middle class grew by over 40 %. In fact, the share of the middle class did not change very much during this period — it was about 38 % in 1961 and about the same in 1983. In 1983, however, the size of the new middle class was more than twice that of the old middle class. There are several specific reasons for this, but the key underlying factor is the one we have already mentioned: the accelerating process of becoming a capitalist society. As in other countries, this process was (is) responsible for the growth and the domination within the middle class of the new middle class component.

Table 3.   Composition of the new middle class in 1961, 1972, 1983 (%)

	Nationality		Gender		Ethnic origin		Age		Education		Immigration	
Categ	Jew	Arab	M	F	Seph	Oth	-30	+30	Elem	High	-48	+48
1961	98	2	61	39	11	89	26	74	55	45	63	37
1972	98	2	60	40	16	84	40	60	5	95	54	46
1983	94	6	57	43	27	73	33	67	11	89	55	45

It has already been noted that the new middle class was growing steadily and became the dominant component of the middle class during the studied realms. Mobility into this class was increasing for two reasons: the expansion of positions and the growing supply of graduates of high institutions, partly produced in Israeli universities, partly imported by immigration. Primarily, the formation of the new middle class is attributed to substantive changes in the economy, such as the expansion of high-tech industries, the expansion of personal services, and the growth of the self-employed section of the Israeli market. The growth of this class into a significant category in the class structure was anticipated because of the same process that affected the old component of the middle class, that of becoming a capitalist society, and because of the shifting options of/across the particular realms. The decline of the old middle class and the rise of the new middle class were both the result of structural changes that occurred between 1948 and the early 1980s. Eventually, the structure comes first, and the context of the realm determines the concrete possibilities of the old and the new middle class component.

V. The formation of the middle class is almost inevitable; at least in empirical terms it appears that in every capitalist society, the future of the present has already been decided, the old middle class is declining and the new middle class is growing. Moreover, even though the middle class is a minority, it constitutes an inevitable component of the entire class structure. It is suggested here that we can account for this by the general process of becoming a capitalist society, and by a more particular explanation, through the use of realms of opportunities. The latter allows us to look more closely into the association between two processes of class formation: that which creates class positions in the economy, and that which allocates individuals into these positions. It was argued above that the former is independent of the latter, and that the concrete effects of the process of allocations is contingent on certain intermediate factors that relate the realm options to class formation by means of mobility of individuals in and out of the middle class components.

The following section examines the relative effects of the factors presented above on the mobility of individuals, in association with particular realms. One may suspect that the association between a certain factor and either the old or the new component of the middle class is influenced by the absolute effect of that factor. That is, the real effect of a factor is 'overshadowed' by its marginals. Thus, in absolute terms, women constituted about 25 % of the labour force in 1961, and about 37 % in 1983. Arabs constituted about 6 % of the labour force in 1961, and about 10 % in 1983. Sephardim constituted 26 % of the labour force in 1961, and 40 % in 1983. In addition, the absolute figures of veterans and individuals below and over the age of 30 probably had an absolute effect on their standing in the middle class.

Thus, the immediate question here concerns the estimation of the net effect of each of the above factors. The procedure is carried out by using the distribution of individuals in middle class positions in two consecutive periods, 1961-1972 and 1972-1983. Odd values specify whether or not the changes in the size and the composition of the class positions/volume, during the above compared periods, had any association with the factors that mediate between the realm's options and individual mobility in and out of the middle class.

The odds ratio is considered to be a good measure of association. The advantages of this measure make it highly productive despite the defects cited in the literature (Tyree 1973). The outcome of calculating odds is straightforward: the closer the value of an odds ratio to unity, the more perfect is the mobility (in and out of the middle classes), and the less is the association between mobility, middle class and the particular factor which is selected for comparison in the specific case under examination. The logged-odds ratio indicates the relative 'in-mobility' of the group which is reflected by the factor first listed in the comparison. A negative value indicates larger 'in-mobility' of this group.

**Table 4.   Odd ratios of ethnic origin, gender and nationality:
'old' and 'new' middle classes in 1961-1972, 1972-1983**

Class	Old middle class				New middle class			
Period	1961-1972		1972-1983		1961-1972		1972-1983	
Category	odds	logged*	odds	logged	odds	logged	odds	logged
Seph	1.672	-.387	2.308	-.763	1.418	-.406	2.418	.671
Ashk.	.854	—	.641	—	.948	—	.824	—
Male	.988	.052	1.015	.072	.993	.016	.951	.136
Female	1.047	—	.939	—	1.259	—	1.072	—
Jews	.939	.202	.984	.187	1.000	.010	.958	.174
Arabs	.829	—	1.179	—	1.001	—	3.157	—

*Logged-odds ratio.

Interpretation of the odds and logged-odds ratios in Table 4 supplies us with information about the relative advantage or disadvantage of a specific sub-group of ethnic origin, gender or nationality. It must be noted that the odds-ratios in this Table do not specify the exact component of the realm that had the effect that relates a realm's class to a certain factor. However, it points to the fact that structural changes that occurred in the realm or that matured in the realm, have a concrete influence on the 'effectivity' of certain factors regarding mobility in or out of the middle classes.

The formation of the old middle class was effective for, or supportive of, the sociological 'minorities', Sephardim, females and Arabs. There are some variations between the compared realms. For instance, the 1972-1983 realm was less in favour of females than the previous realm. But the general picture is as stated, considering the sign of the logged-odd ratios: 'minorities' were relatively more effective within the old middle class, although in absolute terms Ashkenazim, males and Jews dominated this class (see Table 2) in every individual realm. The decline of this class was therefore relatively to the disfavour of Sephardim, females and Arabs. Nevertheless, these subgroups were compensated by the accelerating formation of the new middle class. The odds ratios of Sephardim, females and Arabs, as shown in Table 4, indicate their relative advantages regarding 'in-mobility' to the new middle class.

Clearly, the process of becoming a capitalist society affected the middle class in two different directions: it enforced a shrinkage of the old component of this class, and it enhanced the growth of the new one. However, it is possible to identify some specific effects as well, such as the effect of a realm on the composition of the middle class, on the relative effects of certain intermediate factors, and on individual odds of 'in' or 'out' mobility regarding both the elements of the middle class.

Three other factors, *education, age,* and *year of immigration* (omitted from Table 4) behave in a different way: for the old middle class the effect of the education parameter decreases over the realms, but it increases regarding the new middle class. The parameter of age decreases over the realms for both middle class components. Also, the year of immigration parameter decreases over the realms regarding both middle class components. However, education remains effective over the realms in both components of the middle class, that is, education is still an important factor in affecting odds of mobility, while age and year of immigration become quite immaterial in the third realm.

It has been argued here that the formation of the middle class is forged by the options available to the realms. This partly explains the high proportion of the petty bourgeoisie in Israel in the first realm. The same reason explains the decline of the old middle class in the second and third realms and the growth of the new middle class. In capitalist systems, the major and most critical changes that influence the class system occur in the economy. In fact, these changes are differentially reflected in the various sectors of the economy: some sectors undergo deep changes, while others undergo minor changes within and over the realms of opportunities. For instance, the history of agriculture in capitalist societies after World War II exemplifies a sector that was heavily reformed by economic change. The history of industry and of private and public services during the last two decades of the present century — the so-called 'post-industrial' era, or the realm of monopoly capitalism — is another example of the differential effects of the development of the economy.

The following section deals with shifts in the sectors of the economy — the industrial shifts — and the associated shifts that occurred in the composition of the middle class, vis-à-vis its two sections, as before. The strategy employed is intended to decompose the total changes in the sectors of the Israeli economy (9 sectors) into two components. First, the industry-shift effect is estimated in order to assess the changes in the middle class due to changes in the overall sectoral distribution of the labour force across sectors between the realm of 1961 to 1972, and that of 1972 to 1983. Second, the class-composition effect is estimated in order to assess the changes in the middle class due to changes within a given sector over the same two realms.

The strategy of analysis of class-cum-sector is as follows: structural changes are decomposed into the following components: a) a sector-industry effect, b) a class composition effect, and c) an interaction effect. The sectoral shift-effect refers to the changes in class structure that result from changes in the overall sectoral distribution of the labour force across industries. Thus, the decline of agriculture in terms of employment at the end of the 1950s and during the 1960s — a definite change in the structure of the Israeli economy — probably had some effect on the relative size of various classes. The class composition shift-effect refers to the changes in the class structure that result from changes within given sectors of the economy, independent of the relative size of these sectors. Table 5 shows the decomposition for pairs of realms: for each pair, the three effects are calculated separately.[4]

Table 5. Decomposition of changes in the old and new middle classes, 1961-1972; 1972-1983

Sector & class	Sector shift effect	Class composition & interaction effect	Class shift effect	Sector & interaction shift effect
		1961-1972		
Old	90.0	10.0	17.0	83.0
New	27.0	73.0	-26.0	126.0
		1972-1983		
Old	36.0	64.0	-21.0	121.0
New	74.0	26.0	22.0	78.0

For the old component of the middle class, during the first period compared, 1961 to 1972, the sector (of industry) shift effect was much greater than the class shift effect. That is, the relative size of this component of the middle class was influenced by the 'what happened' to the industrial sectors, that is the entire consolidating economy. The new component of the middle class was affected both by the sectoral shift and the class shift, but in fact the effects on this class were still indecisive — the interaction effects (of sector and of class composition) were still dominant.

In the second comparison, the 1972 to 1983 realm, the results reveal only some closeness to the previous decomposition. The effect on the old component of the middle class was mainly the result of interaction shift effects. The new component was affected by sectoral shifts and also by a sectoral interaction shift.

All in all, the changes in the economy were transmitted to the old and new components of the middle class (as well as to other classes) by means of the reorganization of the industrial sectors in Israel at that time. The effects of these changes, such as the decline of the size of employment in agriculture, the consolidation of industry and the acceleration of various public and private services, were elaborated and transmitted by the realm. Thus, the main effect across the realm was that of the sectoral shift. That is to say, as anticipated, both components of the middle class were influenced primarily by the realm's economic options. The decline and the growth of certain sectors were more important regarding the formation of the old and the new middle classes, than the class composition by itself. That is, the differential expansion of employment was more effective than their classification into class positions. This was more prominent regarding the old class in the 1961-1972 period, while in the second period (1972-1983) the sectoral shift was more effective regarding the new, and far less effective regarding the old class (Table 5).

The process of becoming a capitalist society underpinned every major instance in each realm. However, it appears that each realm had certain specific authentic impacts on the formation of the entire class structure, and in particular, on the formation of the middle class(es).

V. The main theme of this paper is that 'structure comes first'. It was argued at the outset that when one is considering class formation and associated factors such as mobility, consideration of structural effects must take precedence over other sources of effects. Structural effects are treated as contingent on the realm of opportunities. These arguments have been applied to this study of the old and the new middle class formation in Israel. Practically, the leading question is not what happened to certain people, but what happened to these classes, and then, what were the options of mobility in and out of these classes. It is suggested that the realm of opportunities determines the options as well as the actual effects of certain factors on individual odds of joining the old or new middle classes, retaining a position in these classes, or leaving them.

Thus, while dealing with formation, structure is of primary importance. It is necessary to begin by identifying the dominant realm of opportunities in the studied society. Capitalism is a proper title, but it is also too big to describe the concrete situation in society. Therefore, the identification of realms is advised here. This leads to the identification of the class structure, the real composition of this structure, and each class in this structure. These are also the basic steps for dealing with the options of class formation by means of mobility. What remains is to study the immediate factors in the realm(s) that mediate between options and the actual people.

The study of the middle class in Israel is embedded in the unique history of this society. The point of departure of the present study is the assumption that during the period in question, Israel was undergoing a process of becoming a capitalist society. The first realm was specified by being protected by the state. This was a period of incubating capitalism. The second realm was still specified by the influence of the state, and by industrialization of the Israeli society. The third realm was specified by the growing influence of the market economy. Each realm had a decisive influence on the formation of the class structure and on the old and new components of the middle class. Just as anticipated in a developing capitalist society, the petty bourgeoisie was declining and the new middle class was growing. Certain factors in certain realms had more influence on one's odds of mobility regarding these components. But some elements did not change dramatically in spite of the shifts in the structure of the economy and those which took place in politics and other instances: males, Jews and Ashkenazim remain in a dominant position in the old and the new middle class. The middle class remains, as before, a minority in the Israeli society, though its composition has changed in favour of the new middle class. Eventually, as in other countries, what had been anticipated regarding the formation and position of this class was realized in Israel.

Notes

1. Marx and some of his more conservative disciples were not very optimistic about the future fate of the petty bourgeoisie; see Kautsky 1971; Berenstein 1966; Cuneo 1984; Nicolaus 1970.
2. Different studies have dealt with education, ethnic origin, gender, and year of immigration as factors which facilitate (or inhibit) an individual's class and status in Israel. It appears that these factors have had an important, sometimes even critical, influence on the individual's mobility in this society.
3. These factors are dichotomized for the purpose of the present presentation. A more refined treatment of some of these factors, such as education, supports the results of Tables 2 and 3 in the following section.
4. The decomposition process was executed first for 1961-1972, and then for 1972-1983. For each comparison pair, the three effects were calculated separately. The information in Table 5 shows the effects of class, economic sector and interaction. The procedure by which these results were obtained is based on sample information. Therefore it is not possible to give absolute numbers of growth or decline. See Ben-Porat 1993; Stenmetz and Wright 1989.

Bibliography

Becer, E.H. (1984), 'Self-employed workers: An update to 1983', *Monthly Labor Review*, 107; 7.

Barkai, H. (1983), *The Genesis of Israeli Economy* (in Hebrew), The Maurice Falk Institute, Jerusalem.

Ben-Porat, A. (1989), *Divided We Stand*, Greenwood Press, Connecticut.

Ben-Porat, A. (1993), *The State and Capitalism In Israel*, Greenwood Press, Connecticut.

Ben-Porat, A. (1994), 'What Make Them Proletariate', *Israel Social Science Review*.

Berenstein, E. (1966), *Evolutionary Socialism*, Schoken, New-York.

Bradly, I. (1982), *The English Idle Class Are Alive and Kicking*, Collins, London.

Bruc-Briggs, B. (ed.) (1979), *The New Middle Class?*, Transaction, New Jersey.

Burris, V. (1986), 'The Discovery of the New Middle Class', *Theory and Society*, 15, pp. 317-349.

Burris, V. (1980), 'Class Formation in Advanced Capitalist Society: A Comparative Analysis', *Sociel Praxis*, 7(3/4), pp. 147-179.

Charchedi, G. (1977), *On the economic identification of social class*, Routledge and Kegan Paul, London.

Clegg, S., Borneham, P. and Dow, G. (1986), *Class politics and the economy*, Routledge and Kegan Paul, London.

Cuneo, C.J. 'Has the traditional petite bourgeoisie persisted?', *Canadian Journal of Sociology*, 9(3), pp. 269-301

Crossic, G. (ed.) (1977), *The lower middle class in Britain*, Croom Helm, London.

Dale, A. (1985), 'Social class and the self-employed', *Sociology*, 20(3), pp. 430-434.

Dale, J.L. (ed.) (1985), *Middle classes in dependent countries*, Sage, Beverly Hills, Cal.

Enzensberger, H.M. (1976), 'On the irresistibility of the petty bourgeoisie', *Telos* 30, pp. 161-166.

Gagliani, G. (1981), 'How many working classes?', *American Journal of Sociology* 87,(2), pp. 259-285.

Giddens, A. (1973), *The class structure of the advanced societies*, Hutchinson, London.

Goldthorpe, J. (1980), *Social mobility and class structure in modern Britain*, Clarendon Press, Oxford.

Gruski, G.D. (ed.) (1994), *Social Stratification*, Westview Press, Boulder.

Hauser, M.R. and Featheman, D. (1977), *The process of stratification: trends and analysis*, Academic Press, New York.

Hazerling, L.E. and Garnier, M.A. (1976), 'Occupational mobility in industrial societies: a comparative analysis of different access to occupational ranks in seventeen countries', *American Sociological Review* 41, pp. 498-511.

Hindess, B. (1987), *Politics and class analysis*, Basil Blackwell, London.

Kautsky, K. (1971), *The class struggle*, Norton, New York.

Patenkin, D. (1976), *The Israeli economy: The first decade*, The Maurice Falk Institute, Jerusalem.

Poulantzas, N. (1975), *Classes in contemporary capitalism*, New Left Books, London.

Przeworski, A. (1985), *Capitalism and democracy*, Cambridge University Press, Cambridge, Mass.

Robinson, V.R. (1984), 'Structural changes and class mobility in capitalist societies', *Social Forces* 63, pp. 51-71.

Rose, G. (1978), 'Marxism and the middle classes', *Theory and Society* 5, pp. 163-191.

Scase, R. (1982), *The entrepreneurial middle class*, Croom Helm, London.

Simkus, A. (1984), 'Structural transformation and social mobility: Hungary 1938-1973', *American Sociological Review* 49, pp. 291-307.

Steinmetz, G. and Wright, E.O. (1989), 'The fall and rise of petty bourgeoisie: Changing pattern of self-employed in the postwar United States', *American Journal of Sociology* 94(5), pp. 973-1018.

Tyree, A. (1973), 'Mobility ratios and association in mobility tables', *Population Studies*, pp. 577-588.

Toivonen, T. (1987), *The rise of self-employment and industrial structure*, Egos Colloquium, Antwerp.

Wancquand, L.J.D. (1991), 'Making class: The Middle class(es) in social theory and social structure', in S.G. McNall, R.F Levine, and R. Fantasia (eds.), *Bringing Class Back*, Westview, Boulder, pp. 39-64.

Wright, E.O. and Martin, B. (1987), 'The transformation of the American class structure, 1960-1980', *American Journal of Sociology* 93(1), pp. 1-29.

Wright, E.O. (1985), *Classes*, New Left Books, London.

9 Intragenerational Mobility and Middle Class Formation in Estonia[1]

ELLU SAAR AND JELENA HELEMÄE

Introduction

Economic reform in Estonia has been extremely radical as regards its liberal economic principles and the modest role of the state. However, the social cost of reforms in Estonia has been one of the highest among all the economies undergoing the transition to market economy. The key issue in promoting social stability is thought to be the strengthening of the middle class (Estonian Human Development Report 1995).

In this paper we examine the patterns of intragenerational mobility in two age groups in the early days of economic reform in Estonia. Was there any evidence of changes in opportunities for trained sections of the age groups? Were people stabile or mobile; did intragenerational mobility tend to rise with the start of economic reform? Which types of mobility predominated, structural or circulation, upward or downward? What were the factors that caused the most educated members of two age groups to become managers and professionals? To address these questions we use data from two longitudinal studies of the most educated persons born in 1948-49 and 1964-65. The studies were carried out in Estonia by researchers from the University of Tartu and the Institute of International and Social Studies of the Estonian Academy of Science (under the leadership of M. Titma).

We found that most members of these age groups occupied fairly stable positions within occupational categories. The middle of the scale of occupational categories was more stable than the top (managers) and bottom (unskilled workers). This material was from the early years of economic reform (1989-1993), but the picture which emerged was quite similar to that based on material 20 years earlier (1972-1976). Professionals and managers — our categories of interest — in the younger age group had came to their positions by 1993 from a background that was rather similar to that of the older age group when they were the same age. The emergence of the private sector as the most important dimension of contemporary economic life in Estonia did not bring about any major changes in the mechanisms governing movement into the status of professionals, and very slight changes for managers.

Social Mobility and Economic Reforms

In Estonia, as well as in other post-socialist societies, the emergence of the new middle class has been associated with the development of economic reforms. One of the most important ingredients of these reforms are structural changes of the economy.[2] Some of the main consequences of these structural changes for the labour market are a decline in the proportion of full-time employees in the whole population, especially in heavy industry and agriculture; a growth of employment in the service industries; an a growth of employment in the private sector.[3]

To examine the pattern of social mobility as a context of middle class formation in the early years of economic reforms, our analysis focused on two age groups. Both of these groups are by definition the trained sections of the relevant larger age groups because of their higher level of education: general secondary in the case of the older age group and three types of secondary education (vocational, specialized and general) in the case of the younger age group. Because of the high degree of educational selectivity in the former Soviet Union, these groups ought to provide a balanced representation of the middle class.

The older age group, in its early forties, may be considered to have reached the apex of its life career. It represents the most stabilized part of society, with substantial accumulated and largely realized human capital. The younger age group represents the part of society that is most open to change, its initial human capital also sizeable but not yet realized.

Economic reforms may be seen as a source of two types of change: on the one hand, of a broadening spectrum of opportunities and voluntary changes of social positions and primarily upward mobility; and on the other hand, of a rise in vulnerability to forced changes of social positions, especially downward mobility.

The market orientation of the Estonian economy inspired greater labour mobility.[4] However, we suggest that for the most trained sections of all age groups — those near the top of their life career — opportunities of upward mobility are restricted because of their already high status and the scarcity of even higher status places. We also expect them to suffer less downward mobility or forced loss of jobs (which we suggest to be one type of downward mobility). We suggest that

H1-1: The beginning of the economic reforms did not bring about a rise in mobility for the older age group examined.

Under conditions of social transformation a different picture emerges for the younger age groups. Firstly, many of them had not attained a stable position by 1989; secondly, those with a higher educational dimension of human capital expected to have new opportunities to realize this capital with the beginning of economic reforms; thirdly, because of a lack of job experience they might suffer forced downward mobility, especially loss of jobs. We suggest then that

H1-2: The younger age group examined had a high rate of mobility during the period from 1989 to 1993.

Since the beginning of the economic reforms there had been no significant migration into Estonia (Statistical Yearbook 1994, p. 80-81). In 1991 the restructuring of the economy was still only just beginning and there is no reason to expect it would have changed the structures of occupational categories in the advanced middle-aged groups. We suggest that the older age group had the opportunity to maintain its privileges and:

H2-1: The older age group examined was not involved in structural mobility during the period from 1989 to 1991.

The younger age groups might be involved in structural mobility for the following two reasons:

— their higher vulnerability to forced changes of jobs and corresponding social positions;

— the new economic structures that appeared by 1993, which might prove quite attractive to young people and offer an opportunity to change their social position. We hypothesize that

H2-2: Economic reforms during the period from 1989 to 1993 brought about a slight increase in structural mobility in the younger age group examined.

How are these general trends in mobility connected with the formation of a middle class? Quite obviously, mobility governs the composition of classes, or in Goldthorpe's (1987) words their 'demographical identity'. Stability and recruitment patterns — measured by the actual percentages remaining in and joining different classes — were to Goldthorpe the 'absolute rate of mobility' (Goldthorpe 1987). Therefore, absolute rates govern the potential for class actors to realize their interest (Sorensen 1991).

To measure the demographic identity of classes Goldthorpe, like most mobility researchers, concentrated on the analysis of intergenerational mobility. We chose to focus on intragenerational mobility in order to address the question of the relationship between mobility and class formation during the transformation of the Estonian economy. Firstly, life course data provide opportunities for direct measurement of the 'demographic identity' of classes as stability of class membership over real time (not 'generations') (Sorensen

1991). Secondly, it seems a more adequate measure for the formation of a *new* class that could only emerge after 1989.

There are many different definitions of middle class (for an overview see Blom 1995; Kivinen 1995). We tend to understand middle class as a conceptual construct and measure it here through occupational categories. We also realize that although the age groups we examined as wholes are in fact the most trained sections of the relevant age groups, their 'top' should not be the top of society as a whole; we do not suppose that the real elite or upper class is adequately represented in our samples. We do consider the scales of occupational categories for the age groups concerned to have managers at the top and unskilled workers at the bottom of the scale, but in reality we expect managers in the groups examined to be rather upper middle class.

It is a widely held view in contemporary Estonia that a top and a bottom have just been formed for a 'new' society. These two extreme groups have begun to recognize and express their group interests in society, but those social groups which fall between the two extremes are the most controversial and fluid (Estonian Human Development Report 1995). This view about the contradictory nature of the middle of society corresponds to Goldthorpe's analyses (Goldthorpe 1987). However, as mentioned, Goldthorpe concentrated on the analysis of *inter*generational mobility. For our *intra*generational measurement we suggest that the 'middle' position of the 'middle age group' becomes quite stable by their late thirties, and the very beginning of economic reforms could not alter this situation. However, the younger age group had not been stabilized before the beginning of reforms and they tried to use the new opportunities. There was also a possibility that they might suffer under the labour market forces. We also take into account the large 'mobile' aggregate of those who moved into or out of the labour force (first the young mothers, but also people who completed their studies after 1989, and those made redundant). We suggest then that

H3: The older age group attained middle positions in society by 1989 and became stable by 1991. The younger age group was mobile during the period from 1989 to 1993.

The higher level of mobility in younger age groups in Estonia could have been due to economic changes as such. Part of this mobility could be explained by the stage of their life cycle. The two age groups we examined were at very different stages in their life at the time of the survey: members of the older age group had reached their middle age by 1991, members of the younger age group were still in their late twenties in 1993. To assess the influence of life cycle — whether the pattern of mobility for the younger age group in 1989-1993 differed from the norm for people of their age in Estonia under the old economy — we study two groups of the same age but in very different social circumstances: the older age group in the 'era of stagnation' of the socialist party-state, and the younger age group under conditions of radical transformations in the political, economic and social systems.

In state socialist societies the allocation mechanisms of social structure were under direct bureaucratic control. Thus, this allocation mechanism acted to 'limit the scope of mobility through administrative regulation, standardization, and bureaucratic obstacles' (Mach, Mayer and Pohoski 1994). Allocation mechanisms in capitalist societies are usually characterized by greater freedom in differentiating social mobility.

We used the Sorensen-Kalleberg theory of labour market matching and attainment processes (Sorensen and Kalleberg 1981; Eliason 1995) as a basis in formulating hypotheses about social mobility of different groups at the same age. This theory rests on the structure of control over market positions as open and closed position systems (Sorensen 1983, 1986). Open positions are seen as characteristic of competitive homogenous labour markets — market competition is the mechanism of access to these kinds of positions. Open positions are freely available to anyone who meets whatever requirements exist for access. Only the personal resources of candidates should determine access to a position. Changes in abilities and qualifications will lead to a move to higher positions. In an open positions system, future allocations are not determined by past allocations.

In a closed positions system the allocation mechanism shall be referred to as vacancy competition (Sorensen 1977), and the system is governed by the logic of institutional and/or organizational rules (Eliason 1995). In this system, movement depends on the availability of vacancies at the next level. New allocation can take place only when positions are vacated by previous holders or when new positions are added to the system. The timing of the creation of vacancies has nothing to do with the human capital factors of the candidates for vacant positions. The ability and efforts of all candidates desiring the vacant position have an important impact on the chances of any candidate to obtain the position: the movements are interdependent among a set of candidates. The allocation process is closed to others outside the system. For those inside the system, the opportunity structure reflects the past history of the candidate. Promotion and movements depend on a ranking of candidates for positions that is based on a combination of criteria believed to provide information on future performance through past performance, education, origin and other personal characteristics.

Under state socialism, the highly institutionalized mechanism of access to positions believed itself to have many elements of vacancy competition. In contrast, we consider the allocation mechanism in the period of transition to market economy to have more elements of market competition. Since vacancy competition and market competition are expected to generate different mobility regimes, we hypothesize that

H4: Intragenerational social mobility should be different for two age groups examined at the same age, both by amount and direction.

Under the vacancy competition mechanism, the holder should leave a position only when a higher position is available; the holder can wait for it in the present position (Sorensen and Tuma 1981). Therefore, downward social mobility should be rare. In contrast, 'the declines that would be observed in open-position systems would be declines in physical and mental capacities duly recognized by the market' (Sorensen 1986, p. 188). Thus, according to our conclusions from Sorensen's reasoning, we hypothesize that:

H5: Downward intragenerational social mobility should be greater for the younger age group than for the older age group at the same age but under different economic conditions.

Vacancy and market competition mechanisms both produce upward mobility, but the mechanisms are different. In vacancy competition the upward moves are generated by historically and organizationally specific mobility regimes (Sorensen 1986). The increase in human capital is neither necessary nor sufficient for upward moves. In contrast, in market competition an increase in human capital is a both necessary and sufficient reason for upward mobility.

In the socialist period, the allocation process for the jobs of professionals was characterized by the fact that the state controlled opportunities for achieving a higher school degree (Huinink and Solga 1994). As a result, social mobility into the class of professionals was strictly controlled through the educational system. The candidates for professional jobs were screened primarily for educational — not political — credentials (Walder 1995). Thus, we suppose that although vacancy competition as such does not presuppose an importance of educational credentials — under state socialism organizational rules of a similar system had led to the same result as in market competition — education was and is a necessary reason for upward mobility into the class of professionals. In this sense, we suppose that the pattern of allocation for professional jobs is not changed by the transition to market economy. Our next hypothesis states that:

H6: The patterns of mobility into the class of professionals do not differ between the younger and older age groups.

By dual path model hypothesis (Walder 1995) competition for vacancies in the manager stratum in socialist societies took place according to organizational rules. Political credentials were very important. We hypothesize that:

H7: The patterns of mobility into the stratum of managers should be different for the two age groups.

Material, Variables and Method

We use data from two longitudinal studies. The first Estonian longitudinal study was started in 1966 by the Laboratory of Sociology of Education at Tartu University and the Department of Youth Sociology of the Estonian Academy of Sciences under the leadership of professor Mikk Titma. The initial population of interest was Estonian high school graduates; in 1966 they were 18 years of age. The total size of this age group born in 1948-49 was 18,500; in 1966 7,000 pupils graduated from general high school, and 60 % of them from schools where Estonian was the language of instruction. Our sample thus constitutes about 15 % of the entire age group. The sample was drawn according to the territorial indicator and population in local communities where the secondary schools were located.

This study aimed to cover the period of an age group's integration into social life, i.e. up until the age of 30. Five waves of study were conducted (in 1966, 1969, 1973, 1976 and 1979). Because of crucial changes in the political, economic and social life of Estonia, an 'additional' stage of study was carried out in 1991 to examine the influence of these changes on the life course of a generation. In this paper we use data from the 1991 survey, in which graduates of schools with Russian as the primary language of instruction were interviewed as a control group.[5] The total size of the samples was 1,920.

The second survey, 'Paths of a Generation', is part of a larger set of longitudinal surveys in sixteen regions of the former Soviet Union. This project was started in 1982 by a team also headed by Titma (Titma and Koklyagina 1990). The original population comprised 17-18 year-old graduates of the secondary educational system. The initial samples in 'Paths of a Generation' were selected to be representative of the population of 1983 secondary school graduates in Estonia (which makes up 95 % of the age group according to state statistics, and 75 % to 85 % by the 1989 census). The sample was chosen to reflect the proportion of graduates from each of the three main types of Soviet secondary schools: specialized secondary schools, general academic secondary schools and vocational schools. In this paper we will use data from the second follow-up of this survey: 2,218 respondents were interviewed in 1992-93.[6]

The data contain detailed information on personal characteristics for both age groups as well as their labour force participation from 1966 to 1991 for the first age group and from 1983 to 1993 for the second one.[7]

Method. To capture the main tendencies in intragenerational social mobility as the context of middle class formation in the early days of economic reforms in Estonia, we use life history data of two age groups. 1989 is chosen as the year marking the beginning of societal transformation in Estonia. By 1989 members of the older age group were about forty years old, members of the younger age group about 25 years. The age groups examined were at different stages in their life course. The older age group (born in 1948-49) was expected to represent the stabilized part of society, close to the top of their life career. The younger age group (born in 1964-65) was expected to represent the most active and mobile part of society. Their behaviour might be used — with certain reservations, of course — as an indicator of the more general tendencies related to social mobility in society at large.

To understand the impact of one's life stage on the patterns of mobility, we compare intragenerational social mobility for two age groups at the same age (from 24 to 28 years), but in different periods (for the older age group from 1972 to 1976; for the younger, from 1989 to 1993).

Our analysis will proceed in four steps. We begin by comparing social positions in 1989 and 1993, for the younger age group, and in 1972, 1976, 1989 and 1991, for the older age group. Then we examine the amount of mobility for the two age groups in different periods.[8] Third, we construct mobility tables for both age groups and analyse the outflow and inflow patterns.

The next step is to analyse factors influencing mobility into the strata of managers and professionals for both age groups. The formation of these strata is interesting, while in the international literature the new middle class is associated with 'white-collar workers' and the strata of employees and managers (Gouldner 1979; Pappi 1981). Secondly, moves into the strata of managers and professionals represent two of the most frequent kinds of upward mobility for our age groups. Studies in the former socialist states demonstrate the existence of two distinct career paths that lead to administrative posts and to professional positions, respectively (Szelenyi 1987; Walder 1995). We include in our analysis all members who belong to the concrete stratum in 1993 (or in 1976).

There are numerous alternative ways in which to study predictors of mobility into strata. Our choice is segmentation modelling,[9] which allows us to reveal concrete groups as sources for the stratum examined. The dependent *variables* were defined as dummies with code 1 if belonging to the stratum and 0 if not belonging to the stratum. In constructing tree diagrams we use five categories of predictors: (1) structural variables by the beginning of the period of study — by the age of 24 — (social strata, branch of economy, residential status, political status); (2) human capital variables — also by the age of 24 — (educational level, number of jobs[10]); (3) personal characteristics, including gender and ethnicity; (4) political participation; and (5) characteristics of social origin (education and social status of both parents).

Findings

Amount of Mobility. As we can see in Table 1, structures of occupational positions were quite stable for both age groups examined throughout their life course. The most important changes for the older age group were:
— from age 24 to 28 a reduction in the proportion of those outside the labour force (young mothers and 'later students' came back to work) and an increase in the proportion of professionals;
— from age 28 to 41 and by beginning of the economic reforms, a time of promotion into the manager stratum;
— economic reforms brought about a very slight rise in the number of those out of the labour force.

Table 1. Social position of age groups (%)

Year	1989	1991	1993	1972	1976	1989	1991
Age	24	26	28	24	28	41	43
Manager	3	6	7	4	8	17	18
Professional	14	17	16	29	36	34	33
Semi-professional	17	16	15	12	13	14	12
Clerk	8	8	7	13	12	12	11
Service worker	6	6	5	5	5	5	5
Skilled agricultural worker	4	4	3	2	2	3	3
Skilled industrial worker	31	29	25	14	13	13	12
Unskilled worker	3	3	3	1	2	2	2
Out of labour force	14	11	19	20	9	0.4	4
Total	100	100	100	100	100	100	100

During 1989-1991 the younger age group experienced very slight changes in the structure of occupational categories: there was some increase in the number of managers and professionals but a decrease in skilled industrial workers and those out of the labour force. The next two years helped to clarify some trends. Firstly, the decline in the share of skilled industrial workers continued as an obvious result of economic restructuring. The share of those out of the labour force within the age group increased, contrary to the previous two years of reforms. We tend to interpret changes in the share of people out of the labour force as an interplay of life course and economic restructuring processes, with the former dominating during 1989-1991 (as was the case with the older age group at the same age) and the latter (especially unemployment, but also the preference of some women for the role of housewife) dominating during 1991-1993.

To estimate rates and directions of mobility, we present our results for both age groups in different periods in Table 2. The direction of a move is determined by comparing social status at the beginning of the period with the status by the end of the period. This produces three types of events: immobility (or stability, respondents on the diagonal), upward and downward mobility (respondents over and under the diagonal).

Table 2. Intragenerational mobility of age groups

Age	Younger age group			Older age group	
	24-26	24-28	24-28	28-41	41-43
Year	1989-1991	1989-1993	1972-1976	1976-1989	1989-1991
Stable	78	64	61	59	91
Mobile	22	36	39	41	9
Structural mobility	7	13	13	10	4
Circulation mobility	15	23	26	31	5
Upward mobility	14	17	28	29	3
Downward mobility	8	19	11	12	6

As we see, there is no difference in the share of mobile persons between the younger and older age groups at the same age. As expected, in the same time interval (from 1989 to 1991) the younger age group was more mobile than the older age group. Members of the older age group were at that time in their early forties and had attained a stable social position. In contrast, for the younger age group the time interval from 1989 to 1991 covers their mid-twenties, the age period when people should be at their most mobile.

As expected, we saw no reason to consider the structural mobility of the older age group in its early forties. The younger age group seemed to be more mobile during the economic reforms, but this mobility did not exceed the rate of mobility of the older age group when they were the same age. This means we cannot consider our hypothesis proven for the younger age group.

Table 3.1. Inflow percentages for intragenerational mobility of the older age group (1972/1976)

Social strata in 1972	Social strata in 1972									Total (number of resp.)
	M	P	SP	C	SW	AW	SIW	UW	OLF	
Manager (M)	41	1	-	2	1	-	0	3	3	4 (85)
Professional (P)	27	63	4	4	3	6	2	3	26	29 (551)
Semiprofessional (SP)	5	2	65	3	5	3	3	3	14	12 (231)
Clerk (C)	4	4	5	64	6	9	3	13	12	13 (239)
Service worker (SW)	2	1	4	3	59	9	0	3	3	5 (92)
Skilled agric. worker (AW)	-	0	0	1	1	55	1	-	2	2 (31)
Skilled ind. worker (SIW)	5	2	5	4	6	6	84	10	5	14 (276)
Unskilled worker (UW)	1	0	1	0	-	3	1	52	1	1 (26)
Out of labour force (OLF)	15	27	16	19	19	9	6	13	34	20 (387)
Total	100	100	100	100	100	100	100	100	100	100(1918)

Social strata in 1989	Social strata in 1991									Total (number of resp.)
	M	P	SP	C	SW	AW	SIW	UW	OLF	
Manager (M)	87	2	0	1	2	-	1	-	-	17 (318)
Professional (P)	8	96	-	2	2	2	0	-	28	35 (664)
Semiprofessional (SP)	3	1	98	1	-	-	1	3	20	14 (265)
Clerk (C)	-	1	1	94	2	-	1	4	20	12 (235)
Service worker (SW)	1	-	0	0	93	2	-	-	8	5 (101)
Skilled agric. worker (AW)	-	-	-	-	-	96	0	3	1	3 (49)
Skilled ind. worker (SIW)	1	0	0	1	1	-	95	3	14	13 (243)
Unskilled worker (UW)	-	0	-	1	-	-	0	87	1	2 (38)
Out of labour force (OLF)	0.3	-	-	-	-	-	-	-	8	0.4 (7)
Total	100	100	100	100	100	100	100	100	100	100(1920)

Table 3.2. Inflow percentages for intragenerational mobility of the younger age group

Social strata in 1989	Social strata in 1993									Un-empl.	Total (no of resp.)
	M	P	SP	C	SW	AW	SIW	UW	OLF		
Manager (M)	31	1	1	-	-	-	-	-	1	2	3 (64)
Professional (P)	11	64	2	3	-	-	1	2	10	4	13(286)
Semiprofessional (SP)	10	4	78	8	7	1	2	7	8	16	17(352)
Clerk (C)	2	5	1	74	7	-	-	-	9	10	8(178)
Service worker (SW)	7	-	1	2	60	-	1	3	9	8	6(125)
Skilled agric. worker (AW)	-	-	1	1	1	79	1	6	4	3	4 (82)
Skilled industrial worker (SIW)	15	1	8	4	17	16	93	24	16	43	32(670)
Unskilled worker (UW)	1	-	-	1	4	4	1	48	5	2	3 (65)
Out of labour force (OLF)	23	25	8	7	4	-	1	10	38	12	14(297)
Total	100	100	100	100	100	100	100	100	100	100	100(2119)

	Social strata in 1991								
	M	P	SP	C	SW	AW	SIW	UW	OLF
Manager (M)	44	1	1	1	1	-	-	-	1
Professional (P)	7	68	1	1	-	-	-	-	8
Semiprofessional (SP)	8	2	83	4	6	1	1	5	7
Clerk (C)	2	2	1	84	7	1	-	-	7
Service worker (SW)	4	-	1	1	71	1	-	3	5
Skilled agric. worker (AW)	11	1	6	2	9	94	9	16	8
Skilled industrial worker (SIW)	-	-	-	1	1	1	85	6	4
Unskilled worker (UW)	1	-	1	1	3	1	-	65	3
Out of labour force (OLF)	23	26	6	5	2	1	5	5	57
Total	100	100	100	100	100	100	100	100	100

Table 4.1. Outflow percentages for intragenerational mobility of the older age group

Social strata in 1972	Social strata in 1976									
	M	P	SP	C	SW	AW	SIW	UW	OLF	Total
Manager (M)	78	8	-	5	1	-	1	1	6	100
Professional (P)	8	79	2	2	0	0	1	0	8	100
Semiprofes- sional (SP)	4	7	71	3	2	0	3	0	10	100
Clerk (C)	3	12	5	63	3	1	3	2	8	100
Service worker (SW)	4	6	10	6	63	3	1	1	6	100
Skilled agric. worker (AW)	-	7	3	7	3	58	9	-	13	100
Skilled industrial worker (SIW)	3	5	4	4	2	1	77	1	3	100
Unskilled worker (UW)	4	8	8	4	-	4	8	60	4	100
Out of labour force (OLF)	6	47	10	11	5	1	4	1	15	100
Total	8	36	13	12	5	2	13	2	9	100
(N)	(161)	(690)	(250)	(233)	(99)	(33)	(255)	(31)	(166)	(1918)

Social strata in 1989	Social strata in 1991									
	M	P	SP	C	SW	AW	SIW	UW	OLF	Total
Manager (M)	93	4	0	1	1	-	1	-	-	100
Professional (P)	4	92	-	1	0	0	0	-	3	100
Semiprofes- sional (SP)	3	2	88	1	-	-	1	0	5	100
Clerk (C)	-	2	1	88	1	-	1	1	6	100
Service worker (SW)	2	-	1	1	89	1	-	-	6	100
Skilled agric. worker (AW)	-	-	-	-	-	94	2	2	2	100
Skilled ind. worker (SIW)	2	1	0	1	0	-	92	0	4	100
Unskilled worker (UW)	-	3	-	5	-	-	3	86	3	100
Out of labour force (OLF)	14	-	-	-	-	-	-	-	86	100
Total	18	33	12	12	5	2	12	2	4	100
(N)	(340)	(635)	(238)	(220)	(97)	(48)	(233)	(38)	(71)	(1920)

Table 4.2. Outflow percentages for intragenerational mobility of the younger age group

Social strata in 1989	Social strata in 1993										
	M	P	SP	C	SW	AW	SIW	UW	OLF	UE	Total
Manager (M)	77	5	6	-	-	-	3	-	6	3	100
Professional (P)	6	79	2	1	-	-	1	-	9	2	100
Semiprofessional (SP)	4	4	68	3	3	-	3	2	7	6	100
Clerk (C)	2	9	1	60	5	-	1	-	15	7	100
Service worker (SW)	8	-	2	2	55	-	2	2	21	8	100
Skilled agric. worker (AW)	-	-	2	1	1	69	5	5	12	5	100
Skilled ind. worker (SIW)	3	1	4	1	3	2	69	2	7	8	100
Unskilled worker (UW)	3	1	1	1	6	-	11	52	20	5	100
Out of labour force (OLF)	12	29	9	3	1	1	2	2	36	5	100
Total	7	16	15	7	5	3	24	3	14	6	100
(N)	(154)	(346)	(312)	(143)	(114)	(71)	(501)	(68)	(281)	(129)	(2119)

Social strata in 1989	Social strata in 1991									
	M	P	SP	C	SW	AW	SIW	UW	OLF	Total
Manager (M)	84	3	5	2	2	-	2	-	2	100
Professional (P)	3	88	1	-	-	-	1	-	7	100
Semiprofessional (SP)	3	2	83	2	2	1	2	1	4	100
Clerk (C)	1	5	2	76	5	-	2	-	9	100
Service worker (SW)	4	1	1	2	79	-	3	2	8	100
Skilled agric. worker (AW)	2	-	2	1	2	85	4	1	3	100
Skilled ind. worker (SIW)	-	1	3	1	1	1	78	5	10	100
Unskilled worker (UW)	1	-	1	2	6	-	12	63	11	100
Out of labour force (OLF)	9	31	8	3	1	-	2	1	44	100
Total	6	17	16	8	6	4	29	3	11	100
(N)	(122)	(366)	(348)	(160)	(136)	(76)	(606)	(63)	(225)	(2102)

As assumed, at the same age the rate of downward mobility is greater for the younger age group than for the older age group. From age 24 to age 28 the rate of upward mobility for members of the older age group was more than twice as high as the rate of downward mobility; for members of the younger age group rates of upward and downward mobility did not differ. This is partly due to the fact that the older group constituted a more highly trained part of their entire age group than did the younger group — although only partly. From 1989 to 1991 members of the older age group had a higher rate of downward than upward mobility regardless of their high stability. Assuming that the high rate of downward mobility here does not reflect just differences between age groups, downward mobility observed in a period of transition to the market economy could represent a decline in capacities recognized by the market.

An analysis of the mobility tables of the younger and older age groups reveals that in both cases, the most intensive inflow was into the strata of managers (top of age groups) and unskilled workers (bottom). However, for the younger age group the proportion of newcomers in the stratum of managers was more than two-thirds and in the stratum of unskilled workers one-half, while for the older age group the proportion of newcomers in the relative strata was little more than 10 %. By 1991, the older age group was mainly maintaining its 'pre-reform' social position. We tend to explain this as an interplay of two reasons: the stage of development of economic reforms and the stable position reached by the older age group by the start of reforms. By 1991 the 'middle age' stabile position was a more important factor of intragenerational (im)mobility than were the economic changes. It is worth noting that for the younger age group other strata were also quite stable — their 'stable core' was anything from two-thirds (professionals) to more than 90 % (skilled industrial workers). Our preliminary conclusion is that economic changes had a very slight impact on the social positions of the older age group and a rather slight impact on social positions in the middle of the strata scale for the younger age group. The most evident change in the social position of the younger age group was the movement from being in the labour force to being out of it, a 'new' pattern in these movements.

A comparison of the mobility tables for the younger age group and for the older age group at the same age reveals some surprising discoveries: the intragenerational mobility pattern of the older age group, by its later twenties, was quite similar to the pattern of mobility in the younger age group. The main inflows were into the manager and unskilled worker categories (almost to the same extent); the position of skilled workers was the most stable; and the middle of the occupational categories scale was more stable than the categories of managers and unskilled workers (but this stable core was even smaller than in case of the younger age group!). Therefore the hypothesis regarding differences in intragenerational social mobility between two age groups at the same age receives no support.

Our conclusion is that by the year 1993 we fail to reveal any extensive intragenerational mobility pattern that might be attributed to the consequences of economic reforms with any certainty. To confirm this preliminary conclusion we would need to analyse data from further stages of the research with the two age groups. We would also require data on the careers of a sample representative of the whole population.

Becoming Managers and Professionals

We have taken from segmentation modelling the list of significant predictors for belonging to managers and professionals by the age of 28 for members of both age groups (see Table 5).

The results for managers show that structural variables are the most significant predictors for entry into the stratum of managers for both age groups. We found only a few differences in the predictor lists. One of the human capital variables (number of jobs) had no significant effect on the older age groups' probability of becoming managers. The social origin effect (and mother's social status and education in particular) was more important for the younger than the older age group. We stress the significant effect of party membership on the attainment of a managerial position in the older age group.

As can be seen, the differences in the older and younger age groups' lists of significant predictors for belonging to the stratum of professionals are even smaller. We noticed that the effect of individual variables (especially the effect of gender) is significantly smaller for the older than for the younger age group. A comparison of the predictors for entry into the strata of managers and professionals reveals differences in these lists for the older age group and similarities for the younger age group. To our mind the most important difference in the lists for the older age group is that the effect of CP membership on the attainment of professional position is not significant. Thus, our results are consistent with the findings of Walder (1995) pointing at two different career paths leading to managerial versus professional positions in socialist societies.

Tables 6.1 and 6.2 display the results of segmentation modelling for entry into the manager stratum for the older and younger age groups, respectively. As assumed, the best predictor for both age groups is belonging to the stratum of managers at the beginning of the period of study. In both age groups at least three out of four of those who held managerial positions at age 24 remain in this position until the age of 28 or older. Nevertheless, mobility from other strata into the manager stratum is somewhat higher for the younger age group

Table 5. **Predictor list[1] of belonging to managers or professionals at the age of 28**

Predictors	Older age group (1976)		Younger age group (1993)	
	Mana-gers	Profes-sionals	Mana-gers	Profes-sionals
A. Structural variables by beginning of the period (1972 for older, 1989 for younger age group)				
1. Social strata	***	***	***	***
2. Branch of economy	***	***	**	***
3. Residental status (type of place of residence)	**	***	***	***
4. Political status[2]	***		-	-
B. Human capital variables				
1. Education (in years)	***	***	***	***
2. Number of jobs		***	***	***
C. Political participation				
1. Participation in social life	-	-	***	***
2. Political status[3]	-	-	*	
D. Individual variables				
1. Gender	***		***	***
2. Ethnicity		*	**	***
E. Social Origin				
1. Father's education		***		***
2. Mother's education		***	***	***
3. Father's social status		***		***
4. Mother's social status	**	***	***	***

[1] *** — significant at level 0.001
  ** — significant at level 0.01
   * — significant at level 0.10
[2] CP membership for older age group
[3] Membership of some party or socio-political organization

Table 6.1. Formation of managers in 1976, older cohort

Segments of Cohort where from came ...

51-100 % of managers				11-50 % of managers				0-10 % of managers			
% of managers from segment	Description of segment	% of cohort	% of all managers in 1976	% of managers from segment	Description of segment	% of cohort	% of all managers in 1976	% of managers from segment	Description of segment	% of cohort	% of all managers in 1976
78	Managers in 1972	4	41	32	Men, out of labour force or professionals in 1972, members of Communist Party (CP)	5	21	9	Men, out of labour force or prof's in 1972, non-members of CP	11	12
								7	All strata (excepting managers and prof's), members of CP	8	7
								7	All strata excepting managers and prof's, non-members of CP, whose fathers had medium education	7	6
								2	Women, out of labour force in 1972 or prof's	31	9
								1	All strata (excepting managers and prof's), non-members of CP, whose fathers had high or low education	34	4
Total		4	4			5	21			91	38

Table 6.2. Formation of managers in 1993, younger cohort

Segments of Cohort where from came ...

51-100 % of managers

% of managers from segment	Description of segment	% of cohort	% of all managers in 1993
77	Managers in 1989	3	31
Total		3	31

11-50 % of managers

% of managers from segment	Description of segment	% of cohort	% of all managers in 1993
35	Men, out of labour force or professionals in 1989 with 2-7 work places	4	21
27	Men, semiprof's and service workers in 1989 with 3-4 work places	2	8
11	Women, service workers in 1989, Estonians	4	6
Total		10	35

0-10 % of managers

% of managers from segment	Description of segment	% of cohort	% of all managers in 1993
0	Agricultural workers in 1991	4	0
3	Clerks and industrial workers in 1991	42	18
8	Men, out of labour force or prof's in 1989 with 1 work place	4	4
0	Men, semiprof's and service workers in 1989 with 1-2 or 5-7 work places	3	0
2	Women, out of labour force, prof's and semiprof's in 1989	33	12
0	Women, service workers in 1989, other nationalities	1	0
Total		87	34

than for the older age group. The probability of mobility into the manager stratum is highest for men belonging to the professional stratum at the age of 24 or for men out of the labour force at this age. This group then splits into smaller subgroups. The splitting process is based on different variables for each age group. For the older age group the important variable was CP membership; for the younger age group the number of jobs previously held by the person. We interpret this variable to be the human capital variable. Contrary to ideological claims in the Soviet era that the people who changed jobs were mainly no good as workers, we can definitely say that among those who changed jobs there were the most entrepreneurial and active people. In our view both CP membership (for the older age group) and the number of jobs held (for the younger age group) are indicators of the activity of the person.

We discovered a relatively high percentage of service and trade workers moving into managerial positions in the younger age group. Mobility from other social strata into managerial positions was very rare in both age groups. Our results do not fully confirm the hypothesis about different mobility patterns into the manager stratum for older and younger age groups.

The transition period to a market economy in the former socialist countries can best be described as a clash between two opposing developments (Mach, Mayer and Pohoski 1994). One of them is a continuation of tendencies characteristic of state socialism. A significant proportion of the state economic sector allows the preservation of divisions: firstly, in terms of power with a hierarchic structure, and secondly, in terms of a powerful political and economic elite. The other development concerns the direct consequences of moving away from planned economy. The process of privatization brings about the emergence of private, public and municipal ownership.

We hypothesized that the process of mobility into the stratum of managers should be different for the private and state sectors. To verify this hypothesis, we divide the younger age group into three groups — persons working in the public sector, in state-owned enterprises and in the private sector — and study the process of entry into the stratum of managers in these subgroups, using segmentation modelling. Figure 1 displays tree diagrams.

In the public sector 39 % of managers were managers by the age of 24. Note the high inflow from the category of out of labour force. Respondents from other social strata are divided into two subgroups on the basis of their level of participation in social life. Active participants in social life had a significantly higher probability of mobility into managerial positions than did non-active participants.

For managers who worked in state-owned enterprises, a highly significant factor was belonging to the stratum of managers at the age of 24. Main inflows

Figure 1. Formation of managers in different sectors, younger cohort

Public sector (100%)

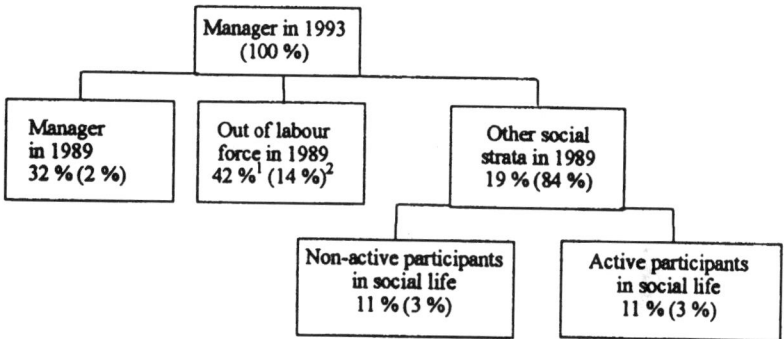

State-owned enterprises (100 %)

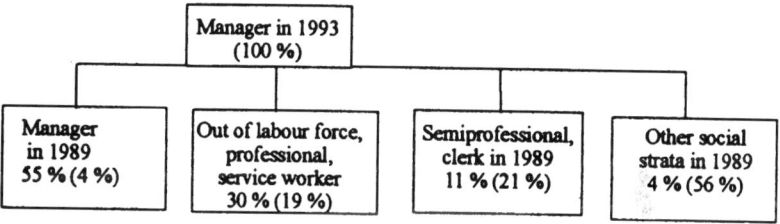

Private sector

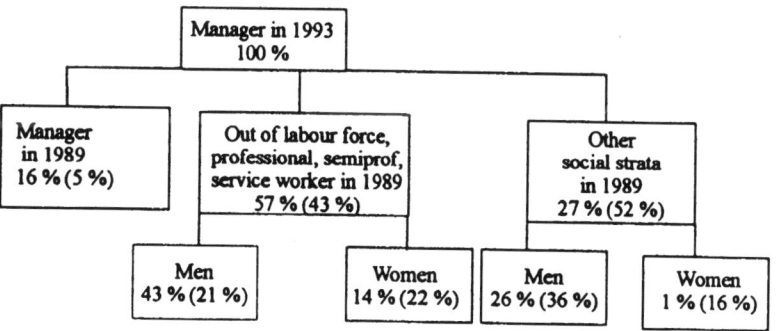

[1] Percent from manager in 1993
[2] Percent from hired in this sector in 1993

into managers hired in these enterprises were from the strata of professionals and service workers and from out of the labour force.

The tree diagram for the private sector differs from the two other diagrams. For other sectors, the best predictor is social stratum in 1989. However, we notice that 87 % of managers in the private sector belonged to other strata in 1989. Thus the inflow into managerial positions was very high in the private sector. The significant variable determining the inflow into managerial position was gender. Men had a great advantage for entry into managerial positions compared to women regardless of their social stratum in 1989.

We turn now to the results on becoming professionals in both age groups. As we see, more than 60 % of professionals belonged to this stratum at the age of 24. The level of inflows into the stratum of professionals was significantly lower than into the stratum of managers. For the younger age group, there were significant gender differences. As indicated earlier, for women the path from being professionals to being managers was closed. 82 % of women who were professionals at the age of 24 remained in the stratum until the age of 28 or over. The development of the private sector had opened new opportunities for men to move from being professionals into being managers. In both age groups the main inflow into the stratum of professionals was from out of the labour force. For other social strata the probability of entry into professional positions was low. The segmentation modelling suggests that the process of becoming professionals did not differ between age groups.

We can conclude that the patterns of access to managerial and professional positions have not yet changed from the socialism period. These patterns are governed first of all by the logic of institutional and organizational rules.

Discussion

Our analyses showed the most people in the two age groups concerned occupied quite stable positions within occupational categories. However, the evidence from other studies suggests that these 'places' as social positions often have a new social quality (i.e. have different social consequences for those holding them). We might consequently suggest that it would be better to say that positions move into a new system of social coordinates than that people change positions. This is true for our 'trained' age groups; but if we take into account the fact that younger age groups are the ones with the greatest potential for social mobility, we assume that this is equally true for the greater part of Estonian society (at least in the early days of reforms). Our data did not cover potential areas of (downward) mobility, i.e. young people with a low level of education and age groups near the end of their working career.

Table 7.1. Formation of professionals in 1976, older cohort

Segments of Cohort where from came ...

51-100 % of professionals				11-50 % of professionals				0-10 % of professionals			
% of prof's from segment	Description of segment	% of cohort	% of all prof's in 1976	% of prof's from segment	Description of segment	% of cohort	% of all prof's in 1976	% of prof's from segment	Description of segment	% of cohort	% of all prof's in 1976
78	Prof's in 1972	27	61	28	Out of labour force with general secondary education	5	4	5	Clerks in 1972, whose mother worked in industrial sphere and 2-7 work places	6	1
68	Out of labour force in 1972, with higher education	5	10	28	Clerks in 1972, whose mothers had mental job or were housewives	3	2	5	All strata (excepting clerks and prof's) with lower than higher education	36	5
54	Out of labour force in 1972, with general secondary education and 0-1 work places	7	12	20	Out of labour force in 1972, with specialized secondary education	3	1				
				17	Clerks in 1972, whose mothers were service workers	5	2				
				17	All strata (excepting clerks and prof's) with higher education	3	2				
Total		39	83			19	11			42	6

Table 7.2. Formation of professionals in 1993, younger cohort

Segments of Cohort where from came ...

	51-100 % of professionals				11-50 % of professionals				0-10 % of professionals		
% of prof's from segment	Description of segment	% of cohort	% of all prof's in 1976	% of prof's from segment	Description of segment	% of cohort	% of all prof's in 1976	% of prof's from segment	Description of segment	% of cohort	% of all prof's in 1976
82	Women, prof's in 1989	11	56	37	Men, out of labour force in 1989	6	14	4	Managers and semiprof's in 1991	20	5
58	Men, prof's in 1989	2	8	22	Women, out of labour force in 1989	8	11	5	Clerks with 1-3 work places	7	3
				39	Clerks in 1989 with 4-7 work places	1	2	0.5	Workers in 1989	45	1
Total		13	64			15	27			72	9

Patterns of mobility for all age groups deserve to be examined carefully on the basis of a database representative of the whole Estonian population.

The middle of the occupation categories scale of age groups examined was more stable compared to its top (managers) and bottom (unskilled workers). These findings are from the beginning of the economic reforms (1989-1993), but in comparison with material from 20 years earlier (1972-1976) the picture is very similar. Professionals and managers — our categories of interest — of the younger age group had come to their positions by 1993, from backgrounds rather similar to those of older age groups at the same age. This shows that old mechanisms of mobility (or even 'stability') did not lose their significance at the start of economic reforms. It might mean that the middle class could become 'new,' in the sense of its role in society becoming new, if not so much in the sense of its membership or the paths for 'becoming middle class' becoming new. The emergence of the private sector as an important dimension of contemporary economic life in Estonia did not bring about crucial changes in mechanisms governing mobility into the stratum of professionals, and it only brought very slight changes for managers. We may suggest then that the mechanism of 'new rules of position attainment' are not yet fully formed. Only the allocation mechanism for managerial positions in the private sector can be characterized as market competition.

There is clear evidence that labour market regimes differ for men and women in the transition period to a market economy. Women reap fewer rewards and experience less protection from market competition than men do.

How will the same individuals cope with the new and different social quality of their social positions and thus with their new social roles? Will they be able to form a new collective with its own socio-cultural (not only 'demographic') identity — these are questions that still remain open for future research and discussion. As regards the transformation of the middle strata of society, we might suggest some important questions: one might try to explain the mechanism of filling empty places, to address the question of how the system of coordinates has changed? If one considers it more important to investigate the formation of social actors, many of the problems call for a rethinking in terms of not only re-stratification, but also in terms of re-identification.

Notes

1. The writing of this paper was financed with a grant from the Estonian Science Foundation.
2. The proportion of trade with the countries of CIP dropped to less than 30 % of all imports and 20 % of all exports from the 85 % of imports and 95 % of exports in 1991 when Estonia was still part of the rouble zone (Estonian Human Development Report 1995).

3. The private sector accounted for over 55 % of Estonia's GDP at the end of 1994 and was increasing rapidly (Estonian Human Development Report 1995).
4. While about 10 % of the workforce changed employers annually prior to the period of economic restructuring, as much as one-third of the workforce either changed jobs or lost their jobs in 1992 (Estonian Human Development Report 1995).
5. This study involved American (Barbara Ann Anderson, Director of the Population Studies Center of the University of Michigan and Brian David Silver, Chairman of the Department of Political Science at Michigan State University) and Estonian sociologists from the Institute of Sociology, Philosophy and Law.
6. The second follow-up of this project was funded by the M. Jacobs Foundation.
7. The time dimensions of our data are 'overlapping' — the 'societal' time (from the 'era of stagnation' in 1979 through to 1991, as the early days of crucial changes, to 1993 as the current era) gets mixed up with 'life course' time (the younger age group in 1993 was even younger than the older age group in 1991). These longitudinal data provide quite good opportunities to learn about intragenerational social mobility over time. At the same time they require that we take into account all complications caused by the 'overlapping' time dimensions.
8. To capture the moves into/out of the labour force — a very important structural change in the transition to a market economy — we take these moves into account in our analysis of mobility. We also suggest that moving out of the labour force has largely been forced and often connected to a loss of job. We interpret this move as downward mobility.
9. Segmentation modelling is a relatively new statistical application. The method divides respondents into two or more distinct groups based on categories of the 'best' predictor of a dependent variable. The splitting process continues until no more statistically significant predictors can be found. The final subgroups are displayed on a tree diagram (Goodman 1991).
10. We consider the number of jobs held as an indicator of human capital in accordance with the logic of researchers who expect higher human capital to increase rates of job shifting early in the work career (Spenner, Kerckhoff and Glass 1990).

Bibliography

Blom, R. (1995), 'In the chase of the middle class', R. Blom, H. Melin and J. Nikula (eds.), *Reformation of the middle classes in the Baltic countries? Social Change in Baltic and Nordic Countries Project*, Working Papers Series 4.

Estonian Human Development Report, 1995.

Goodman, L.A. (1991), 'Measures, models and graphic displays in the analysis of cross-classified data', *Journal of American Statistical Association* 86, pp. 1085-1138.

Eliason, S.R. (1995), 'An Extension of the Sorensen-Kalleberg Theory of the Labour Market Matching and Attainment Processes', *American Sociological Review* 60, pp. 247-271.

Gouldner, A. (1979), *The Future of Intellectuals and the Rise of the New Class*, London.

Huinink, J. and Solga, H. (1994), *From Mobility in Status and Occupation to Simple Job Shifts? Occupational Career Mobility of Men in the Former GDR*, Arbeitsbericht 7, Max-Planck-Institut für Bildungsforschung, Berlin.

Kivinen, M. (1995), 'The middle classes in the Baltic states — theoretical starting points', in R. Blom, H. Melin and J. Nikula (eds.), *Reformation of the middle classes in the Baltic countries? Social Change in Baltic and Nordic Countries Project*, Working Papers Series 4.

Mach, W., Mayer, K.U. and Pohoski, M. (1994), 'Job Changes in the Federal Republic of Germany and Poland: a Longitudinal Assessment of the Impact of Welfare-Capitalist and State-Socialist Labour-Market Segmentation', *European Sociological Review* 10, pp. 1-28.

Pappi, F.U. (1981), 'The Petit Bourgeoisie and the New Middle-class', in F. Bechhofer and B. Elliot (eds.), *The Petit Bourgeoisie*, MacMillan, London.

Sorensen, A.B. (1979), 'A Model and a Metric for the Analysis of the Intragenerational Status Attainment Process', *American Journal of Sociology* 85, pp. 361-383.

Sorensen. A.B. (1991), 'On the Usefulness of Class Analysis in Research of Social Mobility and Socioeconomic Inequality', *Acta Sociologica* 34, pp. 71-87.

Sorensen, A.B. and Kalleberg, A.L. (1981), 'An Outline of a Theory of the Matching of Persons to Jobs', in I. Berg (ed.), *Sociological Perspectives on Labour Markets*, Academic, New York, pp. 49-74.

Sorensen, A.B. and Tuma, N.B. (1981), 'Labour Market Structures and Job Mobility', in D.J. Treiman and R.V. Robinson (eds.), *Research in Social Stratification and Mobility*, JAI Press Inc, Greenwich, Connecticut.

Sorensen, A.B. (1983), 'Processes of Allocation to Open and Closed Positions in Social Structure', *Zeitschrift für Soziologie* 12, pp. 203-224.

Sorensen, A.B. (1989), 'Social Structure and Mechanism of Life-Course Processes', in A.B. Sorensen, F.E. Weinert and L.R. Sherrod (eds.), *Human Development and the Life Course: Multidisciplinary Perspective*, Lawrence Erlbaum Associates, Hillsdale, pp. 177-197.

Spenner, K.I., Kerckhoff A.C. and Glass, T.A. (1990), 'Open and closed education and work systems in Great Britain', *European Sociological Review* 6, pp. 215-235.

Szeleny, J. (1988), 'The Intelligentsia in the Class Structure of State-Socialist Societies', *American Journal of Sociology* 43.

Titma, M. and Koklyagina, L. (eds.) (1989), *Nachalo puti: pokolenie so srednim obrazovaniem* [Beginning of Life Path: Age Group with Higher Education], Nauka, Moscow.

Walder, A.G. (1995), 'Career Mobility and the Communist Political Order', *American Sociological Review* 60, pp. 309-328.

PART III

MANAGERS AND PROFESSIONALS

10 A Russian Middle Class in Formation? Social Strata and Sectional Trade Unionism in the Aviation and Coal Industries

PETER FAIRBROTHER

The debate about the formation of a middle class in Russia is important, with many arguing that such a development is part of the process of democratization contributing to political stabilization. This is against the background that the class structure in the Soviet period was one where a middle class was absent, the intelligentsia comprising a social stratum rather than a class. Thus, the question is whether a middle class is in the process of formation and what are the implications of such a development? However, in order to focus this question, the aim of this paper is to consider one aspect of the debates about the middle class, that of middle class trade unionism, thereby raising questions about class formation and class consciousness. The argument in this paper is that trade unionism is one of the ways in which middle class labour expresses its interests at the point of production. In view of the recent development of sectional white-collar trade unionism in Russia, particularly in the coal and aviation industries, it is reasonable to ask whether this indicates the beginning of a process of middle class formation.

These links between class formation and trade unionism have been examined extensively in the Western literature on advanced capitalist societies. This debate comes out of an attempt to understand class structure and accompanying relations, central to which have been questions about the formation of 'new' classes and the way in which these may be evidenced by forms of trade unionism, as the collective expression of class interests at the point of production. There have been two pertinent questions in this debate. First, is there a 'new' middle class in the process of formation, comprising the technical and supervisory staff as well as administrative and clerical staff, seeking to defend and articulate their interests, usually in alliance with the more traditional working class? Second, and alternatively, is there a 'new' working class emerging in these societies, with routine administrative and clerical staff as well as technical staff constituting this class?

179

Since the 1960s this debate has taken on a particular force with the enormous expansion of white-collar jobs in most of the advanced capitalist societies, so that now non-manual jobs comprise around half of all jobs in these societies. This has been accompanied by the feminization of many areas of employment, particularly the long-term trends in clerical and routine administrative jobs in the public sector. As part of this development, white-collar unions have come to a prominence, organizing staff, including managerial staff and technical cum engineering staff, in the manufacturing sectors, as well in the utilities (electricity, water, gas, telecommunications, and the public sector more generally). In substantive ways, this represents a recomposition of class relations with middle class labour seeking alliances with the working class via their trade unions.

The theoretical questions raised in the debate about these class developments in the West are relevant to a consideration of modern Russia, where it might be argued that a middle class is in the process of emerging. To explore them and to unravel the detail of the changes that are taking place in Russia, the recent history of the aviation and coal industries will be examined. The structure of the paper comprises four sections. In the first section, the Western literature on the question of middle class formation and trade unionism will be presented, noting the way in which class-based forms of unionism have been characteristic of advanced capitalist economies. In the second section, the focus will shift to examine a substantive example of the development of non-manual trade unionism in Russia, focusing on recent developments in the northern coal field of Vorkuta. The argument is that if a middle class is in the process of emerging within enterprises, then this should be expressed in situations where non-manual workers look to union forms of organization to express their interests. Third, non-manual sectional unionism is most advanced in the aviation industry and this will be examined to determine whether this is a process of class in the making. Finally, in the last section, the argument about class formation and the case of non-manual sectional unionism in Russia will be assessed.

Middle Class Labour and Trade Unionism

At a general level, the debates about middle class labour follow three broad trajectories. First, there has been an attempt to locate the middle class as a distinct or partially formed social grouping. Second, there is a long-standing argument about the proletarianization of the middle class, or more accurately sections of it, and a consideration of what this might mean in terms of class relations. Third, a body of writing has been concerned to identify middle class labour in terms of their structural location at the point of production. While the first two strands of argument are important for a comprehensive under-standing of the debates about class, it is the last body of writing which is most relevant to this paper.[1]

Class Location

Taking the question of class location first, the main objective, as far as debates about the middle class are concerned, has been to identify the middle class with reference to the differentiations and distinguishing features of the various social groupings that comprise the middle class, clerical work, supervisory work, professions, such as teaching, social work and the like. Various aspects of work and market circumstance are frequently pointed to as factors of distinction. In the more sophisticated versions of this type of analysis, well represented by the class mapping exercises of Wright (1978 and 1985) or in a different way by Goldthorpe (1982) and Goldthorpe and Marshall (1992), there has been an attempt to identify the contradictory and complicated relations of these social groups. This is best illustrated through Wright's early notion of contradictory locations in class relations (1978), where, in terms of a grid referring to ownership, and various aspects of control, the middle class, or sections of it, are located between capitalist and working classes, and between the working class and the petty bourgeoisie, depending on their situation. In later work, this is extended to include reference to skill and credentialism, thereby developing a more comprehensive schema but one which attempts to account for the complexity of the market and the way this might be expressed at the place of employment and work (1985).

The difficulty of this type of account is that class structure is separated from class practice. Where this leads is best illustrated in the recent debates in Britain about the rediscovery of class, where the argument becomes a methodological one, concerned to identify the way different social groups occupy class positions in the sense that they are located in 'sets of structural positions. Social relationships within markets, especially within labour mar-kets, and within firms define these positions. Class positions exist inde-pendently of individual occupants of these positions. They are "empty places"' (Sorenson 1991, 72).

Following on from this it is then argued that in recognition of class position, sections of the workforce may take steps to identify themselves as constituting a class, and not only acting both consciously and voluntarily in similar ways, but also in class conscious ways, in the sense that they 'have a reflexive awareness of the link between class position and outcome' (Breen and Rottman 1995, 457), although the form this may take is not specified. The necessary step in analyses that define class in terms of position is to define class in terms of some notion of class identity, where members identify themselves as constituting a class, in this sense via their trade unionism (Burawoy 1985; Przeworski 1991). The problem is that this is not a central and integral step in the argument.

The Proletarianization of the Middle Class

Of more pertinence are the arguments about the proletarianization of the middle class (for example, Klingender 1935; Lockwood 1958; Braverman 1974; Gorz 1967 and 1976; Mallet 1975). These analyses can be divided into two types, the first concerned to explain the fate of clerical workers, while that of Gorz and Mallet is concerned more with technical and supervisory staff. Nonetheless, they each argue that a 'new' working class is in the process of making, with important implications for the way in which trade unionism is understood.

In the first set of accounts, the central idea is that class organization and relations have developed in the context of capitalist societies in such a way that there is a polarization between the capitalist class and the working class (Klingender 1935; Lockwood 1958; Braverman 1974). In this circumstance, layers of the middle class, particularly the waged clerical and routine administrative workers are in the process of becoming a 'new' working class. This is because of the routinization of their labour, increased intensification of their work in terms of control relations, and declining status. The major consequence of these developments is to be seen in their trade unionism, so that these workers are now more likely to join trade unions and engage in collective activity in pursuit of their interests. In general, it is assumed that while these trade unions may not be particularly militant they nonetheless constitute part of a trade union and labour movement which at the workplace, and more generally, seeks to secure their interests as part of the labour movement. In this respect it is an argument that there is an alliance emerging, expressed via trade unions and often arbitrated, at least in social democratic societies, through political parties.

The point of these analyses is that they develop arguments about class formation and class consciousness, a class consciousness being expressed through trade unionism. However, the problem with these analyses is that they are grounded in a relatively superficial account of class in that little attention is given to the types of changes that are taking place in the workplace and particularly the reconstruction of managerial hierarchies. Rather they are cast in general terms with reference to shifting occupational relations and the like, with little attempt to locate these developments as part of changing class relations. As a result, there is considerable ambiguity over what is meant by middle class trade unionism.

More interesting is the debate at the end of the 1960s and early 1970s about the technical class, in which Gorz (1967 and 1976) and Mallet (1975) were important contributors. Briefly, these two authors began, from a consideration of production relations, examining the types of changes taking place in the organization of labour at the point of production. The crucial distinction in the case of Mallet was that the working class, in the context of transformations in the modern enterprise, performed the functions of production and were 'separated from the actual direction of the production process' (Hyman 1983, 27). For Mallet both process operators in the increasingly automated manufacturing plants and research centres and the technical workers were part of the working class. These workers have both a strategic overview and practical understanding of the production process, placing them in a position to question the economic base of enterprises and managerial hierarchies. In Mallet's view, this provides the basis for these workers to seek to exercise collective control and to realize versions of workers' participation and control within the industry.

This type of argument was criticized by Gorz, who saw technical worker unionism as the means for the transformation of capitalist society, but who subsequently criticized the Mallet optimism. He pointed to a more critical and discerning view of the technical class in terms of an ambiguity of their position, in relation to workers, as privileged and educated staff and who organized to prevent an erosion of privilege, rather than in alliance with other workers. As Gorz notes:

> More often than not the rebellion of intellectual workers is profoundly ambiguous: they rebel not as proletarians, but *against* being *treated* as proletarians (Gorz 1976, 179).

What this points to is the importance of rooting the explanation of class formation and consciousness in a detailed account of production relations, drawing attention to the relations between different classes and the circumstances of the class condition of middle class labour.

A New Middle Class?

One strand of argument has focused explicitly on the structural ambiguity of middle class relations, pointing to the way in which this is variously expressed in forms of class organization and consciousness. This is the case with Wright's earlier discussion of 'contradictory locations' (1978), the most interesting being that of the technicians and related professionals within enterprise hierarchies. These staff have limited autonomy over work procedures and routines, limited control over subordinates, but are not in command positions within the enterprise and do not have economic ownership of the enterprise. They are thus located somewhere between the capitalist class and the working class. Although they are mental labourers, Wright suggests that active trade unionism can reinforce an identification with the working class and serve to distance this class of workers from the capitalist class, at least in political and ideological terms. While there is a strength in the emphasis on trade unionism as a vehicle for developing a class consciousness, the problem is that this is an analysis which overlooks a more dynamic understanding of class relations at the point of production.

A more satisfactory account is that provided by Carchedi, although it does fall foul of an overly structuralist account of class relations. Drawing on a re-reading of Marx, particularly the arguments about the continued relevance of production and the appropriation of surplus value in class analysis, he develops an argument which points to the structural ambiguity of middle class labour, marked by a perpetual tension between undertaking the functions of labour and capital. Moreover, he addresses the question of productive and unproductive labour and thus develops an analysis of middle class labour which goes beyond the preoccupations with manufacturing and related sectors. While there is an unfortunate abstraction to his writing, he does provide insights that have been taken up in the discussion about middle class unions.

While Carchedi points to the internal relations of the work and employment relationship, developing an innovative account of the class position, thus laying the foundation for an analysis of middle class labour, his thesis suffers from three major deficiencies. First, in practice, the class analysis of middle class employees is made more complex by the wide variations in employment conditions and concrete tasks. The mode of control both by, and of, professional employees (teachers, doctors, social workers) is very different from that of administrative workers. The former has tended to be 'personal' or 'professional', while the latter have been bureaucratic and coercive, although this is not an unambiguous distinction in practice. Second, as with other such writing, this is a formalistic structural account of class relations which overlooks the way in which these relations are experienced and constructed in an ongoing way. This requires a consideration of the internal relations of work in a variety of settings, within the state as well as in manufacturing and related sectors. Third, Carchedi's analysis is very deliberately an economic identification of class relations, ignoring the political and ideological dimensions of these relations. This results in a partial and misleading type of analysis so that, for example, he sees clerical workers as proletarian in their production relations, and petty bourgeois in their ideological and political relations. The problem is that formalism begins to replace an analysis of class formation, consciousness, and conflict in its historical and empirical context (Smith 1987).

While Carchedi has little to say about middle class trade unionism, his main concern being to lay out the bare-bones of an analysis of class structure in contemporary capitalist society, others have taken up the idea of structural ambiguity and developed an argument about middle class labour and trade unionism. In one very interesting study Armstrong (1986) develops the distinction between labour and capital at the point of production and argues that white-collar unionization can be examined via the capital function of middle class labour. What he means by this is that rather than focus on the labour function or the proletarianization of the middle class condition, it makes more sense to examine the way that unionization is part of an attempt, at least in the case of supervisory staff and managers, to restore or reposition themselves in terms of the control functions of capital. This is an approach which derives from the view that these staff have suffered from the growing importance and effectiveness of manual unions in qualifying their position, in their conditions and their involvement in managerial activity. This then becomes an argument for separate representation of the interests of these staff, in support of management. It is thus a strategy for maintaining class power.

The major difficulty with this analysis is that Armstrong tends to develop a straightforward account, placing the supervisors and managers as locked into the performance of capital function. There is no consideration of the ambiguity of function noted by Carchedi and others (see also Smith 1987, 263-64). Others have taken this duality of function as their starting point (Carter 1979, 1985, 1986; Carter and Fairbrother 1995). Starting from the argument that there is an intrinsic duality between the capital and labour functions within the new middle class, Carter goes on to argue that trade unions representing these sections of the workforce combine aspects of division and duality within their unions. The point is that unions may reflect a pressure towards proletarianization as well as an attempt to arrest that movement. Thus the problems that middle class labour experiences in the performance of their tasks, both individually and collectively, are also re-flected in their trade unionism. This leads Carter to consider the distinctive features of white-collar unionism and particularly the cross-cutting cleavages within such unions (for a similar type of analysis on the state of middle class, see Carter and Fairbrother 1995).

The strength of this type of analysis is that it stresses the relation between class and unionism, emphasizing the class basis of unionism as well as the distinctive features of white-collar union practice. They point to the impor-tance of very careful analysis of the middle class labour, taking into account the variation in class location, considering experience and consciousness. Thus it is necessary to consider the difference between clerical workers undertaking the functions of middle class labour, as well as managerial staff undertaking the functions of capital, not ignoring the ambiguity of such relations.

Assessment

This review of the debates about middle class labour raises three separate points to consider in any analysis. First, the point of emphasizing the importance of structural ambiguity is that it draws attention to the way in which individuals and groupings may emphasize different aspects of the class relationships in which they are embedded. Put baldly, middle class labour may emphasize the functions of collective labour rather than capital and vice versa. Out of this, alliances may be forged with senior managers as representatives of capital or the working class and their organizations. This may result in relatively marginal or peripheral features, such as income differentials, acquiring an importance in the making of classes and class consciousness. Equally, situations do change, both immediately at the point of production but also in the context of broader structural and institutional changes in the economy and the politics of the society. These changes may underwrite moves towards a proletarianization of condition, or equally to distinguish and to separate so that privilege and status are maintained.

Second, a related point is that in discussing middle class labour it is important to take into account the variations and differentiations within this class. These may be expressed via skills and credentialism, as some argue, through income and related employment differentials, emphasized in much literature on white-collar unionism, as well as in terms of gender relations, as noted more recently. In addition, it is important to keep in mind that there are divisions both within classes and between them. While managerial hierarchies are often noted, it is equally necessary to take into account hierarchies within the collective labourer in terms of skill, age, gender, and so on. Third, the emergence of trade unionism amongst middle class labour raises difficult questions about the nature and character of such unionism. Too often, the assumption is that trade unionism embodies principles of solidarity and unity, at the most general and idealistic level, or at worst, a narrow economism and defensiveness within a broader trade union movement. But it is also important to extend the analysis and to consider the way in which such unionism may be part of a managerial defence of position, arising out of the struggles taking place at the point of production between a capitalist class and working class. These are the features of condition which are worked out in practice, in the context of the diverse and often contradictory experience of middle class labour.

The Case of Russia

In view of this analysis it is reasonable to ask the question whether such a middle class is emerging in Russia. In the coal and aviation sectors, past power and status hierarchies have been questioned and challenged, with sections of enterprise workforces taking steps to secure their own futures in distinct ways, via sectional trade unionism. In some respects, these developments are part of an ongoing struggle which is taking place within Russian enterprises about the form and organization of the labour process, as different social groups seek either to defend themselves in a period of uncertainty or to advantage themselves. This is part of a challenge to the past status and power hierarchies that made up the labour process of each industry. In both of the cases examined, these developments constitute prototypical cases of the social and political changes that are taking place within the Russian enterprise, where aspects of a possible future are being played out.

The data are drawn from an extensive and detailed study of the Russian aviation and coal industries, both of which are characterized by the emergence of alternative unions.[2] In both sectors an emergent middle class began to express and defend their interests in relation to other sectors of the workforce. The argument is presented in five stages. First, the emergence of a particular form of class control in the coal industry which excluded the middle management is considered. In the case of the Vorkuta region, in northern Russia, there emerged a managerial form of unionism. Second, a history in the aviation industry is presented, pointing to the emergence of sectional forms of professional trade unionism. Third, the implications of these developments for an understanding of class relations in modern Russia is considered.

The Coal Industry

The Russian coal industry is a major state subsidized and controlled sector. Its importance in the Russian economy derives from the fact that it supplies coal to the power stations and steel mills. In part as a result of the strategic importance of coal, and in part because of the solidarity of miners in their isolated and prison-like communities, the miners became one of the most potent political forces in the democratization process in the late 1980s. It was the miners who began to challenge the government and subsequently supported the campaigns by Yeltsin against the old regime. They were amongst the first to experiment with forms of sectional unionism, establishing the Independent Miners' Union (NPG) for underground workers in November 1990 (Rutland 1990, 372-373). Since then the NPG has remained one of the key alternative trade unions in modern Russia (Clarke et al. 1995).

The coal mines in Vorkuta, the second major coalfield in Russia, which are located north of the Arctic Circle, operate under the control and direction of the coal Association Vorkutaugol. There were 13 mines in the Association until 1990, when the largest and most prosperous mine, Vorgashorskaya, withdrew from the Association and dealt directly with Moscow as an independent mine. With the collapse of democratic centralism, there were pressures towards mine autonomy, in the sale of coal and a mine by mine determination of terms of pay and conditions. In 1991, Vorkutaugol became more or less moribund with mine managements increasingly acting independently of the Association. In these circumstances the newly formed NPG began to challenge and question the basis of mine director power, querying the distribution of goods and services (houses and social welfare) as well as seeking to increase wages on the assumption that this would give the miners a freedom in their patterns of consumption.

The leadership of the NPG were able to present the union as the defender of underground miner interests and to argue against what they saw as the social parasitism of the engineers-technical staff (ITR) and related managerial staff in the mine enterprises. The basis for this stance was initially the prospect of individual mine prosperity following a degree of financial mine autonomy in 1992 and 1993. With the end of this prospect, as the realities of the global coal market and the chaos of the domestic market became more apparent, the Association began to reassert itself as the pre-eminent body in the city with the mine enterprises being reduced to the equivalent of shops. In this the Association leadership began to look to an alliance with the underground workers as a way of bringing the mine enterprise directors to heel. As part of this the Association was also prepared to criticize the role and position of the ITR and related staff as a means of levering control over the mine directors.

The ITR and Related Staff as a Managerial Social Stratum

With the beginning of mine independence in 1991 and 1992 and the relative collapse of the Association, the staff in the mines found themselves in a vice between pressures from the management, on the one side, and manual workers on the other. The senior mine directorates relied increasingly on these staff to maintain production, to control and discipline workers, and to ensure the continuity of managerial control within seemingly volatile mine enterprises. In this respect, the mine directors played on their traditional associations with these staff, utilizing grace and favour and coercion to elicit support and create the base for a relatively unified managerial hierarchy in the mines. However, the mine directors had only a brief moment of relative independence from the coal Association between 1991 and 1993, when they were able to take initiatives to consolidate their control over the mines. Even so, it remained in their interests to have the ITR and related staff acting in public and tangible support of the policies pursued by individual mines, but also subordinated to the director and immediate senior staff.

At the same time, antagonism was expressed by the underground workers, particularly in the NPG, towards the managerial hierarchies within the mines, singling out the ITR and related staff for special comment. These staff were identified as 'social parasites' who contributed very little to production and the prosperity of the mines but who sought to exercise a spurious authority over workers and who attempted to advantage themselves, both materially and in terms of status. In some cases there were threats of strikes, and in one case a strike by underground workers took place, demanding the reduction of this stratum of staff.

Not surprisingly, the ITR and related managerial staff saw themselves as scapegoats criticized by underground workers, on the one hand, but not receiving the type of recognition they thought their due from management, on the other. Nonetheless, the senior sections of this stratum, excluding the clerical and routine administrative workers, very much saw their future as integral members of the managerial hierarchy in the mines. They were thus a social group in the 'middle', useful to the senior mine directorate as they attempted to consolidate their positions within the mines, and attacked by underground workers as superfluous and expendable.

In 1994 and particularly 1995, these staff faced further problems when they were also singled out by the Association senior directorate as too numerous, too complacent, and expendable in the 'new' coal world. This occurred in the context of the re-centralization of the mine enterprises under the control of the Vorkuta coal Association. It was a criticism of convenience in that the Association directorate focused on the ITR and related staff in the mines as a way of securing an alliance with the NPG, so as to pressure mine directors to accept the lead and control of the Association in the restructuring that was taking place. The idea was to force the mine directors to turn to the Association so as to justify their policies and staffing practices as well as to unsettle the ITR and associated staff. To this extent, it was a successful ploy and these staff felt further threatened, although some of the mine directors made soothing comments informally on their behalf.

The Union of Managers, Professionals, and Clerks of the Coal Industry

In these circumstances the ITR and related staff began to identify themselves as a distinct and beleaguered social group which looked to trade unionism as one way of countering these attacks. In this they were encouraged by their mine directors who saw an advantage in the ITR and related staff presenting a united voice, defending not only their specific interests but managerial interests in general. However, this was a somewhat fraught exercise since these staff were not a structurally united group, comprising technical workers cum engineers and chiefs of departments, production staff and commercial-economic staff, and senior staff and routine clerical-administrative employees. The outcome was that the union tended to organize the senior layers within the larger non-manual stratum; very few routine clerical and administrative staff joined and the leadership of the union was drawn from the higher levels. As a result, the union remained relatively small, organizing in five unions and recruiting on average between 50 and 80 % of eligible staff.

The idea to establish such a mine began with mine engineers in Vorkutaugol, the Association, in 1991, when the Association was in the process of collapsing as mines acquired a degree of independence. At the time, both the NPG and the City Workers' Committee displayed relatively aggressive attitudes towards mine managements and managerial staffs, with demands on occasion for the 'mass sacking' of such staff. However, this initial attempt came to nothing, and the union was first established in Zapolyarnya mine in December 1991, when the workers at the mine demanded that a third of the office workers be sacked and the wage fund for these workers be reduced by a corresponding amount. Although the director tried to explain that such a reduction would not only threaten the safety of the mine but that such personnel were necessary for the 'normal' working of the mine, it was without effect and the strike occurred on 2-3 December 1991. The ITR and white-collar workers decided to respond with a strike of their own and at a meeting attended by 50 of the 290 staff employees organized legal action against the initiators of the workers' strike and planned their own strike. The strike idea was supported by the director, but before it took place, a compromise was reached and the union was established. In 1994 the primary organization of the union had 185 members (56 women) out of 290 such workers. It was led by a woman who was the assistant director of personnel (for further details, see Ilyin 1996).[3]

The core of the union resides in the primary groups and this form of organization is indicative of the way in which the managers and ITR have sought to develop a union form of organization in alliance with and supportive of senior management, particularly the mine director. At Zapolyarnaya, the initiative for the union came from the director of the enterprise, who saw union organization as one way of strengthening his own position in relation to the Association. At another mine, Vorgashorskaya, the union was established to counter a proposal to appoint a trade union leader as mine director and to secure a director more in the traditional mould. Here the roots of the union lay in a 'Club of Enterprise Officers' which had been formed in the late 1980s composed of the chiefs of departments, deputies and mechanics, to deal with problems relating to the disciplining of these staff. It acted as a support group, occasionally speaking on behalf of members with senior management, but more frequently providing material support and advice to members. In 1992, when a leader of an alternative union at the mine attempted to become the mine director, the Club transformed itself into a primary group of the ITR Union and successfully petitioned Moscow against the appointment of the union leader as director. Instead, they promoted the chief engineer who subsequently worked closely with the union, although not a member.

One of the features of union organization, further buttressing the way in which the union is a managerial organization, is the way in which the leaders of the primary groups utilize their jobs and close working proximity with the director to blur the activity as trade union leaders or managerial staff. Particularly in the circumstances where enterprises have become more like shops within the coal association rather than the relatively independent enterprises of 1991 and 1992, then the impetus for both mine directors and ITR management staff to look to each other becomes more likely. This is further enhanced by the overlap of activities in terms of the organization and operation of the mine labour process, especially at the administrative and technical support levels.

These staff looked to a distinct form of sectional unionism as a means of defending themselves and articulating their class interests as management within the enterprise. They were to a certain extent modelling their unionism on the apparent success of the sectionally based forms of unionism within the mining industry and to a lesser extent elsewhere. Theirs was a sectional union which aimed to mirror and articulate their concerns as non-manual workers in the mine industry, caught between pressures to continue as loyal and supportive staff as well as staff who were vilified and criticized not only by workers but also by sections of the Association management, when it suited them. In these circumstances, senior management encouraged the growth of this form of unionism as formalizing an alliance with managerial staff, including the ITR. This enabled these staff to defend and pursue their particular work and employment interests as trade unionists and as managers.

Assessment

The unionization of the ITR and associated staff is a formalization of their relations as managerial staff. This was not part of a process of class formation at the point of production for a number of reasons. These staff were not a homogenous group which, because of their material and ideological circumstances within the enterprise, saw themselves as having interests in common, against the mine directorate and in sympathy with the working class. Rather they were a divided and beleaguered group, sections of whom sought union representation to articulate their concerns as a distinct layer of management. In this, senior management both encouraged this development as a way of countering the sectional unionism of the underground workers and to legitimate support for these staff as employees in a changing situation.

The paradox is that this form of unionism not only supports management but also creates the possibility of these staff developing interests in line with those of other groups of workers in the enterprise. On the one hand, they organize as managers, via their trade unions, defending their concerns as a section of management, and in alliance with the senior directorate. On the other hand, they are part of a broader trade union movement, negotiating with and alongside other trade unions, and in this respect develop the capacity for articulating distinct sets of political interests as trade unionists. In this respect, they are in a position both to defend their own concerns and to support the development of trade union activity addressing the fate of enterprises in this period of transition.

The Aviation Industry

A different pattern of unionism emerged in the aviation industry where the focus was on the 'middle layer' of the industry social structure, the pilots and air traffic controllers. Each attempted to secure themselves as a social stratum within the framework of a transient and restructured aviation industry (Borisov et al. 1994). The key point in this history is that the restructuring of the aviation industry, particularly with the move towards semi-autonomous airports, and the subsequent division of Aeroflot into separate companies, each based on a particular airport, has placed a premium on pilots attempting to maintain their long-standing privileges. In these circumstances the pilots have attempted to secure their collective future via their own trade union. In this they have been challenged by the air traffic controllers who saw the pilots as threatening in their move to create barriers and marked differentials in pay and conditions between the pilots and the air traffic controllers. Like the pilots, the air traffic controllers looked to a sectionally-based form of unionism to defend their position within the industry.

The aviation industry is organized on the basis of airports, graded in terms of size. It is here that the aviation ministry organized the workforce, comprising airport workers, undertaking all the support and ancillary work, associated with aviation work, engineers and technical support staff, responsible for the maintenance and operation of the airlines and other users of the airports, aircrews, including pilots and service staff, and the air traffic controllers, responsible for the control of flights in and around the airports. In Soviet times the airports and the aviation industry were organized under the auspices of the Ministry of Aviation and complemented by the parallel structures of the Communist Party, organized both in the airports and within the ministry. Historically, one union, the Trade Union of Workers of Air Enterprises (PRAP) was responsible, at a theoretical level, for articulating the concerns and interests of workers in the industry, although in practice, as with other industries, the union worked as part of a troika with airport management and the Communist Party (Clarke and Fairbrother 1994). The airport managerial structure has long been one that provides an avenue of employment for pilots once they have completed their flying service, then moving into management, particularly at an airport level, so that most airports continue to be managed by ex-pilots.

Pilots

The pilots in the Russian aviation industry saw themselves as the core workers, in an elite status position, the highest paid in the industry, with the best prospects for a career in management, and receiving priority treatment in housing and social welfare benefits. Against this background, with the collapse of the Soviet Union the pilots sought to preserve and enhance their elite position. The first step in this process was to create an organizational base which rested on separation from the rest of the aviation workforce, via an alternative trade union based on sectional occupational concerns. The establishment of the Union of Flying Personnel (PLS) allowed the pilots to articulate their interests as an exclusive professional group, distinct from those of other professional groups in the industry, such as the air traffic controllers or the general workforce. This was a policy of securing elite privilege, reinforced by an ideology that this was a modern form of unionism, evident in the 'West', a professional form of unionism, and one that could legitimately argue for privilege and increased salary differentials.

Thus, at the end of the 1980s, pilots attempted to secure their position in the unfolding aviation industry initially in alliance with other professional groups, but then excluding the air traffic controllers as they began to organize as a separate sectional group. Initially, the focus of this policy was to put pressure on the state to distribute the state budget in favour of their industry, but the distribution of the wage fund was to be skewed towards the pilots, even if at the expense of other groups. While there was a period of success in this tactic following the lead by the miners, as the political transformation proceeded and the economic crisis deepened, it became more and more difficult to extract enough money for the whole branch and allow the pilots to secure their position materially. It was much simpler to secure the position of one elite group, and the mechanism to achieve this was by forming a trade union of pilots only. Not only did this allow the pilots as the elite professional group in the industry to lobby the government directly, reinforced by an implicit threat sometimes made explicit, that if the pilots did not get their way then they would wreak havoc on the industry with strike action. As a further consequence this revised policy allowed the pilots to draw a sharper line around themselves as a privileged and elite professional group and to argue for the exclusion of others.

With the moves towards the establishment of independent unions in 1989, and in the general atmosphere of workers seeking sectional union representation, the pilots moved towards the establishment of an association within the official union to defend their interests.[4] In October 1990 the PLS was established, attracting the vast majority of the 65,000 pilots in the USSR. This was part of the continued self-recognition by pilots of their own distinct interests as the elite of the civil aviation industry. As indicated, they were always a privileged group of workers with the majority of senior managers being former pilots and active members of the Communist Party. Since the founding of the PLS they have been relentless in pursuing their own interests, working with the official union, the airport administrations, the Department of Civil Aviation and the Ministry of Transport, at the cost of any unity with air controllers' union, the other major occupational union in the aviation industry. Further, the PLS has been relatively successful in presenting itself as the acceptable face of independent unionism, securing a place on the Russian Tripartite Commission.

What this indicates is the way in which the union form of organization can secure a social stratum within enterprises. The union is defined in exclusive and narrow terms to reinforce the pursuit of terms and conditions of employment which advantage one section of the workforce and a specific section of the non-manual part of that workforce. This was cast in exclusive and hierarchical terms so that the pilots were presented as the focal grouping within the reconstituted aviation industry. In this, unionization of the pilots along sectional qua professional grounds allowed them to oppose the air traffic controllers who pursued a similar policy but in terms of a different rhetoric and union practice.

The Air Traffic Controllers

Air traffic controllers are employed throughout Russia at airports and with relatively large numbers (between 400 and 600) at the air traffic control facilities in Moscow. They occupy a distinct position in the airports, often working in geographically separate areas of the airport. Although initially involved in the control of take-off and landing, this has now been extended to the regulation of air movement in the region, associated in part with increased technical sophistication in air movement. This has been accompanied by an increased job complexity resulting in an intensification of air traffic work. To further add to the work remit of the air traffic controllers, there has been an increase in international air traffic and a shift in the economic significance of air control work since the control of international over flights is paid for in hard currency.

The air traffic controllers are a relatively homogeneous but a low-paid aviation occupational group (relative to pilots) who have distinct sets of interests. They campaigned for recognition as a distinct occupational group and for establishing a unified and centralized system of air traffic control. They pursued these ambitions via their union, the Federation of Air Traffic Controllers' Unions (FPAD), established in 1990 from an association initially established within PRAP in 1989. In pursuit of these objectives FPAD attempted to deal directly with the Ministry and the government, reinforcing their claims with the threat of strikes and on one occasion with a one-day strike. They organized in one pre-strike situation in 1991, another four in 1992, and one national strike on 15 August 1992, as well as a near national strike on at least two other occasions.

During the 1990s, air traffic controllers have sought a new recognition within the industry both in terms of their immediate rewards as well as in terms of the organization of air traffic control. They have sought, via their union, to improve their place on the pay spine as well as to create a separate air traffic control enterprise which would further consolidate their position in the aviation industry as a distinct and separate social group. The problem for the controllers was that the pilots were pursuing a parallel policy which would place the pilots at the peak of the aviation social structure. Nonetheless, the air traffic controllers were supported within the aviation industry by the managers of air traffic control services who saw the realization of the air controllers aspirations as a mirror of their own ambitions in relation to airport managers who also sought control of the revenue prospects of air traffic control.

It could be argued that the ensuing bitterness between the air traffic controllers and the pilots was in effect a struggle for pre-eminence and privilege within the aviation industry (Ilyin 1996). In support of this proposition it soon became clear that the air traffic controllers could not achieve recognition of their interests by remaining within the aviation industry trade union. The establishment of the Association in 1989 thus represented an attempt to delimit and realize the ambitions of both air traffic controllers and their managers. This, however, was limited by the fact that the Association was forced to act within the bureaucratic power relationships of the industry, a particular constraint on air traffic management. In this respect the establishment of the union in 1990 enabled these joint interests to be pursued via the union and eventually in opposition to the pilots who were threatened by the air traffic controllers' initiative.

This was a struggle between two social strata supported by different factions of management. On the one hand, the pilots were committed to defending privilege and position as the elite group of the aviation industry. This was reflected in their trade unionism as well as in the alliances between the pilots and aviation management. On the other hand, the air traffic controllers were both attempting to secure a more privileged position than they had enjoyed previously, although this was a claim for an arguing upwards for an equality with the pilots rather than reintroducing further inequality. In addition, and at least as importantly, the air traffic controllers developed a form of unionism predicated on participation and membership involvement that was unlike any other trade union in Russia. In this respect, the air traffic controllers argued a case for solidarity among alternative unions within Russia and solidarity with equivalent international trade unions which was unusual in Russia. This distinguished their unionism from others in the industry and lay the foundation for these workers developing a form of unionism which more adequately approximates a form of middle class unionism.[5]

Assessment

What is evident from this examination is that both the pilots' union and that of the air traffic controllers were grounded in the material and ideological circumstances of work and employment relations. In the case of the PLS the union reflected and confirmed the pilots as a privileged social grouping within the aviation industry, who came out of a past prominence within the Communist Party at their workplaces. Further, pilots had reasonable expectations of promotion into senior administrative positions within the industry as indicated by the predominance of former pilots amongst such staff. In practice, their move to establish the PLS was an attempt, largely successful, to maintain and reinforce their position within the industry. They used the vehicle of sectional unionism to this end. In this respect, they had little interest or incentive to build a form of unionism that broke with the past, the relatively centralized and remote branch-based unions of the Soviet period. This was a union which was led from the centre with a leadership who were skilled in representing pilots' interests and concerns within airports and state structures in fairly conventional ways, and a union which, despite its occasional militant rhetoric, consistently presented itself as a responsible and co-operative union within the industry.

In contrast, the air traffic controllers looked to FPAD as the mechanism to question the prevailing pay arrangements as well as to defend a view of air traffic control which increasingly ran counter to the policies of the Ministry and the implicit fragmentation of the aviation industry. These were concerns which were rooted in their experience as a cohesive and relatively distinct work group within the employment structures of the industry. To pursue these concerns they built a union which was federally-based, with a relatively accountable leadership and a participative membership. The approach of the PLS in relation to FPAD's policies and the status hierarchy of airports further isolated FPAD within the industry, with the result that the air traffic controllers had the unpalatable choice of making a virtue of their relative isolation or succumbing to the increasingly vehement demands by the PLS that FPAD fall into line behind the pilots. The paradox is that in the event they created the basis for a genuinely independent and oppositional union in the unusual context of modern Russia.

Thus, these unions represent very different sets of interests and forms of organization and are a prism through which more diverse and complex trends may be seen. In one very specific way, the history of unionism in this sector captures part of the dilemma of Russian trade unionism. The choice before workers is whether to develop forms of unionism rooted in the workplace, where workers are able to articulate and express their concerns in the face of hostile managements and manipulative governments or to acquiesce to this coercion and strike accommodations which benefit the few but appear to offer a measure of stability for the many. What the outcome will be in the short term remains uncertain. What is more certain is that both sets of workers looked to unions to articulate their interests, thereby expressing themselves as distinct professional groups.

A Class in the Making?

The focus of this paper is on a specific type of social stratum, namely unionized non-manual workers in two prototypical industries. While there is a long tradition of examining such workers in the West in this way, particularly in the manufacturing sectors, the utilities and the public sector, this has not been the case in Russia. There the history of the state-organized and state-run enterprises has been different, resulting in a distinctive class formation. The question is whether the unionization of non-manual employees in the aviation and coal industries constitute a 'new' middle class in the making.

These industries have gone through considerable change in the last five years, with the collapse of the administrative-bureaucratic state and the changing economic position of Russian enterprises, reflected in part in the complicated processes of change in the aviation and coal industries. However, what is equally clear is that there has been a very uneven process of change within enterprises, with non-manual staff locked into long-established managerialist relationships. Thus it is only in the sense that these staff, ITR and related managerial staff in the coal industry and pilots and air traffic controllers in the aviation industry, occupy a 'middle position in the industries, between a more assertive senior management and a more homogenized working class' (Kozina and Borisov 1996).

The question is, do these social groups constitute a class in terms of their position in the social structure of their enterprises and in terms of their unions? Taking the question of structure first, it is clear that while there has been change within enterprises, this is not part of a class in the making. In a formalistic sense these staff occupy distinct strata within the enterprises. They were all part of the managerial hierarchy of the Soviet labour process, undertaking tasks associated with co-ordination and those of control. In the formalistic sense of the Carchedi type of analysis, they undertook both the functions of capital and labour. However, both ideologically and politically they were firmly part of the managerial hierarchy, although in the case of both the air traffic controllers and the technical cum engineering staff of the coal industry in a socially subordinate position. It is the potential ascribed to their formal position, the economic identification in Carchedi's terms, which gives rise to the view that they may constitute a middle class in the making.

These are social groups whose resort to sectional trade unionism is a reflection of their position in an uncertain managerial hierarchy both within the enterprise and within the industry. In all cases, their unionism was associated with a defensive and exclusive stance within the industry, where they attempted to secure their position as privileged and prominent strata. This in each case was done in alliance with the senior management or factions of management who in turn were also attempting to secure their position. These are strata who have allied themselves, via their trade unionism, with sections of management, and not by attempting to secure their position, either as a distinct stratum or in alliance with a working class that is increasingly subordinated to an assertive senior management. Rather, they were part of a process whereby the managerial hierarchy was being recomposed, with these staff attempting to secure a prominent part within this hierarchy. In line with the long-standing role of trade unions to support management in the Soviet enterprise, this was a form of unionism which took that a step further, with the establishment of sectional managerial unionism. The base for this lay in the managerial hierarchies of these industries, not the structural ambiguity that arises from the development of the public or private enterprise in the advanced capitalist societies.

This pattern of managerial unionism is most evident in the coal industry, where managers created unions or at least provided the conditions for the core of the Soviet managerial structures, the engineers cum technical staff workers, to unionize in supportive sectional unions. In the changing managerial hierarchies in the industry this gave these staff a voice in the debates about the development of the enterprise and the industry, via their trade unions, a form of representation which has more in common with the continuity of the Soviet enterprise. Without this both the staff and senior management were without an organized voice both within the enterprise and the industry. Nonetheless, it is equally important to note that these were trade unions and they increasingly worked with the other trade unions in the industry, forging the basis of an alliance with each other. Still as unions increasingly looked to an alliance with managers this was consistent with the sectional and exclusivist form of unionism that was in the process of making.

For the pilots, their concern was to maintain their privileges as the core non-manual staff in the aviation industry, who benefited from promotion into the administrative stratum, at the end of their operational lives. In addition, they had long occupied prominent positions within the Communist Party which further reinforced their place within the industry. For them the advent of sectional trade unionism was a means to pursue their objectives in a context where there was considerable uncertainty about the way in which the industry was changing. In general, their interest was in securing a unified aviation industry, with pilots inscribed as the core and pre-eminent occupational group, rather than as employees of separate airlines. For a time they pursued these objectives in alliance with air traffic controllers, but broke with them when the controllers began to assert their own distinct interests, in particular for a separate air control facility with its own revenue and administration. Thus the pilots sought to operate as a managerialist union, pursuing the interest of the enterprise and securing their position within it.

The air traffic controllers have long occupied a socially marginal and secondary position within the aviation industry and it was only within the context of the transition that they found themselves placed so as to possibly secure and indeed improve their place in the industry. This is clearly brought out in their long-standing objective to establish a separate air traffic control facility offering control services to the industry and receiving revenue. However, this is not a straightforward stance, because the union has also argued for a unified and separate facility on safety grounds. Equally, this was a union that challenged the government as employer in a series of collective agreements which attempted to defend the place of controllers within the industry. The point is that organizationally and ideologically this was always a union that articulated an ambivalence about the position of air traffic controllers as waged workers and as staff who saw the possibility of securing their future in a restructured industry with managerial opportunities for these staff. However, rather than seeing this as an authentic middle class trade union, it is more accurate to note the way in which they were caught in a managerial struggle and in the context of this came to stress their waged labourer status. They neither saw any prospect of unity with working class sections of the aviation industry as workers nor as trade unionists. In this respect they maintained their exclusivity and thus acted in a way that reaffirmed their sectional interests. Nonetheless, this is a social stratum which articulates the ambivalence of middle class labour, an ambivalence which is reflected in the way the union is organized and operated.

This then was the unionism of distinct stratum within the managerial hierarchies of these enterprises and industries. They acted to defend their interests in the context of division and struggle over the future of the industries. In this respect this was not a process of middle class unionism or an articulation of the middle class in the making at the point of production. For that to happen the labour process would have to be restructured so that the structural ambiguity between the production and labour functions became a central feature. While this may occur eventually, depending on the way in which the Russian enterprise is restructured, at the present moment this does not seem to be happening in any even or systematic way.

Notes

1. As part of these debates about middle class labour, trade unions are often seen as an expression of class consciousness. Depending on the way in which class relations are structured and unfolding, different sets of middle class labour may look to trade unionism as the organized expression of their concerns and interests at the point of production. But this also raises difficult theoretical questions about the nature and character of trade unionism. Nonetheless, there are analyses which reject this link and instead argue that rather than reflecting class interests and concerns, white-collar trade unionism reflects work and employment differentials. In this type of account the emphasis is on the institutional features of industrial relations, the argument being that there is no association between class structure and unionization. Instead they focus on the similarity between union objectives and procedures of manual and white-collar unions, with an implication that white-collar unions are becoming increasingly like manual unions. The assumption is that the market and work conditions of manual and non-manual union members are becoming similar, reflected in employee concentration, the decline of non-manual status, the standardization and routinization of non-manual employment conditions, and the prospect of job insecurity and uncertainty. This is coupled to the way in which employers and the state have increasingly underwritten policies either promoting unionism or have attempted to deal with unions in the same or similar ways (Bain 1970). The problem with

this type of analysis is that it abstracts unions as institutions, devoid of a membership locked into class relations at the point of production.

2. The research began in 1991 and is part of a comprehensive research programme conducted by Simon Clarke and Peter Fairbrother (both Centre for Comparative Labour Studies, University of Warwick, Coventry) along with nearly 25 Russian collaborators. This particular research was conducted principally by Peter Fairbrother, Vladimir Ilyin (University of Syktyvkar, Syktyvkar) and Vadim Borisov (Institute of Comparative Labour Relations Research, Moscow), supported by Simon Clarke. The research relies on in-depth interviews with key informants in the aviation industry and the alternative unions, in particular, as well as three years' research in Vorkuta (north Russia) focusing on the coal unions and managerial restructuring of the coal industry. Altogether over 200 interviews have been conducted, many lasting several hours, in addition to the collection of documents and supporting material as well as observation. The research has been financed by Nuffield Foundation, ESRC, INTAS.

3. The trade union maintains a city office with a part-time office worker. It acts as a vehicle for disseminating information of the different primary groups and gives support to groups of potential members organizing in unorganized mines. In 1995, it had a relatively small membership with 11 primary groups covering five mines, the service for the installation and service of mine equipment, and Vorkutaugol. Altogether they have a little over a thousand members.

4. Not all pilots joined the PLS as a rump group of some few hundred pilots remained in the association. For four years this has been a fairly ineffective union, although over the last year it has begun to grow in numbers and exert some influence within the industry.

5. As confirmation of this commitment to a distinctive form of unionism, FPAD was a federally organized union with a rotating leadership elected for a maximum of two successive two-year periods in office. The federation is comprised of 29 regional organizations, whose senior leaders meet monthly as the central committee of the union. An annual congress attended by 500 of the 7,500 members elects the President and four vice-presidents, who comprise the executive committee of the union. Unusually in the context of Russian unions, official and independent, all the leaders work at their jobs as air traffic controllers while undertaking their union duties. The Moscow office is looked after by the secretary to the executive committee who together with the treasurer are the only full-time employees of the union. In view of these organizational arrangements, there is an incentive for the President and at least one of the vice-presidents to be based at one of the Moscow offices since the union has no national full-time leaders.

Bibliography

Armstrong, P. (1986), 'Work Supervisors and Trade Unionism', in P. Armstrong, B. Carter, C. Smith and T. Nichols (eds.) *White-collar Workers, Trade Unions and Class*, Croom Helm, London.

Bain, H. (1970), *The Growth of White Collar Unionism*, Oxford University Press, Oxford.

Borisov, B., Fairbrother, P., and Clarke, S. (1994), 'Is There Room for an Independent Trade Unionism in Russia? The Case of the Federation of Air Traffic Controllers' Unions and the Union of Flying Personnel', *British Journal of Industrial Relations* 32, 3, September, pp. 359-378.

Braverman, H. (1974), 'Labor and Monopoly Capital', *Monthly Review*, New York.

Breen, R. and Rottman, D. (1995), 'Class Analysis and Class Theory', *Sociology* 29, 3, pp. 453-473.

Burawoy, M. (1985), *The Politics of Production: Factory Regimes Under Capitalism and Socialism*, Verso, London.

Carchedi, G. (1977), *On The Economic Identification of Social Classes*, Routledge, Kegan Paul, London.

Carter, R. (1979), 'Class, Militancy and Union Character: A Study of the Association of Scientific, Technical and Managerial Staffs', *Sociological Review* 27, May.

Carter, R. (1985), *Capitalism, Class Conflict and the New Middle Class*, Routledge & Kegan Paul, London.

Carter, R. (1986), 'Trade Unionism and the New Middle Class — the Case of ASTMS', in P. Armstrong, B. Carter, C. Smith and T. Nichols (eds.), *White-collar Workers, Trade Unions and Class*, Croom Helm, London.

Carter, R. and Fairbrother, P. (1995), 'The Remaking of the State Middle Class', in T. Cutler and M. Savage (eds.), *The New Middle Class*, University College London Press.

Clarke, S. and Fairbrother, P. (1994), 'Post-Communism and the Emergence of Industrial Relation in the Workplace', in A. Ferner and R. Hyman (eds.), *New Frontiers in European Industrial Relations*, Blackwell, Oxford.

Clarke, S., Fairbrother, P., and Borisov, V. (1995), *The Workers' Movement in Russia*, Edward Elger, Aldershot.

Goldthorpe, J.H. (1982), 'On the Service Class: Its Formation and Future', in A. Giddens and G. Mackenzie (eds.), *Social Class and the Division of Labour: Essays in Honour of Ilya Neustadt*, Cambridge University Press, Cambridge.

Goldthorpe, J.H. and Marshall, G. (1992), 'The Promising Future of Class analysis: Response to recent Critiques', *Sociology* 26, pp. 381-400.

Gorz, A. (1967), *Strategy for Labour: A Radical Proposal*, Beacon Press, Boston.

Gorz, A. (1976), 'Technology, Technicians and Class Struggle', in A. Gorz (ed.), *The Division of Labour: The Labour Process and Class Struggle in Modern Capitalism*, Brighton.

Harvester, H.R. (1983), 'White-collar Workers and Theories of Class', in R. Hyman and R. Price (eds.), *The New Working Class? White-Collar Workers and Their Organizations*, Macmillan, Basingstoke, pp. 3-45.

Ilyin, V. (1996), 'Russian Trade Unions and the Management Apparatus in the Transition Period', in S. Clarke (ed.), *Conflict and Change in the Russian Industrial Enterprise*, Edward Elger, Aldershot, pp. 65-106.

Klingender, F.D. (1935), *The Condition of Clerical Labour in Britain*, Martin Lawrence, London.

Kozina, I. and Borisov, V. (1996), 'The Changing Status of Workers in the Enterprise', in S. Clarke (ed.), *Conflict and Change in the Russian Industrial Enterprise*, Edward Elger, Aldershot, pp. 136-161.

Lockwood, D. (1958), *The Blackcoated Worker: A Study in Class Consciousness*, Unwin University Books, London.

Mallet, S. (1975), *The New Working Class*, Spokesman, Nottingham.

Przeworski, A. (1991), *Democracy and the Market: Political and Economic Reforms in Eastern Europe and Latin America*, Cambridge University Press, Cambridge.

Rutland, P. (199), 'Labor Unrest and Movements in 1989 and 1990', *Soviet Economy* 6, pp. 345-384.

Smith, S. (1987), *Technical Workers: Class, Labour and Trade Unionism*, Macmillan, Basingstoke.

Sorenson, A.B. (1991), 'On the Usefulness of Class Analysis in Research on Social Mobility and Socioeconomic Inequality', *Acta Sociologica* 34, pp. 71-87.

Wright, E.O. (1978), *Class, Crisis and the State*, NLB, London.

Wright, E.O. (1985), *Classes*, Verso, London.

11 Managerial Change in Estonia

HARRI MELIN

Introduction

The Soviet Union was a very special kind of industrial society which at once tried to be an affluent and a modern society. The accent in industrial development was decidedly on heavy industries, whereas private consumption had only very limited influence on investments. In state socialist societies the state had close and strict control over the social activities of its citizens: indeed it can be said that the state controlled social life — and anything it could not control it would prohibit. Civil society, as we understand it, was virtually non-existent. However, modernization was an important political doctrine. The Communist Party had ambitious plans to beat the capitalist countries at their own game: in industrial production and consumption (Kagarliski 1992).

The means of production in state socialist countries were not owned by private individuals. Enterprises were owned, de facto, by the state. Although mills and factories were formally structured in the same way as factories in the capitalist world, there were many important differences. Instead of independent economic units, companies were more like branches of industrial ministries. Annual production targets, for instance, were set by ministries. Factories received their raw materials from above, and the output was delivered to 'customers' according to ministry instructions. Enterprises did, however, have extensive autonomy in the realm of production.

In the Soviet context state-owned firms can be divided into four categories. The most important firms were so-called all-union firms, which had great strategic significance. Their headquarters were in Moscow, their staff was highly qualified, and raw materials supply was well organized. Secondly, republican industries served the needs of different Soviet republics. Locally organized enterprises, for their part, used local raw materials and were usually run by cities. The fourth group was represented by enterprises organized by non-industrial ministries, such as a locomotive factory owned by the Ministry of Railways. The administration of industrial production was in the hands of Moscow-based branch ministries which had strategic plants around the country. Secondly, there were republican ministries that were in charge of the production of a particular product category (e.g. shoes) in a certain republic.

The Soviet ideology stressed that all power in the country was in the hands of the working class. Indeed this was not just an ideology; in many respects the Soviet Union really was a workers' state. The industrial working class was seen as a leading economic, political and social force. The working class had considerable autonomy in the workplace and much influence at the shopfloor level. Nonetheless industrial firms in the Soviet Union were organized in the same hierarchic fashion as in the West.

All these social and economic features of the former Soviet Union were universal, i.e. Soviet society was based on the same sets of principles from eastern Siberia all the way to Estonia.

Estonia regained her independence five years ago. Since then the country has witnessed rapid and dramatic social changes. During the past few years Estonia has taken giant steps towards restructuring her economy, legislation and infrastructure. Estonia now has its own, stable currency, even though the mechanisms for regulating banking and fiscal institutions are still not properly in place. By Western standards inflation is still high but falling. Industrial production has started to grow again after a sharp downturn at the beginning of the 1990s (see Blom et al. 1996, 240-243).

There has also been a clear change in the structure of the labour markets and in labour market relations, not only in Estonia but in all Baltic countries. These changes followed the reorganization of political relations as well as property relations. At the same time the role and the functions of management began to change as well. Although the process of privatization has not been easy in any of the Baltic countries and at least the land reform is still under way, the changes that have taken place are significant indeed. Management, as it is understood in the context of the capitalist labour and production process, is now beginning to emerge in the Baltic states.

My intention in this article is to discuss issues of management against the background of social change. I begin with an examination of the development of factory management in state socialism. I then move on to discuss theoretical approaches concerning enterprise management in state socialism: What was the role of managers in manufacturing production? Finally, I shall briefly discuss some empirical findings on managerial change in Estonia.

The Development of Factory Management

During the 1920s there was lively debate in the Soviet Union about strategies of work organization. Several different theoretical approaches were presented (cf. Kiezun 1991). The main drive was to reduce the use of raw materials and human labour and to raise levels of productivity. In many respects these efforts came quite close to Taylorism: theorists and innovators in the Soviet Union also wanted to increase the use of scientific methods of work organization.

Stalin's 'revolution from above' during the early 1930s led to dramatic changes throughout society and also affected industrial management. First of all, forced industrialization caused a sharp increase in the number of enterprises, industrial workers and industrial managers in the late 1920s and early 1930s. New workers were brought in from the countryside, many of them reluctant to work in big factories. Most managers were young men, very few of them with any formal education for their job.

The adoption of the principle of democratic centralism in business companies meant that factories were administered according to a system of 'one-man management'. Managers had exclusive power and control, while decision-making powers and responsibilities were delegated to factory directors. So while the manager, in theory, was in power, in practise the enterprises were divided into separate units each with a fairly high level of operational independence.

The centralized production system caused various problems to daily business operations. The biggest problems occurred on the supply side of production: there was a chronic shortage of machines, raw materials and labour force. Plans drawn up in Moscow rarely met the needs of an engineering plant in Murmansk, for instance. Managers adopted different strategies to resolve these problems. In many cases this meant resorting to unofficial channels, neatly captured in the concept of 'blat': managers would use their personal contacts, extra cash or barter exchange to get whatever it was the factory needed.

This period was also responsible for creating one of the biggest bottlenecks in state socialist industrial production, i.e. bonus systems. Workers as well as managers would be paid a bonus if the unit reached the targets set out in the central administration. To qualify, the unit had to produce 100 % of the target. This system gave rise to much fraud and deception: factories would report back to the central planning organ and say that they had met the targets even if they hadn't and then make up the shortfall later. Sociologists have used the concept of 'storming' to describe this intensive period of catching up.

In principle all spheres of life in Soviet society were governed and controlled by the Communist Party, which was a major force not only in politics and state administration but also in art and in science. Manufacturing industry and factory management were also under party control in that the party had its own representation in enterprises. Each factory had its own party secretary. However, these secretaries were usually 'company men' who were more loyal to the management than to the party organs. This was because their own welfare was dependent, in part, on the factory's performance. They, too, got their bonuses if the production targets were met.

The third corner of the 'power triangle' was the trade union institution. Soviet trade unions were not part of the working class movement, as is the case in the Nordic countries, for instance. Trade unions were not independent, but they were more like servants of the regime rather than independent social actors. One of the chief concerns of the unions was to encourage workers to try and meet the targets set out in the plan. They also had much influence in matters relating to social policy, supplying flats to workers and arranging holiday tours. Unions organized kindergartens and other related activities. On the other hand, unions had no power whatsoever in collective bargaining on wages and working conditions: wages were set in negotiations between the enterprises and planning organs (see Ruble 1981).

On the eve of World War II the Soviet Union was an industrialized country, but the structures of industrial management were very different from the structures in capitalist enterprises. Industrial production was centrally controlled by industrial ministries, which worked closely with central planning organs, most notably Gosplan. The role of managers at the local level was to put these central plans into effect, but they had no say over products or markets — although they did have their power in production-related questions.

After Stalin's death the management of industrial production was completely reorganized. Khrushchev's reforms were aimed at reducing the power of industrial ministries and planning organs: the key idea was decentralization of power. As a consequence the Soviet Union saw an impressive growth of regionalism in the late 1950s and early 1960s. Republics, and regions within the republics, were now given the opportunity to take control. At the same time the power of enterprise managers was increased. Regional planning committees consequently took a greater interest in the needs of their own republic than in the requirements of the national plan. This, in turn, caused serious difficulties for the operation of some other plants in other republics: in the Soviet system enterprises were highly dependent on each other.

Khrushchev's reforms were not very long-lived, however. By the mid-1960s industrial management was engulfed by a new wave of reforms. G.E. Liberman (1976) initiated a programme that aimed to turn the attention of industrial managers more and more towards making a profit out of their operation. Ever since the Bolshevik revolution, profits had been associated with capitalist exploitation; in socialism firms had nothing to do with profits. Liberman's idea was to use the profit motive to inspire managers and to increase productivity through profits.

One of the most important outcomes of the reforms of the mid-1960s was the restoration of industrial ministries system. Additionally, Gosplan assumed an increasingly important role in management. The managerial system that had been created during the period of forced industrialization was reinvented in the circumstances of rapid technical change in the 1960s. As far as managerial power was concerned, managers at the plant level received no new power resources.

The period before *perestroika* is often described as a period of stagnation. Indeed, the old structures and old ways of doing things remained effectively unchanged throughout the 1970s and early 1980s. In the mid-1980s the Soviet Union was a 'ministerial society'. Economic power was vested in industrial ministries and in the planning organs. Another important feature was the inherent contradiction in power relations: on the one hand enterprise managers were stripped of all power in that they had no say in matters concerning the frames of production; on the other hand managers were important social actors at the local level, they were a part of the local power elite and they ran the enterprises.

The Soviet work organization comprised almost exactly the same hierarchic positions as were to be found in capitalist work organizations. Soviet managers had both decision-making power and authority, but the limits to the exercise of that power were set by the production plan. Managerial power was also restricted by other factors. Wage differentials were much smaller in the Soviet Union than in the West. The chronic shortage of qualified labour, combined with labour legislation that was heavily pro-workers, guaranteed blue-collar workers a strong position in the enterprises.

Enterprise managers were an important part of the local power elites (see Andrle 1976): together with the leading party functionaries, they were the real leaders of industrial cities and regions. Their social situation was based on a totally different set of structural elements than the situation of their subordinates. Through their various social networks and their formal positions, some top managers made absolute fortunes during the 1970s and early 1980s. They were not capitalists proper, but in the Soviet context they were immensely rich people.

Perestroika was aimed at a 'revolution from above', just as in Stalin's days. The purpose was to give factory managers more power. Bureaucratic control over business operations had increased considerably since the launch of Liberman's reforms. Computerized planning systems together with the increased resources made available to the planning organs had created a close web of instructions and rules that the firms were required to observe. From this point of view both managers and workers were considered to form a part of the industrial machinery. All this served to undermine, decrease productivity and create a growing sense of pessimism about future prospects.

In spite of all the changes, the basic element of the state socialist mode of production remained untouched: the state owned the factories and state authorities had the final say in all key decisions concerning the enterprises. Managers were still subordinated to the political and administrative authorities.

In principle a 'universal' work organization and managerial strategies prevailed throughout the Soviet Union, in Estonia as well as in Armenia.

Nonetheless, in spite of these principles of universalism, different regions and different branches of economy adopted their own practices with regard to work organization. In the Western literature the Soviet Union is often described as a monolith, yet the regional differences within the Soviet system were quite huge, both in terms of the level of social and economic development and in terms of administrative and managerial practices. The Baltic Sea region was one of the most developed parts of the Soviet Union. Estonia and Latvia were among the most modernized and industrially most developed parts of the country.

There was much social mobility in the Soviet Union. People moved from the countryside into urban areas, from agriculture into industrial jobs. Millions of workers experienced upward social mobility via education. The Baltic republics saw a huge influx of immigrants from other parts of the Soviet empire. All union corporations invested vast sums of money in Estonia and in Latvia. As a result almost half of the labourers in Estonia and in Latvia were immigrants at the end of the 1980s.

The Soviet type of work organization and management structures can be briefly described as follows. Managerial practices attached much importance to the role of the annual production plan and to the centralization of power at the enterprise level. In the Soviet tradition enterprise managers were in many ways executors of the production plan. Their tasks differed quite considerably from those of their colleagues in capitalist countries.

The Role of the Plan

In capitalism managers have a special role to play in business management. In modern large-scale corporations, managers have at least four functions to fulfil. According to A.W. Teulings (1989, 16), these functions are:

1. Ownership function (accumulation of capital)
2. Administrative function (allocation of investments)
3. Innovative function (product market development)
4. Production function (control of the direct labour process)

In capitalism, managers occupy authority positions and at the same time they are responsible for decision-making. This type of social actor did not exist in state socialism. The managers were told in the plan what they were to produce and how much. When the plan was endorsed, it became the law: the firm was to follow, to the letter, the instructions set out. Soviet managers took the plan more or less for granted, never questioning its legitimacy. Red directors negotiated, 'stormed', cheated and did the most amazing tricks — all to meet the targets specified in the plan. The reason for this extraordinary commitment was that until the late 1980s, the whole industrial community was more or less dependent on the plan: if the manager and the factory met the targets, they would get their bonuses; if they failed, the future was less encouraging.

It was the manager's responsibility to negotiate the conditions that were to be recorded in the plan, although the final decisions were taken elsewhere at a higher level. The way in which the plan was executed, however, was left to managers. On many issues management actually had more power than in capitalist countries. Economic rationality, for instance, was not an issue in the Soviet Union. Although management was controlled both from above (through the party and ministries) and from below (the party and trade unions), this control was in practice quite weak and ineffective. The most important tool of control was in fact the plan itself.

The role of the plan in state socialism has been heavily criticized by many Western sociologists (see e.g. Rutland 1985, 56-63). At the enterprise level the central role of the production plan caused a number of difficulties. Firms used manufacturing methods and technologies that were completely inappropriate for their purposes. There was also a marked lack of sophisticated accounting systems, and accounting was indeed more a means of control from above rather than a tool of management. 'Soft budget constraints' allowed the production of goods that were too heavy and too expensive year after year. The price system had nothing to do with actual production costs.

According to the principles of 'democratic centralism', all power in the enterprises was vested in the factory directors. However, different units and departments enjoyed considerable operational independence. At the shop-floor level workers had a high level of autonomy over the labour process.

As regards the centralization of power and the power resources of different managerial groups, Mladen Lazic (1992, 8) has emphasized the importance of the system of nominations. According to Lazic the most important power resource for management was the right to nominate their own subordinates: strip the manager of this right and he, too, falls into a subordinate position. The very possibility to nominate your own workers is an important source of concrete power.

Top groups of enterprise management were part of the economic and political power elite. They were also members of different regional and local elites. In the Soviet Union political positions were more important than economic positions. This was also true at the local level. However, the position of a single manager was very different in, say, Magnitogorsk or Togliatti than in Moscow or Leningrad. At the local level the party elite and enterprise management constituted a very significant political force.

The most important incentive in the Soviet economic system was money. At the centre of the incentive system were different kinds of bonuses paid to management and workers. In the case of management this was a serious problem in that there existed no other systems of incentives.

The role of manufacturing industries was not restricted to the production of goods and commodities; in most cases factories formed the very heart of industrial towns. The towns were built around the factories, by the factories, and it was from the factories that they made their living. A factory could produce tractors or missiles, but it also was responsible for the reproduction of the entire community (Grancelli 1995, 16). Factory managers were important local leaders. These features of the very special role of factories in the Soviet system is described in an exciting way by Stephen Kotkin in his book concerning the city of Magnitogorsk.

Managers operated in the networks of multiple interdependencies. The future of the whole factory, not to mention their own future, was dependent on the action of different partners in these networks (Crowley 1994, 594-595). Within the networks, managers had much influence on decisions concerning the production and allocation of apartments, holidays, etc. At the same time, they depended on the work performance of the central work collectives in the factory. The outcome of the work done at the factory was also dependent on suppliers, whose work was dependent on the performance of some other unit, etc. So one of the main tasks of the managers was to sail successfully within the networks of multiple interdependencies.

Figure 1. An example of a managerial network

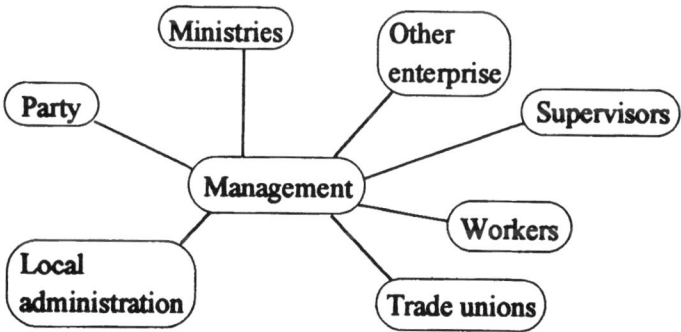

In a planned economy managers had no role at all as 'investors', 'innovators' or 'salesmen'; all these managerial tasks were covered by the plan, and some were actually taken care of by the industrial ministries. In the Soviet Union managers were often seen as passive executors rather than active policy-makers (see Gimpelson and Nazimova 1992, 73).

The Soviet understanding of management contained one inherent paradox: The idea of 'one-man management' said that managers occupy a position of power. On the other hand, managers were not considered responsible for the results of the operation, but simply as part of the ministerial bureaucracy. Historically, Soviet enterprise managers can be divided into three groups. During the first years of the planned economy a manager was more like a leader of his industrial troops and a director without any professional education. The second type was the engineer-manager, a leading figure from a supervisor up to a minister who was familiar with all the necessary technical details, but who had no financial education whatsoever. The third type is something that should have followed the engineer: scientific-technical progress requires also knowledge about financial matters and leadership knowledge. However, this kind of manager type never emerged in Soviet management (see Smeljov 1990, 59-60).

The Soviet management literature presents an idealistic picture of how a centralized administrative apparatus can provide a solid basis for the management of the whole society. This notion is founded in a strong belief in planning. Soviet researchers made generalizations that were based on experiences drawn from the most developed enterprises or regions. They also denied the existence of all other social interests apart from the so-called general interest. Soviet thinking stressed the unity of society. Sociologists did not emphasize the interests of different occupational, ethnic or other social groups that could be found in the factories. Factory management was not as easy an task as the Soviet planning system gave to understand. During the last years of *perestroika*, managers often faced problems that they simply were unable to solve; they did not have the answers to the new questions that were being thrown up by the accelerating process of social change.

Managers in the Early 1990s

The social division of labour, as measured in terms of the occupational structure, was quite similar in the Soviet Union as in advanced capitalist countries. In the late 1980s the share of managerial groups in the Soviet Union was somewhat larger than it was in Finland, for instance (Melin 1996, 108). The proportion of women among Soviet managers was also higher than in capitalist countries. On average managers were slightly older than other major occupational groups, and they were well educated, with more than half having an academic degree.

Official Soviet class theory recognized two social classes, i.e. the working class and the peasantry. The intelligentsia was seen as a social stratum, and managers were part of the intelligentsia. Among wage labourers, Soviet thinking accepted only one internal division, i.e. that between mental and manual labour: the communist ideology was that there existed no divisions based on power resources. Society had reached the stage of mature socialism, and any such divisions had by then disappeared. This basic tenet meant that hierarchic power divisions were not part of Soviet reality.

The discussion below introduces some results of an empirical analysis concerning the social position of enterprise managers in the Soviet Union. The data were collected in spring 1991 in the European parts of the Russian federation (Hout et al. 1992).

The economically active population can be divided into class groups on the basis of their formal position in the work organization. Education or incomes can also be used as the main criteria for stratification. However, I consider this kind of analysis irrelevant to the case of state socialism. Instead, I have divided the respondents into different class groups on the basis of their actual decision-making power (power concerning the whole plant), their supervisory power (how much they can influence the work of their subordinates) and their autonomy at work (how much autonomy they have in their job).

On the basis of these criteria it can be said that at the beginning of 1991, half of the Russians (N=1495) were workers, one-fifth were professionals and just over one-quarter belonged to managerial groups. One half worked in manufacturing industries and the rest in services and in administration.

Looking more closely at the middle class, or at professional and managerial groups, the following generalizations can be made:

— the proportion of women is slightly larger than the proportion of men;
— men occupy top managerial positions clearly more often than women (1/3 vs. 1/5);
— the proportion of men in middle management is slightly larger than the proportion of women;
— there are equally many women as men working in supervisory positions (1/10);
— half of the women and one-third of the men are working in professional positions;
— women in middle class positions work more often in services or in administration, while men work more often in the manufacturing industry (Melin 1996, 120).

One of the first declarations that the communists made after the October Revolution was to say that women and men have equal rights and duties in society. In spite of this heavy ideological emphasis on gender equality, men and women did not have equal positions in Soviet society, but all the really important positions were occupied by men. Although there were large numbers of female managers, they did not occupy the higher positions. This segregation was not due to education. In general, women had better educational qualifications than men from the late 1960s onwards.

In modern societies the vast majority of the economically active population earn their living in the form of wages or salaries. Wages are also a good indicator of class situation: wage level tells us about the importance of a certain occupation/position in a given society. It may also tell us about the division of prestige. In general income differentials were much smaller in the Soviet Union than they are in capitalist societies. Measured on the basis of official monthly incomes, top managers only earned about 35 % more than wage earners.

There were considerable differences in incomes between different branches of the economy. Wages in the manufacturing industry were higher than in services. On average women earned less than men. In managerial positions the gender difference was almost 50 %, in professional occupations about 35 %. This means that equality at the ideological level does not necessarily correlate with real social situations.

Monthly wages do not, however, tell the whole truth about a person's total incomes and life situation. State socialism was a shortage economy. The problem was not so often lack of money as lack of goods, which quite simply did not appear in the shops. The best companies had their own farms and greenhouses. There were company-owned shops, restaurants, cinemas, etc. Firms also had their own networks and channels to gain access to rare consumer goods, which were frequently used as rewards. In general managers were best placed in companies to benefit from these kinds of arrangements. All in all managers lived a much more comfortable life than the average Soviet citizen.

Soviet sociologists often criticized Western mobility researchers for overestimating the prospects for upward social mobility and for neglecting the inevitable downward mobility that also takes place. In the Soviet Union social mobility was a visible phenomenon. In fact Soviet society was very fluid. Soviet sociologists understood mobility as a voluntary phenomenon, workers moved both horizontally and vertically (Aitov 1986, 255).

At the beginning of the 1990s the working class was still the most common social background position even for managers and professionals. However, all managerial groups deviated from the working class, although the differences were not very considerable. About three-quarters of all workers come from a working class background, while about 60 % of managers come from working class origins.

Career mobility is another aspect of social mobility. More than three-quarters of the top managers have had a pure managerial career. On average about half of the cases in managerial groups occupied some managerial post in their previous job as well. There were some interesting differences between different branches. In industry the number of people who have been promoted was smaller than in services. In particular, top management in industry used to get promoted less often than managers in respective posts in the service sector.

Job autonomy is an important power resource at work. The question of autonomy is always closely related to concrete work. In sociological theorizing, job autonomy has been used as one criterion for class divisions (Wright 1978). Compared with capitalist countries, all occupational groups in the Soviet Union had quite extensive autonomy at their work. In the Soviet work organization differences between managers and manual workers were not so wide as they are in the West. In relative terms workers were in better positions than managers. In spite of this managers had considerable influence over their work.

Although managerial power was restricted in many ways, Soviet managers nonetheless held the keys of their enterprises firmly in their own hands. They were the real leaders and decision-makers who could rule the factories. In spite of the plan, managers were autonomous actors in the state socialist production system.

Towards New Managerial Practices in Estonia

In capitalism managers have both authority and decision-making powers. This type of social actor did not exist in state socialism. But how has the situation changed after five years of social transition in Estonia? How do industrial relations appear at the shopfloor level? What are the role and the functions of managers in Estonian manufacturing industries?

Two Case Studies

In autumn 1994 two case studies were carried out in Estonia under the research project 'Social change in the Baltic and Nordic countries'. Working closely with researchers from the Tallinn technical university, we conducted a series of interviews in a textile factory 'A' and in a furniture factory 'B'. The company manager, a line supervisor and an ordinary industrial worker were interviewed. The aim of these interviews was to collect information about changes in industrial relations, the management's labour processes and future expectations of different hierarchic groups.

Company 'A' was a clothing factory established in 1988 by two young men. It is one of the first private manufacturing companies in Estonia. 'A' produces mainly leisure and sportswear for the local markets. It has some export to other Baltic countries and to Finland. The firm is also doing subcontracting work for Finnish companies. At the time of the interviews 'A' had 130 employees, and the figure was steadily growing.

'B' is a furniture factory with a staff of more than 450. It is also one of the oldest industrial enterprises in Estonia. It was privatized immediately after independence in 1991. The company produces bedroom and kitchen furniture. During the Soviet period the company was an important all-union producer of furniture which operated in the all-union markets. Today, it is one of biggest furniture companies in Estonia. It has some export to Russia and subcontracts for Finnish and Swedish companies.

'A' has always been a private enterprise. It has created its own 'line' and its own products. It has made some major investments in new machinery. The company also bought a site for themselves with Swedish funding. In many respects 'A' is a real success story in the Estonian framework, while company 'B' is a typical case of the difficulties that most Estonian firms are facing in the aftermath of privatization.

Our interviews indicate that three important processes are taking place in company management. The first is the growing influence of top management, the second is the growing internal differentiation within management. Thirdly, the distance between workers and management seems to be growing.

The factory manager was the most important figure in the former Soviet firm (Melin 1996), although in many questions his power was very relative. Managerial power was restricted by both external and internal dependencies. Since independence (and privatization), the manager's power has grown. Our survey data reveal that the manager's supervisory power and decision-making authority have increased between 1985 and 1993 (Melin 1995, 36).

What about the qualitative data; what do they say about these changes? Has the power of top management increased? It seems that managers have more independence today than they used to. They no longer have to follow orders from central planning organs or from the party. This, in itself, has meant increased power. The Managing Director of company 'A' describes his day:

> I would not like to describe my usual day because that involves external affairs such as public relations and so on. I work here only when necessary. In general I've tried to free myself from the day-to-day routines.

A supervisor in company 'B' talks about the situation at his factory earlier and today:

> Everything is secret now. The old factory manager with whom I started, I could go to his office and we talked like man to man. He was a good guy. And I knew exactly how much he earned. Today it's difficult to get hold of the manager, and as far as his earnings are concerned, well we just don't know.

On the other hand management's evaluation of the change is a very positive one. They feel that 'in the old times' their days were filled by meetings. Now they have more time to run the company.

The Soviet way of doing things was by commands: the manager issued an order to his deputy, who issued an order to the head of department, who issued an order to the supervisor. Finally, the supervisor told the workers what to do. Managers often complain that it is very difficult to change these practices. People show no real initiative, they have to be told to get even the simplest of tasks done. All this is due to the legacy of how things were done for almost 50 years in the Baltic countries.

What, then, are the most visible changes that have happened in managerial practices? Managing Director of company 'B' described the most important changes shortly as a shift from 'fulfilling orders' to 'managing production'. This change can be seen in the structure of managerial hierarchies. The span of control has simply grown. As a consequence the number of supervisors has decreased. Today there are more workers working under one supervisor than there used to be. This means that the position of lower management is also changing.

On the other hand, firms have hired more personnel to top management positions than there were during the Soviet period. This is due to changes in the environment: companies today are faced with a completely different kind of business environment. They have to plan their production, buy the raw materials and sell their production. New kinds of accounting systems must also be adopted. All this means that industrial firms need personnel with new types of qualifications.

Many firms have had serious problems with the above-mentioned changes. Firstly, their managerial structures were set up with a view to the needs of a centrally planned economy. Secondly, the qualifications of their staff do not correspond to the new requirements. And in general, there is a lack of managerial staff in all post-socialist countries.

Conclusions

Research on the labour process in Russian industry points at both change and continuity. In the Soviet Union the managerial labour process was based on functions imposed by the planning system. Today, the growing influence of market economy is also seen in the work of managers. Managers are now becoming real business managers involved in making important economic decisions. Factory managers are becoming business executives, though the change is a slow process. They have to learn many new skills. Marketing or accounting, for instance, were more or less unknown or even ignored skills in state socialism.

In Estonia this change has already happened. Estonia is a capitalist society that has adopted a very liberal economic policy. However, some elements from the state socialist past continue to live on. We have seen in Estonia a strengthening of economic and political democracy. The future role of managers in Estonia is very different from that of managers in Russia. In Russia the future is just as wide open as the future of Russian society at large. In Estonia managers are, together with the political elite, agents of modernization.

Earlier research has shown that in Soviet Estonia managers had less power resources than Finnish managers in the same position (Melin 1995, 32). On the other hand, other occupational groups had more decision-making power than the respective groups in Finland. Today Estonian managers share the same situation as their Finnish colleagues. Managers are real decision-makers and they have also power over their employees.

It is quite evident that capitalist work relations have replaced old state socialist practices. Estonian managers are agents who are really performing the functions of business management. Differences between occupational groups have increased. Although Estonia is no middle class society, managers are certainly in the core of the new middle classes. Their class situation and their consciousness is clearly different from that of other social groups in Estonia.

Bibliography

Aitov, N. (1986), 'The Dynamics of Social Mobility in the USSR', in Yanowitch (ed.), *Social Structure of the USSR*, M.E. Sharpe, New York.

Andrle, V. (1976), *Managerial Power in the USSR*, Saxon House, Westmead.

Blom, R., Melin, H. and Nikula J. (1996), 'Constant Transition — The Baltic Condition', in R. Blom, H. Melin and J. Nikula (eds.), *Material for Baltic Models of Transformation — National Reports*, Department of Sociology and Social Psychology B:36, Tampere.

Crowley, S. (1994), 'Barriers to collective action. Steelworkers and mutual dependence in the former Soviet Union', *World Politics*, Vol. 46, pp. 589-619.

Gimpelson, V., Nazimova, A. (1992), 'Master of production. Dogma and reality', *Sociological research*, Vol. 31, No 4, pp. 61-74.

Grancelli, B. (1995), 'Organizational change. Towards a new east-west comparison', *Organization Studies*, Vol. 16, No 1, pp. 1-25.

Hout, M. et al. (1992), *Class Structure and Consciousness in Russia*, Survey Research Center, Berkeley, California.

Kagarlitski, I. (1992), *Hajonnut monoliitti*, Orient express, Helsinki.

Kiezun, W. (1991), *Management in Socialist Countries. USSR and Central Europe*, Walter de Gruyter, Berlin.

Lazic, M. (1992), *The decay of socialism and activities of the commanding class*, paper presented at the First European Conference of Sociology, 26.-29.8.1992, Vienna.

Liberman, E.G. (1976), 'The Plan, Profits and Bonuses', in Nowe and Nuti (eds.), *Socialist Economics*, Penguin Books, London.

Melin, H. (1995), 'Work situation of main Estonian occupational groups revisited', in R. Blom, H. Melin and J. Nikula (eds.), *Social strata and occupational groups in the Baltic states. Social change in the Baltic and Nordic Countries, Project*, working papers no. 1, Tampere.

Melin, H. (1996), *Suunnitelman varjossa. Tutkimus yritysjohtajista Neuvostoliitossa ja Venäjällä*, Acta Universitatis Tamperensis no 489, Tampere.

Ruble, B. (1981), *Soviet Trade Unions. Their Development in the 1970's*, Cambridge University Press, Cambridge.

Rutland, P. (1985), *The Myth of the Plan*, Hutchinson, London.

Smeljov N. (1990), *Ennakot ja velat*, Tammi, Helsinki

Teulings, A. (1987), 'Liikkeenjohdon työprosessit organisoidussa kapitalismissa', *Hallinnon-tutkimus*, Vol. 6, No 3.

Wright, E.O. (1978), *Class, Crisis and the State*, Verso, London.

12 On Transition to the Middle Class: Professional Strategies of Young Intellectuals in Russia

VICTORIA SEMENOVA

The development of the middle class in Russia ranks among the most debatable issues both in practice and in theory, since the formation of the professional-managerial class — as a main force of modernization and political stability — has always been one of the vital tasks facing any country embarking on the road of reform (for example, Japan in the postwar period).

This paper is not an exercise in abstract theorizing, but it attempts to advance concrete arguments in the examination of this problem in the labour market: whether young professionals have the objective opportunity and subjective capabilities to become professional managers in marketizing Russia.

The national history of different countries lends evidence to the fact that the formation of the professional-managerial class has depended on three constituents:

1) state policy in the production sphere;
2) employer—employees relationship in the workplace; and
3) the subjective strategies adopted by economic actors themselves.

The following deals with the latter component from the point of view of the market and work situation of young professionals. According to Goldthorpe (1987, 40) market situation consists of level of income and other conditions of employment, job security, and promotion of opportunities; work situation consists of organizational assets (authority and autonomy).

These situations are here analysed from the vantage-point of social-cultural changes in the sphere of production. What I have in mind is transition from the culture and the labour ethics of 'dependency' — when the so-called 'intelligentsia' used to function under the administrative command system (to obey the commands from above, to perform mainly administrative functions) — to the culture and ethics of 'independence' — when managerial staff are pursuing their own professional interests, enjoying a certain autonomy and exercising control over production.

Without going into any theoretical discussions, we shall proceed from the 'working' notion of the middle class as the professional-managerial positions

220

employed in one of the spheres of intellectual labour, having an autonomy and exercising professional control over the production process and receiving certain income out of their professional skill (Ehrenreich and Ehrenreich 1979).

As regards the criteria of the middle class, there is some difference of opinion among different schools and theories (e.g. Wright 1978; Goldthorpe 1982; Giddens 1973; Roemer 1981). Nevertheless, on the level of concrete analysis, all employ similar arguments and examine similar processes. Most theorists share the view that the formation of the middle class is connected with the development of professionalism and managerial functions (as a certain degree of autonomy and control over the production process). Western scholars maintain that one of the main criteria for the new middle class, in its Western interpretation, is employment in the state sector of the economy where they can exert more influence on state policy, on the one hand, and on the production process, on the other (Kivinen 1989).

However, in Russia none of these criteria could be used with regard to the so-called Russian intelligentsia (and mainly its scientific-technical part). As for the so-called 'work situation' in the era of command economics, professionals had no autonomy or control over production processes; everything was controlled from above. As for the so-called 'market situation' (in the absence of labour markets in general), the state was not interested in rewarding professional competencies and there was not sufficient differentiation in incomes between the intelligentsia and other social groups. For example, according to official statistics for 1991, there is little difference in terms of consumer behaviour between poor and middle class families; their space of living was approximately the same and the amount and quality of goods at their disposal was the same: a refrigerator, television set and even a car (Yarigina 1994). They were all similar in terms of economic and consumer behaviour: so-called Homo Sovieticus. Moreover, their consumer psychology had one common feature that could be described as 'minimized effort' to achieve certain positions and rewards fixed by the state and its social and political institutions. The ideological standard of this kind of economic behaviour was 'to be modest and poor, and differ as little as possible from one's neighbours' (Voronkov and Fomin 1995). All these arguments could explain the absence of the middle class in its Western interpretation (Kivinen 1993; Burawoy 1986; Zaslavskaya 1992).

Researchers hold the view that during the transitional stage in Russia, as in other post-socialist countries, a shift towards differentiation in the social structure is mainly connected with the emergence of differences between the state and private spheres. The development of the professional-managerial stratum with its specific value system and psychology is thus possible only within the private sector, where the market situation and competition urgently call for professional skills and where therefore there is a readiness to reward professional abilities on the principles of a market equivalent (Cox 1992). As for state-owned enterprises, they could not use professional-managerial skill and they have no realistic financial possibilities to pay for it (Zaslavskaya 1992).

Through our long-term interest in the cohort of the 27-28 year-olds whom we have observed since they entered the labour market (1985) until now (1993), we have also discovered this discrepancy at the concrete level, i.e. as personal inability.

The majority of the cohort (over 60 %) still remain in their jobs in state-owned enterprises and are quite satisfied with their production functions, indeed even with the failure of the administration to adequately remunerate their professional contribution at market prices (about 30 % of the cohort have an additional source of income outside their professional functions). Moreover, over two-thirds of those who are professionals do not intend to pursue their professional career. Some professionals had given up their professional career altogether and moved into other spheres, e.g. trade or business, where no professional skills are required. In other words the majority of young professionals do not connect their further social advantage with their main professional activity.[1]

Only a small minority of the cohort (3-6 %) moved to owner or manager positions within the private sector. The first in-depth interviews with those who moved to the private sector revealed that they had been attracted not only by the system of remuneration for their professional work, but also by the new system of job relations ('ethics of independence') based on autonomy and the possibility to influence the production process (Semenova 1993), the prospect of professional 'self-realization'.[2]

In our further interviews we concentrated on comparing the strategies of those professionals who had moved to the private sector (10 persons) and those who remained in state enterprises (15 persons).

The focal concern here is with the objective possibilities — the requirements that professionals are expected to meet at state-owned and private enterprises — and the subjective strategies of young professionals, i.e. their orientation to professionalism, autonomy and control over production. Consumer behaviour and lifestyles were also included in the analysis.

According to our basic hypothesis, the middle class (in its Western interpretation) in transitional Russia can only evolve on the existing basis outside the state sector. The private sector offers opportunities not only for adequate pay, but also, and importantly, it attracts the potential of young professionals with an orientation to a different kind of value system and labour ethics.

Our argument is that the individual's professional strategy and identification with the intelligentsia or the professional-managerial class are connected with the general cultural changes and must be examined in the context of the individual's entire life experience (socialization, education, immediate living environment, lifestyle). For this reason the project involves an examination of the respondents' biographies and life stories. The focus is on the similarities and differences between the professional strategies of individuals who have a job in the private sector and in state-owned enterprises, their social identification with the middle class or the intelligentsia.

From the point of view of social and economic policy, the professional strategies of young intellectuals are worthy of interest as an ability of the labour force to take part in the modernization of the production process in state-owned enterprises.

As is shown by experiences from other countries (Tapan in 1946, France in the 1960s), different strategies can be used to counter the absence of sufficient professional-managerial potential within the country: for example, it can be coaxed in 'from the outside' (training abroad, inviting foreign specialists, etc.). This is why it is so important to highlight the internal potential of the young generation.

Methods

The empirical part of our study combines quantitative and qualitative data on the professional strategies of young intellectuals, linking together three data-bases.

First, a secondary analysis of longitudinal data on professional strategies allows us to trace mass trends in the professional changes of the young adults over the past four years and their orientation towards their future professional career (notions of stable/unstable, upward/downward mobility, retraining, use of additional earnings, subjective expectations related to one's job).

Second, we conducted intensive semi-structured interviews (3-4 hours) with 25 respondents selected from the sample on the basis of their professional characteristics and employment in the private/state sector. These also shed light on the respondents' job situation and employer requirements in terms of autonomy and professionalism. Such interviews allow us to trace professional strategies as well as the background of individual life experiences.

Thirdly, a computerized database was formed on basic biographical events in the respondents' work and life histories. Such a database allows us to highlight the similarities and differences in separate professional strategies by various biographical facts (work history and life history, family data and individual data, regional differences, educational career and professional career, etc.).

First Results

Our analysis of the ten life stories of young entrepreneurs indicated that although they had different social characteristics (in terms of education, profession and type of private enterprise), there were certain common features in their decision-making situations.

Their decision to change jobs was not forced upon by them through dismissal from their previous jobs in the state sector, but it was their own free choice, their desire to escape from a dependent status within the state enterprise and to gain some autonomy.

Here are some short excerpts from different interviews:

— 'It was a chance to become a free man'
— 'I don't like bosses'
— 'I can't stand being ordered about'
— 'I was an employee, a hired worker, and the salary was not bad. What I've gained is independence and prospects. I wanted to be independent'
— 'The whole idea was to get free'.

One owner of a small private enterprise emphasized the common spirit of freedom in his firm:

What I like best here are people working together with me. I like to see them change when they come to us and give up their state status for a private one. Many of them show capabilities they never knew they had in themselves. They immediately become internally free people, the very moment they come here. [...] They do what they want to do in their profession, and they find pleasure in performing their job. You might expect them to go home when they are through, but no, they stay on and work hard (Igor, p. 136).[3]

Escaping the system of regulated labour and labour discipline at state-owned enterprises is perhaps the main reason behind the abandonment of such state structures. The notion of labour discipline was overriding in the labour ethics of the totalitarian society system, implanted in the subconscious of every man and woman. For several generations, a breach of labour discipline was regarded as a serious offence (under Stalin's notorious decree arriving at work five minutes late was a criminal offence). Against this background it is not surprising that many of the older generations feel that the demolition of the order of labour discipline will prove to be the ruin of the entire state system.

It was, however, a purely formal discipline of strictly regulated presence at the workplace; it had nothing to do with the intensity of labour.

Paradoxically, many privately employed professionals who used to be against such forced discipline, have now turned out to be much more 'disciplined' — all of them complain that work takes up almost all their time. They toil from early morning until late in the evening and can speak about their job for hours on end.

The motivation of self-realization and escape from mass production is well illustrated by the case of Anna. She was a furrier for several years in a state enterprise where she was making 'mass' products — just as workers at most Soviet state-owned sewing factories.

> What I did at the factory was boring. I felt I was wasting my life away. So the alternatives I had were these: either carry on with my boring job, working hard to meet my planned targets and discipline requirements and bearing in mind that my wages of 140 roubles a month (the average wage for a specialist before the economic reform in 1992) will never go up, or move on to a job where I would be paid three times as much and have flexible hours. My mother was against the change and called me 'the people's enemy', but I still did it... For the past three years I haven't had to worry about money, about whether I can afford to buy what I want. We've also got our own trademark and we've been admitted into the international register of manufacturers of fur-goods. (Anna, p. 43).

It is also clear that Anna has changed psychologically, that she has grown to realize her own identity. She points out that she had always felt 'ashamed' of herself, inferior to others until she became one of the company leaders. Only then did she find her self-respect, feeling that she was attractive to men. 'It all happened after I began to earn a lot of money'.

It is also worth noting that Anna's mother, as a representative of the former psychology of the 'tiny screw', was very firmly against her daughter's decision. This clearly highlights the hostile relations between these two value systems. As noted earlier, the Soviet system did not allow people to get rich, to step outside of the standard habits of consumers.

One of the interviewees, Grigory, a farmer with high agricultural education, stressed the antagonistic relationships between the two systems based on authority and autonomy:

> Even when I was still going to the institute — that was before perestroika — I was well aware I'd never be able to work in this (Soviet state) system: I would either be a thief or try to change something and get it in the neck. I grew up in freedom, I was brought up by my mother in this way — freedom and insubordination are in my blood (Grigory, p. 13).

Our interviewees realized then that their movement from a state enterprise to a private one meant rejecting one value system and accepting another, conflicting system. It is quite possible that such a motivation is more typical of respondents who are educated people with developed spiritual demands. The motive of freedom, however, seems to be the most meaningful to most interviewees. For them the emergence of private enterprise implies an opportunity to get away from state regulation and control, which evoked a certain sense of euphoria in them. This state is clearly considered to be temporary. At the same time, however, they see a real difference in the work situation and labour relations between these two sectors. As one interviewee pointed out, — 'it's a kind of internal immigration':

> The idea is that we're moving to live here in conditions similar to those in which the guys who moved to America are now living — to make the same effort to adapt, to inculcate oneself into the new system... (Leonid, p. 136).

What is the main difference between traditional professional functions in the state system of production and those on the free market, as perceived by those in private employment?

> The administrative-command system has simply stifled people, most of them have no thoughts of their own, no initiative left. And the people educated by this system continue to fill official posts... But what we need most is not empty talk, but work and work at all levels (Igor, p. 142).

While Igor stresses the importance of formal discipline and the absence of initiative as the main features of the Soviet system, other respondents also referred to the absence of an ability 'to figure out financial profits, to calculate the gross economic effect' (Anna), 'most people couldn't do even simple things: arrange meetings, enter into a contract, they are not true to their intentions' (Grigory).

Leonid summarizes his experience in organizing his private business:

> A strange discovery I've made: there are only few people who are capable of doing things that to me seem so simple and obvious, for instance, to sort out certain formalities relating to the start-up of a company. I've realized that there are not very many people, at least among those around me, who can really work — who can use their head, or legs, or get some organizational job done, and so on. The people you address — either because they are too lazy, or even if it's interesting to them to start with, they eventually lose interest when it becomes clear they should actually do something — in 99 % of the cases these people are not true to their intentions... So far I only have one or two partners whom I can trust (Leonid, p. 70-71).

It is clear then why the majority of the cohort are still in their same jobs in the state sector: they could not perform the functions of a manager in a market situation and they are still out of competition because of their low professional skill. This is one of the reasons why they cannot be named the basis for professional-managerial strata.

As was pointed out earlier, the majority of the age cohort occupy a stable position within a state enterprise. These young people prefer to have guaranteed social protection from the state than to take the risks that come with high earnings. In different interviews their position was motivated as follows:

— 'Perhaps it's a good idea to start in a private firm, but it wouldn't suit me. I'm content with my average but stable wages.'
— 'My parents have taught me to be honest. I don't think that those earning big money have got where they are in an honest way.'
— 'We (my husband and I) prefer to earn not great but honest money.'
— 'My parents have always taught me that performing one's duty is the main thing in life.'

This kind of motivation from the role of 'a tiny screw' in the huge state mechanism can be traced back to the mass psychology and job ethics of the 'ordinary Soviet person'. This orientation to bureaucratic dependence, to duty and honesty before state power is a heritage of the socialization system of the so-called Soviet period. While those employed in the private sector are motivated by a work ethics of independence (achievement, risk and individual success), professional activity is motivated by job security, honest fulfilment of one's obligations and a sense of duty before the authorities.

It is also necessary to add that a change in social status from the state to the private sector, in the Russian context, entails not only a change in the means of production relations, but also in one's entire way of life. The milieu of the private sector tends to inspire a new type of commitment and new patterns of consumer behaviour, often bewildering to most poor people. Because of the restrained circumstances, the average young intelligentsia in the state sector have only limited ways in which to spend their spare time. It is not that they do not have such needs, but they simply do not have the money to travel abroad, to engage in high-prestige, to indulge in expensive entertainments, etc. All these opportunities are closed doors to them.

Those in the private sector invest primarily in themselves; other types of capital investments still involve substantial risks. In this connection a specific mode of life, with high everyday expenses, has been noticeable in their milieu.

No matter how hard I try I can't recall what sort of time off I've had during the past six months. It's a tight schedule for every day. However, every Friday from 3 to 5 I go to play tennis, then to sauna — a cherished place that I always manage.

On Sundays I will try to get out to the countryside together with my colleagues and our families (Konstantin).

Sometimes I am a spendthrift but give myself such pleasure. I've started to buy expensive cosmetics and footwear. Two years ago when I bought a furcoat at a fabulous price in a currency shop, my mother almost turned me away from the door. It has become very difficult for me to find a suitable man because I earn much more than the young men I mix with. I can freely invite them to a restaurant they cannot afford. (Anna)

People like me, we have to be 'smart guys', otherwise our trade negotiations will go nowhere. Be self-controlled. Go in for some sport of your own choice. You must show the level of your prosperity in your appearance and clothes. (Michail)

All these patterns of 'grand-style' behaviour are alien to ordinary Russian professionals. The main distinctive characteristic of the identity of the inter-viewed professionals employed in the private sector is that they link them-selves firmly with the new form of ownership. This can be clearly traced in the above statements and in their claims to state-owned services (they, officials, legislators, those who work or follow the traditional patterns of labour). The feeling of professional or social identity is almost completely absent from their statements. Illustrative in this respect is the feeling of being an 'internal emigrant', as stressed by Leonid, or the statement that a profes-sional path will be abnormal and that labour qualities will remain unclaimed by the former ruling system.

According to their professional patterns in the work situation and their living standards and consumer behaviour in the market situation, they are on the way of forming a new social group of professionals employed in market society. It seems that they have only some genetic kinship with the traditional Soviet intelligentsia employed by the state.

Notes

1. A longitudinal study of the age cohort born in 1967-1968, 'The pathways of one generation in Russia'. In the first stage it was headed by M. Titma. The next two stages in 1989 and 1993 were carried out in Russia by L. Koklyagina and V. Semenova. The sample for the two latter stages comprised 800 respondents in the Tulo region, 800 in the Kurgan region and about 700 in Moscow. See: Titma, Koklyagina, Semenova (eds.), The Lifepaths of One Generation (in Russian). Moscow, Nouka, 1992.
2. The early interviews were carried out by V. Semenova on the same cohort (40 in-depth interviews) during the project 'Adaptation to Social Change: Life Stories of One Genera-tion', sponsored by the Central European University in 1993-1995.
3. The set of interviews was collected during the joint Russian-French project 'The Century of Social Mobility in Russia' (under D. Bertaux, CNRS, France). Interviewers: the story

of Anna — M. Malysheva; the story of Grigory — O. Litvinenko; the story of Leonid — O. Yarsteva; the stories of Konstantin and Igor — V. Semenova.

Bibliography

Burawoy, M. and Luckas, J. (1986), 'Mythologies of Work: A Comparison of Firms in State Socialism and Advanced Capitalism', *American Sociological Review*.

Charkhordin, O. (1993), *The Corporative Ethics, The Ethics of Samostoyatelnost and the Spirit of Capitalism: Reflections on Market-Building in Post-Soviet Russia*, reprint.

Cox, T. (1992), *Structural Barriers to Market Reform in Eastern Europe*, paper presented at the Annual Conference of the British Sociological Association, University of Kent.

Ehrenreich, B. and Ehrenreich, J. (1979), 'The Professional—Managerial Class', in P. Walker (ed.), *Between Labor and Capital*, Boston.

Giddens, A. (1973), *The Class Structure of the Advanced Societies*, Macmillan, London.

Goldthorpe, J. (1982), 'On Service Class. Its Formation and Future', in A. Giddens and G. Mackenzie (eds.), *Social Class and the Division of Labor*, Polity, Cambridge.

Goldthorpe, J. (1987), *Social Mobility and Class Structure in Modern Britain*, Clarendon Press, Oxford.

Kivinen, M. (1989), *The New Middle Classes and the Labour Process: Class Criteria Revised*, University of Helsinki, Department of Sociology Research Reports 223, Helsinki.

Kivinen, M. (1993), 'The Perspectives of Middle Classes in Russia' (in Russian), *Sotsiologicheski zhurnal* 1.

Polyanui, K. (1944), *The Great Transformation*, Alfred Knopf, New York.

Roemer, J. (1981), *A General Theory of Exploitation and Class*, Ballinger, Cambridge (Mass.).

Semenova, V. (1993), 'Soziolökonomische Krisen in den Lebenserfahrungen russischer Familien', *BIOS, Helf* 1/1993.

Titma, M., Koklyagina, L. and Semenova, V. (eds.) (1992), *Zhiznennyi Puti Ognovo Pokoleniya* [The Lifepaths of One Generation], 'Nauka', Moscow.

Voronkov, V. and Fomin, E. (1995), 'Tipologicheskie ckriterii bednosti' [The Typological Criteria of Poor], *Sociological Journal*, 2.

Wright, E. (1978), *Class, Crisis and the State*, Verso, London.

Yarigina, T. (1994), 'Bednost v bogatoi Rossii' [The Poor in Rich Russia], *Social Sciences and Modernity*, 2.

Zaslavskaycl, T. (1992), 'Socialism, Perestroika and Public Opinion', *Sociological Research* 4.

13 The Fate of Party Functionaries in Post-Soviet Russia

ALLA BYSTROVA

Russia is undergoing rapid and dramatic changes. Specifically, a new social structure is taking shape in a step-by-step process, which is unfolding by force of nature. The changes were prepared during the period of stagnation, prior to *perestroika*, thus making nonsense of the argument that a totalitarian society cannot be transformed through its own internal development impulses.

This paper describes a research project which is concerned with the fate of party functionaries who were a specific social group in the former USSR, i.e. the nomenclature. The project was supported by the St.Petersburg Mayor's Office; additional funding has now been received from the Russian research foundation in the humanities.

The existence of the nomenclature in the former social structure of Soviet society has been acknowledged by a plethora of researchers. The phenomenon itself has been variably called class, estate, stratum, or elite, although given the complexity of its features it does not in fact correspond to any of these notions in their classical sense. The nomenclature differed from class because of the absence of ownership based on heritage. It also differed from estate because of the absence of heritable rights and obligations fixed by usage or law. The definition of the Soviet nomenclature as elite did not reflect its hierarchic nature and the existence within it of social strata belonging to the managerial stratum of the middle class rather than to the ruling one.

My view is that the functionaries of party district committees belonged to the middle strata. Party statistics show that in St.Petersburg, practically all these functionaries had a higher education, some of them academic qualifications, and the vast majority were of working age (over 90 % were under 50). One in six had a party political education, having graduated from the Higher Party School. Their wages did not differ very much from the average wage in industry. They carried the main burden of managerial low-grade work because they had to lead and survey activities of the basic party organization that was spread all over the society. Therefore they were the first to feel all the changes in the lowest layers of society, the fluctuations of people's trust in the authorities. They were the first address when people were 'in search of the truth', solving all their problems. It was actually here, at party district committees that the leadership personnel was trained: it was difficult to make

230

a career without several years of work in these committees. However, it is important to stress that these functionaries were by no means subjects who made strategy decisions or who influenced such decisions even at the local level.

The disbanding of the CPSU in summer 1991 proved to be an uneasy test for party functionaries. Overnight they lost not only their social status, already damaged by the cancellation of the sixth article of the USSR Constitution on the ruling position of the Communist Party, but also their job — the only means of subsistence for the majority of party workers. What happened to these people, how did they adjust to their new life, where are they now?

In the course of our investigations 20 semi-structured in-depth interviews were conducted with ex-functionaries. In addition, statistical data was analysed. We were interested in the mechanisms of adaptation and the channels of finding a new job, with the directions of mobility (horizontal, vertical), the self-identification of respondents, their evaluation of the economic and political reforms in the country, state of spirit in the market conditions, political preferences and future expectations.

The interviewees were former functionaries of one city district committee in the centre of St.Petersburg. The district is characterized by a scarcity of industrial enterprises, but on the other hand there are several institutions of higher education, many research and development institutes, artistic unions, theatres, and head offices of city authorities.

The respondents were selected not only from amongst the people who were still working within the city district committee in August 1991. Considering that the importance of 'apparatus work' for a successful career had started to decline much earlier, respondents were also recruited from amongst those people who had left their work at party bodies prior to 1991.

Among the 20 respondents, only two were not associated with the district committee singled out for the investigation: one of them had worked for a long time in another city district committee, the other never worked in the district committee but was invited to work in the regional committee from one of the major St.Petersburg schools of higher education. In the course of preparing the interviews, some working hypotheses were formulated:

Hypothesis 1. People belonging to the corps of party functionaries, including party district workers, came to their positions as a result of a process of 'negative selection'. These were individuals who had not been able to find a job prior to party work. Therefore, the fact that the CPSU lost its role and influence in society had a negative impact on their social status. They had major problems with employment and adaptation to the situation. Obviously, they were reluctant to accept the reform and an extremist orientation of political views was appropriate to them.

Hypothesis 2. Party city district workers were professionals in management and understood the necessity of reforms. For them it was normal that the influence of the CPSU on the development of society had to be curtailed. Their proximity to the grassroots level, their good understanding of the situation in the subordinate organizations, and their strong personal contacts helped them to keep their bearings in the new situation. They soon adjusted themselves, and succeeded in keeping or even improving their standard of living. They made up part of the stratum of the 'new Russians'. Many of them anticipated the changes in the position of the CPSU and left their jobs in the apparatus prior to August 1991. Their political passions are on the side of reforms even if they often express discontent with regard to the pace and modes of reform.

Hypothesis 3. The party city district committee consisted of people with different views on the organizational frame of the CPSU structure. One can observe here the availability or reflection of contradictions appropriate to the CPSU and to society as a whole. Party functionaries were to different extents dependent on party work and on the CPSU. Therefore one may assume that after the closure of the CPSU, they have had different fates, different models of behaviour and different strategies of survival.

It is hardly surprising that the real life reflected in the interviews proved to be far more complex and richer than the suppositions of our hypotheses. So who are they, our respondents?

None of the respondents we interviewed was under 35 years of age. Seven were aged between 35 and 40, ten between 41 and 50, and three over 50 years of age. There were fifteen men and five women, of whom two were over 50.

As for the number of years they had served in party bodies, four respondents had worked in these bodies for more than ten years, twelve respondents for 5-10 years, the remaining four less than five years. As regards the level in the party hierarchy on which their party career ended, six of them were in different positions at party city and regional committees, the others at the city district committee in the following positions:

— instructor (8 respondents)
— full-time secretary of a basic party organization (1)
— deputy head of a department (2)
— head of a department (2)
— first secretary of the party district committee (1).

All interviewees had a higher education. The majority had completed technical college qualifications (8), five had a diploma in economics or law, one was a doctor, three had a humanitarian education (history or philology), one was a university mathematics graduate and one (a woman aged 56) had only a party-political education. Four had a doctor's degree (three in economics and one in chemistry). All of them had either completed their doctorate or were preparing their thesis at the time of starting party work.

Among the 20 interviewees, six occupied different positions in the apparatus of the city district and regional committees in August 1991. In the analysis we set them apart in their own group. In this group, all essential steps of the party hierarchy of the mentioned level are presented. Let us now look at the positions held by the participants at the time of the interviews:

— 4 directors of private or mixed enterprises (not owners)
— 4 deputy directors of enterprises and organizations of different kinds (banks, training centres, vocational schools, joint-stock companies in various branches)
— 1 bank employee at middle level (head of a department)
— 2 officials, functionaries at the Mayor's Office and at the city district administration
— 4 owners of private enterprises (in two cases family firms, one limited company and one joint venture)
— 5 formed a group called 'others': a doctor, an employee of a tourist company, a lawyer at the city Lawyers' Board and two teachers at institutions of higher education.

The motives and circumstances of their transition to work in the party apparatus are rather homogenous, i.e. either a party duty or the need to have a party entry in one's CV for a successful career. One of the respondents had been called upon to work for the party twice in his life. The first time round 'I did not want to go, this was in 1980. The alternative they put to me was that I could defend my thesis when I go to work for the party city district. I felt raped and I tried to drop out.' In 1987, during *perestroika*, a time of great expectations and enthusiasm, he was invited to the lecturers' group of the party regional committee, and he got a very different impression: 'Everything was extremely benevolent, it was interesting for me, I went there because it was on a friendly basis, because nobody encroached upon me as a person'.

A respondent who today is a proprietor of a family enterprise for furniture production says it was pure coincidence that he got to work in the party apparatus: 'It's a mystery for me up to the present day'. However, just a couple of minutes later it became clear that he had gone to the party body on the advice of the head of the association where he was working at the time. He had been told (by a former party worker) that if he refused, his prospects of promotion in the company would be gone. All the respondent recalled of the conversation were some of its most ridiculous details; for instance, the former commando from Siberia was told to get rid of his beard. The next step in the party career was worth his moustache. During his move to work for the party, another respondent was advised to change his wardrobe, to wear a grey suit and a white shirt with a tie rather than light trousers and a colourful jacket.

These amusing episodes are actually very significant, illustrating as they do the situation of a party worker as a 'soldier of the party'.

There were also some further circumstances which made a party career an attractive option. First of all it meant an opportunity to get a dwelling.

None of the respondents looked at the transition to the party office as an immediate promotion. Nonetheless it made it possible for them not only to create a career, but also to acquire useful contacts. The interviewees frequently referred to this point: 'The work at the party city district committee did not really provide much in material terms, but it did help to get in touch with people. Incidentally these contacts have proved very useful with my limited company. Experience in human relations'.

Some interviewees said that the party committee provided for real working skills. Several interviewees emphasized the importance of having a close familiarity of the work organization as well as one's own work plus responsibility and honesty, which differentiated positively the former apparatus people (as they assumed) from the new breed of bureaucrats who came in with Yeltsin. These qualities now make it easier to get a good job. One of the respondents evaluated his employer's motives as follows: 'From the district party committee will emerge a responsible and honest man who never will trip anyone up.'

Similar evaluations were made in other interviews as well. It is noteworthy that none of the respondents who lost their job after the suspension of the CPSU had any real difficulty finding a new job. Our respondents were invited into positions of organizers, managers, administrators who can 'work with people', 'solve their problems in life'.

The fact that the respondents had no major difficulties finding employment after the above decree does not mean to say that the respondents survived the events of 1991 without traumas. All of them kept their jobs to the end. Here are some excerpts from their recollections:

> I left when everything was closed, at the last moment. I felt nothing, nothing like fear. But still I communicated with the examining magistrate on particularly grave issues.

The shock was obviously strong enough. In any event the man 'dropped out' for a sabbatical year and built a summer cottage:

> I am very good with my hands and I can do everything myself. I decided that I would not phone anyone, not disturb anyone. If someone telephones me, alright. I would neither bother nor worry. Yes, I left. Not that I hid my head. There was no fear. It was just psychologically... (from the interview of a businessman).

The following excerpt is from an interview with a former full-time party committee secretary at a research institute:

> The events of 1991 came when I was in the position of party committee secretary. The district party committee was practically closed, so was my committee. I did not want to stay on at the institute then. I could have, I could have spoken to the director. No concrete job of course, but I just didn't see any prospects there. The volume of work decreased, the whole atmosphere was such that certain research fields were axed. The whole future of the institute was very uncertain. Plus there were conflicts between the communists and democrats. The democrats were quite influential. It was for this reason that I decided to leave. However I still keep in touch with the institute today. No productive contacts, I know many people who left there as well: to other banks, to other institutions. So the contacts remained.

The respondent said that he had had offers for a job from colleagues in the party district committee, from relatives and from the institute's administration: 'I could have chosen where to go and whom to contact. There were various options'.

The following is from an interview with the former first secretary of the district committee:

> I sat in the suite of the first secretary until February 1st, 1992. All the premises were already occupied, but my office was still there. I went to work regularly, met people. It was towards the end of 1991 that I thought of a new job, looked for a new job. I received many offers from state-owned enterprises. A director's position somewhere was up for grabs and I was invited to compete. At that time, a horrible time, massive cuts were made in the labour force, they still paid your salary but major cuts were made. Of course it was not convenient to show up in these enterprises. And then around came this option with the bank.

As the respondent admitted, he had tried to leave in 1989 for a director's position at an institute where he had been a department head prior to his arrival at the party district committee. However, the party regional committee did not support his nomination, referring to 'rats leaving a sinking ship'. Never again did he approach anyone with such requests: 'And I sank. Everybody left, nobody remained, and I lived through the arrests and searches, and everything else, and the interrogations which lasted up to six hours at a time'.

Yet another respondent (a woman) described her painful experiences as follows:

> I worked till the very end, when the liquidation decision came in. It was a major tragedy, and we suffered morally because we could not understand what sort of privileges and favours we had had that made us work so selflessly, without noticing time pass, sometimes during weekends, overtime. We, as party workers, should not have summer cottages or cars. All this was prohibited. But with our

salaries that would not have been possible. In that situation in 1991 I took a bookkeeping course. I had to work and feed my family. My diploma of higher education is only a diploma. I worked for no more than one year in my speciality.

Finally, a woman who had dedicated her whole life to the young communist league and party work:

> To lose this job was just to lose myself. Those who worked hard survived this collapse, but it was painful. They did not even need to look for jobs.

None of the respondents in our sample who were affected by the president decree on CPSU suspension, remained without a job. They actively sought jobs, asked friends, relatives and former colleagues for jobs. But the opposite happened as well, well-paid jobs came looking for them. They received several offers and were able to make their pick. The search for a job compatible with one's qualifications and abilities (and wage requirements) takes some time. Some of the respondents are not yet satisfied and go to work just to get paid. Others are perfectly satisfied.

For example, a woman who had no higher education apart from party school, had extensive experience in party work which allowed her to take on the position of executive director at the foundation for support of the international banking congress. This position provided her with a very decent income.

None of the respondents in this subgroup returned to their former profession, for various reasons. One respondent, a woman aged 53, (in 1991 she was 50) had a higher technical education, but she lost her professional skills for years.

A mathematics graduate from the St.Petersburg university, as he confesses himself, lost his qualifications but eventually landed in the banking business. He completed his second higher education qualifications in St.Petersburg. He is not completely satisfied with his new job, and this is not only because of lacking skills:

> The values have changed, but clearly not for the better. I'd like to have faith. Not the faith of life or death, 'life or purse'. Faith in something more elevated. I am an optimist, you have to be otherwise life would not be worth living. I have been in situations where everything has seemed to collapse, bandits coming in and starting to clear relationships. But still there is truth and it is not with the bad but with the good.

These very emotional comments were made very quickly and in a very low voice; the respondent fiddled with some small piece of office equipment. His reasoning, however, had a solid foundation: a personal experience of commu-

nication with clients, the periodic appearance of bandits, pity for his wife —
a qualified mathematics teacher at a school of higher education with a pitiful
salary. Hence his bitter words: 'You don't feel very well when you personally
earn reasonably well while others do not have this opportunity'.

A respondent with an engineering diploma did not return to his previous
profession because that would not have made any sense during the recession.
The recession was actually mentioned in a number of interviews as a factor
that narrowed down the job options. On the other hand, many people found
broader scope for self-realization.

Another respondent, a graduate of a technical high school and of the Social
Sciences Academy, is now head of an affiliation of a Moscow bank:

> I am happy with my job. The economy has been my passion for the past 23-24
> years. Therefore my coming here is a first test of the knowledge I gained at the
> Academy. The job itself is very satisfying in terms of its contents. It's very
> interesting. The circumstances that surround the job are not only complicated but
> even dangerous, when every day you are not sure whether or not you will get
> home safe and sound.

The last respondent in the above subgroup graduated from the Engineering
Economic Institute prior to his part-time party work and wanted to change his
profession. He studied at the higher party school and took courses at the
Foreign Trade Academy. When he was at the district party committee and then
at the city and regional party committees, he always conducted analyses of
socio-economic processes in the region. As a result of all this, after 1991 and
a year of 'relaxation' in building a summer cottage, the respondent became
deputy director of a trading house for foreign commerce within a major
production association in the military branch. Very soon he established his
own joint venture (as a co-owner). One gets the impression that he could easily
operate a bigger operation if only he had the resources to do so.

A much bigger subgroup is represented by those respondents who left
their party positions prior to the president decree on the suspension of party
activities. There were two reasons why they left: conflicts with their chiefs on
different issues, or the recognition that the future held no prospects for them,
a lack of motivation to continue in the party job as the party lost its influence
in society. Only two respondents differed from their colleagues: the first is a
doctor who reluctantly came to the district committee and who had difficulty
adapting to the job who therefore left as soon as it was possible. The other is
a bank employee (head of department) who left the district committee with
the process of reorganization. The longer the respondents remained in the
party body after 1991, the less freedom they had in choosing a new job.

Those who left as early as 1990-1991 were not bound by the strict party
discipline. It is necessary to stress that they were not held by anyone as their

predecessors were. Talking about their departure, the respondents recalled the situation of those years in the country and within the party. None of them feel uncomfortable in the new situation, regardless of their evaluation of the state of society and the economy, regardless of their views on the process of economic and political reforms, and regardless of their political persuasions.

Most of those who left the party bodies said that they were not surprised by the August 1991 coup d'etat or the following ban on party activities: the situation in society and within the party was such that 'everything had to come down to that', 'the CPSU just could not lead the reforms'.

Talking about the final phases of the party, the respondents stressed the negative role of some politicians and the forces behind them. Other respondents emphasized the role of the subjective factor. We also met a cautious statement on a possible involvement by an outside enemy: 'Yeltsin received information from the CIA'.

For many party functionaries the events of August 1991 were, however, a shock, followed by fears that 'all communists will be put up against the wall'. The respondents could not rid themselves of such fears for several months. But none of the respondents mentioned anyone suffering from persecutions for political motives.

The majority of the interviewees have seen an improvement in their material standard of living, only a few have remained at the same level of consumption. No one is in financial straits. Many families have acquired summer cottages and cars. Some of the respondents maintain two families and pay for the education of adult children.

Our conclusion is that the respondents continue to belong to the middle strata of society. They have proved highly competitive in the emerging markets of management, although they are not keen on the personal contacts system of employment. Some of them have been able to put to use their formerly acquired skills and abilities in establishing their own businesses.

The respondents have sharply reduced their information intake. They now preferred light reading or whatever they might need for the job (e.g. economic literature). Three of the interviewees continued to read philosophical and classical literature. One respondent reads sociological literature because he is a teacher at a school of higher education and is preparing a thesis in sociology. Only one respondent said he reads newspapers. The rest got whatever information they needed from television. The unique fan of the newspaper information confessed: 'I regularly read "Soviet Russia", "Pravda", "Zavtra". I don't read Szirinovski's papers. "Pravda" is better. Even "Soviet Russia". I get a buzz from reading newspapers'. The circle of leaders for whom the above respondent expresses his support includes Zuganov, Szirinovski and the ideal of a strong leader who 'cared for the nation, the country'. The current president of Russia is judged as a 'vindictive, unforgiving man' whose activities are very much influenced by his 'lack of culture'.

Virtually all respondents had lost their interest in political activity and to great extent in politics on the whole. Many of them had not taken part in elections for several years: 'The last time I went to elections was in 1990. Since then I haven't gone and quite frankly I see no sense in going. Just think of October 1993'. Quite a few respondents said they had no intention of participating in any political activities during the next years.

Confessing no interest in politics, many expressed their views with regard to political reforms in the country. One gets the impression that the majority of the interviewees were rather critical in their evaluations of political reforms in Russia. On the one hand, some said that democracy here and in the West are 'two different things', that it is 'impossible to take a man from one society and transfer him into another'. On the other hand, they stressed the 'absolute passivity of people' in the political process. 'Nothing has changed for the ordinary man, people are still run down'. In this way the respondents stated the unreadiness and unwillingness of the masses to use democratic institutions in order to exert influence on the situation in Russia as well as the impossibility of exerting such influence: 'The authorities don't care about people, they are preoccupied with resolving their own, often personal problems'. The state does not fulfil its functions of providing security for ordinary citizens. Someone pointed out that the leadership of the country has remained with the same people; it is just that they no longer call themselves communists but democrats.

In their statements regarding changes in Russia, the respondents often gave generalized evaluations of economic and political reforms and their close connections. There were some more emotional evaluations of the chaos, the lawlessness, friendly fascism. However, respondents clearly understood that Russian society was in a stage of transition and therefore many referred to the need to 'ascertain' what we are constructing, where we are heading, at what rate and what methods should be applied.

The respondents took a negative view on the role of the authorities in the transformation of society, referring to the reduced standards of living, recession, high taxes: 'Much harm is done to the population, ordinary people. It is hard to accept'. These observations of a female respondent are connected with her professional activity in the district social office. As one bank employee said of the outcomes of the economic reforms: 'The reform is proceeding [...] not to the benefit of the masses, but to the benefit of certain strata.'

The threat of unemployment and more seriously, the worsening situation of ordinary workers was highlighted by many interviewees: 'Ordinary people are left without any protection, all alone.' There are deep feelings of instability and lawlessness in respect of one's own situation as well. Many of the respondents talked about their lack of faith in the future: they could not plan ahead either for their family life or for business. As the owner of a family-owned production firm said: 'I never look more than three days ahead. Yes I do make plans for the future, but how can you predict what is going to happen in present-day Russia?'

Many interviewees expressed sadness at the lack of opportunity to realize their full potential. In some cases this was not made explicit but could be inferred from their manner of speech. It was also manifested in frequent job changes. Many have been forced to move into trade and commerce, but only one, a graduate of the trade institute, talked about this as deserving the attentions of a normal honest man. The majority of the respondents were convinced that they could achieve much more.

Personal experiences of management in the new market situation and the constant struggle to avoid taxes and to deceive the state persuaded many respondents to back the 'Chinese variety of development'. It is interesting to see that this position is taken equally by liberals, social democrats, communists and national patriots. All have their his own views on why the Chinese model is better for Russia than the Eastern European model. But in my view not a reasonable approach has to be applied but a deep conviction, a faith that complex public problems can best be solved by forceful means.

The majority of the respondents had thus succeeded quite well in adapting to their new life situation. They were looking actively for their place in the new structure of social relations primarily through personal contacts. Here their managerial skills, life experience and knowledge were of special value. Some of them got a job in local administration, which means they restored in essence as well as formally their previous status. Many others made radical changes in the sphere and character of their employment. In their own evaluation, the respondents remained within the same social stratum, which is thought to be the middle class. As before they dedicated much time to their work. Now the majority of them are directors of private and mixed enterprises, owners of small industrial and trading businesses, or middle level banking managers. Their incomes and levels of consumption are at the average level or exceed the average to some extent, but they are not luxurious (by Russian standards). Among their priority values, according to the interviews, are professionalism, family and children. These values pushed to the background their former obligations towards the country. Mutual support among friends and former colleagues remained important.

The respondents relied first of all on themselves and their capabilities. Many of them disapproved of the government for its reluctance to support national capital accumulation and industrial growth. Finally, they expected to see greater stability, which would allow them to plan ahead for their life and their economic activity. Apparently they feel that they are partly 'former' functionaries, but their life was increasingly approaching the standards of the middle class in Western society, albeit with distinct Russian characteristics.

Bibliography

Korzhikhina, T.P. and Figatner, Y.Y. (1993), 'Sovyetskaya nomenklatura: stanovleniye, mekhanizmy deistviya', *Voprosy, istorii*, no. 7.

Slomczynski, K.M and Lee, J-H. (1993), 'The Nomenclatura System in Poland, 1978-1987: A Case of Political segmentation of the Labor Market', *Polish Sociological Review* 4 (104).

Socialno-stratifikationnye processy y sovremennom obshestve (1993), Kn. 2, Institut sociologii RAN.

Staricov, Y.N. (1994), 'Socialnaya structura perekhodnogo obshestva (opyt 'inventarizacii')', *Politicheskiye issledovania*, no. 4.

Voslenski, M.S. (1991), 'Nomenklatura. Gospodstvuyushi klass Sovyetskogo Soyuza', *Sovyetskaya Rossiya*, sovm. s MP 'Oktyabr'.

14 The Middle Classes in the Baltic States — Theoretical Starting Points

MARKKU KIVINEN

Introduction

In state socialism, power was said to be vested in the working class. Official doctrine did not admit the existence of a middle class in Soviet-type societies. Today, the situation is very different, with political forces throughout Eastern Europe keen to identify, and identify with, the middle class. Often characterized in moral undertones, the middle class is thought to be brimming with the 'spirit of capitalism'. However, just as there was a permanent tension between the sacred 'proletariat' and the real working class during the Soviet era (Kivinen 1995), a similar tension now seems to be emerging between the idealized middle class and its social and economic reality.

It is now one hundred years ago since Karl Kautsky first called for a distinction between the petty bourgeoisie and the new middle class (neue Mittelstand) (Kautsky 1899). However, in the discussion on the middle class in post-socialism, the problem is often mislocated in the context of ownership, which is supposed to ensure the middle class its political and social independence. State socialist societies have obviously had no propertied middle class because there have been no independent farmers and no urban petty bourgeoisie. The analysis of these class groups and their evolution is an important challenge. However, the vast majority of the economically active population in capitalist countries today are wage earners. If one wants to identify the special characteristics of the middle classes in post-socialism, they must also be compared with the new middle classes in the West: that is, with the privileged group of wage earners. This will draw our attention to such questions as: To what extent do the processes of professionalization vary between capitalism and Soviet-type socialism? The power resources of the new middle classes will now appear as linked up not with ownership but with professional practices and strategies.

Although the position of the Soviet middle strata has in many ways been dependent on their relationship to the *nomenklatura* and to the party apparatus, it would probably be too simplistic and straightforward to define these groups

242

simply in terms of 'serving the *nomenklatura*' (Zaslavskaja 1992). This would amount to the same sort of postulation as we find in service-class theory when it refers to the loyalty of the middle classes to the capitalist class (Goldthorpe 1982). Instead, we need to concentrate in our analyses on the processes through which the preconditions are created for certain wage earners to exercise the authority that has been delegated to them or to apply their special knowledge and expertise. These processes involve various kinds of power resources and strategies, of which professionalization is a very central one. The socialist ideology takes no explicit, systematic standpoint on the problem of professionalization, in any of its versions. As Talcott Parsons points out: 'It was empirically nearly obvious that the "learned professions" had come to occupy a salient position in modern society, whereas in the ideological statement of alternatives, capitalism versus socialism, they did not figure at all' (Parsons 1970, 834). Different versions of the Bolshevist project included different positions on the problematique of mental labour (the egalitarianism of old Bolshevists, discrimination of the traditional intelligentsia, Stalin's critique against '*uranilovka*', etc.). This means that the structuration of different forms of mental labour in Soviet-type socialism was a result of historical strategies and struggles — and that it cannot be reduced to abstract concepts or said to characterize the entire mode of production, as is suggested by John E. Roemer's exploitation theory (Roemer 1982; Blom and Kivinen 1990).

In Western sociology there has been much debate on the 'death of class analysis' (Holton and Turner 1989; Pahl 1989; Crompton 1991; Marshall 1991; Mullins 1991; Pahl 1991; Goldthorpe and Marshall 1992; Pahl 1993; Clark and Lipset 1991; Pakulski 1993a and 1993b; Waters 1994; Hout, Brooks and Manza 1993; Clark, Lipset and Rempel 1993). Although important issues have been raised within this debate, I would be inclined to argue that as far as post-socialist transition is concerned, we have to face the most fundamental, traditional problems in a new light rather than ignore class analysis. By the most fundamental issues I mean those considerations which link class analysis with such critical concepts as exploitation, alienation, domination and mental work. Rather than totalizing all kinds of private property as potentially exploitative, we have to be able to discuss the justification of various forms of ownership. Instead of theorizing on some class interest as sacred and given, we have to be conceptually open to the possibility that class interests are not a zero-sum game. We also have to raise the issue of flawed aspects in the interests and consciousness of all classes — the working class included. There may not be a simple solution to the relationship of mental and manual work, but we have to be aware that several kinds of simple solutions have been proposed.

This paper is a short introduction to my approach to the problematique of the new middle class in the post-socialist Baltic states (cf. also Kivinen 1994a and Kivinen 1994b). I shall begin by describing my theoretical starting points. Secondly, I shall operationalize my own theory using the data of the Nordic-Baltic project. Third, I shall make some preliminary observations as a basis for further analysis.

The Real and the Flawed Universal Classes

For Kautsky, the new middle class has a particular capacity of abstract thought, but on the basis of its own class interest:

> But the most significant difference between the intelligentsia and the proletariat lies in the former's privileged status: the intelligentsia is a privileged class by virtue of its higher education. It is no doubt in the interest of the intelligentsia that the masses are civilized enough to understand the importance of science (...), but they also have a vested interest in restricting these people's access to higher professional education. (Kautsky 1899, 131).

But how important is this specific knowledge for shaping social outcomes? How important is this difference between the proletariat and the new middle class? What is the actual content of the specific interests of the 'intelligentsia'? Is the history of the new middle class of its own making or not (Mills 1956)? All these issues are crucial for sociological theorizing on modern societies. At the same time, they are ultimately significant for a humane social reconstruction in post-socialist societies.

Many theories about the new middle class take into consideration only one form of mental labour, which means this class may be conceptualized as bureaucrats, technocrats or the intelligentsia, for instance. In these terms the class may be seen as either 'good' or 'bad'. Alwin Gouldner's theory of the new class is perhaps the most sophisticated effort to discuss this problem using more specific concepts. Gouldner argues that like any social object, the new class can be defined in terms of both its imputed value or goodness and its imputed power. In most cultural grammars — including Marxist theory of the proletariat — a 'normal' social world is supposed to be one in which the powerful are good and the bad weak. In contrast, Gouldner's left Hegelian sociology accepts the possibility that those who are becoming stronger — such as the new middle class — and to whom the future may belong, are not always the better and may, indeed, be morally ambiguous.

Gouldner distinguishes several conceptions of the new middle class:

1. New class as benign technocrats. John Kenneth Galbraith, for instance, sees the new class as a new historical elite already entrenched in institutional

influence which it uses in benign ways for society. It is more or less inevitable and trustworthy.

2. New class as a master class. Old revolutionaries Mihail Bakunin and Jan Waclaw Machajski see the new class as another moment in a long-continuing circulation of historical elites, as a socialist intelligentsia that brings little new to the world and continues to exploit the rest of the society as the old class had, but now uses education rather than money to exploit others.

3. New class as an old class ally. Talcott Parsons views the new class as a benign group of dedicated 'professionals' who will uplift the old (moneyed) class from a venal group to a collectively-oriented elite and who, fusing with it, will forge a new genteel elite continuous but better than the past.

4. New class as servants of power. Maurice Zeitlin and Noam Chomsky leading the way, many critical sociologists understand the new class only as subservient to the old moneyed class which is held to retain power much as it always did.

5. Gouldner himself sees the new class as an embryonic new 'universal class'. Encompassing both the technical intelligentsia and the intellectuals, the new class comprises bearers of knowledge. However, the new class is profoundly flawed as a universal class. It is elitist and self-seeking and uses its special knowledge to advance its own interests and power, and to control its own work situation. Galbraith and Parsons fail to see how the new class egoistically pursues its own special vested interests. On the other hand, the new class is historically more unique than recognized by Machajski or Bakunin. While protecting its own special interests, it is not bound to the same rationality and morality as the capitalist class and — as Gouldner carefully puts it — at least transiently, contributes to collective needs. The power of the new class is growing. It is definitely more powerful and independent than Chomsky suggests, while still less powerful than suggested by Galbraith (Gouldner 1979, 5-8).

Gouldner says that the two most important theoretical foundations for a general theory of the New Class are, first, a theory of its distinctive language behaviour, its distinctive culture of critical discourse and secondly, a general theory of capital within which the new class's 'human capital' or the old class's moneyed capital will be special cases.

Gouldner's idea of the new middle class as a speech community is very fundamental and worthy of further analysis. Gouldner asserts that the shared ideology of the new class is an ideology about discourse. The culture of critical discourse is an historically evolved set of rules, a grammar of discourse, which is concerned to justify its assertions, but whose mode of justification does not proceed by invoking authorities, and prefers to elicit the voluntary consent of those addressed solely on the basis of arguments adduced (Gouldner, ibid., 28). Gouldner's vision is one of the most important efforts to theorize on the consciousness of the new middle classes. It is indeed a fruitful exercise to raise the issue of the specificity of middle class culture in state socialist and post-socialist societies in terms of this sort of ideal type. However, Gouldner does not address the specific rationality and the specific limitations which characterize the working class consciousness (Willis 1979). We would seem to need a more general theory about the specific rationalities of different classes.

If Gouldner's first theoretical point links up closely with Habermas, the second point is based on Bourdieu's theory of cultural capital. For Bourdieu, economic capital means above all an asset that is used by individual people or families in their reproduction strategies (Bourdieu 1979). It is of course perfectly legitimate to study capital from such a perspective, and in doing so it also seems reasonable to draw an analogy between cultural and economic resources. In particular, such a perspective is justified when we are concerned to study the reasons for why certain people drift into certain positions. However, it is totally inadequate for purposes of explaining the constitution of those positions and the relationship between those positions. Although Bourdieu stresses the importance of analysing work situations, he does not indicate what place this analysis holds in the totality of class analysis. In an implicit rather than explicit way, he takes the struggle for taste and consumption as the key dimension of class struggle. Taste can surely not be an asset in building a privileged position in the production process. The constitution of position requires a collective application of power resources. Therefore instead of power resources held by families, the focus of analysis should be shifted to the power resources of collective subjects and to the positions achieved at the level of 'politics of production' (Kivinen 1989, 70-71). The key strategic solution in my own theoretical attempt (Kivinen 1987 and 1989) is to link up class theory with the sociology of work. In the conceptualization of the collective power resources at the level of the labour process, we must not content ourselves with the simple juxtaposition of two subjects, but also take into account the power resources possessed by the new middle classes and the related forms of organizing the 'relations in production'. This line of reasoning leads to the identification of specific forms of mental labour and to various related processes of class relations. Furthermore, it points very clearly to the historical nature of class criteria. The whole idea that the middle class has power resources of its own is crystallized in professionalization. Indeed, it is exactly in relation to professional autonomy that all other forms of mental labour should be characterized.

In my earlier works I have argued that the development of adequate criteria for the new middle classes requires a thematization of at least the following processes: professionalization, the development of managerial hierarchies, the separation of office work from company management and the consequent changes in the nature of office work, the development of caring work as a specific form of wage labour and the hierarchization of caring work, the changes that have occurred in the position of skilled craftsmen and their qualification requirements, and finally the development of forms of work organization that are characteristic of small enterprises.

It is important to realize that class analysis is more than just the abstract postulation of boundaries between different classes. Most particularly, in order to understand what class analysis is all about, one needs to have a clear picture of its total structure (Blom et al. 1992). Although different schools and traditions may disagree in terms of their abstract class criteria, they may still be dealing with very similar problems and applying very similar lines of argumentation at the more concrete level of analysis. Indeed, it can be argued that there prevails a fairly broad consensus of opinion on certain basic issues concerning the conceptualization of the new middle classes. The emergence of the new middle classes is closely related to the development of managerial positions and professionalization. There are also theories which emphasize state employment as a middle-class criterion, but there are serious conceptual and empirical problems with this line of thought (Kivinen 1989, 238-241).

The differentiation of wage earners has to do with internal relations of dominance within organizations on the one hand, and with professional competence, autonomy and education, on the other. These factors can be combined in different ways in the elaboration of class criteria (the class schemes of Erik Olin Wright 1978 and 1985 and John Goldthorpe 1980 serve as examples of such a project). However, on this basis it is possible to identify a virtually infinite number of class groups. To avoid this, Giddens (1973, 107-112) builds on Weber's concept of social class to develop the concept of structuration, a theoretical conceptualization of how these innumerable class locations are formed into a few concrete collectivities that constitute the basis for class action.

The concept of structuration, as adopted by the Finnish Class Project (Blom et al. 1992), differs from Giddens both on the dimensions of class criteria and structuration itself. Whereas Giddens starts from the Weberian distinction between three types of market capacity (ownership of the means of production, educational or technical qualifications, and physical labour power), my own theory is based on the internal power relations of work organizations and on different forms of mental labour. This means that aspects which for Giddens are sources of proximate structuration are converted into class criteria (Kivinen 1989, 55-57).

For the Finnish Class Project, class analysis is a complex process involving numerous different levels. A basic distinction that needs to be made is between class position and class situation. Class position has to do with the structural relations of domination within production. The concept of class situation, then, refers to more concrete phenomena: reproduction situation (income, education, position on labour market) and working conditions. Any adequate analysis of class consciousness, organization, and the action of class subjects (class formations) must be preceded by an analysis of the links between class position and class situation, i.e. the structuration of class situation.

The Core and the Marginal Groups of the Middle Classes

I have operationalized Baltic class groups on the basis of my own theory, using the criteria of autonomy. My intention has been to create an operationalization that corresponds to my thesis of the composition of the new middle classes in advanced capitalist countries. That is, I have argued earlier that the core of the new middle classes comprises all wage earners representing professional, capital-adequate (managerial) and scientific-technical types of autonomy, irrespective of their managerial functions, and those who have managerial functions in clerical work. Those in performance-level clerical work with some degree of autonomy, as well as craftsmen, care-workers, and workers in small enterprises who do have autonomy, form a group of contradictory class locations which fall in the middle ground between the core of the new middle classes and the working class. In the class situation of these groups, we can detect features which are characteristic of both the core of the new middle classes and the working class. Finally, within these types of autonomy, those in managerial positions come closer to the core of the new middle class.

Table 1 shows the class structure in the Baltic countries and in Finland. We have here two kinds of class criteria connected with job autonomy. First, the core and marginal occupations are classified on the basis of their type of autonomy, as indicated above. Then, only those who really are autonomous have been classified to the core or marginal group number one. The level of autonomy is used as a class criterion on the basis of a coding that was used in Erik Olin Wright's Comparative Project on Class Structure and Class Consciousness.

In this coding system the level of conceptual autonomy could be:

1. High, unambiguous; 2. High, probable; 3. Medium, unambiguous; 4. Medium, probable; 5. Low; 6. None. To be classified as autonomous, the respondent must have autonomy at least on the 'medium, unambiguous' level. High conceptual autonomy indicates that the respondent has to plan or design important aspects of the final product or service. On the level of medium autonomy, the respondent has to be able to plan important aspects of the work procedure: how he/she does his/her work - but not the final product or service. Because in some services it is difficult to make a distinction between the

product and the procedure, the dimension of problem-solving is also used: non-routine problem solving as an essential aspect of work implies high conceptual autonomy, whereas routine problem-solving implies autonomy on the medium level. To address these issues in the Nordic-Baltic Project, each of these dimensions of autonomy was asked separately, using the scale from one to three, and the synthetic coding was carried out by computer according to the original rules of deduction (Kivinen 1989, 295-296).

In this paper two additional marginal groups have been constructed. Marginal group 2 comprises those wage-earners whose occupation would imply a position in the core, but who are not really autonomous. Marginal group 3 is composed of those persons who according to my criteria would be working class, but who could be counted as marginally middle class according to their managerial position in either of Erik Olin Wright's class schemes. In this way the working class has been constructed in as pure form as possible.

Table 1.   Class structure in the Baltic states and in Finland 1994 (%)

	Estonia[*]	Latvia	Lithuania	Finland
Core of NMC	16	12	12	21
Margin 1	4	6	2	14
Margin 2	25	28	29	12
Margin 3	4	6	5	3
Working class	45	40	43	31
Entrepreneurs	5	8	9	20
N	(724)	(791)	(941)	(878)

[*]For Estonia the corrected sample is used because the bias in the original sample would make the middle class too large.

It is clear that this kind of operationalization involves many problems. An adequate operationalization of such historical class criteria would have to be based on extensive comparative analysis of professionalization, work organization, management strategies, etc. However, since this is clearly impossible within the confines of one empirical project, we will have to content ourselves with much more preliminary tools. Therefore the empirical theses and hypothesis presented below are based on the class groups I have identified in my class theory.

Since I have only just started work with the empirical material, the following results are still tentative; their chief purpose is to provide a basis for my further analyses.

The Crystallization or Decomposition of Classes — Preliminary Results and Hypotheses

Table 1 highlights important differences in class structure between Finland and the Baltic states. In Finland the size of entrepreneurial class groups is still essentially larger. There also seem to be many more wage-earners in a clear-cut middle class position. Consequently, the middle classes in general seem to be more important in Finland. On the other hand many professionals and managers in the Baltic states are rather proletarianized. They have no autonomy and in this sense are more alienated than in Finland. The wage earner who does not control his or her labour process is alienated in a very concrete sense. Autonomy is the central goal of all wage-earner struggles concerning the work organization and technology (Kortteinen 1992). The potentially middle class groups have been far less successful in using their power resources in the Baltic states than in Finland. This concerns not only professionals or managers, but craftsmen and women working in care and reproduction are also less autonomous in the Baltic states.

In this sense the new middle classes are much weaker in these countries than in Finland. The same weakness is also reflected in several aspects of class situation. For example, the difference between the incomes of the core of the new middle classes and the working class is significantly smaller in Baltic countries than in Finland.

More generally then, it can be argued that all social classes are weak in post-socialism. A social class is in a strong position when it has achieved stability (1) in terms of ownership or power resources and (2) class situation and (3) when it has powerful organizations to lean back on. In these terms all classes are rather strong in Western Europe. In these countries ownership based on capital is well established, and professional and managerial groups have definite and undisputable privileges over and above the working class. On the other hand, the working class has its own powerful organizations and in this sense forms an important part of civil society. In post-socialist societies, by contrast, the ownership structures are still in the process of taking shape, the wage-earning middle class is weak, and the working class also lacks its own organizations through which it would become incorporated into civil society.

If there were a universal tendency towards fragmentation of stratification and decomposition of classes, post-socialist societies would be much more advanced in this respect than developed capitalist countries. However, a much more fruitful approach is to specify the crystallizing and decomposing tendencies and to try to analyse them both theoretically and empirically in the conditions of post-socialist transition.

According to Jan Pakulski (1993), the recent changes in industrialised West involved:

— the proliferation of small property ownership;
— the credentialization of skills and the professionalization of occupations;
— state regulation, both internal and international;
— increasing consumption and consumption orientations;
— the formation of 'imagined communities' under the impact of the mass media; and
— the mobilization of 'new social movements' and 'new politics'.

In spite of the massive privatization programmes undertaken in the last decade by many Western governments, there is rather little evidence that this would have fundamentally changed the class relations. In the United States and Canada, working class people have long been small shareholders. The same goes now for Britain. The changes in Eastern Europe are definitely far more dramatic. All kinds of small property owners and small shareholders are emerging. How this will affect the relationship between the new middle classes, the petty bourgeoisie and the working class, is largely an empirical issue. Old theoretical disputes about the polarization or blurring of class relations are not very helpful in this context.

Credentialism and professionalism are fundamental processes of class relations. If these strategies are pursued further in the Baltic states, as can be reasonably expected in the light of the empirical results, they will lead towards more crystallized class relations. On the other hand, the economic crisis and the uncertainty that continues to surround educational structures and state employment, for instance, may cause considerable difficulties for professionals and potential professionals. If managers turn their hierarchic positions into real ownership, this could imply a clear class divide within the professional-managerial class. The relationship between the state and private sector may then constitute a key issue with regard to the formation of hegemonic projects (Szelenyi and Szelenyi 1991). Managers and entrepreneurs are currently satisfied with the trends in economic development, whereas professionals are as disappointed as ordinary shopfloor workers.

State interventions have certainly had a fundamental impact on social inequalities and patterns of social conflict in developed capitalist countries. The post-socialist transition is accompanied by a more recent drive towards the expansion of civil rights and open trade.

In Western societies the expansion of civil rights has linked life chances with politically defined and legally protected elements, such as native peoples, racial minorities and women. In the Baltic states issues of citizenship and ethnicity have provided a basis for programmatic identities. It remains to be seen how far these issues will generate permanent cleavages that cut across class identities. It is also possible that the ethnic divisions will come to overlap to a greater extent with class hierarchies, which would fuel forceful political action.

So far the Baltic states have taken a very liberal attitude towards dismantling their protective barriers. However, the rewards and life changes of large categories of producers may be dependent on state-controlled trade protection. This is very much the case with farmers. But this may also serve to unite the owners, managers and workers of particular branches or districts in defence of protective tariffs and state subsidies. In Russia the vast majority of strikes have turned out to be 'directors strikes', with demands orchestrated by senior management and addressed to state bodies of various levels to secure subsidies, tax privileges, cheap state-guaranteed credits, and speedy settlement of the debts to the enterprise (Clarke and Kabalina 1995, 7-8).

'Imagined communities' are worth closer analysis both in the East and in the West. In a sense both consumption and alternative politics seem to be connected to these kinds of identities:

> Under the impact of the mass media, people start to regard themselves as members of communities with shared concerns (for example, Greens), habits (for example, non smokers), tastes (for example, vegetarians) or even some ascriptive characteristics (for example, blacks). Such imagined communities provide identities and even encourage a sense of solidarity and prompt a common action, yet they do not reflect social proximity or shared economic or political position. (Pakulski 1993, 285).

The weakness of classes and other organizations of civil society may make Eastern Europe highly susceptible to a fluctuation of fashions and imagined communities. However, it is also possible that fashions and alternative concerns are for more affluent peoples and individuals. Under the conditions of economic crisis, financial concerns seem more pressing. This may inspire greater political activity among the Baltic people on class-based economic issues such as wage levels, employment security and social welfare policies.

Bibliography

Blom, R. and Kivinen, M. (1990), 'Analytical Marxism and Class Theory', in S.R. Clegg (ed.), *Organization Theory and Class Analysis. New Approaches and New Issues*, Berlin and New York.

Blom, R., Kivinen, M., Melin, H. and Rantalaiho, L. (1992), *The Scope Logic Approach to Class Analysis*, Aldershot & Brookfield USA & Hong Kong & Singapore & Sydney.

Bourdieu, P. (1979), *La Distinction*, Paris.

Clark, T.N. and Lipset, S.M. (1991), 'Are Social Classes Dying?', *International Sociology*, Vol. 6, No 4.

Clark, T.N., Lipset, S.M. and Rempel, M. (1993), 'The Declining Political Significance of Social Class', *International Sociology*, Vol. 8, No 3.

Clarke, S. and Kabalina, V. (1994), *Privatisation and the Struggle of Control of the Enterprise in Russia*, paper for Conference on Russia in Transition: Elites, Classes and Inequalities, Cambridge, 15th-16th December 1994.

Crompton, R. (1991), 'Three varieties of class analysis: comment on R.E. Pahl', *International Journal of Urban and Regional Research*, Vol. 15, pp. 108-113.

Giddens, A. (1973), *The Class Structure of the Advanced Societies*, London.

Goldthorpe, J. (1982), 'On the Service Class, its Formation and Future', in A. Giddens and G. Mackenzie (eds.), *Social Class and the Division of Labour*, Cambridge.

Goldthorpe, J. and Marshall, G. 'The Promising Future of Class Analysis: A Response to Recent Critiques', *Sociology*, Vol. 26, No 3, pp. 381-400.

Goldthorpe, J. (1980), *Social Mobility and Class Structure in Modern Britain*, Oxford.

Gouldner, A. (1979), *The Future of Intellectuals and the Rise of the New Class*, London.

Holton, R.J. and Turner, B.S. (1989), 'Has Class Analysis a Future? Max Weber and the Challenge of Liberalism to Gemeinschaftlich Accounts of Class', in Holton and Turner, *Max Weber on Economy and Society*, London.

Hout, M., Brooks, C. and Manza, J. (1993), 'The Persistence of Classes in Post-Industrial Societies', *International Sociology*, Vol. 8, No 3.

Kautsky, K. (1899), *Bernstein und das Sozialdemokratische Programm. Eine Antikritik*, Stuttgart.

Kivinen, M. (1994), 'Class Relations in Russia', in Piirainen, T. (ed.), *Change and Continuity in Eastern Europe*, Dartmouth, London and New York, pp. 114-147.

Kivinen, M. (1989), *The New Middle Classes and the Labour Process — Class Criteria Revisited*, Department of Sociology, Research Reports 223, University of Helsinki.

Kivinen, M. (1987), *Parempien piirien ihmisiä*, Jyväskylä.

Kivinen, M. (1994), 'Perspektivi razvitija srednogo klassa v Rossij', *Sotsiologitsheskij Zurnal* 2/1994.

Kivinen, M. (1995), *Sosiologia ja Venäjä*, unpublished manuscript.

Kortteinen, M. (1992), *Kunnian kenttä*, Tampere.

Marshall, G. (1991), 'In defence of class analysis: a comment on R.E. Pahl', *International Journal of Urban and Regional Research* Vol. 15, pp. 114-118.

Mills, C.W. (1956), *White Collar. The American Middle Classes*, New York.

Mullins, P. (1991), 'The identification of social forces in development as a general problem in sociology: a comment on Pahl's remarks on class and consumption relations as forces in urban and regional developments', *International Journal of Urban and Regional Research*, Vol. 15, pp. 119-126.

Pahl, R.E. (1989), 'Is the Emperor naked? Some questions on the adequacy of sociological theory in urban and regional research', *International Journal of Urban and Regional Research*, Vol. 13, pp. 709-720.

Pahl, R.E. 'Does Class Analysis without Class Theory have a promising Future? A Reply to Goldthorpe and Marshall', *Sociology*, Vol. 27, pp. 253-258.

Pakulski, J. (1993), 'Mass Social Movements and Social Class', *International Sociology*, Vol. 8, No. 2.

Pakulski, J. (1993), 'The Dying of Class or Marxist Class Theory?', *International Sociology*, Vol. 8, No. 3.

Parsons, T. (1939), 'The Professions and Social Structure', *Social Forces*, Vol. 17, pp. 457-467.

Parsons, T. (1970), 'On Building Social Systems Theory: A Personal History', *Daedalus* 4/1970.

Roemer, J.E. (1981), *A General Theory of Exploitation and Class*, Cambridge. Mass.

Szelenyi, I. and Szelenyi, S. (1991), 'The Vacuum in Hungarian Politics: Classes and Parties', *New Left Review* 187/1991.

Waters, M. (1994), 'Succession in the Stratification System: A Contribution to the "Death of Class" Debate', *International Sociology*, Vol. 9, No. 3.

Willis, Paul (1979), *Learning to Labour. How Working Class Kids Get Working Class Jobs*, Westmead.

Wright, E.O. (1978), *Class, Crisis and the State*, London.

Wright, E.O. (1985), *Classes*, London.

Zaslavskaja, T.I. (1992), 'Socialism, Perestroika and Public Opinion', *Sociological Research* 4/1992.

PART IV

IDENTITY AND LIFESTYLE OF THE MIDDLE CLASSES

15 The Middle Class and Civil Society

MIHAIL CHERNYSH

A Theoretical Background

The middle strata have continued to attract considerable attention among philosophers and sociologists. The challenge of defining the middle class dates back to Aristotle, who was the first to observe the characteristics of the middle stratum and to examine them in the light of their political behaviour. According to Aristotle society is divided into three basic elements: the very rich, the very poor and the mean. The two extreme strata are unlikely to follow a course of moderation and rational thinking. He who greatly excels in beauty, strength, birth or wealth, or on the other hand who is very poor, or very weak, or very much disgraced, Aristotle writes, will find it difficult to follow rational principles. The middle class, on the other hand, is least likely to shrink from rules, or to be over-ambitious. In Aristotle's concept both law evasion and an unrestrained quest for power are 'injuries to the state' (Aristotle 1943). Luxury from the early days of childhood breeds despotic inclinations, poverty is conducive to degradation are therefore probably to violations of the law. Society, torn apart by these two extremes, is likely to be a tyranny where violence is used consistently to enforce the rule of law. The rich are likely to despise the poor, the poor tend to envy and hate the rich and 'nothing can be more fatal to friendship and good fellowship in the states than this'. The use by Aristotle of the term 'fellowship' is notable, for in the parlance of ancient democracies fellowship implied an ability for spontaneous self-organization for the sake of achieving common objectives. It is only by fellowship that things in society are decided peacefully and without causing harm to others. In Aristotle's view the best political community is forced by citizens of the 'middle class and those states are likely to be well-administered'. The middle class is more likely to sustain democracy and democracy flourishes best in states where the middle class is numerous and has a greater share in the government.

The obvious link between the well-being of citizens and their political behaviour has been further researched by polity explorers of modern times. Tocqueville's *Democracy in America* contains a number of passages to this effect. The American nation, he writes, displays a unanimous desire for a better life. Therefore any threat to material prosperity which threatens the Americans' private life causes grave concern. The prosperous part of American society seeks stability and is profoundly interested in maintaining democracy and freedom:

> The Americans see in their freedom a powerful means of achieving greater prosperity. It never enters their head that public matters are not of their concern. On the contrary, they are sure that the main task consists in the formation and support of a government which would allow them to seek out the coveted well-being and which does not ban them from enjoying what they already acquired (Tocqueville 1992, 397).

According to Tocqueville, another basic characteristic of the 'middle strata' worthy of admiration is their respect for professional activity. The dominance of the middle strata breeds in society profound respect for earned money:

> Traditional thinking divides the notions of profit and work. In reality they may be connected and their unity is evident. As soon as work is accepted by all citizens as an inalienable part of human life, it becomes obvious that most citizens work for a salary and therefore, the great gap between professions which exists in aristocratic societies disappears. Although citizens do not become equal they acquire at least one common characteristic' (Tocqueville 1992, 405).

In other words, the professional middle class contributes to the dampening of envy which is detrimental to societal life and inter-class discourse. Like Aristotle, Tocqueville believes that a polarized society breeds political tension. However, he introduces a critical aspect of prosperity dynamics, or mobility as a factor of influence upon the nature of the state and public institutions. Apart from having a certain degree of prosperity, the middle class sustains a system in which a correspondence of workload and earnings is strictly maintained. The link is lost in other types of society where proximity to power or the use of violence become a major source of material well-being.

Observing the values and life patterns of the American middle class, Tocqueville notes that what has been said of the middle class refers to the times of tranquillity when the middle class has a chance to assert its structural position. Not so in the times of crisis. Tocqueville notes that even the democratically-minded Americans display extreme fear of chaos and in times of crisis are likely to give full support to any force with a promise of stability.

The political risks of downward mobility in the middle class have received more attention in modern sociology, which has had the opportunity to observe and analyse the phenomenon. Ralph Dahrendorf speculates at length on the subject in his book 'Modern social conflict' (Dahrendorf 1980). According to him, modern society has for the first time in history come to a situation where state-related professional employment is going down because of new technology. Correspondingly, the middle class is gradually losing its secure position in the middle part of the social hierarchy. Like manual labour, it has to deal with a problem of downward mobility. The result is that in the 1980s, German university graduates found it extremely hard to find jobs compatible with their skills and training. This situation resulted in a growth of alternative lifestyles, particularly in the growth of support for the 'Greens' and other alternative movements. Dahrendorf also links the rise of German terrorism with the middle class crisis of the 1980s. In other words, the middle class maintains and reproduces a system of legitimate entitlements which, if challenged, produce a desire for social change towards more social control, more management, more order.

A more profound analysis is presented by Seymour Lipset in his book *The political man* (Lipset 1981). He argues that the main difference between the middle class and other lower groups in terms of political behaviour is related to three major factors. The first consists in the insecurity of income:

> The relative conservatism of white-collar workers in the United States may be due to their greater job security during the Depression. About 4 % of the white-collar workers were unemployed in 1930 as compared to 13 % of urban unskilled workers. In Germany the middle class group was much more affected by the post-war economic crisis than in the United States. The German white-collar workers tended to turn to the fascist movement rather than to the leftist parties with their doctrinaire emphasis on the proletariat (Lipset 1981, 248).

The second factor affecting the way the middle class contributes to civil society is work satisfaction. By definition middle class occupations are more satisfying than those of either workers or peasants. Therefore there is strong evidence that the middle class is willing to preserve its privileged position by stronger support for the liberal cause. The situation changes when the middle class positions undergo change in the direction of less work satisfaction. In this case the middle stratum is likely to assume a more revolutionary stance with respect to its developmental strategy. Lipset refers to the difference between skilled and unskilled workers in the US: the skilled workers are likely to be more conservative then than the manual workforce (Lipset 1981, 249).

The last factor characterizing the middle class political contribution consists in status assertion. Direct evidence, Lipset writes, of the importance of the status motive in white-collar political behaviour is provided by a study of 'class identification' in the United States where 61 % of white-collar workers called themselves 'middle class', as against only 19 % of manual workers. Lipset quotes German studies which confirm that the white-collar vote swung from the centrist parties to the Nazis under the impact of the

Depression of 1929. There was a strong correlation between the proportion of the unemployed among the white-collar workers in German cities and the Nazi vote. The usual explanation offered by the Germans for this is that the Nazis represented a hope of solving the economic crisis and at the same time for maintaining the status position of the white-collar workers, while the Marxist parties offered them economic gains only at the cost of 'proletarianization'. In other words, the middle class is a 'fair weather' friend of democracy, capable of swinging to other causes if its privileged position in society is challenged by crisis. In these circumstances it shows willingness to support the political force whose agenda is more promising in terms of greater benefits for the middle strata. While in pre-war Germany the alternative was provided by the Nazis, in today's Russia the middle class vote could equally go to the Communists who promise to give more support to state-run enterprises, small-scale private ventures, to provide more subsidies for education and health care, and impose constraints on the expansion of Western culture into the Russian middle class spiritual domains.

It would be wrong to ignore the Marxist perspective of the middle class. This perspective has more most explicitly presented in the works of E.O. Wright (1985). According to his concept, the middle class occupies a set of contradictory positions in a modern capitalist society. On the one hand, it is exploited by the capitalists who use qualified wage earners to raise production efficiency and get more profits. On the other hand, in a new societal situation it possesses skills which enable it to join in extracting a part of surplus value for its own benefits. As a result, in contemporary societies the middle class finds itself in conflictual relationship with the bourgeoisie, but at the same time is unwilling to rock the boat too hard. Its primary interest lies not in the preservation of the status quo, but rather in extending and expanding the dominance of control and intellect. In other words, the middle class is an ambivalent partisan of democracy, capable of political swings if they help to consolidate its power and strengthen its hold over the proletariat.

Summing up the main theoretical assumptions of the above discussion, we may hypothesize that the stance of the middle class vis-à-vis civil society is largely dependent on the ability of democracy to provide conditions for the quantitative economic growth by way of newer technologies and more social control. The crisis conditions threatening the middle class position can destabilize its political attitudes and bring it to the side of either left-wing or, in some conditions, right-wing political forces.

The Russian Democratic Experiment: Middle Class Attitudes

Two theoretical issues deserve attention before we take up the role of the middle class in contemporary Russian society. Firstly, the social discourse in Russia is yet to reach a conclusion on whether there was a middle class in the Soviet Union before the reforms. Unfortunately, the polemics over the issue have been complicated by worsening economic conditions and continuing political tensions. The problem has assumed ideological overtones and any view on the matter is treated as partisan rather than speculative. The clash of ideologies does not provide for a tranquil view of the matter and a rational examination of existing empirical facts. The facts provide reliable evidence of the existence in the Soviet Union of a large group of people who can at least be qualified as quasi-middle class. It was not born out of the labour market as was the middle class of the developed world. It was rather deliberately created to render patrimonial service to the Soviet state, its functions of social control and defence. Prior to the period of reform, the Soviet population held an impressive stratum of educated wage earners, amounting to 25 % of the whole population. The percentage was even higher in Soviet cities, where the educated stratum came second after the Soviet working class. Six out of ten Soviet citizens lived in their own apartments or houses.[1] True, the quality of Soviet high-rise apartments became a by-word among the critics of Soviet society. Nevertheless, it should be borne in mind that the similar standard of living is yet to be reached by the middle class in many developing countries, including such success stories as China and Mexico. Housing construction and massive migration into private apartments have undoubtedly contributed to the embourgeoisement of the Soviet educated class with concomitant changes in attitudes to a functioning market. The Soviet quasi-middle class had access to a number of other tangible material privileges: almost 25 % of educated Russian citizens had land plots and summer cottages. Over 50 % used privileged access to various leisure facilities. The value system of the Soviet educated class to a large extent incorporated a standard set of middle class values. Education and hard work were viewed as prime movers of success in life. In line with Russian traditions, service to society was regarded as the main value of life. In the wake of reforms the Soviet quasi-middle class had to come to terms with a dramatic change of life patterns and, in many cases, with a shift towards a lower standard of living.

Secondly, the other important issue discussed today, no less vehemently, is whether there is a middle class in contemporary Russia. Using empirical evidence we may say that there is a group of population which fits the material standard of middle class existence. It is not large, no more than 10 % of the population. However, it is certainly an important agent of both economic reform and political change. Let us examine its contemporary attitudes.[2]

Economic Agenda

The data show that the Russian middle class is strongly in favour of liberal economy. When asked whether there should be more state control over private business, the middle strata, unlike other lower strata of the population, came firmly against state interference.

Table 1. Will state control over the private sector contribute to improvements in the economic situation? (%)

Attitude	Middle stratum	Lower stratum
Will contribute	62.9	36.9
Will not	24.5	54.3
Don't know	12.6	8.8
Total	100.0	100.0

The middle stratum is less inclined to support assistance for ineffective enterprises.

Table 2. Should enterprises receive assistance from the state? (%)

Attitude	Middle stratum	Lower stratum
Fully agree	36.1	42.2
Agree to some extent	23.7	27.8
Disagree to some extent	19.5	18.7
Fully disagree	10.0	7.0
Don't know	10.7	4.4
Total	100.0	100.0

The possibility of transferring enterprises into the ownership of their workers receives more support from the middle stratum than from other population groups.

The middle stratum does not favour any limitations on imports. Over two-thirds or 67.2 % of the group believe that restrictions will not improve the situation in the economy. In the lower group the corresponding proportion is substantially smaller at 46.5 %.

Table 3. **Must enterprises be transferred into ownership of those who work there? (%)**

Attitude	Middle stratum	Lower stratum
Fully agree	24.8	34.9
Agree to some extent	27.3	24.9
Disagree to some extent	23.1	20.4
Fully disagree	11.9	15.5
Don't know	12.8	4.3
Total	100.0	100.0

The more global orientation of the middle stratum is further confirmed by its attitude towards the possibility of foreign capital investment in the Russian economy. While in the lower strata of the population 38.2 % come out in favour of it with 36.9 % being against, in the middle stratum 69.4 % stand in favour of foreign investment and only 17.0 % are opposed to it.

There is a substantial difference between the middle stratum and the rest of the population in terms of attitudes towards unemployment. 59.5 % believe that it is acceptable and even desirable. In lower stratum this attitude is shared by only 29.2 %.

The middle class favours differences in income if they are stipulated by concomitant labour input: 86.5 % of the strata claim it is acceptable compared to 64 % in other strata.

Summing up, we can say that the middle stratum is more likely to endorse a classical liberal agenda than any other stratum of the population. Its system of economic values is very similar to the corresponding views of the middle class in other countries.

Political Behaviour

The political attitudes of the middle class are less prominent. In the absence of a functioning civil society, the middle class finds it hard to choose its favourite on the political scene.

The proportion of the middle class voting for the party of former Prime Minister Egor Geidar was the largest. The second largest vote fell with Yabloko, another proponent of liberal reforms. One in ten of the middle class stratum voted for Zhirinovsky's Liberal Democratic party, a bad omen for the future. It is obvious that the middle class is unlikely to vote for any party of communist orientation. Another bad omen consists in a large-scale non-participation in elections, testifying to growing apathy.

Table 4.   Which party did you vote for in the last elections? (%)

Party	Middle class	Lower strata
Choice of Russia	19.1	23.5
Liberal Democrats	10.6	9.9
Communists	7.9	3.7
Agrarian party	2.7	0.8
Women of Russia	6.2	1.4
Yabloko (Yavlinsky bloc)	8.6	9.6
PRES (Party of Unity)	1.7	0.8
Democratic party	5.2	4.4
Other	3.7	3.0
Did not vote	34.4	42.7
Total	100.0	100.0

Conclusion

It is obvious that the budding Russian middle class shows the same inclination to support the liberal cause as its counterparts in other countries. However, its numerical weakness does not allow it to exert substantial influence upon the political situation in the country. Potentially, it is a stabilizing force which may guide the development of the country in the right direction. But today, its influence is marginal and in many cases it cannot yet find its own spokesmen on the political scene.

Notes

1.   From here onward, the empirical data will be drawn from the Russian monitoring study based on a representative sample of the Russian population.
2.   The further analysis is based on the data from the Russian monitoring study.

Bibliography

Aristotle (1943), *Politics*, Modern Library, New York, pp. 190-77193.

Tocqueville, A. (1992), *Democracy in America*, Progress, Moscow.

Dahrendorf R. (1980), *Modern Social Conflict*, London.

Lipset, S.M. (1981), *The political man. The social bases of polities*, Johns Hopkins University Press, Baltimore.

Wright, E.O. (1985), *Classes*, Verso.

16 Capitalism and Democracy in Two Baltic Countries

JOUKO NIKULA

Introduction

The collapse of socialism in socialist countries was followed, not initiated, by expectations of the development of market economy and democracy, where democracy was seen both as an inevitable precondition for and as a by-product of market economy. In neo-liberalist thinking the causal necessity of market economy for democracy is based on the simple assumption that in societies where the development of market economy takes place through true openness and competition, political forms will also follow suit. Politics is thus seen as an analogous sphere of society to the economy — openness and reduced control give rise to competition and alternatives. It is up to the consumers, to the people which economic or political actors gain supremacy.

In the economic sphere the governments of most post-socialist countries have followed the path of IMF orthodoxy or four '-izations' (Cowan 1995), with conflicting results. In the sphere of politics and interest representation the situation in the Baltic countries (as in many other countries) is much bleaker, the political field is highly unstable and fragmented, the social movements are weak and large segments of the population are disenchanted with the results of the reforms. In all the Baltic states the nature of politics has been elitist and technocratic, with very weak links to the grassroots level. Other common features have included a strong demagogic flavour in political programmes and a visible ethnic division among the parties. The practical background for this type of 'authoritarian populism' (Hall 1988) has been provided by the emphasis on the role of strong governments to implement the necessary economic reforms and avoidance of fierce political struggles, which would have, according to theorists of 'shock therapy', hampered or even jeopardized the reforms. The price for the success of economic reforms has come in the form of limited opportunities for the organizations of civil society to influence and to articulate their interests.

Richard Rose and his research groups have produced a series of barometers from the post-socialist countries since 1991 with the humble intention of 'measuring the fever of the patients' (and neglecting the causes of the disease?). At least two distinctive features have emerged from the barometers:

265

(1) high levels of support for democracy and market economy during the first year(s) of transition (including the growth of social inequalities), and (2) a growing discrepancy between the support for democracy and support for market economy during the last years. This means that although people are still willing and prepared to support democracy and some of the political institutions (parliament, government, president, etc.), their support for the present economic system has sharply declined to the extent that in most countries, the previous economic system is held in higher regard than the present one.

In this paper I shall be looking at some of the above issues in the context of the Baltic states. The questions I address are as follows: (1) to what extent, if at all, is political legitimacy dependent on material legitimacy; (2) to what extent have previous beliefs or attitudes about social equality and social justice disappeared and been replaced by new, individual, market-oriented beliefs and attitudes; (3) what are the social bases of various social attitudes/beliefs in the Baltic countries: to what extent have the attitudes become detached from one another?

The data sets used in the analyses are the 1993 three-country data that were collected by the Baltic-Nordic project, and an almost identical data set collected by Richard Rose and William Maley in the three Baltic countries in 1993.

Is the Growth of Social Inequalities a Necessary Part of Transformation?

One of the 'systemic sins' of socialism was a distorted mode of equality or egalitarianism: the fact that success and personal wealth was not socially acceptable, and even if it was accepted in some spheres, it was based on non-meritocratic criteria, party-membership, membership of some influential social network in the official economy or the second economy. One form of this distorted equality was the determination of wages on the basis of factors other than skills, competence or education.

There was much confusion among the respondents over the key determining factors of wage levels.

Overall effort and skills were considered the most important issues, i.e. in this respect the respondents did not differ significantly from 'Western values'. However, the collapse of socialism does not represent the rebirth of social justice and equality for people in most post-socialist countries: the majority of them believe that effort and skills are not rewarded (but speculation and activity in the informal economy are), that opportunities to get ahead are far from equal, that people do not get what they need.

Table 1. Factors determining wage increase according to social class, Estonia only (%)

Factor	Professional	White-collar	Blue-collar	Total
Gender	21	12	19	19
Seniority	52	55	46	50
Responsibility	56	60	56	56
Effort	38	44	41	40
Working conditions	50	53	46	49
Education	51	54	45	49
Family size	10	19	17	15

Source: International Project of Social Justice data

Table 2. Opinions on economic justice by country* (%)

Country	Income differentials too large	Effort rewarded	Skills rewarded	People get what they need
Hungary	61.2	33.2	14.5	12.5
Poland	47.7	17.4	19.3	9.3
Russia	38.9	21.8	19.6	4.4
Estonia	43.9	14.1	6.2	2.1

* Adopted from Mason et al. 1995, 121.

Since the transformation mainly affects the economic situation of ordinary citizens, I took overall satisfaction with the economic situation as a criterion variable. In general, people were not satisfied with their economic situation, three respondents out of four said they were rather or very dissatisfied with their economic situation. Those who were satisfied were more often men than women, young (16-29) than older, more likely to be members of the petty bourgeoisie or managers than semi-autonomous workers or workers. Ethnic group did not play any role in this regard.

In both countries managers and the petty bourgeoisie had a more optimistic view of the development of their financial situation than other groups, but for the majority the expected changes were predominantly negative. A very significant difference is seen between Estonia and Latvia: while in Estonia the estimations varied clearly between the classes, there were practically no class differences in Latvia. In this respect it could be argued that these two countries were in totally different phases of the transformation process: in Estonia the process had already started to give rise to social differentiation, while in Latvia all social groups were still experiencing the effects of a declining economic system more than effects of the evolving new system.

Table 3.   Estimation of the development of financial situation since 1988 according to class in Estonia and Latvia (%)

	Improved	Remained same	Declined	Don't know
Petty bourgeoisie				
Estonia	42	13	27	18
Latvia	19	14	54	14
Managers				
Estonia	28	16	40	16
Latvia	17	18	54	11
Semi-autonomous workers				
Estonia	22	12	52	15
Latvia	5	12	67	16
Supervisors				
Estonia	11	25	52	11
Latvia	9	12	70	9
Workers				
Estonia	15	13	61	11
Latvia	9	13	70	9

Legitimation and Material Well-Being

According to Bruszt (1994) there are two major positions concerning the relationship between social and political legitimation. The first, incompatibility thesis, has rather broad support in politological and sociological studies, proposing that economy counts most. Claus Offe (1991) and Jon Elster (1992) have both argued that the transition processes involve closely interwoven processes — a process of rebuilding a nation-state, a process of changing ownership relations (market economy) and a process of establishing functional institutions of regulation and political participation (democracy). According to incompatibility theses, democracy and economic reform are mutually exclusive goals, one or the other must be sacrificed in order to achieve the other. As Blom et al. (1995, 5) note:

> From an 'integration perspective', social integration and system integration are hardly supportive of one another. If social integration focuses on actors and their cooperative or conflictual relationships and system integration on institutions and the compatibility of different structural logics, the time schedules of their changes are very different (Lockwood 1964; Mouzelis 1991; for the concepts of integration, legitimacy and regulation, see Blom 1993).

Difficulties in social integration may arise from two main sources: first, from insufficient and inadequate experience and knowledge about the systemic change attempted; and second, from the increasing separation of market reform, social security and welfare, and so on. Weakening system integration, then, acts to undermine social integration. Time is a very decisive element. If the (hegemonic) societal projects change rapidly and results are slow to come, there is bound to be increased insecurity.

The alternative thesis claims that this is not necessarily the case, but politics has an independent role to play in the transition. This means that even if necessities of economic reform require undemocratic forms of rule, people do not necessarily turn against democracy or the present economic system as long as there are guarantees that their interests are taken into account in one way or another and that they see that there are political alternatives. So, in short, in the evaluation of the economic and political system, the quality of democracy counts at least as much as the state of the economy and material well-being. Bruszt has backed up the latter thesis by producing results according to which support for democracy is significantly higher in Eastern and Central European countries than in Western countries, despite the fact that preconditions for democracy in the former socialist countries are much more undeveloped and despite the fact that the majority of people in these countries consider the former economic system as better than the present one. According to Bruszt the political economy of patience has a wider basis than just the short-term personal evaluations of past and present: it is based on trust on those who coordinate the transformation process. In addition it requires, as already noted, knowledge of and belief in intra-systemic alternatives (that they exist), the cultural or historical socialization of expectations and an ability to cope with unfavourable situations (shortages in socialism, declining levels of living in the present situation, etc).

According to Bruszt then, there is no direct link between the material level of welfare and support for democracy, as Przeworski (1993) has maintained, but the support for democracy is an interplay between political culture, political structure and political performance.

The assumption drawn from the previous paragraphs is that even if the majority of the people are dissatisfied with their economic situation and with the present economic system in general, that does not necessarily mean that they do not support democratic institutions and democratic principles.

Table 4.   Evaluation of economic systems in Latvia and Estonia by social group (%) *)

	Estonia White-collar	Estonia Blue-collar	Latvia White-collar	Latvia Blue-collar
Past	52	69	58	67
Present	43	40	23	22
Future	83	75	70	71

* only those who evaluate the system as better

Source: Nationalities in the Baltic countries data set (1993).

In both countries the past economic system is held in higher regard than the present one, but in Estonia the present system has more legitimacy than in Latvia, which lends further support to the picture of a differential pace of transformation in the respective countries. In both countries only one in five respondents were pleased with the present political system. This is also consistent with the result according to which the level of trust in both countries was generally very low regardless of social class, ethnic group and level of satisfaction with the economic situation.

Table 5.   Support for political institutions according to economic satisfaction in Estonia and Latvia (%)

	Satisfied Estonia	Satisfied Latvia	Unsatisfied Estonia	Unsatisfied Latvia
Trust				
Parliament	30	31	17	25
Government	31	33	19	26
Trade unions	14	20	15	14

The levels of trust differ somewhat between those who are satisfied and those who are not, but more important than that is the finding that the level of trust is low even among the former. Differences in levels of trust are greater in Estonia than in Latvia, which probably has to do with the fact that the reforms started much earlier in Estonia than in Latvia. Therefore the consequences are more clearly felt in Estonia than in Latvia, where the situation at that time was more 'frozen'.

However, the above results imply that support for democracy — measured in terms of trust in its institutions — is not to any great extent dependent on economic satisfaction or dissatisfaction. People's confidence in the political elite and in their ability to coordinate the transformation process was not very high at the time of the survey, indeed one could argue that democracy came close to the verge of losing its legitimacy. This interpretation is supported by the result that one-fifth of white-collar and blue-collar workers in both countries saw that the suspension of Parliament might be possible and almost two in three respondents felt that a strong leader would be better than Parliament for the development of the country. However, only a minority of respondents would have been prepared to accept the suspension of the parliamentary system.

Social Goals and Social Justices

The issues of social justice are closely interwoven with the above issues of support for democracy and the market economy, with the extent to which a newly-born democracy guarantees the realization of social justice. The second important issue is the extent to which the concept of social justice is understood in the same or in different ways in different social groups and by people in post-socialist and 'Western' countries.

If prevailing notions of the 'mentalities' and social attitudes of people in post-socialist countries were correct, then those people would probably be more paternalistic than they are, i.e. they would attach more importance to the role of the state in the provision of social welfare, employment etc., and they would attach more importance to equality than to the importance of social differences and individual responsibility. On the other hand, it is clear that these attitudes are directly linked to the person's social position and to the amount of social and other forms of capital accessible to that person so that low-skilled and elderly workers are more paternalistic and egalitarian than high-skilled workers and entrepreneurs.

The level of economic satisfaction does not influence attitudes towards various social goals, but both groups consider privatization and market economy as important. Interestingly enough, both groups also consider full employment and satisfying the population's basic needs as paramount, which may seem to be at variance with the goals of market economy and privatization. There is a clear difference between the indigenous population and ethnic minorities in that the former attaches far more importance to market economy and privatization, whereas Russians, for example, consider full employment and basic needs as much more important than privatization or market economy. All groups stressed the importance of combating crime and problems of social order.

Table 6. **Evaluation of social goals according to level of economic satisfaction in Estonia (E) and Latvia (L) (%)**

Goals	Satisfied		Unsatisfied	
	Estonia	Latvia	Estonia	Latvia
(important/very imp.)				
Market economy	84	83	79	75
Privatization	80	84	70	68
Political democracy	60	65	54	54
Full employment	73	79	80	84
Basic needs	89	90	94	91
Social order	90	94	90	90

Table 7. **Opinions about social priorities according to level of economic satisfaction in Estonia (E) and Latvia (L) (%)**

	Satisfied		Unsatisfied	
	Estonia	Latvia	Estonia	Latvia
Favours				
A) Equal standard of living	8	14	13	22
B) Differences	75	72	61	63
A) Income equality	14	16	17	30
B) Differences	71	60	50	50
A) Individual responsibility	35	42	17	27
B) Social safety-net	53	43	71	61

Opinions concerning social priorities were also very similar in both groups: both accepted the growth of social inequalities in standards of living and in incomes, and both favoured state-sponsored safety nets instead of full individual responsibility for well-being. From these two tables the conclusion can be drawn that (1) at least so far the differences in opinions have not grown very wide, and (2) people are quite willing to accept market economy and all its consequences, provided that they are guaranteed the means for coping with the negative consequences.

Differences of Opinion and Their Determinants

Intuitively, one could argue that attitudes towards market economy, privatization and consequently confidence in democratic institutions are inversely related to one another, so that the worse off you are, the less you have faith in market economy and democratic institutions. The discussion below looks at these in Estonia and in Latvia, addressing the question of how far such structural aspects as class, sex, education or age are related to attitudes towards market economy, privatization, full employment, etc. and how far these issues are related to economic satisfaction. The other aspect discussed is the relationship of the above issues to confidence in such institutions as parliament and government.

The results clearly suggest that in Estonia, attitudes towards market economy, democratic institutions and the results of the transformation process are more clearly differentiated according to social position than is the case in Latvia, where no such distinctions can be made (see Appendix).

In both countries the level of trust in parliament and government are closely related to subjective evaluations of personal economic situation (beta-value for Estonia -.15, for Latvia -.12). Other variables such as class, level of vocational training, age and gender show a very weak or no relationship to the level of confidence in either country. This result implies that it is the level of material welfare or material legitimation that largely determines the level of confidence in democratic institutions.

This interpretation is supported by the latest results from various elections in Hungary, Poland, Estonia, Lithuania, etc., where the determining factor for political changes has been popular disappointment with the results of privatization and the negative impacts of the reform on their standard of living. However, economic satisfaction only explains 12 % of the variation in the attitudes, so there still remain other factors that determine attitudes apart from economic satisfaction. I am inclined to agree then with the standpoint of Bruszt rather than with the views of those who consider legitimation merely as a question of material well-being.

The overall picture that emerges from the results is that attitudes both in Estonia and even more so in Latvia are rather mixed. On the one hand there is a clear and strong commitment to market economy and democracy, but at the same time authoritarian forms of government are quite widely supported. There is also much support for heavy state intervention in social policy instead of individual responsibility. In Estonia entrepreneurs (young and male) together with managers (and to some extent also farmers) seem to be the most eager supporters of market economy, and they also seem to be relatively satisfied with the direction and the results of the transformation. This confirms earlier findings and interpretations (Szelenyi 1991; Toth 1990) according to which these two represent the most dynamic groups in the reconstruction of market economy in post socialist societies because they have the relevant social capital (networks, knowledge and financial resources).

The mixture of pro-market and paternalist attitudes do not represent anything like post-communist 'schizophrenia' or confusion, but are more a reflection of the actual situation where strong demands to dismantle most of the welfare systems were voiced by the ruling political elites of these countries.

I agree with Morawski (1994, 126-128) who maintains that it is not a matter of the remnants of state-socialist mentality or populism of any sort, but rather clear-headed pragmatic realism: people wish to have some certainty about their living conditions. This interpretation is further confirmed by the information on people's estimation on responsible actors in various social services: they believe that the municipality (and also the state) should take care of housing, child care, education, elderly and medical care.

People in general have nothing against private ownership or market economy, but they are not convinced by the statements of 'ultra liberals' who claim that a total dismantling of state ownership is a precondition for future prosperity. The state and market are not seen as mutually contradictory, but rather as complementary institutions. According to Morawski the state is expected in all post-socialist countries to be active in the social sphere. As Morawski writes:

> People seem to be prepared to support the institutional system and its programs of transformation on the condition that the system takes care about their own problems, above all their social problems. (Morawski 1994, 124).

Bibliography

Blom, R., Melin, H. and Nikula, J. (1995), 'The Green Banana of the Baltic countries — Obstacles to capitalist development', in R. Blom, H. Melin, J. Nikula (eds.), *Between Plan and Market*, de Gruyter, Berlin.

Bruszt, L. (1994), *Why on Earth would Eastern Europeans support Capitalism — Democracy, Capitalism and Public Opinion*, mimeo CEU/Budapest.

Cowan, P. (1995), 'Neo-liberal Theory and Practice for Eastern Europe', *New Left Review* no 213/September, pp. 3-60.

Elster, J. (1992), 'The Necessity and Impossibility of Simultaneous Economic Reforms and Political Reform', in Greenberg et al. (eds.), *Constitutionalism and Democracy*, OUP/New York.

Hall, Stuart (1988), *The Hard Road to Renewal*, Verso, London.

Kluegel, J.R., Mason, D.S. and Wegener, B. (1995), *Social Justice and Political Change — Public Opinion in Capitalist and Post-Communist States*, de Gruyter, New York.

Morawski, W. (1994), 'Citizenship-Building in Former Socialist Countries', in *The Transformation of Europe — Social Conditions and Consequences*, IFIS Publishers, Warszawa.

Muller, K. (1992), 'Modernising eastern Europe', *Archives Europeannes de Sociologie*, XXXIII, no 1/1992.

Rose, R. and Maley, W. (1992), *Nationalities in the Baltic states: a survey study*, University of Stratchlyde, Centre for the Study of Social Policy, Working Papers no 222, University of Stratchlyde.

Appendix

Table 1.   Beta-values of background variables in relation to attitudes in Estonia and Latvia

Privatization	Estonia	Latvia
Age	.05	-.02
Vocational training	-.06	-.07
Class (Wright)	.12	-.06
Gender	.10	.06
Economic satisfaction I	.11	.06
Economic satisfaction II	-.03	-.11

Market economy		
Age	-.04	-.03
Vocational training	-.05	-.03
Class	-.11	.09
Gender	.02	.14
Economic satisfaction I	.10	.06
Economic satisfaction II	.00	-.04

Full employment		
Age	-.17	-.09
Vocational training	.11	.14
Class	-.15	.00
Gender	-.08	-.08

Trust to government		
Age	.05	-.04
Vocational training	-.01	-.02
Class	.00	-.03
Gender	-.01	.02
Economic satisfaction I	-.01	-.02
Economic satisfaction II	-.16	-.12

Confidence in parliament		
Age	.03	-.06
Vocational training	.00	.00
Class	.02	-.02
Gender	-.00	.01
Economic satisfaction I	-.01	-.00
Economic satisfaction II	-.15	-.12

Table 2.   **Opinions about social priorities according to social group (%)/Variables q009-q015**

Priority:	Estonia White-collar	Estonia Blue-collar	Latvia White-collar	Latvia Blue-collar
Equality	7.8	10.9	9.0	11.3
Inequalities	90.0	87.5	88.9	84.1
Individual responsibility	51.7	42.2	47.3	45.7
State responsibility	44.2	55.4	47.6	47.3
State ownership	10.4	14.2	8.8	14.1
Private ownership	75.6	72.0	72.0	68.6
Economic efficiency	57.0	41.0	57.0	46.4
Security	39.9	55.0	36.5	44.4
Tax relief	33.6	35.2	23.1	27.6
Social services	54.8	52.8	59.1	49.7
Threat = prices	62.2	53.7	22.3	24.7
Threat = unemployment	33.7	43.3	62.8	67.5
N	569	606	553	529

Source: Nationalities in the three Baltic countries, Rose & Maley 1993.

Table 3.   **Estimation of the development of financial situation according to the extent of satisfaction to financial situation**

	Satisfied		Unsatisfied	
	Estonia	Latvia	Estonia	Latvia
Improved	58	44	6	2
Unchanged	25	29	8	6
Declined	10	13	79	80
Don't know	7	14	7	12
Total	100	100	100	100
N	209	159	950	1179

17 Class Differences in Consciousness and Reproduction in the Baltic Countries

RAIMO BLOM

Phases of Change

The post-socialist transformations in Eastern and Central Europe have given rise to widespread hopes of a better life. The expectations have comprised both the basic rights of freedom and association and material living conditions. Although the polarization of reproduction conditions and the worsened economic situation of large parts of the population was the rule during the progress of transformation (for an overview of the studies, see Srubar 1994), social consciousness changed in a different way and often cyclically.

In the first phase the change has been a process of value unification. This is true most particularly of the Baltic countries. The reasons lay not only in the hopes attached to the formation of a market society and political democracy, but also in the sense of community that grew up out of the struggle for independence, socio-cultural autonomy and the process of nation-building. The feelings of historical foe and historical justice strengthened that value cohesion.

The story told in Polish and Hungarian studies, however, was one of rapid unilinear change of social consciousness. Yet the changes were not random. The deficits of material well-being were penetrating into people's consciousness. Promises were not being kept. The waiting span shortened. Interests were now shaped mainly by the immediate situation and 'by personal experience rather than by hopes and apprehensions. The myth of the market was replaced by the privatization of the state sector, unemployment, recession, shops full of goods and many empty wallets' (Kolarska-Bobinska 1994, 134).

There are plenty of reasons affecting the evaluation of the new situation. These include the immediate economic difficulties in family reproduction, worries about jobs, lacking opportunities for social mobility, lost personal hopes, indecision and socio-political apathy.

However, there are also many reasons to argue that support for reforms and the worsened personal situation are different things. People assess the impacts of the transformation process on the economy as a whole more positively than the effects it had on their own situation and that of their families (Kolarska-Bobinska 1994, 129-131).

On the basis of an extensive literature review Laszlo Bruszt (1995) identifies two lines of theoretical argumentation in the explanations offered in support of capitalism in post-socialist countries. The first theory (the 'incompatibility thesis') says that the support is determined by the changes in structural position and the short-term payoffs that the reforms are capable to deliver. The second theory (labelled by several authors as 'the political economy of patience') says that the support is not a direct function of changing socio-economic positions, and furthermore the democratic polity is not about mere re-presentation of people's short-term interests.

Both these theories need the state. The first considers the autonomous transformative state as necessary, but democracy undermines the autonomy that is required of the state. In the second line of thought the democratic state is the prime mediator between the changing economy and lasting support for capitalism. The democratic process itself has plenty of means to influence the support. The main thing is trust in political institutions and in actors playing a key role in the political process. There are also several other factors that are capable of inducing toleration and patience, such as perceptions of past experience, (low) evaluations of alternative routes, etc.

Bruszt's analysis of data from 11 nations seems to support the 'patience thesis'. His empirical analysis also confirms the primary importance of the trust variables in explaining the support of capitalism in Eastern Europe.

Underlying different theories are also questions about class and the social differentiation of positions and consciousness. Even if they have no direct influence on support for social reforms, they certainly do have an impact on the space of possible political/democratic manoeuvring, i.e. on initiatives, mechanisms of inclusion, feelings of responsibility and on the presentation and evaluation of alternative programmes. This is the point where our empirical diagnosis comes in.

Problems and Analysis

Our empirical analysis is concerned with attitudes and beliefs related to societal goals, future social threats and risks and social alienation. These are examined below through factor analysis, which also provides the basis for our consciousness scales. The next step is to examine class differentiation consciousness by using the class model proposed by Erik Olin Wright. Then, the amount of class differentiation in consciousness and in reproduction (incomes) is compared. Finally, group differentiation within the economically non-active population and the relative influence of common background variables (sex, age, education, place of residence) are compared with the effect of class. The main problems addressed in the empirical analysis are as follows:

1. Dimensions of consciousness
2. Class differentiation of consciousness
3. Comparison of class differentiation in the fields of consciousness and reproduction
4. Importance of class compared with (a) cleavages within the non-active population and (b) the importance of social background factors.

In addition to the questions of class differentiation, the analysis aims to add fragmentary pieces of evidence towards the diagnosis of change in the Baltic countries.

Dimensions of Consciousness

The purpose was to describe the mental atmosphere in the Baltic countries and then proceed to construct new variables (scales) for comparative and structural analysis. The starting point was provided by the materials collected from the three Baltic surveys as one single data set. This means that the analysis does not exactly fit any individual Baltic country. On the other hand, if it does yield meaningful dimensions, it will make possible the comparative treatise.

The attitude variables covered the following areas (for the questions used, see Appendix):

— the most urgent goals of social development
— how important are certain things for getting ahead in one's society
— main risks and threats of the transition period
— the demands for future economic and political elites
— individual vs. social responsibility
— attitudes to politics and power.

The first step of factor analysis was to count Pearson's correlation coefficients, then to calculate factor matrices using the principal component method, and finally to rotate the factors to find maximally different dimensions. The rotation method was orthogonal. Varimax converged in 14 iterations.

There appeared to be nine factors that could be interpreted meaningfully. They explained 41.5 % of the variance; the first factor explained 10.4 %, the second 6.8 % of the variance. The ninth factor explained 3.0 % of the variance.

The following presents a brief interpretation of the factors, followed by a comparisons of the Baltic countries according to the factor-based scales.

The following symbols are used in the presentation of the factors:
E = elite; the desired features of the new elite
G = goals; the importance of different goals of social development
R = risks; seriousness of the goals and threats of the transition period
S = success; importance of different conditions (factors) influencing success

I Factor: ORDER AND NEEDS (ORD)

93/9	G:	Fighting crime	.78
93/8	G:	Elementary needs	.68
93/4	G:	Social order	.66
93/10	G:	Human rights	.58
93/6	G:	Full employment	.47
93/11	G:	Settling of national relations	.37

The first factor is very clearly the dimension of two related sets of societal goals: (1) to secure the social order and (2) to take care of social needs. These tasks reflect hopes attached to two basic functions of the state: the original repressive order securing the Leviathan and the later welfare state.

II Factor: SOCIAL SECURITY (SEC)

99/4	R:	Poverty	.76
99/3	R:	Decline of social security	.74
99/1	R:	Unemployment	.70
99/2	R:	Pollution	.49

The second factor describes the main risks and threats to Baltic societies. The three most important of these risks point at shortcomings of social security. The fourth variable brings environmental considerations into the picture.

III Factor: ETHNIC CONFLICTS & POLITICAL INSTABILITY (ETH)

99/5	R:	National conflicts	.74
99/7	R:	Uncertain political situation	.72
93/11	G:	Settling of national relations	.54
99/8	R:	Influence of foreign capital	.49

This factor combines the problem of national conflicts to the threat of political instability. It is interesting that the risks seen in the influence of foreign capital also appears in this dimension.

IV Factor: MODERN STATE (MOD)

93/2	G:	Privatization	.70
93/1	G:	Market economy	.66
93/5	G:	Integration into the EU	.63
93/3	G:	Political democracy	.61

This is the locus of the main goals of post-socialist transformation. The formation of capitalist market relations and political relations called (Western) democracy are expected to materialize. The topical question of EU integration is now also part of the pattern.

IX Factor: APATHY

82/3	Apathy 2	.69
82/1	Apathy 1	.69
82/7	Consumer consciousness	.49

The feelings of powerlessness and low citizenship competence are combined with an anti-corporation attitude within this factor.

The first two factors cover about 41 % of the covariance explained by the nine factors that could be interpreted. They cover about 62 % of the covariance explained by the five factors used here as the basis for the attitude scale.

The attitude scales used in the following are constructed out of sum-scales according to the best weights of each factor.

The first two factors focus on the basic material conditions of social life, different aspects of security and the satisfaction of basic needs. The first and the most important factor moves at the level of needs. The second focuses on comparable aspects of social life that are seen as future threats.

It is interesting to observe that the main aspects raised in the public debate on 'transition' do not appear until the fourth factor where we find a combination of markets (including the EU) and liberal democracy. A comparison with the importance of the first two factors suggests that security and material reproduction are now more important to the respondents' everyday life than the ideals of a liberal state.

The dimension of social apathy is also included in the analysis. The main reason for this is that this aspect has been widely examined in earlier studies on post-socialism.

Variation in Social Consciousness and Reproduction Conditions by Class Groups

The indicators of consciousness are the five attitude scales formed on the basis of the dimensions discussed above. The main indicator of the level of reproduction is that of net incomes. It is clear that it is not the best possible indicator even in the case of the economically active population, and obviously it cannot be used for an examination of the group differences of the economically non-active population.

The following tables show that the differences between the (Wrightian) class groups[1] (for an operational definition, see Melin 1995, 31) in consciousness variables are quite small. In addition, the patterns of these differences are not regular. The directions of the differences are mainly consistent with expectations. The working class receives higher means on the security scale and the apathy scale than the petty bourgeoisie and managers and lower means on the dimension of modern state. The Wrightian intermediate class groups of wage workers vary in their location by dimension and by country.

Before moving on to compare the findings a brief comment is in order on the class group differences on each attitude dimension.

Table 1. Means of ORD by class group in the Baltic countries

	ESTONIA		LATVIA		LITHUANIA	
Petty bourg	25.2	(61)	26.5	(58)	26.6	(79)
Managers	25.5	(155)	26.7	(109)	26.3	(102)
Adv managers	26.0	(80)	26.8	(27)	26.6	(31)
Non-hier dm	26.9	(77)	27.1	(75)	26.6	(85)
Superv	26.6	(68)	26.4	(42)	26.2	(41)
Semi-auton empl	26.6	(97)	27.0	(43)	26.7	(39)
Working class	26.6	(558)	26.5	(424)	26.3	(557)

On the ORD dimension Estonia differs to some extent from the cases of Latvia and Lithuania. Managers and the petty bourgeoisie are less concerned about the societal goals of order and the satisfaction of basic needs than the other groups. In Latvia and in Lithuania, the differences by class groups are rather small.

In Estonia SEC is even more important to semi-autonomous employees and to non-hierarchical decision-makers than to the working class. In Latvia and Lithuania only managers proper differ from the rest of wage workers.

Table 2.   Means of SEC by class group in the Baltic countries

	ESTONIA		LATVIA		LITHUANIA	
Petty bourg	16.2	(62)	17.5	(59)	17.5	(80)
Managers	16.2	(160)	17.2	(109)	17.1	(102)
Adv managers	16.6	(80)	17.9	(28)	17.1	(32)
Non-hier dm	17.4	(79)	17.7	(78)	17.6	(85)
Superv	16.9	(68)	17.8	(43)	17.1	(41)
Semi-auton empl	17.4	(98)	18.1	(45)	17.7	(39)
Working class	17.1	(571)	17.9	(425)	17.6	(558)

Table 3.   Means of ETH by class group in the Baltic countries

	ESTONIA		LATVIA		LITHUANIA	
Petty bourg	13.7	(62)	15.2	(58)	14.3	(80)
Managers	13.6	(160)	14.7	(108)	14.0	(101)
Adv managers	13.5	(80)	15.4	(28)	14.9	(32)
Non-hier dm	14.8	(78)	14.2	(77)	14.5	(84)
Superv	14.5	(68)	15.1	(43)	14.4	(40)
Semi-auton empl	14.4	(98)	15.5	(44)	14.6	(39)
Working class	14.6	(566)	15.1	(422)	14.1	(558)

On the dimension of ETH the dividing line runs between both managerial groups and the petty bourgeoisie vs. other class groups. In Latvia and Lithuania there are no significant differences.

Table 4.   Means of MOD by class group in the Baltic countries

	ESTONIA		LATVIA		LITHUANIA	
Petty bourg	16.2	(62)	15.8	(56)	15.6	(80)
Managers	15.7	(159)	16.0	(107)	15.6	(102)
Adv managers	15.2	(79)	15.6	(27)	15.3	(32)
Non-hier dm	15.1	(77)	15.1	(76)	14.8	(85)
Superv	15.9	(67)	15.0	(43)	15.5	(41)
Semi-auton empl	15.6	(97)	15.5	(43)	15.4	(39)
Working class	15.0	(563)	15.0	(421)	14.5	(556)

On the dimension of MOD the supervisors are allied with the petty bourgeoisie and managers in supporting markets and democracy. In Latvia we find that supervisors and in Lithuania non-hierarchical decision-makers do not differ from the working class in MOD.

Table 5. Means of APAT by class group in the Baltic countries

	ESTONIA		LATVIA		LITHUANIA	
Petty bourg	10.7	(61)	12.0	(59)	11.2	(78)
Managers	10.5	(160)	11.1	(108)	11.1	(101)
Adv managers	11.2	(78)	11.5	(28)	11.5	(30)
Non-hier dm	11.6	(77)	11.5	(78)	11.3	(83)
Superv	11.8	(68)	11.7	(43)	11.9	(40)
Semi-auton empl	11.7	(97)	11.4	(44)	11.5	(39)
Working class	12.1	(568)	11.7	(425)	11.7	(556)

In APAT the differences between managers (and the petty bourgeoisie) from the working class and also from other wage worker groups are bigger than in the other Baltic countries.

To make the overall picture clearer I have added (net) incomes and counted the differences between the means of the working class and managers divided by the (total) standard deviations by country. The main point, as far as I can see, emerges clearly enough from the table even if in some cases the petty bourgeoisie differs more from the working class than managers and in some cases the other wage worker groups (mainly non hierarchical decision makers and semi-autonomous employees) do not differ from the working class.

Table 6. Class effect on reproduction and consciousness measured by the difference between the working class and managers in relation to the standard deviation in each country

	ESTONIA	LATVIA	LITHUANIA
Incomes	.83	.79	.85
ORD	.35	-.09	.01
SEC	.32	.32	.22
ETH	.34	.12	.03
MOD	-.27	-.40	-.42
APAT	.66	.29	.29

There are some clear empirical findings to be made from the table. The class differences in consciousness scales are quite small. They are somewhat larger in Estonia than in the other Baltic countries, and very small in Lithuania. The exception to the rule is the clearly greater class difference in ORD and APAT in Estonia than in Latvia and Lithuania.

The main finding, however, is that the differences in incomes (in reproduction) are wider than the differences in consciousness. As far as reproduction is concerned the result is in line with earlier findings (Blom 1995a and Blom 1995b) where the strata differences between managers, skilled workers and unskilled workers are compared with a larger set of variables (autonomy and mental and physical stress at work, possibilities of career mobility and job security, sources of incomes, etc.) describing different aspects of work and reproduction situation. In these earlier analyses the general conclusion was that there has emerged a cumulative hierarchic model in the distribution of work and reproduction conditions in the Baltic countries (Blom 1995a, 16).

The Baltic countries have a huge economically non-active population. Within this population one can detect greater differences in consciousness than between the class groups of the economically active population. The main differences are those between students on the one hand, and pensioners and the unemployed, on the other (see Appendix Tables 2-6). The differences are bigger than those between class groups in the economically active population at least in ORD in Estonia and Latvia, in SEC in all countries, in MOD in Estonia and Lithuania and in APAT in Latvia and Lithuania, as measured by the difference between students vs. pensioners/unemployed.

Class, Social Background and the Differentiation of Consciousness and Reproduction

Tables 7 and 8 compare the significance of class with that of social background variables. The class variables are dichotomized dummy variables. In the group of reproduction variables, there are in addition to incomes three variables that are based on more subjective evaluations of one's situation.

The correlation tables tell four general things: (1) the correlations of at least some background variables are as high as those of class variables and in many cases higher. (2) Measured by the correlations of background and class variables with incomes, the differences in reproduction are bigger than those in consciousness. (3) The correlations of class variables show that the main and the only clear division line based on class group runs between managers (and in many cases the petty bourgeoisie) and the working class. The correlations representing the middle class groups are insignificant. (4) In most of the cases the correlations are higher in Estonia than in Latvia and Lithuania.

Table 7. The correlations between social background & class and consciousness

	ORD			SEC			ETH			MOD			APAT		
	EST	LAT	LIT	EST	LAT	LIT	EST	LAT	LIT	EST	LAT	LIT	EST	LAT	LIT
Ethnicity	-.30**	-.12	-.20	-.23**	.03	-.11	-.41**	-.16**	-.26**	.13**	.17**	.06	-.25**	-.02	-.00
Gender	-.08**	.00	-.04	-.18***	-.13**	-.08*	-.09**	-.06	.01	.11**	.15**	.04	-.10**	-.06	-.05
Age	.11**	.09*	.06	.14***	.09**	.10**	.04	.01	.00	-.04	.01	-.03	.11**	.01	.03
Place of residence	.12**	.02	.15***	.01	-.09**	-.07*	.18***	.00	.08*	-.01	.00	.10**	.16**	-.09*	-.06
Vocational education	-.06*	-.06	.09**	-.08**	-.21***	-.06	-.06*	-.06	-.01	.10**	.10**	.20**	-.09***	-.09***	-.05
Petty bourgeois	-.09**	-.01	.02	-.07*	-.03	-.00	-.05	.02	.01	.09**	.06	.09**	.05	.05	-.05
Managers	-.11**	.02	-.01	-.11**	-.10**	-.06	-.10**	-.04	-.02	.06*	.12**	.10**	-.09*	-.09*	-.08*
Advisor managers	-.03	.01	.01	-.03	.01	-.04	-.08*	.03	.05	-.01	.03	.03	.00	-.01	-.00
Non-hier. decision-m.	.06	.05	.02	.05	-.01	.01	.04	-.09*	.03	-.02	-.02	-.01	.02	-.02	-.03
Supervisors	.02	-.02	-.01	-.00	-.00	-.04	.01	.01	.01	.06	-.02	.05	.01	.00	.04
Semi-autonomous	.03	.03	.03	.06*	.03	.01	.01	.04	.03	.03	.02	.04	.01	-.03	-.01
Working class	.08**	-.05	.03	.06*	.07*	.06	.10**	.03	-.04	-.12**	-.11**	-.16**	.19**	.06	.09**

* — Signif. LE .05
** — Signif. LE .01
The direction of 'ethnicity' is native — non-native and 'place of residence' urban — rural.

Table 8.   Correlations between social background & class and reproduction situation in the Baltic countries

	INCOMES			WORRIED ABOUT JOB			CHANGE OF ECON. SIT.			SATISF. WITH ECON. SIT.		
	EST	LAT	LIT	EST	LAT	LIT	EST	LAT	LIT	EST	LAT	LIT
Ethnicity	-.04	-.05	-.04	.35**	.14**	.02	.12**	.03	.09**	.10**	-.01	.02
Gender	.22**	.23**	.27**	.14**	.04	.06	.14**	.07	.15**	.11**	.10**	.13**
Age	-.01	-.03	-.08*	-.10**	-.03	-.08*	-.30**	-.14**	-.27**	-.02	-.00	-.14**
Place of residence	.16**	.15**	.22**	-.11**	-.00	-.02	.04	.06	-.03	-.01	.05	-.05
Vocational education	.18**	.13**	.10**	-.01	.11**	.05	.08*	.10**	.07*	.03	.11**	-.02
Petty bourg.	.18**	.15**	.26**	.12**	.06	.15**	.15**	.07	.19**	.09**	.04	.20**
Managers	.19**	.20**	.23**	.12**	.11**	.10**	.18**	.16**	.18**	.15**	.12**	.14**
Advisor-managers	.06	-.01	-.01	.10**	-.05	-.00	.05	-.07	.04	.06	-.05	.02
Non-hier. decision-m.	-.05	-.01	.01	-.02	.06	.02	-.03	.08*	.02	-.01	.02	-.00
Supervisors	-.02	.04	.07*	-.04	-.03	.00	-.02	-.03	.02	.00	-.02	.01
Semi-auton.	-.02	-.04	.00	.02	.05	.04	.02	-.05	.02	-.01	-.02	-.00
Working class	-.20**	-.20**	-.31**	-.17**	-.13**	-.18**	-.20**	-.13**	-.26**	-.17**	-.07*	-.21**

* — Signif. LE .05
** — Signif. LE .01
The variables grow to the directions 'high incomes', 'not worried about the job', 'positive change in economic situation after 1988' and 'satisfied with economic situation'.

This concerns particularly the correlations of ethnicity and also those of sex and place of residence. Likewise, the difference between managers and the working class is usually bigger in Estonia than in the other Baltic countries.

The correlations are not of the same magnitude with the different consciousness and reproduction variables. On the other hand, the directions of the correlations are mainly consistent with expectations.

The correlations with ethnicity are clearly higher in Estonia than in Latvia and Lithuania. In ORD, SEC, ETH and APAT they vary from .25 to .41, i.e. higher than the correlations with any other class or background variables.

We can pick up some more detailed results here. In ORD place of residence shows a noticeable correlation in Estonia and Lithuania but not in Latvia. Class (correlation of managers compared with that of working class) matters only in the case of Estonia.

The relations of social background and class with SEC are quite similar to those with ORD. However, sex and education are an exception, showing higher correlations. The significance of vocational training is particularly high in Latvia.

Place of residence matters in ETH only in Estonia. Workers are more concerned about the prospect of ethnically-based political instability than managers.

The correlations with MOD are opposite to those found for SEC (and ORD): here managers are the supporters and workers are against. Men (except Lithuania) and the educated are probable supporters of markets and the modern state.

Correlations with APAT are clearer in Estonia than in Latvia and Lithuania. In Estonia women, the elderly, rural dwellers and workers are more inclined to apathy than others. In Lithuania it is only the class difference between managers and the working class that matters. In Latvia female sex and a low level of education also shows positive correlations with apathy.

In the group of reproduction indicators the most objective indicator, i.e. incomes, shows rather high correlations. The dividing line between managers (and the petty bourgeoisie) vs. working class is very clear. The difference of correlation varies from .40 to .55. The correlation with sex, highlighting the weaker position of women compared to men, is also high (from .22 to .27). In addition, place of residence and level of education (especially in Estonia) matters.

The other correlations with reproduction variables are less clear than those with incomes. The correlations with the variable 'worried about job' are in most cases country-specific. Sex and place of residence matter only in Estonia, education only in Latvia and ethnicity in Estonia (.35) and Latvia (.12). The middle class group variable 'advisor managers' (being less worried about job) has significance only in Estonia.

The correlation with change of economic situation reveals the significance of age. In the case of the elderly, the change has been worse than in the group of the young. The extent of the class difference between managers and the working class is also noticeable. The differences of the corresponding correlation vary from .32 (Latvia) to .44 (Lithuania).

On the dimension of satisfaction with the economic situation, the correlations are weaker than in the evaluation of change. The significance of sex emerges clearly, with men being more satisfied than women. Age correlates with satisfaction only in Lithuania. The dividing line between managers and the working class is less distinct than in the case of the change of economic situation, and the correlations are clearly lower in Latvia than in the other Baltic countries.

Proceeding somewhat further with our generalizations, an interesting picture begins to emerge from the results — even though it is possible to offer different interpretations.

Unity of consciousness is still higher than equality in reproduction situations, the exception being the impact of ethnicity in Estonia on consciousness. The class dimension of managers (and partly the petty bourgeoisie) vs. the working class is clear in both cases. It is strongest in the case of incomes.

Among the class variables the indicators of middle class have no significance, however. It is hard to make a strong case for the existence of a middle class society or a middle class based hegemonic project. On the other hand, it is possible to suggest that the high level of unity in consciousness does point at a middle class society. According to this interpretation the middle class groups are indeed in the middle and do not differentiate themselves from anything.

The same level of correlations found for social background and class refers also points at the weakness of class society in the sense of numerous possible crossing lines of structural differentiation.

Finally, we can revert to the question of what it means that the differences in reproduction are greater than those in consciousness. The obvious immediate answer is that we can expect consciousness to change with increasing differentiation and growing cleavages. Another possible line of interpretation is to assume that the problems revealed by the analysis of consciousness are so common and so important that they can withstand relatively major differences in reproduction situations and preserve, with some assisting mechanisms, this function for a relatively long time. The final chapter below shall look at these mechanisms (conditions) in closer detail.

Many authors have suggested that legitimation beliefs are not directly related to socio-economic position. Beliefs in democratic institutions and their performance potential and social identification can change and mediate the impact of the position (Bruszt 1995; Fuch and Roller 1994).

Performance beliefs are the most important in Latvia. In SEC they also carry significance in Estonia and Lithuania, in ETH in Lithuania and in MOD in Estonia.

Privatization attitudes have the greatest impact in Estonia. This applies to both attitudes. In Latvia and Lithuania a correlation is mainly seen only in the case where it is considered necessary to limit privatization. The only and clearly uniting feature is the high and natural correlation of the positive attitude to privatization in each country with MOD. It can be inferred then that attitudes to privatization have broader scope in the case of Estonia than in the other Baltic countries as regards to the structuring of consciousness.

Class identification matters only in Estonia. In the case of group identification only identification with managers and entrepreneurs has some significance. The exception is identification with farmers in Estonia in ETH. It needs to be noted that identification in the case of the middle class (those with 'white-collars' and 'intelligence') has no major impact on consciousness.

Performance beliefs have a meaningful impact only in the case of 'worried about job' in Estonia. In most cases privatization attitudes correlate with reproduction indicators.

Class identification shows a clear relationship with reproduction variables. The correlations are highest in the evaluation of the changing economic situation and in satisfaction with the economic situation. Managerial identification shows positive correlations with the success of reproduction. The highest correlation of 'middle class' identification is the negative correlation of white-collar identification with incomes in Lithuania.

There are some country differences in the correlations of group identification variables with reproduction indicators. The most interesting of these is the higher level of positive correlation of entrepreneur identification with the level of (evaluated) reproduction in Lithuania than in the other Baltic countries.

On average the differences of correlations between worker identification vs. manager (or entrepreneur) identification are bigger in reproduction variables than in consciousness variables.

As expected the attitude variables show correlations with the consciousness scales. The most obvious example is the high correlation of positive privatization attitudes with the societal goal of modern state and market society. There are also marked country differences. The figures on performance beliefs of consciousness mainly in Latvia and the effect of entrepreneur identification is surprisingly higher in Lithuania than in the other Baltic countries in reproduction.

Looking at the effect of the above-mentioned performance beliefs, privatization attitudes and identification variables on the correlations of class and social background variables with consciousness scales and reproduction

Table 9.   Correlations between performance and privatization beliefs and class and group identifications with consciousness in the Baltic countries

	ORD			SEC			ETH			MOD			APAT		
	EST	LAT	LIT	EST	LAT	LIT	EST	LAT	LIT	EST	LAT	LIT	EST	LAT	LIT
Perf.belief: government	.01	.20**	.07*	.02	.10**	.05	-.07*	.14**	.06	.11**	.11**	.03	-.03	-.01	.07*
Perf.belief: parliament	.01	.18**	.10**	.00	.05	.08*	-.08*	.09*	.09**	.13**	.11**	.05	-.04	-.03	.08*
Perf.belief: president	.06	.16**	.10**	.07*	.13**	.11**	.05	.19**	.11**	.08*	.07	-.07*	-.03	-.04	-.11**
Priv1	-.18**	-.01	.03	-.16**	-.05	-.04	-.20**	.01	.00	.40**	.30**	-.44**	-.21**	-.03	.00
Priv2	-.19**	-.16**	-.08*	-.17**	-.12**	-.16**	-.26**	-.23**	-.13**	.21**	.14**	.19**	-.20**	-.16**	-.14**
Class identity	-.11**	-.07	.03	-.15**	-.05	-.04	-.08*	-.00	-.02	.14**	.04	.08	-.32**	-.07	-.21**
Workers	.08**	.01	-.04	.10**	.09*	.11**	.12**	-.00	.03	-.08**	-.13**	-.20**	.15**	.11**	.06
White-collar	.05	.01	.07*	.06	.03	-.00	.03	.04	.01	-.03	.03	.08*	-.09**	.01	.02
Managers	-.07*	-.03	-.01	-.07*	-.08*	-.14**	-.05	-.03	-.01	.06*	.09**	.10**	-.11**	-.13**	-.03
Intelligentsia	-.03	.01	-.01	-.08*	-.03	-.04	-.06*	-.03	-.07*	.08*	.07*	.07*	-.12**	-.08*	-.11**
Farmers	-.09**	-.06	-.03	.01	-.08*	-.02	-.12**	-.04	-.04	.01	.01	.01	-.05	-.00	.01
Entrepreneurs	-.07*	-.04	.00	-.15**	-.16**	-.08*	-.05	-.01	.00	.04	.08*	.12**	-.15**	-.10**	-.04

*.— Signif. LE .05
**.— Signif. LE .01

Table 10. Correlations between performance and privatization beliefs and group identifications with reproduction in the Baltic countries

	INCOMES			WORRIED ABOUT JOB			CHANGE OF ECON. SIT.			SATISF. WITH ECON. SIT.		
	EST	LAT	LIT	EST	LAT	LIT	EST	LAT	LIT	EST	LAT	LIT
Perf.belief: government	-.03	-.03	.02	.11**	.04	-.01	-.04	.01	.02	-.07*	.03	-.00
Perf.belief: parliament	-.03	-.03	-.01	.15**	.05	.00	-.02	-.00	.00	-.06	.03	-.02
Perf.belief: presid.	-.03	-.01	-.01	.08**	-.00	-.04	-.04	.01	-.02	-.05	.04	-.06
Priv1	.10**	.06	.03	.23**	.09*	.12**	.19**	.14**	.18**	.15**	.12**	.11**
Priv2	.10**	.11**	.13**	.11**	.05	.10**	.11**	.10**	.15**	.03	.10**	.12**
Class identity	.22**	.15*	.04	.20**	.17**	.12*	.28**	.26**	.28**	.32**	.24**	.23**
Workers	-.09**	-.06	-.07*	-.05	-.14**	-.12**	-.14**	-.16**	-.21**	-.07*	-.09**	-.09**
White-collar	-.04	-.04	-.17**	-.12**	.02	-.02	-.08*	.04	-.05	-.03	.02	-.09**
Managers	.16**	.24**	.14**	.07*	.08*	.06	.17**	.19**	.13**	.12**	.15**	.07*
Intelligentsia	.01	-.04	.01	.07*	.05	.04	.05	.01	-.00	.01	-.03	-.04
Farmers	-.05	-.02	.01	.07*	.11**	.10**	.00	-.05	.13**	-.02	-.01	.12**
Entrepreneurs	.15**	.15**	.37**	.12**	.09*	.14**	.24**	.19**	.36**	.11**	.13**	.27**

indicators, it emerged that the partial correlations generally deviate only very little (from .00 to .05) from the original correlations of Table 7 and 8 when every attitude and identification variable is kept constant each in its turn. This helps to confirm the reliability of the original results.

Diagnosis of Change

During the 1980s the foundations and the significance of the middle classes in capitalist market societies were subjected to a broad and critical re-evaluation. The main target of the exercise was the new wage labouring middle classes (see e.g. Carchedi 1977 and 1983; Abercrombie-Urry 1983; Wright 1980 and 1985; Kivinen 1989; and for an overview, Blom et al. 1992, 63-72). In one of the latest studies on the middle classes it has been suggested that the social importance of these classes has probably been underrated (Savage et al. 1995). In the Baltic countries the middle classes and middle class society are now in the process of developing. Its independence and 'causal powers' (Abercrombie and Urry 1983) are just a possibility (see Blom et al. 1995c).

Our results, combined with earlier studies on the post-socialist condition, suggest that middle class groups will be losers in the transformation process, at least in the short term. Furthermore, the results also suggest that they have rather dispersed locations in different fields of consciousness. The extreme poles are the petty bourgeoisie and managers vs. the working class. It follows that no clear picture of a middle class society emerges from the results.

The inconsistent status of the emerging new middle classes has also been considered a reason for future social conflicts and the reactivation of the opposition between inherited egalitarianism and increasing social differentiation (inequality) required by capitalistic market development (Machonin 1995, 16). The same line of argumentation is also confirmed by the differentiation within the economically non-active population and the relative size of the effects of non-class background factors.

The differences in reproduction are greater than those found in consciousness. On this basis it can be speculated that (1) the phase of 'value mobilization' or the 'period of grace' is not entirely over and/or (2) the other factors uniting consciousness (associated to the democratic process or a new hegemonic national project) have some uniting effect.

Apart from sectoral interests, the high level of support for the goals of social and material security and social welfare lies at the heart of the common consciousness. In addition, there is also some class polarization in security issues and in support for the modern state and market orientation. The situation is also very nearly the same in social alienation and apathy.

Given the high level of uncertainty that continues to surround economic development, political leadership and political projects, we can expect to see a social development which is characterized by slow and cyclical advances. In addition, although democracy, both as a value and as a structure, enjoys as much support in the Baltic countries as in most post-socialist countries in East Central Europe, this does not hold true when it is assisted from the perspective of performance (Fuchs and Roller 1994). In most countries assessments of the performance of democracy are low and have continued to show a declining trend since 1990/91 (ibid, Table 10). In 1993 the number of those with a positive assessment of the performance of democracy in Estonia and Lithuania was 36 %.

There are opinions which underline the fact that a democratic development in post-socialist countries is not the only possible option; other possible alternatives include the formation of new non-democratic or autocratic regimes or societal anarchization (see Ekiert 1991, 287-288). In any event legitimation is by no means automatic; the research evidence indicates that evaluations of the performance of the political system (democracy) are closely related to the performance of cabinet (Fuch and Roller 1994).

Many developments will be crucial for how the short-term future and its modernity project(s) will shape out. In particular, reference must be made to the provision of basic social and material welfare, interest group and mass party formation, the mechanisms of democratic socio-political inclusion, and the ways in which social differentiation or polarization emerge into people's consciousness (either in the shape of changing status or in the form of new and relatively lasting class and strata divisions). Many things also depend on 'the interpellation' (Althusser) of structural cleavages. If class, gender, place of residence and generation can to a great extent represent and strengthen one another, the deficits of material legitimation will rise into people's consciousness.

Note

1. Operationalization of Wright's typology:

   Petty bourgeoisie: under 10 hired employees, control over (minor) investments and physical capital and workers' labour power.

   Managers: Wage earners with decision-making authority in matters concerning the whole organization (including authority to suggest approval of matters).

   Advisor-managers: authority to give advice in matters concerning the whole organization.

   Non-hierarchic decision-makers: decision-making authority in matters concerning the whole organization but not control over other people's labour.

   Supervisors: no decision-making authority but influence on the pay, promotions and discipline of other workers.

Working class: excluded from control over investments, use of physical capital and other people's labour power.
Semi-autonomous employees: as above, but have control over own work process.

Bibliography

Abercrombie, N. and Urry, J. (1983), *Capital, labour and middle classes*, London.

Blom, R. et al. (1992), *The scope logic approach to class analysis*, Aldershot: Avebury.

Blom, R. (1995a), 'Social strata and the structuration of work in Estonia', in R. Blom, H. Melin and J. Nikula (eds.), *Social strata and occupational groups in Baltic states. Social Change in Baltic and Nordic countries, Project*, Working papers 1, Tampere.

Blom, R. (1995b), *Industrial relations and work situation in post-socialist societies: The case of Baltics*, paper for V World Congress For Central and East European Studies, Warsaw, 6-11 August 1995.

Blom, R. et al. (1995c), *Reformation of the middle classes in the Baltic societies. Social Change in Baltic and Nordic Countries, Project*, Working Papers 4, Tampere.

Bruszt, L. (1995), *Why on earth do Eastern Europeans support capitalism. Democracy capitalism and public opinion*, paper of the Political Science Department, Central European University, Budapest College.

Carchedi, G. (1977), *The economic identification of social classes*, London.

Carchedi, G. (1983), *Problems in class analysis*, London.

Ekiert, G. (1991), 'Democratization process in East Central Europe: A theoretical reconsideration', *British Journal of Political Science* 21, pp. 285-313.

Fuchs, D. and Roller, E. (1994), *Cultural conditions of the transition to liberal democracy in Central and Eastern Europe*, unpublished paper, Wissenschaftscentrum für Sozialforschung, Berlin.

Kivinen, M. (1989), 'The new middle classes and the labour process', *Acta Sociologica* 1, 1989.

Kolarska-Bobinska, L. (1994), *Aspirations, values and interests. Poland 1989-94*, IFIS Publishers, Warsaw.

Melin, H. (1995), 'Conceptualizing classes in the Baltic context', in R. Blom 1995c, ibid.

Savage, M. et al. (1995), *Property, bureaucracy and culture. Middle class formation in contemporary Britain*, Routledge, London.

Srubar, I. (1994), 'Variants of the transformation process in Central Europe. A comparative assessment', *Zeitschrift für Sociologie* 3, 198-221.

Wright, E. (1980), 'Varieties of Marxist conception of class', *Politics and society* 3.

Wright, E. (1985), *Classes*, Verso, London.

Appendix

Table 1.   Eigenvalues and explained variance

	Eigenvalue	% of variance	cumul. %
Factor I	5.0	10.4	10.4
Factor II	3.2	6.8	17.2
Factor III	2.1	4.4	21.6
Factor IV	1.9	4.0	25.6
Factor V	1.7	3.7	29.4
Factor VI	1.5	3.3	32.7
Factor VII	1.4	3.1	35.8
Factor VIII	1.4	3.0	38.7
Factor IX	1.3	2.7	41.5

Table 2.   Means of ORD in different groups of non-active population in the Baltic countries

	ESTONIA		LATVIA		LITHUANIA	
Pensioners	26.7	(138)	26.6	(457)	25.5	(314)
Students	25.2	(101)	24.7	(70)	25.7	(98)
Unemployed	25.8	(57)	26.6	(179)	26.4	(72)
Housewives	26.3	(50)	25.6	(95)	24.8	(34)

Table 3.   Means of SEC in different groups of non-active population in the Baltic countries

	ESTONIA		LATVIA		LITHUANIA	
Pensioners	18.0	(135)	18.3	(459)	18.0	(317)
Students	16.1	(102)	17.0	(68)	16.5	(98)
Unemployed	17.3	(60)	18.2	(180)	17.3	(72)
Housewives	16.6	(51)	17.7	(96)	17.7	(34)

Table 4.   Means of ETH in different groups of non-active population in the Baltic countries

	ESTONIA		LATVIA		LITHUANIA	
Pensioners	14.9	(136)	15.4	(453)	14.0	(317)
Students	14.2	(102)	14.6	(68)	13.9	(98)
Unemployed	14.5	(58)	15.6	(177)	13.6	(71)
Housewives	14.9	(51)	15.0	(94)	14.2	(34)

Table 5.   Means of MOD in different groups of non-active population in the Baltic countries

	ESTONIA		LATVIA		LITHUANIA	
Pensioners	14.9	(137)	14.8	(455)	13.5	(314)
Students	15.3	(102)	14.8	(70)	15.4	(98)
Unemployed	13.9	(58)	15.0	(179)	14.1	(72)
Housewives	15.0	(49)	14.8	(95)	14.4	(34)

Table 6.   Means of APAT in different groups of non-active population in the Baltic countries

	ESTONIA		LATVIA		LITHUANIA	
Pensioners	12.0	(138)	11.9	(457)	11.5	(312)
Students	11.2	(101)	11.0	(70)	11.2	(94)
Unemployed	12.3	(59)	11.9	(179)	12.0	(72)
Housewives	11.7	(50)	11.4	(94)	12.1	(34)

18 Increasing Differences? Social Background and the Breakthrough of Affluence in Finland 1955-1966

TIMO TOIVONEN

Introduction

The post-war period from the late 1940s up to the 1990s has been described as 'the short dream of eternal prosperity' (Lutz 1984). Hidden in this expression is the idea of an *even* process of economic growth and the *equalization* of welfare disparities between socio-economic groups. However, during this period there have also been economic upswings and recession and it is by no means self-evident that the differences between socio-economic groups have diminished. One of these periods of radical change was the mid-1950s.

The images of the decades of the 1950s and the 1960s differ quite profoundly from each other. The 1950s was a period of materialism, of family orientation and private interests, while the 1960s has been described as a decade of grassroots action in the form of youth protests, civil rights movements, etc. (e.g. Hirschman 1982). However, changes of epochs will hardly wait for the beginning of a new decade, and in this case it is reasonable to argue that the 1960s actually began in the mid-1950s.

From the mid-1950s onwards the world was beginning to shrink very rapidly in both political and cultural terms. One of the reasons for this was the phenomenal growth of communication, specifically television. News such as the popular uprising in Hungary in 1956, the Suez crisis in the same year, liberation movements in Africa, particularly the liberation of Belgian Congo in 1960, the Cuban crisis in 1961, the erection of the Berlin Wall in 1961, and the murder of President Kennedy in 1963, all these events shocked people all around the world. At the same time a new distinctive youth culture was springing up all over the world. Devotees could be recognized by their unique way of dressing and by their music, rock'n'roll. There were, however, some minor country differences: in England these youths were known as 'Teddy boys', in Scandinavia as 'leather-jackets' and 'flat-hats'. One of the most important factors behind the growth of this culture was the rising standard of living. For example, according to a British survey discretionary consumption by young people was 100 % higher in the mid-1950s than it had been before the war (Abrams 1959, 9).

In the 1950s Finland was one of the most predominantly agrarian countries in Europe: 46 % of the economically active population was engaged in agriculture and forestry. In 1950, only 32 % of Finnish people lived in towns or urban areas; most European countries (excepting Portugal and some countries in Eastern Europe) had reached this rate of urbanization by 1930 (Kirk 1946, 14). However, the pace of change that was to follow in Finnish society was extraordinarily rapid. In 1960 the agrarian sector accounted for 35 % of total employment, in 1970 for 20 % (Toivonen 1988, 68). The proportion of Finns living in urban areas also grew very rapidly: in 1960 the figure was 38 %, in 1970 as high as 51 % (SYF 1992, Table 14).

Figure 1 highlights the rapid growth of per capita private expenditure in Finland from the mid-1950s to the-mid 1960s. Following a short dip in 1957 and 1958, the rise was very rapid indeed, reaching up to 10 % a year. The proliferation of two consumer durables had a decisive impact on the growth of private expenditure. The first was television: in summer 1956 only 500 out of Finland's 1,400,000 households owned a TV set. In the autumn of the same year, the figure had climbed to 3,000 (IS 6.8.1956). Ten years later, in 1966, 822,000 or 59 % of all Finnish households had a TV set, in urban areas the figure was 75 %. The proliferation of television is clearly reflected in the growing proportion of household appliances out of total expenditure (Figure 1). In the US 86 % of all families owned a TV set as early as 1956 (Cross 1993, 191). Finland thus lagged at least ten years behind the United States in this respect.

Ownership of cars also expanded very rapidly throughout the country. From 1955 to 1965, the number of private cars increased from 85,000 to 454,000, marking an increase of 434 % (Leppänen 1973, Table 9; SYF 1991, Table 227). The pace of growth was faster than ever before in history; nor has it been parallelled since. The impression of growing wealth is further reinforced by the structural changes that took place in the import of cars. We only have access to figures from 1959 to 1966, but during this seven-year period the import of cars from the socialist bloc grew by no more than 7 %, while imports from Western countries went up by 435 %![1]

Ownership of various other consumer durables such as refrigerators, tape-recorders, etc. also increased rapidly. The growth of tourism must likewise have been phenomenal, but no detailed figures are available because since 1954, Finnish people have not needed a passport when travelling to other Scandinavian countries (Denmark, Norway and Sweden). However, the period of most dramatic growth in tourism did not take place until ten years later (SYF 1957, Table 217; SYF 1977, Table 206).

Figure 1. **Volume index of some main categories of private expenditure in Finland (1950-1970)**

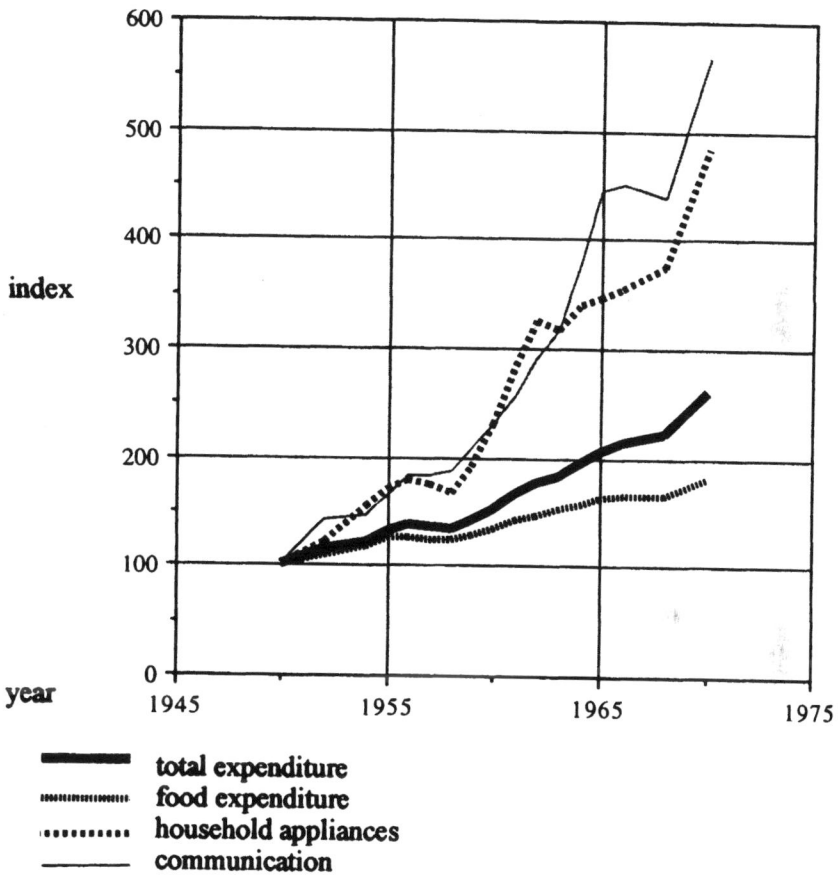

total expenditure
food expenditure
household appliances
communication

All in all, the growth of conspicuous consumption items such as these must have had a major impact on people. Firstly, given that these items are clear examples of superfluous consumption, people certainly recognized the increase in wealth. Secondly, it is also evident that the growth of affluence was not restricted to the upper classes: although the new, highly educated service class was continuing to expand, the growth was never proportional to the proliferation of the consumption items mentioned above. We may assume then that the proliferation also gave the impression of greater equality in consumption. 'It is unbelievable that Finland has risen to the top of the list of welfare states', a professor of social policy exclaimed, but without making any actual comparisons (Siipi 1967, 210). However, both these processes, the rapid growth and the tendency towards equality in consumption, may have given a false picture.

First of all, the consumption items mentioned are single items. In 1966 only 8 % of total consumption expenditure was spent in vehicles and entertainment electronics. This might suggest that the differences between socioeconomic groups, family types etc. were not reduced so dramatically after all with regard to expenditure *as a whole* or in main expenditure categories such as food, housing etc. Secondly, it is not certain that class differences in the consumption of items such as those mentioned above, were actually reduced. All depends on the process through which proliferation happens. One possibility is that expenditure devoted to communication increased more rapidly among other than the upper classes. In this case the popular conception would be right. This was also the view of Georg Simmel: 'Above all, the economic upward movement of low strata in the speed that they take on in the metropolis must favour the rapid change in fashion' (Simmel 1957/1904, 556).

It is also possible that expenditure grew in all social classes but more rapidly among the upper classes. In this case the popular conception is wrong. It may also be wrong because people (this is only my assumption) will more readily recognize increases or decreases in class differences, whereas it is less easy to recognize such changes between family types, age groups etc. The growing impact of age groups on consumption patterns can be expected in a 'Simmelian' sense, because those classes and individuals who gain the advantage from change over others 'find in fashion something that keeps pace with their own soul-movements' (ibid., 556). If it is true that people observe social differences in the world 'in class terms', it would also be interesting to know what lies behind that. However, this question falls beyond the concern of this study.

Starting out from the above facts, this study set out to investigate the development of consumption differences by socio-economic, income and age groups between 1955-1966. At the same time it addresses the question of whether the period mentioned above was epoch-making in Finnish consumption history.

Data and Variables

The data consisted of original material drawn from a 'Consumption Investigation' on 1955 and a Household Survey covering two years, 1966 and 1971. All surveys were conducted by the Central Statistical Office of Finland. The representativity of the first study was rather limited. First of all, it was restricted to households with an economically active head, i.e. households of pensioners, students, etc. were omitted.

There were also two other major restrictions. Firstly, only those households living in towns and in so-called market towns were included. Secondly, the survey was restricted to wage earners and salaried employees. However, in the mid-1950s, Finland was still one of the most agrarian countries in the developed world. It is estimated that urban employees comprised only 30 % of *the economically active population* (Toivonen 1988, 172-179). Thus it follows that a considerable bulk of *households* — mostly farmers and their helping family members — were excluded from the survey. The reason for this may have been that in the mid-1950s one of the most important goals of consumption studies was still to uncover possible deficiencies in nutrition. This was not, of course, a problem for families living in the countryside. Responses were received from 492 households.

The samples for 1966 and 1971 were representative for all Finnish households. However, for the present purposes of comparison the samples had to be restricted to those corresponding to the 1955 survey. The size of the restricted sample for 1966 was 1,001 and for 1971 920 households.

There are several possibilities for establishing a set of variables to measure the available income variable. One way, and perhaps the most common one, is to take the available income per household as the indicator. However, this method tends to give a biased picture at the household welfare level. The standard of living of a single person living alone with a specified available income 'A', is different from the standard of living of a household of five at the same level of available income. The method adopted here — taking *the available income of a household and dividing it by the number of its members*, has been used to counter this bias. However, this method also requires some caution in that it may result in a bias in the opposite direction due to the effects of 'economies of scale'. To minimize this latter risk while still avoiding the former, household income has usually been divided by the number of consumption units. In the present case this method was not adopted because consumption unit calculations for 1955 were not available. In addition, there exists no unanimously accepted definition for what constitutes a consumption unit (van der Gaag and Smolensky 1982).

The central variable in this study was the household head's socio-economic group, defined as worker, lower white-collar employee or upper white-collar employee. The term 'service class' is not easy to use in this context because in several cases it would have been extremely difficult to draw a dividing line between upper and lower white-collar employees.

Socio-economic classifications in household surveys are based on data relating to economic activity, occupation, industrial status and education. In the 1980s the CSOF (Central Statistical Office of Finland) published a paper outlining its classification principles (1983). These principles are not, however, compatible with any coherent theory or research. The practical classification of occupations is based mainly on the judgements by the household survey staff of prestige and the level of education required by the occupations. It is unfortunate that education is already given in the definition of the top layer of employees: 'upper-level employees with a university degree', which meant it was not possible to control for education in the analysis. It is also interesting, from a theoretical point of view, to consider the question of how we are supposed to understand the term 'social class' if it is controlled in all its dimensions, a situation which is not uncommon in such research contexts.

Statistical classifications are very often criticized for the above reasons. The criticism focuses specifically on the boundary lines between upper- and lower-level employees and between workers and other employees. The discriminatory power of these boundaries in the studies mentioned above could have been better than that of a theoretically argumented classification.

One potential pitfall in using data compiled by the CSOF lies in the fact that the office's socio-economic classification of households is based on the socio-economic position of the head of the household, which in most cases is the husband: the head of household is defined as 'the person chiefly responsible for the economic maintenance of the household or in households where both spouses are economically active, as the spouse who has the highest income' (CSOF 1984). This phenomenon is known among marketing researchers as 'the husband only fallacy' (Shimp and Yokum 1981), among sociologists as 'the conventional view' (Goldthorpe 1983). The point is that the measurement of social class has been based exclusively on the class position of the household head, who is typically the husband, and the husband's social class is the sole determinant of a household's class standing. In contemporary advanced societies, however, wives very often work outside the home. Moreover, it has been stressed that spending patterns are also reflected in the consumption of the person who controls the money within the household (wife, husband or both) and not only in the socio-economic position of spouses (Pahl 1990).

Household consumption is defined, for survey purposes, as the consumption of goods and services necessary to meet the household's needs. The classification of goods and services is based on international recommendations (United Nations 1977; CSOF 1988:4, 11).

The dependent variables in this study were the household's total expenditure and expenditure in main consumption categories. The content of the main expenditure categories is usually evident from the name of the respective category (Tables 1-3). However, the following points should be made:

'Food' includes food in restaurants; 'Housing' includes costs of leisure residence; 'Household equipment' includes the costs of furniture, household appliances and domestic help; 'Communication' includes purchases and uses of vehicles and postage, telephone, etc. costs; 'Recreation and education' is a heterogeneous category, comprising, firstly, leisure items and entertainment electronics; secondly, books, newspapers, etc.; thirdly, betting and money spent on sports events, concerts, theatres etc; and fourthly, nursery fees.

Table 1. **Beta coefficients for total consumption by interaction variables (socio-economic variables*year)**

	1955	1966	1971
Age			
-30	.21***	-.02	-.05**
31-45	.44***	-.09***	-.09***
Disposable income quintile			
V	.11***	.26***	.23***
IV	.08***	.13***	.13***
Socio-economic position			
service class	.19***	.04*	.03
lower white-collar	.08***	-.01	.07***

Adjusted $100R^2 = 49.6$

Table 2. **Beta coefficients for housing consumption by interaction variables (socio-economic variables*year)**

	1955	1966	1971
Age			
-30	-.01	-.04*	-.08***
31-45	-.03	-.09***	-.05**
Disposable income quintile			
V	.27***	.29***	.33***
IV	-.07***	.17***	.23***
Socio-economic position			
service class	.11***	.06**	.06**
lower white-collar	.07***	.06***	.15***

Adjusted $100R^2 = 33.5$

Table 3. **Beta coefficients for household consumption by interaction variables (socio-economic variables*year)**

	1955	1966	1971
Age			
-30	.01	.05**	.00
31-45	.01	.04*	-.01
Disposable income quintile			
V	.19***	.23***	.18***
IV	.04*	.10***	.13***
Socio-economic position			
service class	.09***	.08***	.10***
lower white-collar	.04	.04	.10***

Adjusted $100R^2 = 15.4$

The 'Miscellaneous' category includes costs of personal hygiene, jewellery, hotel and package tour expenses.

The dependent variables were measured so that the average expenditure per capita of all households was given the value of 100 in each year. This was because the aim of this paper was not to study the growth of consumption expenditure, but the differences between groups in different years.

On the Development of Income Differentials

One of the most decisive factors influencing consumption differences between groups is of course the difference in disposable income. Figures 2 and 3 describe the income differentials between those socio-economic groups and age groups who are included in this study.

The decrease in income differentials between social classes from 1955 to 1966 was not quite as dramatic as during the next 10-year period, particularly during 1971-1976. The relative position of service class households weakened markedly. This was due, among other things, to the fact that social security systems, financed through heavier and more progressive taxation, were developed at an accelerating pace from the 1950s through to the 1970s (see e.g. Hellsten 1993). In any case, we can expect that consumption differences between socio-economic groups also diminished considerably between 1955 and 1966.

Figure 2. **Disposable income per capita of households by employee category (all households = 100)**

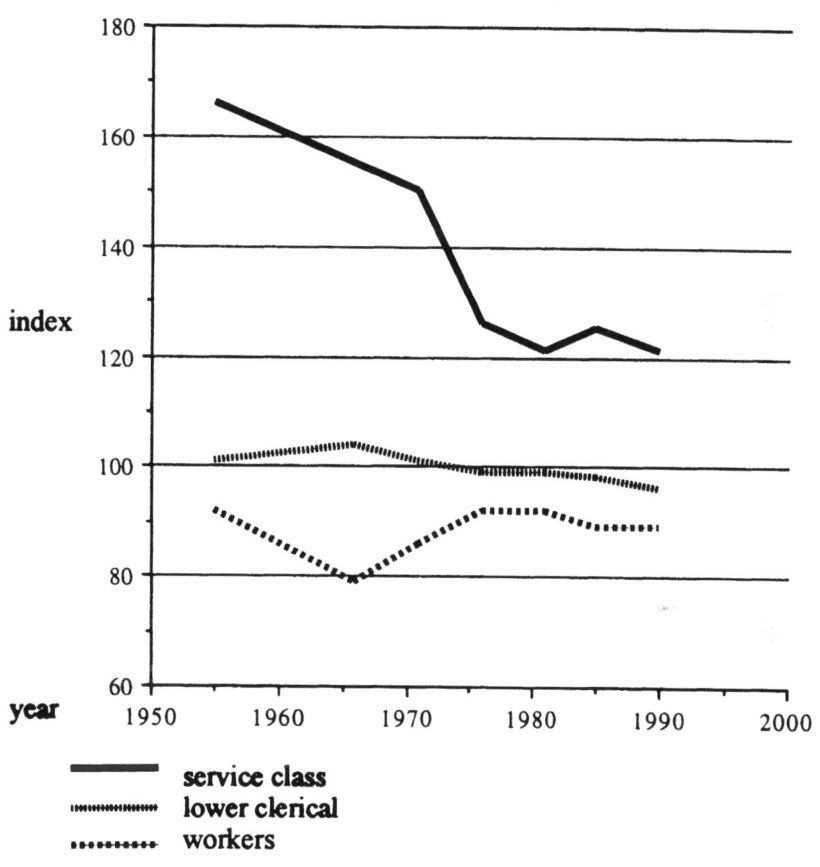

In the groups categorized by the age of the head of household, the disposable income of the oldest age group grew in comparison with other age groups. This change was due to the entry into force of public health insurance and pension reforms in the early 1960s (ibid.). On this basis it can be assumed that the differences between age groups grew during the period under scrutiny.

**Figure 3.   Disposable income per capita by age of head of household
(all households = 100)**

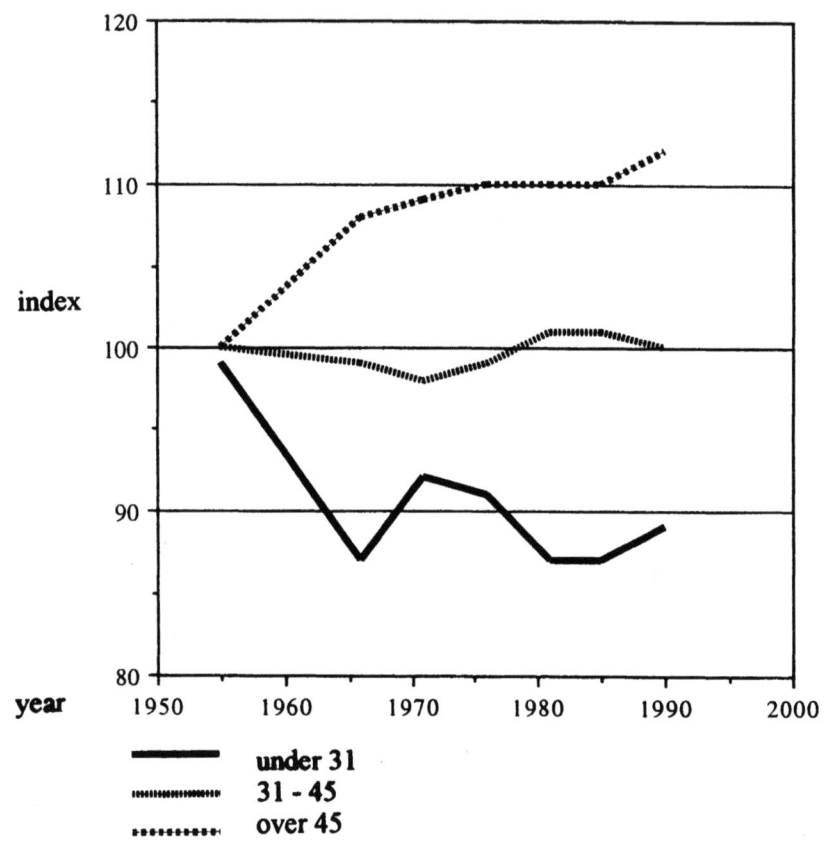

Results

The differences in the grand mean of different social background categories
are shown in Tables 1-3. The range between socio-economic groups and the
explanatory power (eta) of socio-economic groups in 10 out of the 11 main
expenditure categories was bigger in 1955 than in 1966. In the case of income
quintiles, the corresponding figure was 9. However, in the case of age groups
the result was the exact opposite: in 8 main expenditure categories eta was

bigger in 1966 than in 1955. In the case of medical care the decreasing effect of the age of the head of household is easy to understand in the context of the development of social security systems mentioned above. In this case the result seems to be consistent with the images mentioned above. However, this approach is too simplistic because of the possible multicollinearity of background variables.

Multiple regression analysis was selected as a tool for a closer analysis. For this purpose it was necessary to dichotomize the categories of independent (background) variables: if the social class of the head of household was 'service class', value 1 was given to the variable 'service class', otherwise 0; if the social class was 'lower white-collar', value 1 was given to the variable 'lower white-collar', otherwise 0, etc. 'Year' was also included in the equations in the same way (for example, variable '1955' had the value 1 if the year in question was 1955). As we can see, 1971 was also included in the equations for reasons of comparison. In this way we can also compare the extent of the changes between 1955-1966 and 1966-1971. In regression analyses the categories of independent variables were included in the equations in a non-hierarchic sequence.

Analysis of change was based on the following strategy: Every background variable was in fact an interaction term. For example, in the table variable 'service class' in column 1955 is in fact the variable 'service class*1955'. This kind of use of multiple regression analysis helps us to focus not only on the known independent variable in general, but also on a known category (or categories) of an independent variable and on a known year. For example, if the variable mentioned above had a significant coefficient on total consumption, then we know that in that precise year service class households had a higher total consumption than households on average. Whether the selected strategy is the best possible is of course open to debate — as is always the case in the analysis of pooled time series data (Sayrs 1989).

One pitfall of this method is that we can take into account only $(1-n)$ of (n) categories of a known independent variable because of the linear dependence. For example, if we know the effect of three categories of an independent variable with four categories, the effect of the fourth category is logically dependent on these former three categories.

The impact of the household's available income per capita was important in every year in every main expenditure category. This is not surprising in view of the fact that the expenditure categories were counted by absolute indexes. A more interesting finding is the general trend which shows that the impact of service class on differences in the main expenditure categories decreased between 1955 and 1971. However, this trend seemed to be quite even without any major break between 1955 and 1966. Only the equations concerning those main categories where the impact of service class was significant in 1955, are documented here for reasons of economy. However, in the case of total consumption expenditure and in the case of communication expenditure, the results show quite a dramatic drop in the impact of service class between 1955 and 1966 (Tables 4-6).

Table 4.   Beta coefficients for communication consumption by interaction variables (socio-economic variables*year)

	1955	1966	1971
Age			
-30	.05*	.07**	.09***
31-45	.03	.05*	.03
Disposable income quintile			
V	.18***	.21***	.16***
IV	.03	.13***	.11***
Socio-economic position			
service class	.05**	.05*	.02
lower white-collar	-.01	-.01	.04

Adjusted $100R^2 = 10.2$

Table 5.   Beta coefficients for recreation consumption by interaction variables (socio-economic variables*year)

	1955	1966	1971
Age			
-30	.04	.09***	.07**
31-45	-.01	.03	.05**
Disposable income quintile			
V	.22***	.17***	.15***
IV	.04*	.13***	.10***
Socio-economic position			
service class	.09***	.10***	.07**
lower white-collar	.06**	.06**	.10***

Adjusted $100R^2 = 33.5$

Table 6. Beta coefficients for miscellaneous consumption by interaction variables (socio-economic variables*year)

	1955	1966	1971
Age			
-30	-.00	-.02	.11***
31-45	.03	-.05*	.05**
Disposable income quintile			
V	.37***	.18***	.32***
IV	.08***	.06**	.16***
Socio-economic position			
service class	.09***	.05**	.11***
lower white-collar	.06**	.02	.13***

Adjusted $100R^2 = 35.7$

The impact of age increased markedly between 1955 and 1966 in the case of category of household appliances, in that of communication and in that of recreation. The variable 'young' became significant in these cases. New consumer durables (e.g. refrigerators, cars and TVs) belong to these categories. It is also worth noting that the growing impact of age was not in evidence in the cases of household appliances and recreation at the expense of the diminishing impact of service class.

Neither class nor age variables seemed to have an impact on such categories as alcohol and tobacco. Perhaps one of the reasons for this is that although the impact exists, it is highly complicated. For example, the connection between age and expenditure on alcohol[2] is conditioned by socio-economic group. Only those young households who belong to the service class can afford to drink in expensive cocktail lounges (and have such a lifestyle). Therefore, preliminary tests were conducted with second-order interaction terms such as service-class*young*1955.

In this case and some others significant beta coefficients were found. In general, the inclusion of second-order interaction variables did not increase the explanatory power of regression equations to any significant extent. In the case of some statistically significant second-order interaction variables there were also difficulties with interpretation. In a statistical sense, these kinds of higher-order interactions are doubtful because the number of degrees of freedom decreases[3] and many of these interaction terms are without cases (Schaninger and Danko 1993, 580-594). Therefore, no detailed examination was carried out on these terms here.

Conclusions

The main finding of this study is that the consumption pattern of Finnish households did not change dramatically, nor did class differences disappear from the mid-1950s to the mid-1960s. In general, the impact of socio-economic groups decreased quite evenly from the 1950s to the 1970s. It is important to observe that the impact of social class remained strong on those main expenditure categories which include modern consumer durables (e.g. refrigerators, dishwashers, cars, TVs, tape recorders). The sole exception was the expenditure category of 'communication'.

It is also evident that the impact of the age of the head of household increased over the years. This is true most particularly in the case of the modern consumer durables mentioned above. This means that in these cases there was in fact no sweeping movement towards more equal consumption as discussed in the introduction. On the contrary, the dissemination of modern consumer appliances was connected not only with the social class of the head of the household, but also with the age of the head of the household.

This is not surprising. The adoption of new patterns of consumption, such as new work methods, new ways of thinking, etc. is based not only on a person's material resources, but also on a person's mental resources and role models (young, educated, upper class).

Notes

1. This was due to the fact that during the period of reconstruction Finnish foreign trade with other countries had been bilateral, i.e. exports and imports had to be balanced out. This requirement ended in 1957.
2. This is not the same thing as the volume of alcohol consumption.
3. In this study the inclusion of second-order interaction terms increases the number of independent variables to 45.

Bibliography

Abrams, M. (1959), *The Teenage Consumer*, London Press Exchange, London.

Bakker, B.F.M. (1989), 'Gender, Family and Social Class in the Netherlands', in Jansen, W., Dronkers, J. and Verrips, K. (eds.), *Similar or different?*, SISWO, Amsterdam.

Consumption Investigation of Finland from 1955/56, Original data.

Cross, G. (1993), *Time and money. The Making of Consumer Culture*, Routledge, London.

CSOF (Central Statistical Office of Finland) (1983), Classification of Socio-Economic Status, *Central Statistical Office of Finland, Handbooks 17*, Helsinki.

CSOF (1984), *Household Survey 1981*, Vol. 1.

CSOF (1988), 4, 11, *Income and consumption*.

Davis, N.J. and Robinson, R.V. (1988), 'Class Identification of Men and Women in the 1970s and 1980s', *American Sociological Review* 53, 1, pp. 103-112.

Gaag, J. and Smolensky, E. (1982), 'True household equivalence scales and characteristics of the poor in the United States', *The Review of Income and Wealth* 28, pp. 17-28.

Gilly, M. and Enis, B.M. (1982), 'Recycling the Family Life Cycle: A Proposal for Redefinition', in Mitchell, A.A. (ed.), *Advances in Consumer Research 9*, Ann Arbor Mi: Association for Consumer Research, pp. 271-276.

Goldthorpe, J. (1983), 'Women and Class Analysis: In Defence of Conventional View', *Sociology* 17, 4, pp. 466-488.

Hellsten, K. (1993), *Vaivaishoidosta hyvinvointivaltion kriisiin*, Research Reports, Department of Social Policy, University of Helsinki.

Hirschman, A.O. (1982), *Shifting Involvements: Private Interests and Public Action*, Princeton University Press, Princeton, NJ.

Household Surveys of Finland from 1966, 1971, 1976, 1981, and 1985, original data.

IS (Iltasanomat, a newspaper) 6.8.1956.

Kirk, D. (1946), *Europe's Population in the Interwar Years*, League of Nations, Geneve.

Leppänen, S. (1973), *Liikenne Suomessa 1900-1965* [Traffic in Finland 1900-1965], Kasvututkimuksia V, Suomen Pankki, Helsinki.

Lutz, B. (1984), *Der kurze Traum immerwährender Prosperität*, Campus Verlag, Frankfurt/Main.

Pahl, J. (1990), 'Household spending, personal spending and the control of money in marriage', *Sociology* 24, 1, pp. 119-138.

Sayrs, L.W. (1989), *Pooled Time Series Analysis*, SAGE, Newbury Park.

Schaninger, C.M. and Danko, W.D. (1993), 'A Conceptual and Empirical Comparison of Alternative Household Life Cycle Models', *Journal of Consumer Research* 19, 4, pp. 580-594.

Shimp, T.A. and Yokum, J.T. 'Extensions of The Basic Social Class Model Employed in Consumer Research', in K.B. Monroe (ed.), *Advances in Consumer Research 8*, Ann Arbor: Association for Consumer Research.

Siipi, J. (1967), *Ryysyrannasta hyvinvointivaltioon*, Tammi, Helsinki.

Simmel, G. (1957/1904), 'Fashion', *The American Journal of Sociology* 62, 6, pp. 541-558.

SYF, *Statistical Yearbook of Finland 1957*.

SYF, *Statistical Yearbook of Finland 1977*.

SYF, *Statistical Yearbook of Finland 1991*.

Toivonen, T. (1988), *Structural Change 1930-1985. Data and Material on Transformation of Gender Structure, Industries, Social Classes and Strata*, Publications of the Turku School of Economics, Series A-1.

United Nations (1977), *Provisional Guidelines on Statistics of the Distribution of Income, Consumption and Accumulation*, New York.

19 From Status to Class: The Emergence of a Class Society in Russia

TIMO PIIRAINEN

Introduction

During the last couple of decades of its existence, the Soviet Union appeared to be a very egalitarian country compared to Western market economies, at least if social equality was measured with such standard measures as income distribution (see e.g. Melin 1996). International comparisons showed a greater degree of social equality in the Soviet Union than in the West. This greater equality was above all manifest in the even distribution of income, resources, and life chances among different professional groups and other population groups. Paternalistic social equality was conceivable in the planned economy, as resources and life chances were not allocated among the population primarily by market forces but by central planning and public policy that followed explicitly egalitarian objectives.

In view of this history of egalitarianism it is quite surprising to see that after only five years since the disintegration of the Soviet Union and the end of planned economy, Russia now ranks among the countries with the biggest disparities in income and standard of living in the industrialized world. At the beginning of 1994, the Gini coefficient measuring income inequality was 0.46 for Russia (Poverty in Russia 1995, 30).[1] The disparities in 1994 were comparable to those observed in such countries as Argentina (0.46), the Philippines (0.46), and Turkey (0.44) — and the trend is one of steady further growth.

How has this sudden shift from extreme egalitarianism to blatant social inequality been possible? In its rapidity, the redistribution of property, wealth and life chances in the former socialist countries of Eastern Europe is something quite unprecedented in history. Appearing to be a qualitatively new phenomenon in history, the rapid process of social stratification in Eastern Europe also presents a dilemma for social research. What theoretical framework can be meaningfully applied to the study of social stratification in the post-Soviet social space, and what are the methodological tools that can be used in empirical research?

One possible solution to both these problems is presented in this essay. It opens with a discussion on the problems of macrosocial theory in the study of social stratification in transition countries. A basically Weberian view is adopted. A general conceptual framework for steering empirical research of social stratification in societies in transition is then formulated. This general framework is, in principle, an application of a theory tradition known as rational choice theory. In the last sections of the paper, the basic findings of a major empirical research project (Piirainen 1997) applying the above-mentioned theoretical points of departure are briefly reported. The research project took place in St. Petersburg, Russia, during 1992-1996. However, within the confines of this short space it is not possible to present in detail the empirical results.

Transition and Social Stratification: A Weberian Point of Departure

The basic conceptual point of departure in this study is Max Weber's distinction between elementary principles of social stratification (Weber 1978). Weber makes a distinction between three different stratification principles: class, status and party. According to Weber,

> We may speak of a class when (1) a number of people have in common a specific causal component of their life chances, in so far as (2) this component is represented exclusively by economic interests in the possession of goods and opportunities for income, and (3) is represented under the conditions of the commodity of labour markets. (Gerth and Mills 1948, 181.)

Stratification into classes happens through the workings of the market: the life chances accessible to different groups of the population are distributed unevenly as a collective outcome of the activity of individual economic agents who differ with regard to their power in the market. Weber gathers the multitude of logically possible and empirically appearing class positions under the concept 'social class', which 'makes up the totality of those class situations within which individual and generational mobility is easy and typical' (Crompton 1993, 29). In Europe at the beginning of the twentieth century, Weber located four general social classes: (a) the working class; (b) the petite bourgeoisie; (c) the propertyless intelligentsia and specialists, and (d) 'the classes privileged through property and education' (Weber 1978, 305).

Status, by contrast, is not associated with market activity, but with honour and prestige, and correspondingly, status positions are distributed, not by the market, but according to traditions, rules, norms, prescriptions and public policies. In Weber's analysis, a feudal lord or abbot would not belong to a dominant class but to a privileged status group, since membership of the nobility or clergy was not determined by the market power of the individual in question but was acquired via descent or through apprenticeship and initiation. Status group membership is determined by mechanisms of social closure.

The members of the Soviet nomenclatura, the political and economic elite, were selected and initiated into the elite through a procedure that was similar to the one that was applied by the medieval clergy in recruiting new members. In the Soviet Union life chances of individuals were not in the first place determined by their market power but through their membership of status groups of different kinds. The division of the population into various social strata in the Soviet Union happened to a far greater degree through procedures of status ascription and social closure than was the case in Western market economies. Following the Weberian logic, Soviet society is in this essay regarded as a status-ordered society and not a class society. Accordingly, the transition from Soviet socialism to a market economy is considered to imply a fundamental shift in the pattern of social stratification, that is, a shift from status-ordered society to a class society.

Four basic reasons can be given for the choice of the Weberian view on social stratification in transition societies. First, a Weberian approach makes it possible to use other criteria besides production in the study of social stratification and class formation. Second, this approach is better suited to the study of societies in transition, because alternative approaches presuppose a society that is relatively stable. Third, it enables the researcher to focus to a greater extent on social actors than, for example, neo-Marxian class analysis. And fourth, the final strength of Weber's ideal-type contrast between status-ordered societies and market-ordered societies lies in the fact that it reflects, in essence, the sense of transition, the dichotomous contrast of past and present, that is, in fact, inherent in most of classical sociology (see e.g. Holton and Turner 1989, 184). The concepts of classical sociology were created for the understanding of a transition, that is, of the shift from the traditional order towards a society that was perceived to be more modern. And since transition is the subject of this study, too, it is indeed appropriate to make use of the conceptual tool kit that was originally designed for that specific purpose — even though it would be a gross simplification to claim that modernization and the decline of Soviet socialism are essentially one and the same thing.

The neo-Marxian approach has for decades been dominant in class and stratification research. Sophisticated class analyses have also been made on the Soviet Union (e.g. Kivinen 1994). The results of these analyses, based on large survey materials, emphasize the similarities between the class structures and patterns of social stratification in Russia and the industrial countries of Western Europe and North America. According to Kivinen (1994, 130-131), the relative sizes of the working class and middle classes did not differ significantly between Russia and the Western industrial countries in 1991 (for detailed empirical descriptions of social stratification in the Soviet Union, see also e.g. Gordon and Nazimova 1986; Zaslavskaya 1992; Melin 1996). However, an analysis that locates class positions and determines stratification patterns with the individual's occupational status and his or her position in the labour process as the single criterion may — and is even likely to — produce ambiguous or trivial results when it is applied to a society whose logic differs considerably from that of Western industrial countries, that is, from the logic of the societies for whose analysis the approach was originally designed. Depending on the context, the fact that the Soviet Union employed proportionately as many librarians and engineers as Canada may be regarded as an interesting finding — but it does not tell us very much about the fundamental similarities or differences in social structures. From the point of view of stratification research, it is more important to know about the basic processes of power distribution, for instance, how social and economic elites are formed, how status group memberships are assigned, and how privileges and obligations of various social groups are determined. In order to attain that objective, the focus of the study must obviously be shifted to other institutions than solely production and the labour process.

The results of this kind of neo-Marxian and Wrightian class mapping turn from trivial to absurd if the approach is applied not to Soviet society but to the transition societies that have developed in its place after the demise of the Soviet Union. The results of a survey may indicate that the composition of the class structure in Russia is similar to the ones in Western Europe with large middle classes — at the same time as the newspapers announce that two-thirds of the population live below the poverty threshold and official income statistics show that the average salary of an engineer or a research scientist barely exceeds the officially calculated subsistence minimum! Besides position in production, aspects of consumption, way of life, and possession of resources must obviously be included among the criteria that define class position if class analysis is to make any sense at all.

Contrary to Marx, Weber identifies the source of class formation to be the relationships in the market, not in production. For Weber, it is the asymmetries in the exchange in various markets that are the very source of social stratification, that is, the uneven distribution of life chances, in modern societies. Production may be the locus of surplus value creation, as Marx thought, but the asymmetrical power relation between the employer and the worker in the labour market is an essential precondition for that exploitation, and thus the primary foundation of the inequality (Crompton 1993, 29-32; Holton and Turner 1989, 179-185).

For empirical research on transition societies, the advantages of the Weberian approach are obvious. If we are to study a society that is characterized by a rapid and seemingly chaotic change of nearly all its important social institutions — and this dynamic and volatile state seems to be especially evident in the areas of production and the labour process — then it is of course better if the theory allows us to observe a multitude of exchange situations, to try to make sense of the flux by looking at it from several different angles, instead of just concentrating our attention on one single aspect, production.

The second reason mentioned for the preference of a Weberian point of departure was that alternative approaches require a relatively stable society as the subject matter of the study. The clustering of a multitude of different occupational groups into clear-cut classes and sub-classes, as in the Wrightian class-mapping approach (Wright 1978, 1985), is possible only in circumstances of stable labour relations, that is, when the relation between capital and labour is relatively stationary. During the first half of the 1990s, Russia was undergoing a violent process of primary capital accumulation — and this hardly is a situation where occupational groups and social classes are waiting patiently out there in order to be located and mapped by the neo-Marxian sociologist.

Somewhat paradoxically, the second basic condition for the valid application of a neo-Marxian approach in the empirical study of social stratification appears to be the stable and homogeneous nature of consumption patterns in society. This homogeneity may refer either to stable class-specific differences in consumption patterns ('The working class starves while the bourgeoisie lives in luxury') or to a diffusion of certain consumption patterns and lifestyles throughout society ('In post-industrial welfare states, everybody, irrespective of social position, wears blue jeans and eats in Chinese restaurants.'). Whichever the case, a relatively high degree of constancy in the sphere of 'reproduction' is indispensable for the simple reason that only in the case of this constancy does it become legitimate for the analyst to neglect the sphere of consumption and to build an explanation on the single factor that is perceived as a variable, i.e. production. In transition societies, however, assuming this *ceteris paribus* condition is hardly appropriate. What is, for instance, the class position of a university professor who is forced to spend all his spare time growing potatoes and raising chickens at his *dacha* in order to make ends meet? Or that of a surgeon at a prestigious hospital whose salary is not sufficient even to meet the most elementary needs of his family? Or that of his nineteen-year-old son who earns ten times more than his father by selling bananas on a street corner, thereby supporting the whole family?

A similar reservation applies to the Bourdieuan approach. The advantage of a Bourdieuan approach (1977, 1979, 1980) to class analysis is that the focus is not entirely fixed on structures, as in the neo-Marxian theories, but the social order is perceived to be created and re-created through an interplay of actors and structures. Unlike most other approaches that seek to combine actor and structural perspectives, for example the Giddensian structuration theory (e.g. Giddens 1986) that is next to worthless from the point of view of empirical research, Bourdieu has managed to build a powerful unity of theoretical insight and critical research practice. But nevertheless, the range of application of the Bourdieuan approach, too, is to a large degree limited to societies that are relatively stable.

The Bourdieuan actors may accumulate various sorts of capital in various fields or try to alter the rules of these fields to their own advantage, and the analysis of such activity makes sense as long the basic contours of the fields remain clear and the mediating habituses remain unambiguous. The Bourdieuan sociologist is a master in revealing the reproduction of a social order through various established institutions, for instance the education system, art, or public media, but if the subject of the study is a revolution — the overthrowing of the existing institutions and the creation of a radically new social order — then the approach becomes problematic. In order to perform his or her analysis, the Bourdieuan sociologist needs a relatively fixed and stable set of coordinates that is rooted in continuity and tradition. Besides, the emphasis given in the Bourdieuan approach to the symbolic mediation of economic power, the symbolic reproduction of class positions, presupposes the existence of a single dominant set of symbols, speech acts, and cultural distinctions whose proper use would then legitimate economic power.

In transition societies, fields that would have the function of such stable sets of coordinates are found relatively seldom. Instead, the outlines of the fields are most often blurred, and the rules governing the activity of these fields may change fundamentally in a short period of time. Unexpected social trajectories may emerge: habituses that used to enable an actor to occupy a central position in a field may suddenly appear anachronous and marginal, and actors that were considered marginal during the *ancien régime* may quickly gain dominance over a field. Anyone who has followed Soviet and Russian media for any length of time has also surely noticed the rapid transformation of the Russian language and ways of writing, communicating and conveying information (Ferm 1995; Dunn 1995). The emergence of free speech and free media since 1991 has dissolved the uniform discoursive space that prevailed in the Soviet Union. The new discoursive practices that have evolved in place of the old hegemonic discourse are, at the moment, in a very dynamic state, and such a dominant language game or a set of speech acts that would function as a source of cultural legitimation to class power hardly exists in today's Russia.

Old and matured class societies, such as France or Britain, with their traditional social divisions and their established class-specific cultural patterns are ideal sites for Bourdieu-inspired social research. Besides the study of old and traditional capitalist countries, analysing the Soviet Union from a Bourdieuan perspective would most likely also have produced fertile results. Since Bourdieu, in contrast to Weber, does not distinguish between class and status, but makes instead a distinction between different types of capital, the Bourdieuan conclusion would, in principle, be that since the significance of economic capital for the life chances of an individual was rather limited in the Soviet Union, the significance of the remaining two capital types — social and cultural capital — was, correspondingly, greater than in the market economies. (A Weberian conclusion would be that, since the market did not officially exist at all in the Soviet Union, inclusion in privileged status groups was most essential for the enhancement of the life chances of an individual, and for that purpose, symbols of identification with the privileged status groups were important. 'Social capital' may already *per se* be interpreted to mean status group membership.) (See Calhoun, LiPuma and Postone 1993.)

Capitalist Russia of the 1990s is, however, very different in this respect. The exquisite game of distinction-making, the refined play with symbols of social and cultural capital that was characteristic of the groups that sought to distinguish themselves in the stationary Soviet society, seems in capitalist Russia often to have been replaced by the most brutal and elementary language of money. Certain groups of intellectuals still seem to play these traditional distinction games, but these groups are becoming increasingly marginalized. The transformation of these marginalized fields could well be studied with the Bourdieuan approach, and this would, without doubt, be an interesting endeavour. But in order to gain an overall view of social transformation, some more broadly applicable conceptual points of departure must be found. In this respect, a somewhat analogous case with transition countries are, for instance, the Nordic countries: if the Bourdieuan tools are uncritically imported to societies characterized by rapid social mobility and a pronounced ideological emphasis on social equality, the results may easily turn out to be very ambiguous (as an example, see Roos 1985 on Finland).

The third of the above-mentioned points in favour of a Weberian view on social stratification is the fact that his notion of class makes it possible also to focus on individual activity. The Marxian approaches, by contrast, concentrate on social structures and neither pay attention to individual actors or to the resources they have at their disposal as they strive to enhance their life chances in the market. Marx fails to 'leave any theoretical space for the analysis of social mobility as it is affected by the distributional dimensions of market inequality. Marx similarly leaves no space for an understanding of private consumer strategies, as they relate to saving and to the purchase of life-enhancing goods and services, such as homes, means of transport, travel, and so on.' (Holton and Turner 1989, 182-183). If the objective is to study a society that appears to be in flux, the possibility of focusing on actors instead of concentrating solely on social structures gives the researcher some firm ground under foot. Since the social structures in a transition society appear to be volatile and amorphous, sufficient theoretical hypotheses concerning structures to guide the research work may not be available. The Bourdieuan social theory would, of course, make possible an even more explicit focus on social actors, but because of the limitations in its range of application that were discussed above, we are forced to reject this otherwise analytically powerful approach in this context.

The fourth and final reason for the theoretical preferences expressed in favour of a Weberian view is the notion of transition, the contrast between past and present, that is inherent in the distinction between status and class. Holton and Turner (1989, 184) write:

> It is also important to emphasize that the class-status-party framework did not emerge from micro-level empirical accounts of the complex basis of the modern social structure. It grew, rather, out of the historical orientation of German social thought, and from a sense of the dichotomous contrast between past and present. Tönnies' dichotomous contrast in terms of the *Gemeinschaft/Gesellschaft* contrast is parallelled in Weber's ideal-typical contrast between status-ordered societies and market-ordered societies. Here status order and market represent alternative bases of social organization. The former is based on ascriptive forms of cultural evaluation and action — strategies of social closure — the latter on the universalistic logic of calculative exchange among self-interested individuals structured through concentrations of market power.

The distinction between status-based stratification and class-based stratification implies the contrast between status-ordered and market-ordered societies — and eventually, between traditional and modern forms of social organization. This analytical distinction does not, however, mean a separation of these two principles of social stratification in the empirical world. These two stratification patterns may coexist in various and complex ways. Social stratification based on status ascription and social closure may, however, be attributed as a predominant feature of traditional societies. Stratification that is created through the working of the impersonal market is, on the other hand, typical of modern societies.

Weber expresses, however, rather vaguely his own view concerning the coexistence of status and class in contemporary society. He suggests that class tends to be the predominant stratification principle in periods of economic expansion, as new wealth and an expanding market provide new opportunities and disrupt existing bases of power. In periods of stagnation, by contrast, individuals strive to consolidate their positions by seeking status identity and social closure.

In this essay the change of the stratification patterns, that is, the shift from a status-ordered society to a class society is regarded as a central dimension of the transition in Eastern Europe. Assuming this basic view, it is indeed tempting to underline the character of the process that began with *perestroika* and continued with the dissolution of the Soviet Empire as a bourgeois revolution. From this angle, the parallels of the demise of the *ancien régime* in the Soviet Union with the corresponding process that took place in France exactly two hundred years before it, appear striking.

The younger generation of educated professionals was the most committed proponent of *perestroika*. The stratum of educated professionals, the 'technical intelligentsia', had during the post-war decades grown in size and importance, and in the 1980s the occupational structure of the Soviet Union resembled to a considerable degree that of the developed market economies. Unlike their Western counterparts, the Soviet professionals were, however, discriminated against in terms of income and other privileges in favour of other occupational groups (see e.g. Kivinen 1994; Melin 1996). From the point of view of professionals, the life chances were more unfavourably distributed in the status-ordered Soviet society than they would have been in the market-ordered Western countries. It was, above all, in the interests of the Soviet professionals to adhere to *perestroika* and to demand the decentralization of the economy, the enlargement of the freedom of the individual, and a greater freedom of expression. All these developments promised to change Soviet society towards an increasingly market-ordered pattern and thereby strengthen the relative positions of the technical intelligentsia.

Were the professionals the 'Third Estate' of the Soviet Union? The inferior position of the bourgeoisie in the status-ordered *ancien régime* of France did not match its rising power that was acquired through the market. The French Revolution was a manifestation of modernization in the Weberian sense: a universal and impersonal distribution principle — the market — displaces a contingent and particular status order. The bourgeoisie acted as the carrier of this universal rationality. Analogously, the stratum of professionals — or 'the new middle classes' — acted as the carrier of this universalism against the particular status order in the Soviet Union. According to this reasoning, both the revolutions of 1789 and 1989 may well be interpreted as outbursts of modernization, as breakthroughs of the universal.

Households as Rational Actors: A Micro View on Transition

The traditional approach in sociology has been first to examine and outline the social structures and, thereafter, to locate the individuals or some other social actors in these hypothetical structures. But what if the structures appear amorphous, complex and constantly changing to such an extent that their outlines are very difficult to trace? Or what if the subject matter of the study is historically so unique that no existing theory fully covers it, that is, the theory that is needed to guide the empirical research is still waiting to be developed? From the point of view of empirical social research, the new social reality brought about by the transition in Eastern Europe implies, in principle, the need to adopt an inductive and theory-generative approach instead of the usual deductive approach that presupposes the existence of a relatively solid body of theory concerning the subject matter of the study. In order to overcome the problem of the lack of theory tradition concerning transition societies, two basic solutions have been applied in this study.

First, the empirical research is done with qualitative methods. Qualitative methods of social research usually imply a more inductive and theory-generative approach and research setting, whereas the logic of statistical inquiry has a more deductive nature, leaning typically on the testing of existing theory (see e.g. Strauss 1987). If the destination of a research expedition is a theoretical *terra incognita* — for instance, post-Soviet social reality in the 1990s — the qualitative approach may then with good reason be expected to produce more fertile results than the application of statistical techniques and methods of survey research.

Second, the attention is focused primarily on the activity of social agents and not on the social structures — since we do not yet know enough about these structures and what they are like. The rapid emergence of new social divisions in post-Soviet society can be perceived as restructuration, that is, social agents are responding to structural change and producing qualitatively new social structures as a collective outcome of their responses and actions. In this context, it is useful to begin the study by paying attention to agency, to the everyday activities of ordinary people who try to cope with the changing circumstances.

Theoretical propositions concerning social structure can be considered to be more historically specific than basic propositions concerning the conduct of micro-level agents. General theories on the behaviour of social systems do exist, but these general theories — such as Parsonsian functionalism (Parsons 1937) or Luhmannian systems theory (e.g. Luhmann 1984) — usually postulate the existence of a self-regulating social system that strives towards equilibrium. By so doing, these general theories are not particularly helpful in describing and explaining states of social disequilibrium, for instance, a revolution or a rapid social restructuration during a crisis. As was already noted in the previous section, the Bourdieuan general framework, concentrating on the study of relatively stable patterns of reproduction of social power, also fails to function as an adequate theoretical and methodological basis when the study is concerned with a major social upheaval.

Basic propositions concerning the behaviour of individual agents, for example, the simplified propositions of neo-classical microeconomics, are more universally applicable (see e.g. Becker 1976; Coleman 1990). These basic propositions concerning agency may be better applied in extreme situations — and in situations where the structures dissolve they may also be the only ones that are available. From the point of view of the methodology of social research, Jean-Paul Sartre (1961) makes a good heuristic point when he claims that relations between members of a society are always 'serial' relations, except in periods of revolution. Unmediated collective action, for instance, is, according to Sartre, possible only during a revolution, as the actors are for a moment not imprisoned in the constraining social structures. And correspondingly, we may conclude, revolutions may be studied adequately only if we pay sufficient attention to the social actors and their decisions.

Starting from agency, the approach of this study therefore comes close to the basic views expressed in the theoretical tradition that is known as rational choice theory (e.g. Coleman 1990). The purpose is to study how the actions and choices of individual actors combine to produce social outcomes. A central concept in this approach is the notion of optimization: actors are assumed to behave rationally in the sense that they tend to choose action that maximizes the differences between benefits and costs. In acting rationally, an actor is always engaging in some kind of optimization. This optimization may in some cases be perceived as an aim to maximize utility or minimize cost; sometimes it may be expressed in various other ways. The collective outcome of this tendency to optimize at the level of individual actors does not, however, by any means have to be socially optimal. In this respect, the rational choice approach differs radically from, for example, functionalist social theories that postulate optimization or equilibrium at the systemic level and then proceed to explain how various social institutions contribute to the maintenance of this equilibrium (see e.g. Coleman and Fararo 1992).

The adoption of a qualitative, inductive and theory-generative approach was mentioned above as one of the basic solutions to be applied in a research situation that is characterized by the absence of a sound body of theory. But even an inductive research strategy cannot function without any theoretical propositions or hypotheses at all. If total inductivism was set as an ideal, then, for instance, designing a concrete research setting or organizing data gathering would obviously be impossible. In any case, at least some general assumptions must be made prior to the actual research process. The following four idealized general propositions concerning agency have been formulated to guide the research process in this study.

1. Individuals and households are actors who make rational choices. This rationality manifests itself in the actors' pursuit of optimization: the actors

strive to gain access to a maximum amount of life chances with a minimum amount of investment and risk.

2. The actors possess various kinds of assets that can be invested in various objects. The actors tend to choose their investments so that maximally large returns, i.e. a maximum amount of life chances, may be expected with a minimum of cost.

3. In an environment characterized by uncertainty, the actors seek to minimize the risks involved in their investments by dividing them between several objects, that is, the actors seek to build investment strategies of various kinds. The form of these strategies depends on the quantity and quality of the assets that the actors have in their possession.

4. In a period of transition, new social relations evolve to replace the old ones. These new relations are created as a collective outcome of individual investment strategies. When these social relations have become institutional-ized, they can be called social structures.

The Weberian concept of *life chances* occupies a fundamental position in the propositions formulated above. This terminological choice corresponds to the Weberian view of treating social stratification as an uneven distribution of life chances across groups of population. Another basic concept is the notion of *asset*. Assets are here defined as resources, properties, qualifications, or activities that can be used to enhance an actor's life chances.

Individual households are perceived as actors in this study. The household has been selected as the basic unit of the study. Households may choose various patterns of activity in order to enlarge their life chances, in other words, they usually have the choice of investing their assets in various different ways. Optimizing is characteristic of the conduct of a prudent investor in the stock market: in order to secure stable returns and to minimize the risks involved, the investor builds a portfolio that consists of asset placements of several different kinds. Analogously, a household seeks to place its assets in several objects — for instance, by dividing its activity between wage labour, informal economy and the welfare state — in order to optimize between expected returns and risks. Forming this kind of 'portfolio of econo-mies' (Rose 1991, 1992) or multi-faceted 'reproduction model' (Mingione 1983, 1987) is especially important in an environment, such as the Russia of the 1990s, that is characterized by change and unpredictability. In this study, the concept of *strategy* — or 'household strategy', 'investment strategy' or 'survival strategy' — is used to denote the concrete patterns of asset place-ments that the household has chosen to build (Piirainen 1994a; 1994b).

'Strategy' is the key concept that bridges the micro level of individual actors and the macro level of social structures. The last of the above-presented basic propositions is the most daring of the four: it attempts to jump across the gap between the micro and macro levels, while the first three merely gather speed for the leap by specifying the nature of the micro-level activity. The formation of a new social order and new social structures is observed through the study of the investment strategies of individual households. Different strategies yield access to different sets of life chances, and the limits of strategy choice are, in the last instance, determined by the quantity and quality of the assets households have in their possession. Similarities can be perceived in the asset possession and the strategy formation of different households, and distinct strategy differences between various social groups can also be observed. According to strategy type, households and groups of households may be — in Weber's manner — clustered together into 'social classes', that is, into segments of population that have access to markedly different sets of life chances.

One of the key reasons for choosing the Weberian concepts of 'status' and 'class' was the fact that this dichotomy reflects the transition from a status-ordered to a market-ordered society, from the traditional towards the modern. In contrast to the old order, the new social stratification may be perceived as being created through the market-mediated distribution of life chances. Whereas status, that is, status ascription by state policy, was during the *ancien régime* the predominant basis for life chance distribution, it is now replaced by market as the predominant principle. The restructuration process of Russian society may thus be observed as a change of the basic distribution principle and as a corresponding shift from one social stratification pattern into another.

The dissolution of the old social order implied by no means the creation of a kind of a 'zero hour' of social development, that is, a situation where all the members of society would have been on an equal footing as the race towards the market-ordered society began. Quite the contrary: the inequalities contained in the old social order are, more often than not, transmitted to the new order, and not infrequently, the old disparities may have grown deeper in the course of the transition. To use the concepts developed above: the actors have to a varying extent been able to carry their assets from the status-ordered society to the market order and to convert them into new assets that are valid in the new environment. In this study, 'conversion of assets' is one of its central concepts: the assets that gave an actor access to a wide range of life chances in the Soviet society may no longer do so in the market-ordered society, but they must be converted to new assets that are valid in the market order. For instance, an extensive net of social relations — that is, membership of various important status groups — which undoubtedly was an important asset in the status-ordered Soviet society, may no longer suffice to secure the same standard of living as before, and money and private property are required instead. As the wealth of the society is being redistributed in the course of the transition, this social capital may, however, be useful or indispensable for the acquisition of economic capital. Assets are converted into assets of a different type; in this example, social assets are converted into economic ones.

A household strategy consists always of various *components* and it is formed within an *opportunity structure* (see e.g. Merton 1976) that is unique for every actor. The shape of the opportunity structure depends on the quantity and nature of the assets that an actor holds. The opportunity structure — the potential that includes the totality of possible economic activity accessible to an actor — may be seen to consist of a multitude of individual *objects*, that is, concrete institutions, enterprises, activities, and the like, in which actors may invest their assets. Within a given opportunity structure, the preferences of the actor guide the selection of the actual investment objects, that is, the composition of the actual strategy. For example, cultural factors guiding decision-making are regarded in this context as preferences. The assumption about the propensity of actors to optimize was set as a central postulate of the approach; the actors weigh the alternative costs of their choices as they select, having a certain set of preferences, the actual strategy out of the opportunity structure.

Before closing this section, it may be appropriate to emphasize the methodological nature of the approach and of the four basic postulates presented above. These postulates that have served as cornerstones of the approach and guided the gathering of empirical data and its analysis should not be regarded as propositions of an ontological nature, that is, as assumptions concerning human nature and human conduct, but rather as methodological choices and principles that may prove useful in structuring the research process. The objective here is by no means to assume the position of rational choice theorists with an ontological twist and, for instance, claim like Jon Elster (1989, 248) that 'there are no societies, only individuals who interact with each other'. Since the purpose here is not to write a treatise on social philosophy, it is, in fact, quite uninteresting to make any strong statements concerning the fundamental nature of either the world, the society, or the human beings as social actors. The attachment to the postulates formulated above is motivated above all by methodological considerations, that is, by the anticipation that they will prove to be very useful baggage to carry around during a research expedition into a *terra incognita*, into the post-Soviet social reality that has hitherto largely remained virgin territory for serious empirical social research.

The four postulates leave aside institutional or cultural factors as direct primary explanatory factors and let them come into the analysis only indirectly, mediated through the concepts of preference, opportunity structure and asset possession, and as such, these basic postulates undeniably appear to be extreme idealizations and simplifications — but entering unexplored terrain, it is nevertheless better to be equipped with tools which are crude but which have a wide range of applicability than with ones which are very elegant and sophisticated but which are designed for only a few specific purposes.

While adopting the fundamental assumptions of the rational choice approach for methodological reasons, it is also easy to see the limitations of the approach. Richard Münch (1992, 159-160) writes:

> Rational choice theory is a welcome advance in sociological theory. It contributes to improving its explanatory power inasmuch as we are concerned with the economics of social life. We can also freely admit that economics is everywhere, particularly in our modern social life, where economic rationality penetrates virtually every sphere of society. For this reason, it is easy for rational choice theorists to demonstrate the working of their approach with reference to a wide array of social phenomena beyond the economic sphere in its narrower sense. They fail, however, inasmuch as they take this demonstration to represent the whole story of social life. In this process, they simply reduce the whole complexity of social life to terms of economic calculation and transaction, the complexity of modern society to the simplicity of liberal society. Rational choice theory covers only a limited realm of social life. Its explanatory power is limited to the economic dimension of that life. A comprehensive sociological theory must interconnect rational choice theory in a greater framework with theories that are more adequate to deal with the realms of social life outside the economic sphere.

Given the limits of its basic assumptions, rational choice theory can hardly be a comprehensive social theory or even the basis of one. As James Bohman (1992, 225) says, 'even good rational choice explanations must be supplemented by an account of macroinstitutional structure that explains the interdependency of actions and the mechanisms of preference formation'. The Weber-inspired theory of transition as a shift from a status-ordered society to a class society forms the core of this 'account of macroinstitutional structure' which supplements the rational choice approach. Consequently, many of the concepts used in the rendition of rational choice theory that is tailored to the needs of this study are derived from this Weber-inspired macrosocial theory.

In the context of this study, the objective for the application of rational choice approach is far less ambitious than the production of 'the whole story of social life'. The purpose is not to reduce all social life to economics, but to use the approach only in that limited realm where its application is valid, that is, in the study of market situations through which life chances in post-Soviet Russia are redistributed. At best, the critical application of rational choice theory can make it possible for us to establish a firm foothold in the shifting social reality, and after achieving this first stage, we may proceed, as Münch suggests, by 'interconnecting rational choice theory in a greater framework with theories that are more adequate to deal with the realms of social life outside the economic sphere'. The first stage of analysis consists of the application of a universal theory with the purpose of establishing a firm theoretical core, which is then in the further stages of the work complemented by more specific theories concerning, for instance, Russian culture and Soviet social institutions with the objective of building a more comprehensive description of the post-Soviet social reality.

Research Setting and Data Collection

The empirical research project referred to in this essay has been carried out as a case study in St. Petersburg. The site of the case study was one of the administrative districts *(raion)* of the city, a suburban area with approximately 350,000 inhabitants. The research data consist of semi-structured interviews with families; either one or more of the adult members of the household were present at the moment of the interview. The interviews were carried out during the years 1993-96. In total, a sample of one hundred household interviews was collected. Twenty of the families were interviewed twice with an interval of 2-2.5 years between the two interviews. However, within the confines of this space it is not possible to describe the interview data at any length; only the very basic conclusions are briefly reported (for a detailed treatment of the study, see Piirainen 1997).

The interviews were collected for the purpose of gaining an overview of the everyday life of each of the families that participated in the study. The aim was to study the economic activity of ordinary households during a time of rapid transformation of social structures and institutions. How do micro-level actors allocate their resources and what kind of strategies do they build in order to cope with the change? As the research data grew larger and households of different kinds were sampled into the data, different types of household strategies as well as the ensuing class positions, i.e. social positions that yield different sets of life chances, were compared. An analysis of the class structure, emerging in the capitalist Russia as a collective outcome of household choices and strategies, was then made on the basis of these comparisons.

Among the most central interview themes were income and standard of living of the household, participation in wage labour, division of labour between genders, entrepreneurship and additional sources of income, activity in the shadow economy, attitudes towards the Russian 'welfare state', the relation between work and leisure, and consumption patterns and the structure of consumption. On the basis of these themes dealing with the everyday activity of the families, descriptions of household strategies could be constructed. Among other important themes were the changes caused in the life of the family by the transition, the interviewees' opinions concerning the future, social problems in Russia and in the city of St. Petersburg, the social and political orientation of the interviewees, and attitudes towards public authorities, the state and politics.

The interviewees were sampled according to certain theoretical criteria. At the first stage of data collection, a sample of twenty interviews was gathered with households that were considered to be the most 'representative', that is, two-parent families with one or two children, in which both parents were working and had relatively high professional qualifications. After establishing this homogeneous background consisting of relatively 'representative' cases, variation was created in the data in the second stage of sampling by altering such background variables as the age, education, occupation, family composition, and the housing situation of the interviewees. In this second stage of sampling, predominantly those families that differed from the 'representative' background data were interviewed, for example large families, retired people, single-parent families, marginalized families with low professional qualifications, as well as entrepreneurs and people active in the new commercial sector of the economy.

Data collection and analysis followed roughly the prescriptions of grounded theory, a well-known technique for qualitative social research (see Glaser and Strauss 1967; Strauss 1987; Strauss and Corbin 1990). In its emphasis on creative inductivism and theory generation, grounded theory served especially well as a general guideline for the actual research process.

Strategy Type and Social Class

So far the reasoning has been the following. Each household possesses a variety of different assets — time, labour force, professional qualifications, money, social connections, capital goods, and so on — that it can invest in different objects of economic activity. The households seek to share the investment of their assets among different sectors of economic activity in a way that promises them an optimum ratio between risk and returns. The sum of the total investments makes up the economic strategy of a household. The strategies of different households vary depending on the quantity and nature of the assets in their possession. When a strategy becomes a pattern that has continuity in time, it serves as the basis of the social trajectory of the household. The basic approach of the analysis is to trace — or extrapolate — these trajectories to the social positions, that is, class positions, to which they appear to be leading. The economic strategy can be treated as a factor determining a household's social class as we are studying a rapid process of social restructuration — a process that above was thematized as a shift from a status-ordered society to the predominance of the market.

The environment for the Russian households' economic activity can, in principle, be divided into three distinct sectors. These sectors of activity can be called 'the Soviet economy', 'the market economy', and 'the informal economy'. The Soviet economy comprises the public sector of the economy, that is, all the economic institutions that were created during the Soviet Union to operate according to the principles of the planned economy. The market economy consists of all the new economic institutions that have been created after the demise of the planned economy and that follow the logic of market-based exchange. The informal economy consists of institutions and activities that are related to production, consumption, or economic exchange outside the official and monetary economy; home production of goods and services is a prime example of activity in the informal economy. In the Soviet economy, the predominant principle that guides exchange and resource allocation is planning and policy, whereas in the market economy, this principle is, obviously, the market. In the informal economy, the corresponding principle is reciprocity (for more details, see Piirainen 1997, 136-150).

Two basic household strategies in encountering the emerging capitalism in everyday life and adapting to the coming of the market economy can be outlined. The first one seeks to integrate the household closer into the market economy and to compensate for the disparity between the Soviet wages and the market prices by increasing activity in the market economy, that is, by bringing in more money in order to cover the deficit in the household budget, and correspondingly, by withdrawing assets from the Soviet economy. The second basic strategy can be called 'defensive traditionalism'. The objective of this strategy is the opposite: to detach the household as much as possible from the market economy, to escape the onslaught of the market, and to compensate for the disparity between Soviet wages and market prices by minimizing the household's monetary expenses.

A part of the people seeks to become increasingly integrated into the market economy while another, and perhaps an even larger, part of the population tries — or is forced — to withdraw from it in order to defend itself. The first segment of the population aspires towards the consumption patterns of the Western middle classes, while the second resorts to traditional methods of securing subsistence. To a certain extent, the defensive traditionalism is, undoubtedly, a transitory phenomenon: as the market economy expands and assumes a more stable and civil character, more and more people will abandon temporary traditionalism and shift their assets gradually from the informal economy to the market economy. The point is, however, that the choice between the market and traditionalism is not, ultimately, merely a question of will: not everybody possesses assets that are valid in the market economy.

'Conversion of assets' was above mentioned as one of the key concepts: in order to shift assets from either the Soviet or the informal economy to the market economy, they must first be converted to a valid form. For example, social connections, a valid asset in the informal economy, may be used to obtain money and private property, or professional qualifications that are valid in the Soviet economy may be supplemented to make them meet the demand in the labour market. But conversion of this kind is not feasible for everybody. It is particularly difficult for the older generations. In Russia which, despite the loss of the empire, still is territorially the largest nation in the world, regional factors also play an especially important role. The case study which is referred to in this article took place in St. Petersburg, a city of five million inhabitants and a major industrial and commercial centre in the uttermost western corner of Russia. The European metropolis offers a wide variety of opportunities for asset conversion as well as a rapidly expanding market economy where these freshly converted assets can be invested. The degree of traditionalism is necessarily much larger in the innumerable smaller cities and towns in the vast provinces, where such chances are much fewer, where the overwhelming majority of the Russian population live — and where the political future of the Russian nation is, ultimately, decided.

The future economic development in Russia will, of course, eventually determine the proportions and persistence of traditionalism in the society in the long run. If the market economy expands steadily and if this expansion is accompanied with stabilization of the national economy, structural adaptation of the domestic industries, and the shift of the emphasis of the economic activity in the new market sector from commerce to production, then the percentage of those who will resort to traditionalist strategies will obviously be lower.

Integration and traditionalism may be defined as the two basic approaches in encountering the market. The placement of assets in various sectors of the economy can also be used as a criterion when household strategies are to be typified further. On the basis of the interview data describing the households' economic behaviour, three general ideal-typical strategy patterns can be constructed. These strategies are hereafter called *the market-oriented strategy, the traditionalist strategy* and *the proletarian strategy*.

In the empirical world, clear-cut cases of these strategy types are, of course, more difficult to find.

The data consist of urban households, and urban life necessarily implies asset placements at least to some degree in the market economy, no matter how strong the traditionalist aspirations of the household may be. Traditionalist and market-integration propensities merge in the real world, but nevertheless, most of the interviews collected for this study convey the basic tendency of the household in question, that is, the main direction of its social trajectory.

The possession of relatively large numbers of assets that are valid in the market economy is characteristic of the households that follow a market-oriented strategy. As was noted in the previous section, the households do not usually want to invest all their assets solely in one single sector of the economy, but seek to divide their asset placements among economies in order to achieve an optimum ratio of risk and promised returns. A household following the market-oriented strategy divides its assets mainly between the Soviet economy and the market economy. Asset placement in the Soviet economy brings continuity and predictability to the life of the household, while the assets that are invested in the market economy yield returns that render possible the rise above poverty level and an ascent towards a pattern of consumption that is characteristic of the middle classes in Western industrial countries. The most typical example of household asset division between Soviet and market economies is a family where the husband works in the new market economy while his wife remains in old Soviet sector employment.

The households that follow a market-oriented strategy always invest assets in the informal economy, too. For the subsistence of the household, these asset placements in the informal sector have, however, an increasingly minor significance. Vegetables and potatoes may still be grown at the *dacha*, and home-preserved foodstuffs may still be made, but the economic relevance of these activities is diminishing. Gardening, for instance, assumes the character of a pastime or of a ritual reverence to the old way of life, but the activities that are important and necessary for the family economy take place elsewhere. Home-grown food or home-made articles may be of help in managing the household budget, but they do not have a decisive importance. Increasing the monetary income of the household is for a market-oriented household the most important and realistic objective. These households seek also to actively obtain more assets that are valuable in the market economy, for example, to acquire new professional skills or learn foreign languages.

The market-oriented households belong most frequently to the younger generations. Persons who have specific professional skills and qualifications that are needed in the market economy are obviously among the ones who are able to pursue a middle-class strategy, as well as people who have a large network of influential or useful social contacts. Individuals who held key positions in the Soviet Union are also among those that had a head start when the race towards the market order began.

The traditionalist strategy implies the allocation of asset placements primarily between the Soviet economy and the informal economy. The household members still have their permanent employment in the Soviet economy, and the additional resources that are needed to lift the household from poverty are acquired through activity in the informal economy, for instance, by substituting market goods and services by home production and by mutual assistance between relatives and friends. While the middle-class strategy strives to increase market consumption, the major objective of the traditional strategy is to decrease market consumption to a minimum. Especially in an urban environment like St.Petersburg, small asset placements in the market economy, such as spontaneous and small-scale entrepreneurship and occasional extra jobs, also belong to the picture. The life chances and well-being of the traditionalist households do not, however, primarily depend on the returns that may be acquired from these asset placements in the market economy, as is the case with the market-oriented strategy.

A basic feature that both the traditionalist and the market-oriented households have in common is the possession of assets that can be invested outside the Soviet economy — although in the case of the traditionalist households these assets are, as a rule, not valid in the market economy, but can only be placed in the informal economy. In more rare cases, the households may also voluntarily choose not to place their assets in the market economy, preferring to increase their activity in the informal economy instead. This is the case, for instance, with people of the older generations, who, having once internalized the Soviet ethics and values, do not want to become active in 'bazaar capitalism', even if offered a chance to do so.

In many respects the traditionalist strategy signifies the continuation of the Soviet patterns of household behaviour. In the Soviet Union, too, the households tried to allocate as much assets as possible to the informal economy. The usually quite lax working pace in the Soviet Union permitted to quite a high degree the 'flexible' use of working hours for private purposes. Since the quantity of life chances available for the household was not to be significantly augmented through effort at work, it was only rational to shift all excess assets to the informal economy. This optimization behaviour of Soviet workers was combatted by recurring Stakhanovite campaigns — and during Stalin's regime, by discipline and terror — but it is well-known that in the vast majority of cases these campaigns had far from impressive results.

The market economy existed in the Soviet Union, too, having the character of a shadow economy, but since market activity was criminalized and black marketeers were severely punished, a Soviet household that sought to optimize had an obvious reason to avoid large asset placements in it: the returns might have been great but even greater were the risks. Clever minor asset placements in the shadow market were part and parcel of the art of managing everyday life in the deficit economy of the Soviet Union — but a major re-allocation of assets in favour of the market economy certainly did not promise a stable social trajectory for an ordinary Soviet household.

For the 'non-ordinary' households, by contrast, the circumstances of 'advanced socialism' — not to mention the three final years of the Soviet Union — opened up magnificent opportunities for market operations. The members of the nomenclatura were able to use simultaneously the mechanisms of social closure that were characteristic of the strict Soviet status order as well as the mechanisms of the market to their own advantage. During the late Brezhnev era, the result of this double strategy was a large-scale symbiosis between corporate power and the shadow market. During 1989-1991, this opportunity for the nomenclatura to shuttle between the disintegrating status order and emerging market led to the spontaneous privatization of Soviet state property to the advantage of a group of *apparatchiks* in the high echelons of the status hierarchy. (For an excellent description of this mechanism, see e.g. Gaidar 1995, 140-150; see also Frydman et al. 1996; Åslund 1995, 43; Åslund 1996, 12-16.)

The informal economy also had an important role in the Soviet Union. It had the function of compensating for the shortcomings of the planning and distribution system of the Soviet economy, and large asset placements in it were essential for the well-being of ordinary households. The well-being could be further augmented by clever small investments in the — then illegal or semi-legal — market economy. The basic strategy of traditionalist households has remained analogous after the collapse of the Soviet socialism and central planning. The shortcomings of the Soviet economy — which now are manifest in the form of low wages and not of the deficit of goods — are even today compensated for by the shifting of assets to the informal economy and by making small asset placements in the market economy — which may now have either a legal or illegal character. The methods and practices familiar from the Soviet era are also currently in use. Some of these traditional practices, such as small-scale farming for private use, have experienced a heyday, as the economic and political liberalization has granted new freedoms. Some of these 'informal' practices are, by contrast, transforming and becoming increasingly monetarized; for example, barter with goods and services in social networks is becoming increasingly monetarized and losing its reciprocal character (e.g. Jyrkinen-Pakkasvirta and Poretskina 1995).

The most important feature that characterizes the proletarian strategy, the third general strategy type mentioned above, is the absence of assets that could be invested either in the market economy or in the informal economy. Because of this lack of valid assets, major asset placements are made solely in the Soviet economy, and the allocation of asset placements among different sectors of the economy is difficult or impossible. As the returns from investments in the Soviet economy are usually not sufficient to cover all the necessary expenses of a household, poverty is an inevitable consequence of this pattern of asset placement.

Single-parent families and pensioner households are most typical examples of households that have a limited amount of assets and, consequently, difficulties in dividing asset placements among different sectors of economy.

A sole supporter may not have enough time and energy to invest in activities other than wage work and child care; if she does not have the possibility of getting support from her family, the opportunities for engaging in extra activities either in the market economy or in the informal economy are small. Pensioners who do not have help from their children or relatives may also easily be in a difficult position, as the value of the average pension has during 1995 fallen even below the minimum subsistence level (Poverty in Russia 1995; Kosmarskii and Maleva 1995, 13). In Russia it is usual that the elderly live together with their children; this extended family is an important source of support. As the retirement age is low — 55 years for women and 60 for men in 1995 — a large percentage of pensioners also work in order to supplement their small pensions. The pensioners whose age or health does not permit them to work any longer have difficulties in making ends meet if they are not helped by their families.

According to poverty research that is based on statistical information, the largest group among the poor in present-day Russia consists, however, of the working poor, i.e. two-parent families that are dependent on income from low-paid wage labour (e.g. Poverty in Russia 1994). The problem with the statistical poverty studies is that they take into account only the returns from asset placements in the official monetary economy, while the returns from other sectors of economy remain unobserved. Although the poverty of Russian families is most likely not so deep and widespread as these studies suggest, a large number of families, especially those with three or more children, face an increased risk of proletarianization. The lack of professional qualifications is also a factor that increases the risk of poverty.

Each of the three basic strategy types imply a specific pattern of production and consumption, a specific way of life, specific value orientations, a specific habitus, a specific set of life chances, and a specific social trajectory. The once relatively homogeneous Soviet 'middle strata' seem to be segmented into distinct social classes that increasingly diverge from each other with regard to all these factors. The origin of this new class division can be seen to be the economic activity of individuals and households and their power differentials in the newly established market.

On the basis of the above overview of household strategies, the Russians can be seen to be diverging into three major social classes. These classes that are in the process of formation may be named The Middle Class, 'The People' and The Proletariat. In addition to these three major social classes, the new political and economic elite, people who are popularly called the 'new Russians', also forms a distinct class whose life chances are far better than those of the three first-mentioned classes. This new elite is, however, not very large in number, consisting of only about 0.5-2 per cent of the Russian population (cf. Zaslavskaya 1995, 1996; Poverty in Russia 1995, 30).

The former members of the nomenclatura who, during the period of privatization of state property, have successfully converted their old power assets to capital, form the core of the new elite. This core is surrounded by a larger stratum of upwardly mobile new entrepreneurs who in most cases are, to varying degrees, nourished by the 'nomenclatura capital' (e.g. Frydman et al. 1996; cf. Kryshtanovskaya 1992; Radaev 1994; Ershova et al. 1994).

The acquisition of middle-class positions — and the subsequent formation of a middle class in Russia — is based on market-oriented household strategies. The households that augment their asset placements in the market economy and increase their consumption of market commodities are coming ever closer to the consumption patterns and lifestyles of the urban middle classes of the industrialized West. The quantity of assets possessed by this class is, however, essentially smaller than that of the elite, whose members may expect a completely different set of life chances as a return from their investments in the market economy. The middle class, allocating its investments prudently between the market and Soviet economies, occupies a 'middle position' between the newly rich elite and 'the people'. Its strategic behaviour, its life chances, and its aspirations differ from those of the elite that does not need the Soviet economy any longer as an insurance.

The obvious fact that merely the adoption of a market-oriented strategy does not automatically guarantee a household an affluent middle-class position may, however, be worth emphasizing. The market-oriented strategy may or may not be successful. It may lead to a dominant or a marginal social position. There is quite obviously a difference between the social positions of a bank owner, a factory worker, and a street vendor, even though they all had placed their assets in the market economy. The quantity of the assets that the household possesses and is able to invest in the market economy is, of course, decisive in determining the actual class position. But whatever the case, adopting the market-oriented strategy implies, in the transitory situation, to a certain degree a commitment to a pattern of economic activity and consumption, which, in its paradigmatic form, may be labelled as 'middle-class'.

'The people' — *les classes populaires* — allocate their assets mainly between the Soviet economy and the informal economy. The way of life and consumption patterns of 'the people' contain, even in an urban environment, many features that are characteristic of traditional and rural life. Thus, 'the people' differ markedly in important respects from the market-oriented middle-class. The traditionalist strategy adopted by this class yields, however, in most cases a somewhat tolerable level of living — a fact that remains hidden from the statistical studies that measure poverty with the income from official sources as the sole criterion.

The members of the third large social class that is emerging in Russia, the proletariat, have no other options than to place their assets mainly in the Soviet economy. Since returns from the Soviet economy are, however, usually no longer sufficient to secure the elementary standard of living, poverty and deprivation is characteristic of this large class.

Figure 1 contains a schematic presentation of strategy types and class division.

Figure 1. Strategy types and social classes

	SOCIAL CLASS	ASSET PLACEMENTS
	The elite	Market economy
	Entrepreneurial middle class	Market economy (+ Soviet economy)
	Wage working middle classes	Market economy + Soviet economy (+ informal economy)
	'The people'	Soviet economy + informal economy (+ market economy)
	The proletariat	Soviet economy (+ informal economy + market economy)

A Summary of the Discussion

The environment of economic activity was divided into three spheres. These three economies were called 'the Soviet economy', 'the market economy' and 'the informal economy'. In the Soviet economy, the predominant principle that guides exchange and resource allocation is planning and policy, whereas in the market economy, this principle is, obviously, the market. In the informal economy, the corresponding principle is reciprocity.

Households were seen as rational actors that invest their assets in objects in all three sectors of economic activity, forming different strategies as they allocate their asset placements among these economies. The quantity and nature of assets in a household's possession determines, in the last instance, the form of the household strategy. Three basic household strategies were detected in the interview data. The first one was called 'the market-oriented strategy'. In its most typical form, the market-oriented strategy consists of the allocation of asset placements between the market economy and the Soviet economy. The traditionalist strategy was the second of the basic household strategies. The essence of this strategy is the division of a household's asset placements between the Soviet economy and the informal economy. The third major strategy type was named 'the proletarian strategy'. The lack of any major quantities of such assets that could be placed outside the Soviet economy is characteristic of this last-mentioned strategy. As the returns from asset placements in the Soviet economy are usually not sufficient, the proletarian strategy implies social mobility downwards, the gradual narrowing of the household's life chances.

The strategies were found, to a large degree, to be specific to corresponding social classes that are in the process of formation in Russia as the old status-ordered society changes into a market-ordered one. A successful market-oriented household strategy serves as the basis of a social trajectory that leads to a middle-class social position. A well-functioning traditionalist strategy implies a position in another social class that is distinctly different from the middle class. This class was in this chapter named 'the people'. And finally, the proletarian strategy implies a social trajectory that leads to a position in a new proletariat, a large and deprived underclass that is being formed from the millions of households that are dependent mainly on the asset placements in the Soviet economy.

Note

1. The Gini coefficient was calculated on the basis of a representative sample collected by the Moscow-based research institute VTsIOM. For the last quarter of 1993, the coefficient calculated on the basis of the data of the Russian central bureau of statistics, *Goskomstat Rossii* was lower (0.40), whereas a coefficient as high as 0.49 was derived from the Russian Longitudinal Monitoring Survey data, collected as a joint initiative by *Goskomstat Rossii* and the World Bank (see Poverty in Russia, pp. 29-31).

Bibliography

Becker, G. (1976), *The Economic Approach to Human Behavior,* The University of Chicago Press, Chicago, Ill.

Bohman, J. (1992), 'The Limits of Rational Choice Explanation', in J. Coleman and T. Fararo (eds.), *Rational Choice Theory. Advocacy and Critique*, Sage Publications, London.

Bourdieu, P. (1977), *Outline of a Theory of Practice*, Cambridge University Press, Cambridge.

Bourdieu, P. (1979), *La distinction. Critique sociale du jugement*, Iditions de Minuit, Paris.

Bourdieu, P. (1980), *Le sens pratique*, Iditions de Minuit, Paris.

Calhoun, C., LiPuma, E. and Postone, M. (1993), 'Introduction: Bourdieu and Social Theory', in C. Calhoun et al. (eds.), *Bourdieu: Critical Perspectives*, Polity Press, Cambridge.

Coleman, J.S. (1990), *Foundations of Social Theory*, Harvard University Press, Cambridge, Mass.

Coleman, J.S. and Fararo, T.J. (1992), 'Introduction', in J. Coleman, and T. Fararo, (eds.), *Rational Choice Theory. Advocacy and Critique*, Sage Publications, London.

Crompton, R. (1993), *Class and Stratification. An Introduction to Current Debates*, Polity Press, Cambridge.

Dunn, J. (1995), *Kak russkii yazik perestal byt' yazikom sovetskogo tipa i prevratilsya v yazik zapadnogo tipa*, a paper presented at the 5th Congress of Central and East European Studies, Warsaw, 6-11 August 1995.

Elster, J. (1989), *The Cement of Society. A Study of Social Order*, Cambridge University Press, Cambridge.

Ershova, N.S. (1994), 'Transformatsiya pravyashchei elity Rossii v usloviyakh sotsialnogo pereloma', in T.I. Zaslavskaya and L.A. Arutyunyan (eds.), *Kuda idyot Rossiia*, Mezhdunarodnyi simposium, Moskva, 17-19 dekabrya 1993 g.

Ferm, L. (1995), *Razvitie politicheskoi metafori v postsovetskii period*, a paper presented at the 5th Congress of Central and East European Studies, Warsaw, 6-11 August 1995.

Frydman, R., Murphy, K. and Rapaczynski, A. (1996), 'Capitalism With a Comrade's Face', *Transition* 2.

Gaidar, E. (1995), *Gosudastvo i evolyutsiya*, Izdatelstvo 'Evrasiya', Moskva.

Gerth, H. and Mills, C.W. (eds.) (1948), *From Max Weber*, Routledge and Kegan Paul, London.

Giddens, A. (1984), *The Constitution of Society*, Polity Press, Cambridge.

Glaser, B.G. and Strauss, A. (1967), *The Discovery of Grounded Theory: Strategies for Qualitative Research*, Aldine de Gruyter, New York.

Gordon, L.A. and Nazimova, A.K. (1986), 'The Socio-occupational Structure of Contemporary Soviet Society: Typology and Statistics', in M. Yanowitch (ed.), *The Social Structure of the USSR*, Recent Soviet Studies, London.

Holton, R.J. and Turner, B.S. (1989), *Max Weber on Economy and Society*, Routledge, London and New York.

Jyrkinen-Pakkasvirta, T. and Poretskina, E. (1995), *Transformation, Social Networks and Daily Life in St. Petersburg, Russia*, a paper presented at the ISA World Conference of Sociology, Bielefeld, Germany, 18-23 July 1994.

Kivinen, M. (1994), 'Class Relations in Russia' in T. Piirainen (ed.), *Change and Continuity in Eastern Europe*, Dartmouth, Aldershot.

Kosmarskii, B. and Maleva, T. (1995), 'Sotsialnaya politika v Rossii v kontekste makroekonomicheskoi reformy', *Voprosy ekonomiki* 9.

Kryshtanovskaya, O. (1992), 'The New Business Elite' in D. Lane (ed.), *Russia in Flux. The Political and Social Consequences of Reform*, Edward Elgar, Aldershot.

Luhmann, N. (1984), *Soziale Systeme*, Suhrkamp Verlag, Frankfurt am Main.

Melin, H. (1996), *Suunnitelman varjossa. Tutkimus yritysjohtajista valtiososialismissa*, Tampereen yliopisto, yhteiskuntatieteellinen tiedekunta, väitöskirja, Tampere.

Merton, R.K. (1976), *Contemporary Social Problems*, 4th edition, Harcourt Brace Jovanovich, New York.

Mingione, E. (1983), 'Informalization, Restructuring and the Survival Strategies of the Working Class', *International Journal of Urban and Regional Research*, vol. 7, 3.

Mingione, E. (1987), 'Urban Survival Strategies, Family Structure and Informal Practices' in M. Smith and J. Feagin (eds.), *The Capitalist City*, Basil Blackwell, Great Britain.

Münch, R. (1992), 'Rational Choice Theory: A Critical Assessment of Its Explanatory Power' in J. Coleman and T. Fararo (eds.), *Rational Choice Theory. Advocacy and Critique*, Sage Publications, London.

Parsons, T. (1937), *The Structure of Social Action*, Free Press, New York.

Piirainen, T. (1994), 'Survival Strategies in a Transition Economy: Everyday Life, Subsistence and New Inequalities in Russia' in T. Piirainen (ed.), *Change and Continuity in Eastern Europe*, Dartmouth, Aldershot.

Piirainen, T. (1997), *Towards A New Social Order in Russia. Transforming Structures and Everyday Life*, Dartmouth, Aldershot.

Poverty in Russia. An Assessment (1995), The World Bank, Report No. 14110-RU, Washington, D.C.

Radaev, V.V. (1994), 'Revolyutsiya raznochintsev' in T.I. Zaslavskaya and L.A. Arutyunyan (eds.), *Kuda idyot Rossiia*, Mezhdunarodnyi simposium, Moskva, 17-19 dekabrya 1993 g.

Roos, J.P. (1988), *Elämäntavasta elämänkertaan*, Tutkijaliitto, Helsinki.

Rose, R. (1991), *Between State and Market. Key Indicators of Transition in Eastern Europe*, University of Strathclyde, Centre for the Study of Public Policy, Glasgow.

Rose, R. (1992), *Toward a Civil Economy?*, University of Strathclyde, Centre for the Study of Public Policy, Glasgow.

Rose, R. (1994), 'Getting by without Government: Everyday Life in Russia', *Daedalus* 3.

Sartre, J.-P. (1961), *La critique de la raison*, Gallimard, Paris.

Strauss, A.L. (1987), *Qualitative Analysis for Social Scientists*, Cambridge University Press, Cambridge.

Strauss, A. and Corbin, J. (1990), *Basics of Qualitative Research. Grounded Theory Procedures and Techniques*, Sage Publications, London.

Weber, M. (1978), *Economy and Society*, 2 volumes, University of California Press, Berkeley, California.

Wright, E.O. (1978), *Class, Crisis and the State*, New Left Books, London.

Wright, E.O. (1985), *Classes*, Verso, London.

Zaslavskaya, T. (1992), 'Socialism, Perestroika and Public Opinion', *Soviet Sociology*, vol. 31, 4.

Zaslavskaya, T. (1995), 'Struktura sovremennogo rossiiskogo obshchestva. Ekonomicheskie i sotsialnye peremeny: monitoring obshchestvennogo mneniya', *VTsIOM*, 6.

Zaslavskaya, T. (1996), 'Stratifikatsiya sovremennogo rossiiskogo obshchestva. Ekonomicheskie i sotsialnye peremeny: monitoring obshchestvennogo mneniya', *VTsIOM*, 1.

Åslund, A. (1995), *How Russia Became a Market Economy*, The Brookings Institution, Washington, D.C.

Åslund, A. (1996), 'Reform vs. "Rent-seeking" in Russia's Economic Transformation', *Transition*, vol. 2, 2.